THREE THOUSAND FUTURES

*The Next Twenty Years
for Higher Education*

*Final Report
of the Carnegie Council
on Policy Studies
in Higher Education*

Contents

*The following technical reports were published by the Carnegie
Council on Policy Studies in Higher Education.*

The Carnegie Council Series

*The following publications are available from Jossey-Bass Inc., Publishers,
433 California Street, San Francisco, California 94104.*

The Federal Role in Postsecondary
Education: Unfinished Business,
1975-1980
*The Carnegie Council on Policy
Studies in Higher Education*

More Than Survival: Prospects for
Higher Education in a Period
of Uncertainty
*The Carnegie Foundation for the
Advancement of Teaching*

Making Affirmative Action Work
in Higher Education: An Analysis
of Institutional and Federal
Policies with Recommendations
*The Carnegie Council on Policy
Studies in Higher Education*

Presidents Confront Reality: From
Edifice Complex to University
Without Walls
*Lyman A. Glenny, John R. Shea,
Janet H. Ruyle, Kathryn H. Freschi*

Progress and Problems in Medical
and Dental Education: Federal
Support Versus Federal Control
*The Carnegie Council on Policy
Studies in Higher Education*

Low or No Tuition: The Feasibility
of a National Policy for the
First Two Years of College
*The Carnegie Council on Policy
Studies in Higher Education*

Managing Multicampus Systems:
Effective Administration in an
Unsteady State
Eugene C. Lee, Frank M. Bowen

Challenges Past, Challenges
Present: An Analysis of
American Higher Education
Since 1930
David D. Henry

The States and Higher Education:
A Proud Past and a Vital Future
*The Carnegie Foundation for the
Advancement of Teaching*

Educational Leaves for Employees:
European Experience
for American Consideration
*Konrad von Moltke,
Norbert Schneevoigt*

Faculty Bargaining in Public
Higher Education: A Report and
Two Essays
*The Carnegie Council on Policy
Studies in Higher Education,
Joseph W. Garbarino, David E.
Feller, Matthew W. Finkin*

Investment in Learning: The
Individual and Social Value of
American Higher Education
*Howard R. Bowen
with the collaboration of Peter
Clecak, Jacqueline Powers Doud,
Gordon K. Douglass*

THREE THOUSAND FUTURES
The Next Twenty Years for Higher Education
The Carnegie Council on Policy Studies in Higher Education

Copyright ©1980 by: The Carnegie Foundation
for the Advancement of Teaching

Jossey-Bass Inc., Publishers
433 California Street
San Francisco, California 94104

Jossey-Bass Limited
28 Banner Street
London EC1Y 8QE

*Copies of the full report are available from Jossey-Bass, San Francisco,
for the United States and Possessions, and for Canada,
Australia, New Zealand, and Japan.
Copies for the rest of the world are available
from Jossey-Bass, London.*

Library of Congress Cataloging in Publication Data

Carnegie Council on Policy Studies in Higher Education.
    Three thousand futures.

    Includes bibliographical references and index.
    1. College attendance—United States. 2.   Educa-
tion, Higher—United States.   I.   Title.
LC148.C29   1980   378′ .1059′73   79-9665
ISBN 0-87589-453-4

Manufactured in the United States of America

JACKET DESIGN BY WILLI BAUM

FIRST EDITION
          First printing: May 1980
          Second printing: August 1980
          Third printing: February 1981
          Fourth printing: October 1982

Code 8014

THREE THOUSAND FUTURES

The Next Twenty Years for Higher Education

Jossey-Bass Publishers

San Francisco • Washington • London • 1982

Introductory Note on the Carnegie Council on Higher Education

The report that follows is the last in a series of topical reports issued by the Carnegie Council on Policy Studies in Higher Education, 1974–1980.[1] This series has followed one by the Carnegie Commission on Higher Education, 1967–1973.[2]

The Council owes a debt of deep gratitude to the members of its staff whom we list below with their titles:[3]

Margaret S. Gordon, *Associate Director*
Verne A. Stadtman, *Associate Director and Editor*

[1]A *Summary Report on the Carnegie Council on Higher Education* (forthcoming) contains a digest of each report of the Council and of each research study published by the Council. It also lists the prior reports of the Commission and sponsored studies undertaken for the Commission. In total there have been 40 reports and 120 sponsored studies.

[2]For a summary of the work of the predecessor Commission, see *Priorities for Action: Final Report of the Carnegie Commission on Higher Education* (1973a); *A Digest of Reports of the Carnegie Commission on Higher Education* (1974); and *Sponsored Research of the Carnegie Commission on Higher Education* (1975).

See also Mayhew (1973); Wren (1975); Pifer (1975); and, for a European point of view, Embling (1974).

[3]This list includes all persons who have served half-time or more for two years or more of the Council's existence, or who served for the last six months of the Council's term.

Charlotte Alhadeff, *Research Specialist*
Robert O. Berdahl, *Senior Fellow* (1974 to 1976)
Nancy A. Blumenstock, *Editor*
William Carmichael, *Research Assistant*
Earl F. Cheit, *Associate Director* (1974 and 1975)
C. E. Christian, *Research Fellow*
Florence Eisemann, *Administrative Assistant*
Sandra Elman, *Research Assistant*
Marian Gade, *Postgraduate Researcher*
Ruth Goto, *Postgraduate Researcher*
Sura Johnson, *Survey Coordinator*
Barbara Jordan, *Secretary* (1974 and 1975)
Maureen Kawaoka, *Administrative Secretary*
Martin Kramer, *Senior Fellow*
Arthur E. Levine, *Senior Fellow*
Sandra Loris, *Secretary*
Jeanne M. Marengo, *Secretary* (1973 to 1978)
Lillian North, *Secretary*
Thomas Phalen, *Research Assistant*
Nanette Sand, *Librarian*
Karen Seriguchi, *Editorial Assistant* (1973 to 1976)
John R. Shea, *Senior Fellow*
Katrine Stephenson, *Office Manager*
Rachel Volberg, *Research Assistant*
Claudia White, *Secretary*
Scott Wren, *Research Associate*
Sylvia Zuck, *Secretary*

The present membership of the Council is shown in the signatures to this introductory note. Other persons who served as members of the Council, with their dates of service, have been:

William G. Bowen, 1974 to 1977
Ernest L. Boyer, 1974 to 1977
Philip R. Lee, 1976 to 1977
Pauline Tompkins, 1973 to 1976
William Van Alstyne, 1973 to 1976
Clifton R. Wharton, Jr., 1973 to 1975

Serving as members of the Council in all but title, attending all meetings, participating in all discussions, commenting upon all reports, and being helpful in many other ways have been the following members of the staff of The Carnegie Foundation for the Advancement of Teaching:

E. Alden Dunham, *Secretary*
David Z. Robinson, *Vice-President*
Richard H. Sullivan, *Treasurer*

We also greatly appreciate the attendance at several of our meetings of Jack W. Peltason, President of the American Council on Education. David Riesman of Harvard has similarly attended quite regularly and has gone over each report in great detail in advance, making comments that draw on his unique knowledge of American higher education. We all, particularly the members of the staff, have learned greatly from him.

The Council has met on the following dates and in the following locations, benefitting on most of these occasions from opportunities to meet with many leaders of higher education, literally hundreds of them in total:

Dates	*Location*
December 17, 1973	New York, New York
April 1, 1974	New York, New York
April 15, 1974	Claremont, California
May 29, 1974	New York, New York
October 8-9, 1974	Berkeley, California
January 9-11, 1975	Berkeley, California
February 6-7, 1975	Berkeley, California
April 14, 1975*	Salt Lake City, Utah
May 5-7, 1975	Princeton, New Jersey
June 18-19, 1975	New York, New York
October 10-11, 1975	Washington, D.C.
November 19, 1975*	New York, New York
January 8-9, 1976	Tampa, Florida
February 5-6, 1976	Berkeley, California
March 25-26, 1976	Berkeley, California
April 12, 1976*	Ann Arbor, Michigan

* Joint meeting with The Board of Trustees of The Carnegie Foundation for the Advancement of Teaching.

June 14–15, 1976	Albany, New York
October 21–23, 1976	Toronto, Canada
January 6–8, 1977	Berkeley, California
February 17–19, 1977	Tempe, Arizona
April 17, 1977	Nashville, Tennessee
June 15–17, 1977	Fairbanks and Anchorage, Alaska
September 7–8, 1977	New York, New York
November 16–17, 1977	New York, New York
January 11–13, 1978	La Jolla and San Diego, California
April 15–16, 1978	Wellesley, Massachusetts
June 14–16, 1978**	Nortre Dame, Indiana
October 10–11, 1978	Washington, D.C.
November 15–16, 1978	New York, New York
February 8–11, 1979	Ajijic, Mexico
April 24–25, 1979	Berkeley, California
June 20–22, 1979	Missoula, Montana
October 4–6, 1979	West Greenwich, Rhode Island

The Council has had the advantage of good advice on several of its reports, including the present one, from members of the Technical Advisory Committee whose names and affiliations are:

Professor Frederick E. Balderston
Chairman
Center for Research in Management
University of California, Berkeley

Professor Earl F. Cheit
Dean
School of Business Administration
University of California, Berkeley

Professor Lyman Glenny
School of Education
University of California, Berkeley

** Joint meeting with members of Carnegie Commission on Higher Education.

Professor Charlotte Kuh
Graduate School of Education
Harvard University

Professor Eugene C. Lee
Director
Institute of Governmental Studies
University of California, Berkeley

Professor Lewis Mayhew
School of Education
Stanford University

Professor T. R. McConnell
Professor Emeritus, School of Education
University of California, Berkeley

Professor Roy Radner
Department of Economics
University of California, Berkeley

Professor Neil J. Smelser
Department of Sociology
University of California, Berkeley

Professor Martin Trow
Graduate School of Public Policy
University of California, Berkeley

The Trustees of The Carnegie Foundation for the Advancement of Teaching have given us excellent support throughout. At each of their two annual meetings, the Council has met with the Foundation Trustees to discuss the contents of one or more reports. Trustees have reviewed these drafts most carefully and given their advice. Several of the reports have been issued in their name. The membership of the Trustees has been as follows, with the titles they held at the time they served:

Elias Blake, Jr.
President
Clark College

Ernest L. Boyer*
Chancellor
State University of New York

Kingman Brewster, Jr.
(Chairperson 1973)
President
Yale University

J. Richardson Dilworth
Rockefeller Family and Associates

Cecelia Hodges Drewry
Assistant Dean of the College
Princeton University

Stephen M. Dubrul, Jr.
Partner, Lazard Frères

Nell P. Eurich*
Senior Consultant
International Council for
*   Educational Development*

Daniel J. Evans*
President
The Evergreen State College

John T. Fey
Chairman of the Board
The Equitable Life Assurance
*   Society of the United States*

Robben W. Fleming
(Chairperson 1978 and 1979)
President
Corporation for Public Broadcasting

Elbert K. Fretwell, Jr.*
(Chairperson 1976, 1977)
Chancellor
The University of North Carolina
*   at Charlotte*

Donald N. Frey
Chairman of the Board
Bell & Howell Company

William Friday
President
University of North Carolina

Robert F. Goheen
Chairman of the Board
Council on Foundations

Hanna H. Gray
Provost
Yale University

Sheldon Hackney
President
Tulane University

Theodore M. Hesburgh
President
University of Notre Dame

John G. Kemeny
President
Dartmouth College

Clark Kerr*
Chairperson and Director
Carnegie Council on Policy
*   Studies in Higher Education*

* Also member of the Carnegie Council.

Leslie Koltai
Chancellor
Los Angeles Community
   College District

Marigold Linton
Professor of Psychology
The University of Utah

Herman H. Long
President
Talledega College

Candida Lund
President
Rosary College

Richard W. Lyman
President
Stanford University

Margaret L. A. MacVicar*
Associate Professor
   of Physical Science
Massachusetts Institute
   of Technology

Sterling M. McMurrin
Dean of the Graduate School
University of Utah

Malcolm C. Moos
President
University of Minnesota

Barbara W. Newell
President
Wellesley College

Frank Newman*
President
University of Rhode Island

Robert M. O'Neil*
Vice President
Indiana University
   at Bloomington

Rosemary Park*
Professor of Education, Emeritus
University of California,
   Los Angeles

James A. Perkins*
Chairman of the Board
International Council for
   Educational Development

Alan Pifer*
President
The Carnegie Foundation for
   the Advancement of Teaching

Joseph B. Platt*
President
Claremont University Center

Tómas Rivera
Chancellor
University of California,
   Riverside

George L. Shinn
Chairman of the Board
First Boston Corporation

* Also member of the Carnegie Council.

Stephen H. Spurr*
Professor
LBJ School of Public Affairs
University of Texas at Austin

Pauline Tompkins
(Chairperson 1974, 1975)
President
Cedar Crest College

Sidney J. Weinberg, Jr.
Partner
Goldman, Sachs & Co.

Clifton R. Wharton, Jr.
President
Michigan State University

O. Meredith Wilson
Director
Center for Advanced Study
in the Behavioral Sciences
Stanford University

The main library (and several of its branches) at the University of California, Berkeley, has been most helpful in making its excellent collections readily available to us and in the spirit of the greatest of goodwill.

Jossey-Bass Inc. has been the publisher for the Council, and we thank the staff for their advice, cooperation, and service.

Above all, the members of the Council wish to express profound appreciation to The Carnegie Foundation for the Advancement of Teaching for giving us a privileged opportunity to learn more about American higher education, and to express our opinions about its course of development and about the public and private policies we think may best advance its welfare.

Members of the Carnegie Council
on Policy Studies in Higher Education

Nolen M. Ellison
President
Cuyahoga Community College

Nell P. Eurich
Senior Consultant
International Council for
Educational Development

Daniel J. Evans
President
The Evergreen State College

E. K. Fretwell, Jr.
Chancellor
The University of North
Carolina at Charlotte

Margaret L. A. MacVicar
Associate Professor of
*   Physical Science*
Massachusetts Institute
*   of Technology*

Frank Newman
President
University of Rhode Island

Robert M. O'Neil
Vice President
Indiana University
*   at Bloomington*

Rosemary Park
Professor of Education, Emeritus
University of California,
*   Los Angeles*

James A. Perkins
President
International Council for
*   Educational Development*

Alan Pifer
President
The Carnegie Foundation for the
*   Advancement of Teaching*

Joseph B. Platt
President
Claremont University Center

Lois D. Rice
Vice President
College Entrance Examination
*   Board*

William M. Roth

Stephen H. Spurr
Professor
LBJ School of Public Affairs
University of Texas at Austin

Clark Kerr
Chairperson and Director
Carnegie Council on Policy Studies
*   in Higher Education*

THREE THOUSAND FUTURES

FUTURES

*The Next Twenty Years
for Higher Education*

1

The Fears of Some
and the Hopes
of Others

Since 1870, enrollments in higher education have grown at a compound annual rate of 5 percent; ahead of the total population growth of 1.6 percent. Resources used by institutions of higher education have increased from what we estimate was 0.1 percent of the GNP in 1870 to 2.1 percent presently (not including construction).

During the next 20 years, enrollments may fall even as the total population continues to rise; real resources available to and used by colleges and universities also may decline, even if and as the total GNP keeps increasing.

This dramatic new situation has given rise to a great sense of uncertainty within higher education, to many fears and to some hopes.

We set forth some of the fears expressed by individuals within higher education without endorsing them but rather as one possible, if extreme, scenario. We do the same, with the same qualification, for some of the hopes that have been set forth. In each case, we wish to emphasize, these are views set forth by others and are not necessarily our findings. We then note that this report will discuss our own view of the future, which relates to both some of the fears and some of the hopes, and that it will comment on which of the fears and which of the hopes we think are most likely to be realized—and we believe, as our analysis will show, there will be some of each. We also set forth courses of action we believe may reduce some of the fears and give realization to more of the hopes. What is certain is that, at this turning point in the history of higher education, the new uncertainties have given rise to an explosion of expressions of both fears and hopes.

Fears in the Outlooks of Some

- Enrollments will fall even more than the size of the historic college-age cohort (18-21) because a glut of former college students in the labor market is driving down the salaries of college graduates. It has been projected that the combination of a smaller age cohort and reduced prospects for college graduates in the labor market may cause enrollments to decline by 40 or even 50 percent.
- The combination of tax limitation movements plus other higher priority competing claims on public expenditures will reduce the resources available to higher education. At the same time, inflation raises the costs of providing a higher education more than other costs rise because there is no gain in productivity, as there is in most other sectors of society, to help offset these higher costs. The return on endowment has already declined drastically and may virtually disappear as a source of income. 'The financial situation of higher education is therefore even more threatening than are its enrollment prospects.
- Colleges and universities will compete for ever more scarce students in destructive ways—including false advertising, easy academic credits, soft courses, grade inflation. To an alarming degree, some of this has happened even *before* total enrollments started to go down. Public confidence in higher education erodes. Controls increase.
- Faculty members first refuse to recognize the gravity of the new situation and then react in rigidly defensive ways, through collective bargaining and attacks on presidents and trustees, when adjustments are proposed. Faculty members are becoming older and farther removed from the students, are mostly white men

blocking women and minorities from employment, are more tenured-in.

- Both the number and quality of persons willing to serve as administrators decline as the positions become more difficult and subject to more harassment.
- Students, with their new-found influence through choice of where and in what they enroll, increasingly guide institutional developments toward lower standards of academic conduct and quality. The counter-culture of the students overwhelms the high culture of the academics. Students drop in and drop out; now here, now there.
- Public authorities will penetrate ever farther into the internal life of institutions, increasingly determining what shall and shall not be done. They will undertake to manage the decline of enrollment by direct intervention both quantitatively and, more ominously, qualitatively.
- The private sector of higher education will be decimated because it cannot compete owing to its higher tuition; meanwhile, public controls and public financial support make it only quasi-private — reducing its rationale for continuation.
- The future of institutions is only marginally in their own hands.
- Research is adversely affected because young scientists are no longer hired and older scientists tend to become less productive.
- All institutions of higher education are becoming or will become less dynamic in their development; more torn by internal stresses and strains in a Hobbesean world of "every man against every man"; more creatures of the public will expressed through bureaucratic controls than free-standing, self-governing entities.
- Campus governance is already turning from a tone of cooperation and mutual tolerance to one of competition and mistrust.
- The electronic revolution of cassettes and computers and TV sets tied into satellites makes classroom-type higher education increasingly obsolete; and colleges fight rather than embrace the new technology, driving it into commercial channels.

This is not just a series of Lamentations by a few academic Jeremiahs. Some of these fears are already actualities, and there are many people in higher education who are expecting the worst.

Hopes in the Outlooks of Others

- Enrollments do not fall all that much; they might even rise—
  perhaps as much as 25 or even 40 percent. Older persons and
  foreign students take the place of the missing 18-21 year olds.
- Resources go down, but not as much as enrollments, as tuition
  rises and states and the federal government continue their historic
  good support of higher education—and they can afford to do this
  because per capita income keeps rising and they are realizing
  savings anyway on the reduced enrollments.
- Higher education is politically influential enough to hold on to its
  current share (2.1 percent) of a rising GNP, like farmers holding
  on to parity. Vastly increased student financial aid makes it pay to
  be a student; and unemployment in the labor market impels youth
  into the colleges. Enrollment never falls; it may even rise significantly. Universal attendance is the next historic stage of development after the realization of universal access. All it takes is large
  enough federal and state subsidies of students.
- Colleges and universities develop codes of fair practices, through
  the leadership of the American Council on Education and other
  national associations and regional accrediting agencies, and
  preserve the academic integrity of higher education.
- The end of expansion, and even the discipline of moderate
  contraction, allows institutions to turn their energies to the quality
  of education. More time and thought can be given to educating the
  new and ever more diverse student body, and to new ways of
  linking research and public service to instruction.
- Faculty members develop realistic expectations and place the
  long-term welfare of their institutions above sectional and private
  interests. Imaginative personnel policies make it possible to keep a
  small flow of high-quality young faculty members entering the
  system, including women and minorities.
- Trustees choose administrators more carefully for their leadership
  talents and give them better support; they also work harder to raise
  more private funds.
- Students want a good education by and large, and they are
  intelligent consumers. They choose the best academic institutions
  and the best programs, and these areas of higher education prosper.

They will, in any event, constitute a more buoyant generation facing better prospects in the labor market.

- Public authorities will exercise self-restraint in further intrusion into the internal life of institutions.
- The private sector has great strength to start with, and both the states and the federal government will give it increasing support without reducing its autonomy. Only the weakest institutions, both private and public, are shaken out, and this actually strengthens the system as a whole.
- The federal government, perhaps in concert with industry, steps in to assure an adequate flow of young scientists into universities; and gives greater support to basic research generally.
- Colleges and universities stay flexible and preserve the quality of their internal life.
- Colleges and universities use this period as a time for reshaping their organization and philosophies to the needs and challenges of the twenty-first century.
- The new technology supplements older forms of instruction but does not replace them.
- The nation surges ahead with renewed vitality, and higher education makes central contributions to this forward thrust.

This is not just a utopian vision. There are those within and without higher education already acting as though it were the reality of the future.

Which Future?

Either of these scenarios could happen in relatively full measure, or large elements of one could be combined with large parts of the other.

Which is the more realistic scenario? Or, better, which parts of each scenario may be the more realistic possiblities?

What can be done by individuals and institutions to help realize the hopes and eliminate the fears?

These are the central questions to which this report is addressed. Many others, of course, already have addressed, are addressing, or will address these same questions and come up with different answers than those we give. There are many differences concerning both what may happen and what should be done. We base our views on the studies we have made and the many discussions we have held over the past six years.

We recognize full well the hazards of trying to describe the unknown and unknowable, but we believe that the views people hold of the future, both when they turn out to be right and when they turn out to be wrong, help to shape that future in fundamental ways. The purpose of all policy is to change the future and, thus, how we see the future affects how we seek to change it. Policies adopted by both public and private bodies, based on the views they hold, can affect the future for better or for worse. We set forth a selected list of policies that we are convinced will lead to better results for a crucial segment of American society so that higher education may serve more effectively the people and the institutions of the United States. We express our judgment about what is most likely to happen and about what should most urgently be done.

We address this report:

- To the leaders of each institution of higher education — trustees, presidents and faculty—with the message that there are some long-term problems ahead that require early attention to long-term solutions.
- To state planners with the message that a too negative view of the future may turn out to be a self-fulfilling prophecy, and that creation and use of fair competition in the student market is a better alternative than increasingly detailed state control in managing a decline in enrollment.
- To the federal government, which can take some highly useful but not very costly actions.
- To all those who can contribute private funds to colleges and universities (alumni, corporations, foundations) with the message that their contributions are the best guarantee of continued autonomy for all of higher education and of high quality in its most future-oriented functions of scholarship, of training the highest skills, and of commenting constructively on the functioning of society.

We give special attention in this report to enrollments, not for their own sake or for the sake of survival of institutions or some of their component parts, per se, or out of pity for the plight of an over-

expanded industry. We are concerned, rather, that in a largely enrollment-driven system of higher education decreasing enrollments can potentially have unfortunate impacts on academic excellence, on accumulation of scientific knowledge, on future capacity to interpret the past culture and the current human predicament, on the tone and spirit of an essential segment of American society, on the survival of private initiative and institutional autonomy.

There are other major axes along which higher education is developing in addition to the demographic, including:

- The axis of greater equality of access to higher education for minorities, women, and adults; and of improving opportunities for youth outside of higher education
- The axis of innovation: new ways and new times and new places to undertake higher education via both traditional and non-traditional colleges and what we call later the Second and Third Sectors of postsecondary education, and via the new technologies
- The axis of greater governmental impact on higher education through control of institutions, public support of both public and private colleges, public support of students in meeting their costs, intervention by way of regulation, and intervention by the courts.

We make reference to each of these axes in this report.[1]

Discussions of the future of higher education, in our judgment, are often too dominated by gloom and doom, even by a sense of panic: all certain changes are said by some to be for the worse, and uncertainty additionally is said to be unlimited. Some of these observers seem to have been unprepared for any unfavorable changes in the status quo ante. For too long they seem to have expected that

---

[1]We call attention to three forthcoming reports by members of the staff, separately published, which discuss in more detail topics treated briefly in this report: *The Venture Capital of Higher Education: The Public and Private Sources of Discretionary Funds* by Martin Kramer; *When Dreams and Heroes Died: A Portrait of Today's College Student* by Arthur Levine; *Academic Adaptations: Higher Education Prepares for the 1980s and 1990s* by Verne A. Stadtman.

The Council also undertook a special survey of developments in and opinions about higher education involving replies from 570 carefully selected institutions. A description of this survey (identified in the text as Carnegie Council Surveys, 1978) appears in Appendix A. This appendix also describes other Carnegie surveys upon which we have drawn. Appendix B defines some technical terms we use in this report.

everything would get better and better, that continuation of the Golden Age of higher education was a matter of right, and they seem to have forgotten the age-old cycles of advance and retreat, the long history of new problems following on old solutions.

Our version of the future is, instead, that problems, even severe problems, lie ahead, but that there are reasonable solutions to most, if not all, of them; that it is better to plan to meet the future effectively than just to fear it as a new dark age. The performance of higher education becomes ever more important to the welfare of the nation, and thus it becomes ever more important for the nation to insure the continuing welfare of higher education—this is both highly necessary and reasonably possible. Becoming somewhat smaller is, we believe, compatible with becoming somewhat better.

2

Base Point: 1980

Much has been happening to and within higher education in recent years. These developments form the background from which the rest of the twentieth century is approached. Reference to these trends also helps to make the point that the ensuing period may also bring many changes; that the status quo of today will not be the status quo of tomorrow.

Heredity can be a strong force in higher education[1]—the Catholic Church and the early universities of Western Europe are, among all the institutions in our historical tradition, the ones that have continued least changed in form and function.[2] Yet institutions of higher education do change, including when, as in the United States, they are heavily connected to a fluctuating student market as compared with when they are more tied to the conservative influence of the academic guild of the professors or to an established state ideology and plan. And student markets in our society will be even

---

[1]For a discussion of the major role of heredity in higher education, see Ashby (1967). He states that it is much more profitable to reflect on the "future of heredity" than on the "future of the environment of universities." However, in this report, the Council does reflect on those parts of the future environment that are already more or less known, or, at least, can be speculated about with some caution.

[2]Taking, as a starting point, 1530, when the Lutheran Church was founded, some 66 institutions that existed then still exist today in the Western World in recognizable forms: the Catholic Church, the Lutheran Church, the parliaments of Iceland and the Isle of Man, and 62 universities. Universities in the past have been remarkable for their historic continuity, and we may expect this same characteristic in the future. They have experienced wars, revolutions, depressions, and industrial transformations, and have come out less changed than almost any other segment of their societies.

more overwhelming in their impact in the two decades ahead. Institutions of higher education also change rapidly, of course, in the process of civil revolutions and in the process of economic development.

We start this analysis of the contemporary situation of higher education in the United States by taking a retrospective view of the 1970s.

Some Myths About the 1970s

We would like to challenge the conventional wisdom about the 1970s—that it was a decade of disaster for higher education. We believe a new perspective is needed about where we have been and where we are now. How true are some standard assertions?

"Most institutions lost enrollment." Actually, most institutions (59 percent) gained full-time equivalent (FTE) enrollment. Only 29 percent lost enrollment. The remainder stayed more or less even. Total enrollment rose by 24 percent (see Table 1 for these and other data).

"The private institutions have been badly hurt." Actually, enrollments (FTE) overall increased significantly—by 16 percent. Enrollments in the private sector declined as a percentage of the total but, if this sector is looked at on its own, it prospered overall in the 1970s. Private institutions were still spending one-third more per student-credit-hour on instructional costs than were public institutions. The situation of institutions per se is less clear. If all institutions, as classified by the U.S. National Center for Education Statistics (NCES), are included, it appears that there were substantially more private institutions by 1978-79 than in 1970. This, however, is mainly due to two factors: (1) These figures include specialized institutions, most commonly theological seminaries, and (2) they also include, as new additions, pre-existing institutions that became newly accredited. Our own analysis, which excludes both of these categories, shows a decline of private institutions by about 100. We believe this is the more significant figure (see the data in Table 1, Section B).

"Institutions have been starved for money." Actually, expenditures on instructional costs per student in constant dollars remained steady.

"*Rising tuition has really hurt the middle class.*" Actually, privately paid tuition has not risen as fast as disposable family income.

"*The federal government has been carrying an increasing share of the burden of financing institutions of higher education.*" Actually, the federal share for educational and general purposes (which excludes auxiliary enterprises like residence halls, service activi-

Table 1. Selected data on higher education in the 1970s, United States

A. All Institutions
National Center for Education Statistics (NCES) Universe

	1970	*Latest year*	*Percentage change*
Total enrollment (FTE)	6,738,000	8,372,000 (1978-79)	24.3%
Enrollment in private institutions (FTE)	1,785,000	2,069,000 (1978-79)	15.9
Total number of institutions	2,817	3,125 (1978-79)	10.9
Number of private institutions	1,504	1,660 (1978-79)	10.4
Ratio of expenditures per student on instruction in private colleges versus public	1.34	1.34 (1976-77)	0
Real expenditures per student on instruction (Average for the 1960s = $2,500)	$3,070 (1969-70)	$3,166 (1976-77)	1.5
Privately paid tuition as a percentage of per capita disposable income			
Public institutions	10.5%	9.6% (1976-77)	-8.6
Private institutions	50.3%	44.5% (1976-77)	-11.5
Federal share of institutional expenditures for educational and general purposes	22.5% (1969-70)	16.4% (1976-77)	-21.7
State share of institutional expenditures for educational and general purposes	36.6% (1969-70)	41.6% (1976-77)	13.7

(continued on next page)

Table 1 *(continued)*

B. Selected Categories of Institutions[a]
Carnegie Universe

	All institutions		Public		Private	
	Number	*Percentage*	*Number*	*Percentage*	*Number*	*Percentage*
FTE enrollment changes						
Gainers	1,256	59%	771	68%	485	48%
Losers	630	29	236	21	394	39
Stable	259	12	129	11	130	13
Total	2,145	100	1,136	100	1,009	100
Institutional changes						
Openings	111		80		31	
Closures, mergers, and shifts in control	186		56		130	

[a]Specialized institutions are excluded. They include professional schools such as theological schools, medical schools, schools of engineering and technology, business, law, and other specialized institutions at the four-year level. Also excluded are institutions already in existence (but not counted, in accordance with NCES practice) in 1970 that gained accreditation in the 1970s. These are, however, reflected in the number of institutions in 1978-79 shown in Section A of this table. Enrollment changes could be analyzed only for these 2,145 institutions which reported enrollment in 1970 and 1978; 249 institutions which closed, merged, or otherwise did not report for both years are not included.

Sources: Section A: U.S. National Center for Education Statistics (NCES) (1970; 1971; 1973; 1978a; 1979b). *Section B:* NCES (1971; 1979d).

ties, and construction) went down from 23 to 16 percent (mostly because research support declined comparatively). The federal share of direct student aid, however, increased.

"The states have not done their share." Actually, the states' share rose from 37 to 42 percent of expenditures for educational and general purposes.

The 1970s, despite the "New Depression" (Cheit, 1971) period of recession early in the decade and the OPEC crisis in the middle, and contrary to the impression left by the many complaints and some cries of anguish, was a good decade for higher education. It was possibly the best decade in all of history, in terms of institutional progress, except for the 1960s. Higher education ended the 1970s generally in good shape. For example, college presidents (Carnegie Council Surveys, 1978), reported improvement in the quality of the faculty, among other on-campus improvements. Reports about a few losses in selected areas have obscured this basic fact: Higher education concluded the decade in better condition, by and large, than it entered it.

The 1970s were a decade, both for the nation and for higher education, when bad news was more likely to be featured than good news. An impression, both inside and outside higher education, of its threatened condition was created by:

Student unrest at the beginning of the decade that shattered confidence on campus and support in the community

The decline of male participation rates with the end of the military draft

The first impact on the labor market of the new outpouring of college graduates, coincident with recurring recessions

The deep recession and dramatic rise in oil prices in 1974-75 that sent many colleges into financial deficits.

These shocks were widely reported and deeply felt. What was not so evident was the underlying growth in enrollments and the sustained financial assistance, particularly by the states. The quiet, almost unnoticed favorable developments, by the end of the decade, had more than balanced the shocks along the way.

We note misconceptions about the 1970s for two reasons. One, they demonstrate a negative tendency of some academics when they comment on the situation of higher education—a tendency to see only the worst aspects. Their views need to be discounted.[3] Two, a presentation of the actualities shows that higher education enters the 1980s from a relatively high level of performance—not from a badly

---

[3]See Kerr (1975). The titles of a number of recent books are cited, including *Academics in Retreat, Death of the American University,* and *Fall of the American University.*

weakened situation; and is generally in a position of substantial strength as it faces the future.

To get more accurate images of the future we need more accurate perceptions of the recent past.

Important Contemporary Trends

So much has been happening to higher education in recent times that it is difficult to select a short list of the most important developments. However, we do advance the following (and incomplete) list:

1. *Rise of the public sector.* Not so long ago, in 1950, higher education was half public and half private as measured by enrollments. Nationally, it is now four-fifths public and one-fifth private, with great state-to-state variations. The question must now be raised, for the first time in our national history, as to whether or not the private sector might become too small in relative terms to act as an adequate check and balance to the public sector, to act as an effective model for the public sector, and to serve as an adequate competitive spur to it. Table 2 shows the trends overall and by major institutional category. The public community colleges have been the great gainers over the past two decades in terms of enrollments. While the private sector has lost proportionately, it has, however, gained absolutely.

2. *Transition from free sector to regulated industry.* Higher education, including the so-called public institutions, was once largely a self-governing, autonomous part of American society. Increasingly, including the private institutions but to a lesser extent, it has become subject to many forms of regulation and is taking on the status of a regulated industry. Even its internal records on students and faculty are now subject to controls. Less policy is set by faculties and by boards of trustees and more by state governments, and by federal law and agencies. The courts are also more and more being drawn into what were once the internal affairs of higher education; and when drawn in are intruding more deeply into these affairs. This increase in public regulation and influence is blurring the distinctions between the public and private sectors, particularly at the federal level. It might be more accurate to say that we have a public and a quasi-public sector.

3. *Changing sources of financial support—more public money.* Two long-term changes (since 1930) have taken place in the source of

Table 2. Enrollment shares among sectors of higher education

	Share of total headcount enrollment (in percentages)			
	1950	*1960*	*1970*	*1976*
Total, all institutions				
Public	50.0	59.1	74.8	78.4
Private	50.0	40.9	25.2	21.6
By category				
Research Universities and				
Doctorate-granting Universities:				
Public			23.7	21.4
Private			7.8	6.0
Liberal Arts Colleges:				
Public			0.5	0.2
Private			7.6	4.6
Comprehensive Universities and Colleges:				
Public			23.3	21.3
Private			6.1	7.1
Two-Year Colleges:				
Public		13.9	26.0	34.2
Private		2.4	1.6	1.4
Other Categories:				
Public			1.3	1.3
Private			2.1	2.5
	Total Headcount Enrollment (in thousands)			
	1950[a]	*1960*[a]	*1970*	*1976*
All institutions	2,281.3	3,582.7	8,580.9	11,012.1
Public	1,139.7	2,115.9	6,428.1	8,653.5
Private	1,141.6	1,466.8	2,152.8	2,358.7

[a] Degree-credit enrollment only.

Sources: U.S. NCES (1979a); and Carnegie Council.

funds for institutions of higher education: a major redistribution from private to public funds; and the rise of the federal government as a major contributor of public funds. More recently (the past decade), however, private funds have gone down only moderately on a comparative basis. Among private funds, the biggest change since

1930 has been the collapse of endowment as a source of income. The big recent change has been the decline, on a percentage basis, of federal funds as less money comparatively has been spent on research. Figure 1 shows these changes since 1930.[4]

The sources of institutional funds shown in Figure 1, however, do not reveal total federal expenditures on higher education, because major portions of federal student aid—especially under the Basic Grants, veterans' educational benefits, and social security benefits programs—do not flow to institutions but are allocated directly to students, who may use the funds in large part for subsistence (often entirely outside of institutional facilities). Moreover, a portion of tuition payments included in Figure 1 is actually met through student aid income of institutions. Figure 2 indicates changes in the sources of total monetary outlays for higher education, including total student aid expenditures of federal and state governments. (Private student aid is included under philanthropy.) Students and families are now meeting a considerably smaller proportion of total expenditures than in 1929–30, partly because of the growth of public student aid and partly because of the relative growth of enrollment in public institutions with their lower tuition charges. The share of state and local governments (primarily state) has risen in recent decades, as has the share of the federal government, if we include all federal student aid expenditures (which have increased enormously).

We see two trends now in prospect. One is a stabilization of federal support. We foresee no further decline of support to institutions as compared to state support since we believe and recommend that research support will and should be increased by the federal government. We also believe that student aid support will roughly level off. And we see no totally new federal program coming along. The other is somewhat heavier reliance on private support, reversing the historical trend, as resistance to taxation rises and other priorities attract public attention, and as some elements in the population may question the comparatively larger subsidies that go to those young persons attending college.[5] Financial support from the states we see as the most dependable component in the future as in the past.

[4]See also Supplement A, *Sources of Funds for Higher Education.*

[5]See preliminary study by Congressional Budget Office (U.S. Congress, 1979). College students receive about four times the federal subsidy of "all youth," including college students with their high subsidies.

Figure 1. Changes in sources of income of institutions of higher education for educational and general purposes,[a] 1929-30 to 1976-77

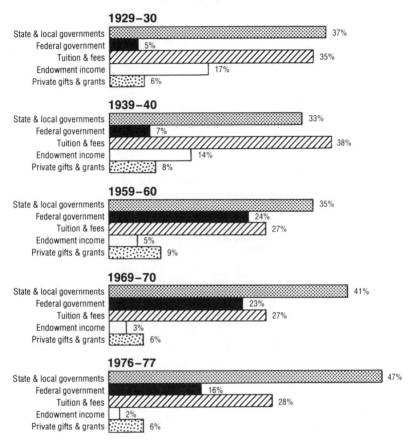

[a]Includes current income received for educational and general purposes, including research; does not include such items as sales and services of educational activities, sales and services of auxiliary enterprises, and sales and services of hospitals, and construction. Tuition represents gross tuition and includes, especially since 1969-70, some tuition expenses met from student aid.

Source: Supplement A, Table A-1.

Figure 2. Changes in sources of monetary outlays for higher education, including support of students, 1929-30 to 1976-77

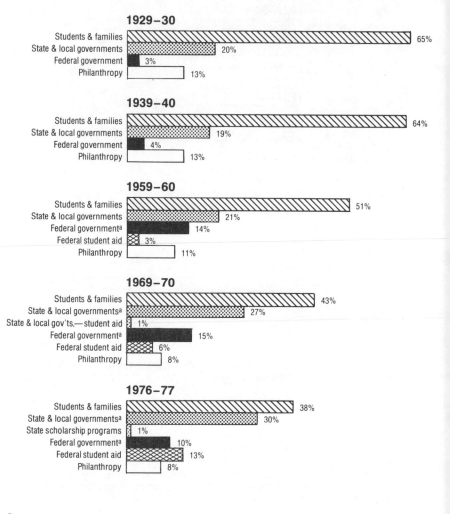

1929–30

Students & families	65%
State & local governments	20%
Federal government	3%
Philanthropy	13%

1939–40

Students & families	64%
State & local governments	19%
Federal government	4%
Philanthropy	13%

1959–60

Students & families	51%
State & local governments	21%
Federal government[a]	14%
Federal student aid	3%
Philanthropy	11%

1969–70

Students & families	43%
State & local governments[a]	27%
State & local gov'ts.— student aid	1%
Federal government[a]	15%
Federal student aid	6%
Philanthropy	8%

1976–77

Students & families	38%
State & local governments[a]	30%
State scholarship programs	1%
Federal government[a]	10%
Federal student aid	13%
Philanthropy	8%

[a]Not including student aid.

Source: Supplement A.

4. *Increasing role of large institutions.* The large institution has come to dominate enrollments in higher education. Primarily, this has been the result of student choice and not of intentional public policy. But the choice has been affected by the fact that most large institutions are public, with tuition substantially below levels in private institutions; by the improved academic quality of many public institutions, and by their concentration on attractive occupational subjects; by the shift from student bodies drawn heavily from upper-income groups oriented toward private and small-scale higher education to mass attendance; by the shift of population to the South and West where large public institutions have long been elite institutions that are often the first choice of the academically able and financially well-to-do. But the shift to larger institutions (but not to the largest) has occurred in the private sector also. It is the small institution that has become endangered. Despite all the rhetoric to the contrary, larger size has become predominantly the more preferred by students. What was once called the "curse of bigness" has now become the "curse of smallness." (See Figure 3 for recent trends.) Campuses with more than 10,000 students accounted for one-quarter of all enrollments in 1955 and one-half in 1977; campuses with fewer than 500 students accounted for 8 percent in 1955 and 1.5 percent in 1977.

Correlated with the growing size of institutions are some other developments. More and more institutions are comprehensive, in the sense that they offer several or even many professional and technical programs and not just teachers' education or just liberal arts. A substantial number of less selective liberal arts colleges have shifted to the comprehensive colleges category; fewer are either specialized (teacher education) or general (liberal) in their approach. Fewer institutions also have an exclusively collegiate atmosphere partly because of larger size, partly because of more part-time employment by students, and partly because more students live off campus.[6]

[6]The number living on campus has dropped from about 60 percent of all students in 1960 to about 20 percent in 1979.

Figure 3. Institutions of higher education by control and size of (headcount) enrollment, percentage distribution, 1955 and 1977

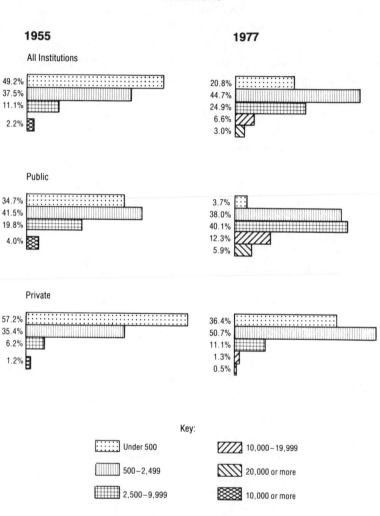

Institutions

1955   **1977**

All Institutions

49.2%
37.5%
11.1%
2.2%

20.8%
44.7%
24.9%
6.6%
3.0%

Public

34.7%
41.5%
19.8%
4.0%

3.7%
38.0%
40.1%
12.3%
5.9%

Private

57.2%
35.4%
6.2%
1.2%

36.4%
50.7%
11.1%
1.3%
0.5%

Key:

Under 500   10,000–19,999

500–2,499   20,000 or more

2,500–9,999   10,000 or more

Figure 3 *(continued)*

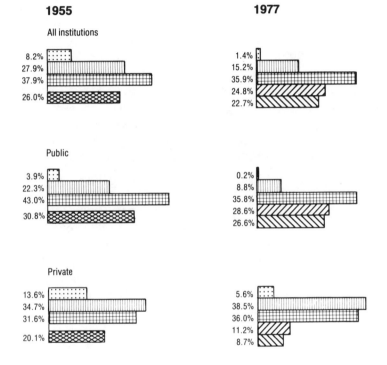

Size of Enrollment

1955

All institutions

8.2%	
27.9%	
37.9%	
26.0%	

1977

1.4%	
15.2%	
35.9%	
24.8%	
22.7%	

Public

3.9%	
22.3%	
43.0%	
30.8%	

0.2%	
8.8%	
35.8%	
28.6%	
26.6%	

Private

13.6%	
34.7%	
31.6%	
20.1%	

5.6%	
38.5%	
36.0%	
11.2%	
8.7%	

Sources: U.S. Department of Health, Education, and Welfare (1958, p. 54); and U.S. NCES (1979a, p. 107).

The very small college has declined in comparative importance. So also have the single-sex, the rural, and the religious colleges. They all represent an earlier America of local attendance patterns, of greater regional variation in attitudes and style, of more parental choice of college. The market is now more cosmopolitan, the dominant culture more uniformly spread, the choices made more by students themselves. And student choices have been increasingly for the comprehensive institution of large size—the choice Americans as a whole also have made in locating increasingly in comprehensive cities. The diversity of American higher education used to be found between and among institutions with conformity within each of them; now diversity is more often found within institutions, with the institutions in their entirety being more alike. Fewer institutions have their own strong individual personalities. Yet there are some new diverse institutions for Native Americans and Hispanics; the black colleges and the fundamentalist Protestant colleges are holding their own; and new types like Empire State in New York and Metropolitan State in Minnesota and the University Without Walls at several locations have come along. Additionally, the new Third Sector[7] brings in other forms of variation as noninstructional institutions take on instructional activities. But, overall, proportionately more students are in the same types of environments than ever before.

Not only the students, by their choice of campus, but also faculties press for conformity with the standard pattern. Many an academic reform of the 1960s and early 1970s foundered on the constant pressure of faculty members to conform toward the standard

[7]We identify the Third Sector as institutions that give postsecondary instruction as an adjunct to noninstructional activities: instruction by a corporation, a research agency, a museum, a trade union, the armed forces. The First Sector is made up of nonprofit colleges; the Second of profit-making institutions. The boundaries of the First Sector have become more imprecise as nontraditional programs are added, and the growth of the Second Sector and the addition of the Third Sector mean that the edges of the total universe of postsecondary education are softer than ever before; the definitions of it are more blurred. The Second Sector and the Third Sector are nibbling away at the enrollments of the First Sector, as well as tapping new markets. These developments make it harder to estimate both the totality of future First Sector enrollments and their distribution among institutions since some institutions are much more affected by these changes than others.

model. The alumni are the great force for preservation of elements of historical diversity where they exist, and their financial support is almost directly related to the traditional distinctiveness of the institution.[8]

Along with concentration of enrollments in larger institutions has gone the growth of systems.[9] For example, in 1978, only 21 of the 141 member institutions in the National Association of State Universities and Land-Grant Colleges were still governed by their own individual boards. This has many implications for the concentration of decisions in the process of governance.

5. *Changing public confidence.* Public confidence in higher education historically has been very high. It fell drastically around 1970 but, compared with that of other institutions, has recovered. It is still low, as is true also for all other American institutions, as compared with earlier periods. It now rates, however, at the highest level among American institutions, along with TV news broadcasts (Figure 4). This relative ranking is an enormous asset. We see a major threat to it, however, as we shall note below, in a declining reputation for integrity of conduct. Public confidence is basic to public financial support, and currently it constitutes a comparatively strong base.

6. *Changing rates of growth.* Higher education has been subject to substantial shifts in rates of enrollment increases over the past 20 years. On the way up, the problems were those of obtaining new physical facilities, and of recruiting added faculty members to the existing system with a resultant explosion in the capacity to train them. In the leveling-off phase, a major problem has been an overcapacity to train new faculty members. The number of additional faculty members required fluctuates more than total enrollments, although institutions do smooth out their demands over a period of several years. A small increase or decrease in the rate of change of enrollments, however, usually means a bigger increase or decrease percentagewise in new faculty hires.

[8]For a discussion of changing patterns of diversity and other transformations in the 1960s, see Hodgkinson (1971); for transformations in the 1970s, see Stadtman (forthcoming).

[9]See the discussions in Lee and Bowen (1971; 1975).

Figure 4. Percentage expressing high confidence in selected major American
institutions (February 1979)

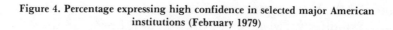

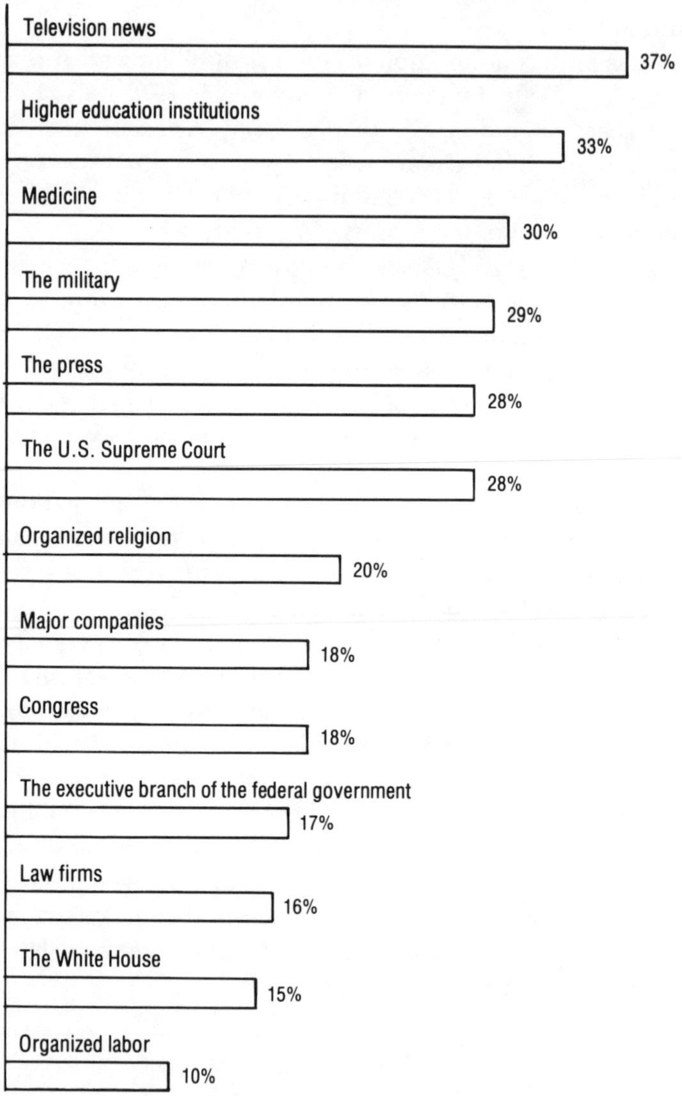

Television news

37%

Higher education institutions

33%

Medicine

30%

The military

29%

The press

28%

The U.S. Supreme Court

28%

Organized religion

20%

Major companies

18%

Congress

18%

The executive branch of the federal government

17%

Law firms

16%

The White House

15%

Organized labor

10%

Source: Reprinted from the ABC News-Harris Survey by permission of the Chicago
Tribune-New York News Syndicate, Inc.

We note in passing that a common academic attitude when facing expansion was "bigger is worse"; now it is "smaller is disastrous." Bigger, by and large, turned out not to be worse, and somewhat smaller may not turn out to be so disastrous. Certainly, however, changing rates and directions of growth are worrisome.

Federal research funds have also been made available in changing amounts. A large decrease, in real terms, occurred in the late 1960s and continued into the 1970s, but this has been reversed in recent years.

Changing rates of growth in enrollments, faculty acquisition rates, and federal research funds have been upsetting factors for higher education.

7. *The older faculty.* The percentage of older faculty members with tenure keeps rising as the rate of new hires goes down. The last heavy period of faculty hiring was from 1960 to 1970; the next will be from 2000 to 2010. The modal age of tenured faculty members in four-year institutions in 1980 will be 36 to 45; in 2000, 56 to 65 (Figure 5). In the latter year, there will be far more faculty members 66 and over than there are faculty members 35 and younger. An older faculty is a higher paid faculty—adding to costs; less resilient in adjusting to new fields that come along; farther removed from the age of the students. On the other hand, more faculty members will be of the home guard type, tied by years of service to the welfare of their own institutions; fewer will be transients who are eager to be on their way somewhere else. This will add to stability in governance and attention to campus welfare. It may also add, however, to the number of time servers on campus.

8. *The institutional stance: from offense to defense.* The tone of the Golden Age of the 1960s was one of euphoria, of expansion, of new endeavors, of overall "telic" and purposeful reform,[10] of additional piecemeal experimentation, of a frantic chase after excellence. The new tone of the advancing demographic depression is now more one of concern and even despair, of concentration on contraction, of avoidance or abandonment of telic reforms, of a single-minded emphasis upon survival. Signs of the new emphasis on survival are legion, including:

---

[10]See the discussion in Grant and Riesman (1978).

Figure 5. Age distribution of tenured faculty in four-year colleges and universities, 1980, 1990, and 2000

AGE
GROUP

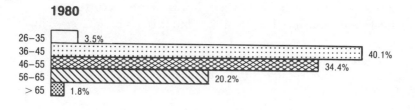

1980

26–35	3.5%
36–45	40.1%
46–55	34.4%
56–65	20.2%
> 65	1.8%

1990

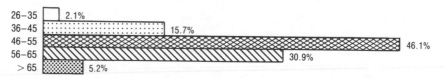

26–35	2.1%
36–45	15.7%
46–55	46.1%
56–65	30.9%
> 65	5.2%

2000

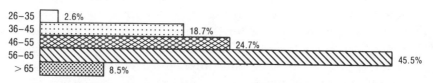

26–35	2.6%
36–45	18.7%
46–55	24.7%
56–65	45.5%
> 65	8.5%

Source: Carnegie Council estimates.

The lowering of admissions requirements

The search for nontraditional students, who in the past have been the least preferred

The increased emphasis on retention of students, sometimes regardless of their performance

The rising level of grades to attract and retain students in courses and departments

The turn toward vocational and professional subjects following student demand

The introduction of new fields and courses that are highly popular with students

The faculty interest in collective bargaining to protect tenure and real income, and, sometimes, to resist the impacts of affirmative action

The effort to find top leadership which is good at cost accounting or at recruitment of students or at fund raising or at all three; to find managers for survival who will balance the books, recruit the students, and raise the funds instead of innovators and planners for a different and hopefully better future.

The impacts on institutional behavior are manifold:

It is more difficult to start anything new with a nonmarket orientation, or to preserve the telic reforms of the 1960s

Supporting personnel—recruiters, admission officers, student financial aid officers, student counselors, for example—are becoming more important

Top leadership is more cautious, less visible

Consultation within the campus is more total, the search for consensus more insistent, the avoidance of controversy and of alienation of any important constituency more avidly sought, the status quo more enshrined

Internal tensions, nevertheless, are exacerbated; departments compete to survive; and coalitions form over where the cuts should or should not be made.

The ambience was once one of overall excitement; now it is more one of tenacity, of holding on within each little academic fortress.

The increasing intrusion of public policy and public regulation adds to the defensive attitudes.

9. *The new students.*[11] The students of today enter on the average with lower levels of developed aptitude.[12] Test scores on entrance have declined (1963–1979) as follows:

Verbal   11 percent

Quantitative   7 percent

Students have changed in other ways:

They are concentrating more on professional and vocational subjects.[13]

They are less active politically. Large-scale political activism died in the summer of 1970 and has never been successfully resurrected. The "far left" has declined by over one-half (1969 to 1978) from 4.5 percent of freshman students to 1.8, and the "middle-of-the-road" group increased by nearly one-half from 42 to 58 percent (Creager and others, 1969; Astin and others, 1978).

Political activity, to the extent it exists, is oriented more toward specific issues than toward overall social reform, and it follows accepted methods of persuasion.

They are less interested in academic reforms. Their efforts at impacts on campus are more of a trade union variety: no increase in tuition, better counseling, and so forth.

They are overwhelmingly choosing large institutions in metropolitan settings.

They are less respectful of rules and regulations—there is more

---

[11]For a detailed discussion of the new generation of students, see Levine, forthcoming.

[12]The average score on the verbal portion of the Scholastic Aptitude Test (SAT) dropped from 478 in 1963 to 427 in 1979; the average mathematical score declined from 502 to 467 (*Higher Education Daily*, 1979, p. 1).

Scores of college graduates on entrance examinations for graduate school (Graduate Record Examination, Graduate Management Admissions Test) have dropped about 5 percent; although Medical College Admission Test scores have risen slightly (data from Educational Testing Service, Princeton, N. J.; and Golladay (1977).

Early in the 1970s, Cross (1971, p. xiii) recognized that ". . . the distinguishing characteristic of the young people seeking postsecondary education in the 1970s is their low level of academic achievement on traditional measures in traditional curricula."

[13]See The Carnegie Foundation for the Advancement of Teaching (1977, p. 103). Professional and vocational majors among undergraduates rose from 40 to 60 percent between 1969 and 1975.

cheating, more vandalism, more defaulting on student loans.[14]

They are, if anything, less hopeful about the world.

They are, on the other hand, if anything, more confident about their own individual futures.

10. *The supremacy of the market.* The orientation of higher education has changed substantially over the past nearly three and one-half centuries. At first, it was toward preparation for the ministry, for teaching, and for community leadership in a frontier nation, with curricular emphasis on the Bible and the classics. Later it added preparation for the other ancient professions, specifically law and medicine. Then, after the American Civil War, attention was turned toward agricultural and industrial production, toward science, engineering, and later business administration. Increasingly in the past two decades, training has been added for policemen, firemen, nurses, and several of the skilled manual trades, among other additional occupations. More recently the mass student market has become more important, particularly for the community colleges, but most colleges have placed additional emphasis upon it. Under the conditions of the next two decades, consumer sovereignty may well prevail largely undisputed in most institutions.

Consumer sovereignty is not the only way to set the agenda for higher education, and consumer sovereignty itself will express quite different tastes in an elite as compared with a mass system of higher education. In addition to consumer sovereignty, there are two other major ways of setting the agenda. One is by the academic guild of the professors, as historically has been the situation in England and in the United States—particularly in the Ivy League and the most selective of the liberal arts colleges. The other is by external authority, which can be quite varied. It may be the state, as in Russia with concern for technology and ideology, or as in France with emphasis upon the civil service and French culture, or as to some extent in the United States with the emphasis of the federal government on encouraging science. It may be the church, as in many early American institutions and some even today. It may be a class, in a class-dominated society, as in England in centuries past

[14]See Carnegie Council on Policy Studies in Higher Education (1979a).

and much of Latin America in more recent times. It may be industry dominating schools of technology or business administration.

So there are alternatives; and there are changing mixtures as there have been in the United States; and the interests of student consumers, faculty producers, and public controllers are partially in harmony as well as partially antithetical. The clear trend, however, perhaps more than ever before, in the 1960s and 1970s, has been toward the student market. The enduring reforms have been the "popular" reforms that follow shifting student interests (Grant and Riesman, 1978, chap. 6). Academic guild interests have been best protected by private endowments, alumni support, and federal research funds; and public interests by earmarked funds such as those for agriculture or health care or mineral technology. But most public funds follow the student market through formulas based on enrollment and through direct aid to students, and so do most private funds in the form of tuition.

We have a largely enrollment-driven system. Such a system works better in a period of expansion than of contraction; and we now face a time of contraction. In a period of expansion, among other things, money can be more easily siphoned off to support academic guild interests. Declining costs per additional student help this with state financing based upon higher average costs, with a resultant gain for the institution in between. In contraction, costs climb back up the steeper marginal cost curve, as fixed overhead is spread over fewer students, and put on pressure to cut into nonessentials—nonessentials in attracting and holding students.

The road to survival now leads through the market place. A new "academic revolution" is upon us.[15] In the 1960s, the revolution consisted of many institutions trying to become research universities and mostly failing (Jencks and Riesman, 1968). In the 1980s and 1990s, it will take more the form of following the long-time example of the community colleges in adjusting to the market, and often succeeding. Excellence was the theme. Now it is survival. Institutions were trading up; now they are trading down.

---

[15]See the discussion in the forthcoming volume by Riesman.

Summary

Thus, we enter the 1980s with a system of higher education characterized by:

Increasing concentration of students in public institutions

More and more regulation by governmental agencies of both public and private institutions

More and more dependence on public sources of financial support

Heavy concentration of students on large campuses of traditional form

Substantial public confidence in higher education on a comparative basis

Slowing and uncertain rates of enrollment growth

An aging faculty

More and more defensive reactions internally

A new generation of students

More and more pressure to serve the student market.

These factors place the old and the new, the static and the dynamic in dramatic conflict. Most of these factors support the old and the static more than the new and the dynamic. But there are contradictions and inherent conflicts in the developing situation. The more dynamic factors are (1) the added emphasis on the student market, which (2) consists of a new generation of students. Higher education, to the extent it changes, will be changing mostly in response to these new students making their choices. A short time ago, higher education was particularly following decisions made in Washington. And, on balance, the circumstances of that day supported more the new and the dynamic. The scientist and the academic institution builder were in the forefront of the procession; today it is the uncommitted students casing their alternative opportunities. It has been a long time since voting in faculty meetings fundamentally set the new course for most institutions of higher education. This form of leadership is by now more a cherished illusion than a reality. The quiet student now leads the way.

Some of the drama of the next two decades will center around the natural and strong efforts of many within the academic community, and particularly among faculty members, to hold on to what they cherish most from the past, and the necessity, felt more strongly by administrators and trustees, to adapt to the new realities of the student market.

3

A Judgment About
Prospective Enrollments

The most dramatic feature of the next 20 years, as far as we now know, is the prospect of declining enrollments after more than three centuries of fairly steady increase (see Figure 6). Points of enrollment acceleration in history have been 1870 with the increase of growth after the Civil War and following the introduction of the land-grant college movement; 1945 with the G.I. Bill of Rights; and 1960 with the "tidal wave" of students following the high birthrates after World War II. Now there is a deceleration point, with the abrupt and substantial demographic decline in the numbers of young persons. Two points of change, with movements in opposite directions, will have occurred within one 20-year period. This has never happened before in American history.

How sharp this deceleration will be has great impacts on how the future is viewed and on what preparations are needed for it.

Were there to be an overall increase in enrollments of 25 percent, as one projection has suggested, almost no institution would be in trouble between 1980-2000 except for problems arising from inflation (A on Figure 7).

Were there to be an overall decrease in enrollments of 25 percent, a large proportion of institutions would be in trouble (C on Figure 7).

Figure 6. Generalized View of Enrollments in Higher Education, 1640 to 2010

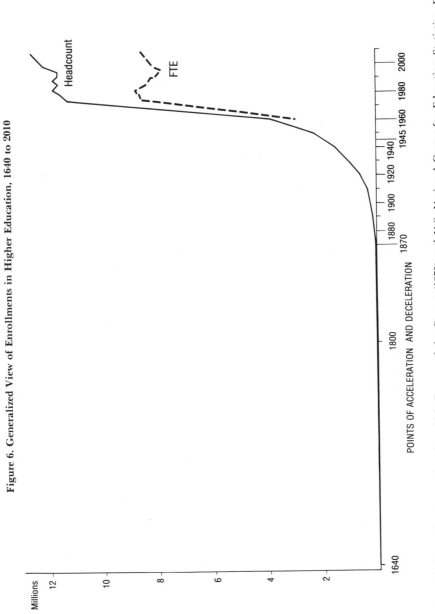

Sources: Carnegie Council estimates based on U.S. Bureau of the Census (1975) and U.S. National Center for Education Statistics, *Fall Enrollment*, appropriate years.

Were there to be an overall decrease of 40 percent, as several predictions foresee, or over 50 percent as one model indicates, then all or nearly all institutions will be in trouble (D on Figure 7).

The first of these projections is based on the assumption that long-term trends for increasing participation rates by youth will reassert themselves, with the 1970s set aside as a special period that is not consistent with more permanent and more favorable tendencies, and that there will be a substantial increase in attendance by adults. The second of these predictions builds on the decline of 25.6 percent in the size of the traditional college-attending age cohort (18-21 years of age) from 1978 to 1997. In the third, the decline in the size of the age cohort is compounded by the impact of a deterioration in the private rate of return in the labor market on investments in higher education. A decrease of about one-third in this rate of return did occur from the mid-sixties to the mid-seventies. Thus, there will be both fewer young persons and a smaller proportion of them will find it advantageous to go to college, in this view.

We see a fourth possibility (B in Figure 7) of a decline within a range of 5 to 15 percent for undergraduate enrollments. We shall explain this estimate below.

The "A" view implies a continuation of current activities with a sense of assurance; "D" suggests preparations for drastic cutbacks and phase-outs.[1] "A" means that institutions can largely rely upon their own actions; "D" that governments may need to step into detailed planning and direct intervention as never before. Our view, "B," emphasizes selective impacts within and among institutions and selective remedial actions by both individual institutions and by governments.

A caveat: In setting forth our own enrollment projections for the future we do not wish to help create any "delusions of certainty"[2] or to suggest that we have any illusions of certainty. We only wish to suggest the variable weather view of the future that we hold as against alternative views that range from disaster

---

[1]This is the "dark ages" scenario of Froomkin (1978, p. 31): "The 1980s may well become the Dark Ages of higher education."

[2]See Boulding (1979).

Figure 7. Potential basic directions of enrollment trends

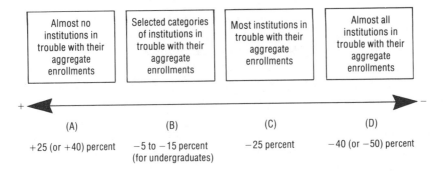

| Almost no institutions in trouble with their aggregate enrollments | Selected categories of institutions in trouble with their aggregate enrollments | Most institutions in trouble with their aggregate enrollments | Almost all institutions in trouble with their aggregate enrollments |

| (A) | (B) | (C) | (D) |

| +25 (or +40) percent | −5 to −15 percent (for undergraduates) | −25 percent | −40 (or −50) percent |

Source: Carnegie Council estimates.

warnings to all-clear signs; to advance the idea that some constructive actions are needed as against contrary advice that either extreme measures are imperative or that business may proceed as usual. Decisions are already being made and actions taken based on views of the future. To help guide these decisions and actions, we set forth our own views. Errors can be made by either expecting too little or too much by way of prospective enrollments, and by either doing too much or too little. We advocate a course of action based on long-run confidence in the future of higher education, moderated by short-term concerns; a course of adherence to continuing basic purposes[3] while adjusting flexibly to temporary changes in circumstances. It is not a time for either panic or euphoria.

Hazards in Enrollment Predictions

Enrollments in higher education are now subject to many changing forces. Gone is the day when the size of the fall freshman class

[3]The Carnegie Commission (1973a) set forth these purposes, and the Council endorses this listing, as follows: (1) the education of the individual student and the provision of a constructive environment for developmental growth; (2) advancing human capability in society at large; (3) educational justice for the postsecondary age group; (4) pure learning—supporting intellectual and artistic creativity; and (5) evaluation of society for self-renewal through individual thought and persuasion.

could be predicted nationwide with great precision based on the number of graduating high school seniors of the June just passed.[4] It is no longer enough to look just at the size of the age cohort, or at changing high school graduation rates, or at private rates of return in the labor market on investments in a college education, or at long-term historical trends, helpful as each of these is.

We set forth in this section a variety of factors we have considered in making our projections. This presentation may serve two purposes: One is to allow others making overall projections to match their detailed judgments against ours; and the other is to serve as a checklist of possibilities to be considered in individual situations, which may be of use to state planning agencies and to planners in individual systems and institutions of higher education.

In advance, however, we should note how precarious it has become to make predictions. Some of the factors that make predictions more difficult are the following:

The new phenomenon of stop-outs and stop-ins

Reduced dependence of young people on parental wishes and financial support

Higher proportions of adults attending college

Higher proportions of part-time students

Higher percentages of students in two-year colleges who have more marginal commitments to attendance shifting with circumstances

Higher proportions of students at graduate levels, particularly the M.A. level, tied to immediate job prospects which fluctuate

Changing inducements to attend college in the form of veterans' benefits, student subsidies, and opportunities in the labor market

Changing private rates of return on a college education

Changing military recruitment policies

The historic shift from assured class to less certain mass attendance

The rise and fall of geographic areas

---

[4]The rule was that 50 percent of white males and 40 percent of white females who graduated from high school entered college the next fall and this, along with rather steady but lower percentages for nonwhites, essentially determined the size of the freshman class (Jaffe and Adams, 1964-65).

The addition of quality-of-life objectives of a recreational and
social nature to professional and vocational objectives
More nontraditional institutions catering to specialized markets.

Only about 40 percent of all students are hard-core partipants, defined as second-generation attendees within their family
histories who are enrolled in four-year colleges. This is the group
most likely to attend on an assured basis.

The other 60 percent of enrolees are in the softer fringe of first-generation attendees, second-generation attendees in two-year colleges, and M.A. level vocational students. The high percentage of
soft-core students makes it necessary to expect wide fluctuations in
enrollments, and particularly in those institutions and subject
matters that many of these students prefer.

Undergraduate Enrollments[5]

1. We start with the prospective decline of the 18-24-year age group
   by 23.3 percent by 1997.
2. We adjust the impact of this decline by 20 percent, because about
   20 percent of undergraduate enrollments (FTE) are by students
   over the age of 24. The resultant impact is to reduce the prospective
   decline to 19 percent.
3. We offset this by the prospective increase in enrollments of persons
   25 and over. Their enrollments have been increasing over the past
   decade. They are likely to increase considerably more because there
   will be bulges in the size of the older age groups, and because more
   of these older persons already have attended college and such
   persons have a much higher historic participation rate in additional college attendance than the population as a whole. This
   offset amounts to about 9 percent. We note that participation rates
   for adults with prior college attendance may rise to even higher
   levels than past practice might indicate (this applies to the
   graduate level as well) because of the great competition of many to
   get ahead within the bulge of young adults, because of the desire of
   some to change jobs in the face of this competition, and because
   of the impulse of a few to escape the competition by attention to
   nonvocational interests.

[5]See Supplement B, *Carnegie Enrollment Projections*, for more detail on potential
undergraduate and graduate enrollments.

The resultant figure is a prospective decline of 10 percent (A in Table 3).

4. Next we look at males 18-24. They constitute about 40 percent of all current enrollments. Their participation rates have gone down in the 1970s with the end of the Vietnam war and the more recent decline in the number of veterans in college. We expect current participation rates to stabilize. We are not certain of this but do believe that any further decline will not exceed an impact of more than -5 percent on total enrollments. Added to the figure just given above, this would result in -15 percent, the low end of our range (B in Table 3).

We are hesitant about enrollment rates for 18-24 males for several reasons:

- They might stabilize at present levels. Present levels of participation for 18-21 year olds are at about the 1964 level before all of the impacts of the Vietnam war on the draft and avoidance of the draft, and on veterans' benefits. They are slightly higher than 1964 for the 22-24-year age group. The 1964 level and levels since 1973 seem like a reasonable base for estimations about the future (see Figure 8). Some forecasters may have been misled by looking too exclusively at the 1969 to 1973 trends or, alternatively, at 1964 to 1969 trends—the former leading to visions of continuing declines, the latter to visions of resumption of increases (see Figure 9). (Note that both of these figures include graduate enrollments. This inclusion does not affect the 18-21 age group, but has some impact on the 22-24 age group. It is not possible to separate undergraduate and graduate enrollments by age prior to 1970. Figure 9 does separate these enrollments beginning with 1970.)
- They might go down. Attendance by veterans has already fallen by one-half and will fall some more. The military will be taking a higher proportion of eligible males from the smaller age cohort, although this may be offset, after a lag, as a result of educational benefits for those who have served in the armed forces. The labor market for young persons will be comparatively good for the smaller age cohort and may draw marginal attenders out of college. High school graduation rates have been going down slightly.

Table 3. Potential decline in full-time equivalent undergraduate enrollment, 1978 to 1997, with contribution from each factor in projection model.

	Percentage	Reference in text
Decline in 18-24 age cohort	-23.3	
Adjusted for the 80 percent that this age cohort constitutes of all enrollments	-19	
Adjusted for increase in population 25 and over at constant participation rates (+4 percent)	-15	
Adjusted for increase in percentage of population 25 and over with college experience and resultant higher participation rates (+5 percent)	-10	(A)
Adjusted for potential further decrease in participation rates by males 18-24 (-5 percent)	-15	(B)
Adjusted for changes in other components:		
More blacks and more participation by blacks (+2 percent)		
More participation by majority women 18-24 (+4 percent)		
Increased retention (+4 percent)		
Impact of increasing proportion of part-time enrollment (-5 percent)		
Net: +5 percent		
Applied to (A)	-5	(C)
Applied to (B)	-10	(D)

Source: Carnegie Council estimates.

- They might rise. The private rate of return on a college education has gone down substantially since the high levels of the 1960s but has started to rise again. The "ratio of mean income of college and high school graduates" reached a peak level for full-time workers aged 25-34 of 1.38 in 1968 and 1.39 in 1969. It fell to 1.16 in 1974 but had risen again to 1.24 in 1976 (Smith and Welch, 1978)[6] and is likely to rise some more. The percentage of the labor force in

[6]For a discussion of the effects of the job market on enrollments in the past, see Gordon (1974) "Introduction."

Figure 8. College participation rates, men in selected age groups, 1947 to 1978 (includes graduate enrollment)

Excluding the Vietnam war period.

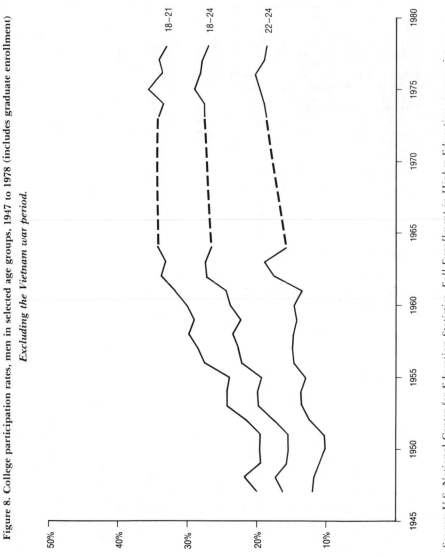

Source: U.S. National Center for Education Statistics, *Fall Enrollment in Higher Education,* appropriate years.

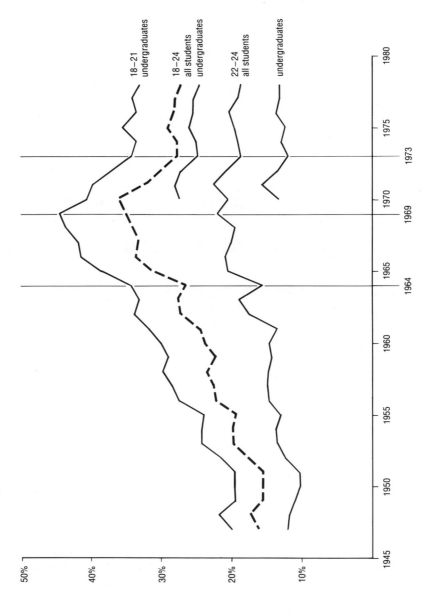

Figure 9. College participation rates, men in selected age groups, 1947 to 1978

18–21
undergraduates

18–24
all students
undergraduates

22–24
all students

undergraduates

Source: U.S. National Center for Statistics, *Fall Enrollment in Higher Education,* appropriate years.

"managerial" and in "professional and technical" occupations has been rising rapidly (it is now 25 percent of the total) and will rise even higher. These occupational groupings draw heavily on persons who have attended college.[7] Also, more persons intent on entering the skilled crafts and public service occupations (like that of police) are going to college, although often for only two years. Additionally, graduation rates from high school and attendance rates in college may continue to rise toward the national average in some states in the South and elsewhere, raising the national average.

5. We turn next to a consideration of other enrollment components:

- More majority females. Their numbers have been rising to match those of men, and we expect their participation rates to rise above those for men. One reason is that new opportunities are opening to them. Another reason is that to obtain good jobs with substantial pay college degrees are more important to women compared to men who can also get such jobs without a college education as commercial farmer, as skilled craftsman, as over-the-road truck driver, and so forth.[8] Females, in general, now graduate from high school at a rate 3.3 percent above that for men.

- More blacks. Opportunities for blacks are especially improved by college attendance, and they have a long tradition of placing a high value on education. We expect that their attendance rates will equal those of whites. They already exceed those for whites within the same income ranges. We expect attendance rates for blacks in the top half of the overall income range to exceed those for whites in the top half of the overall income range, but we expect attendance rates for blacks in the bottom half of the overall income range to remain below those for whites in that half of the overall income range. Some parts of the black community are moving

[7]For a discussion of these and other considerations, see Supplement C, *The Labor Market and Higher Education.* It should be noted, in particular, how different rates of economic growth, for example 2 or 3 or 4 percent in GNP, make a very great difference in the employment market for youth.

[8]An offsetting factor, however, may be a rise in the birthrate which would keep more women at home and out of both college and the labor market. See the discussion in Easterlin (1978).

ahead faster than others. Blacks, also, are becoming a higher proportion of all youths.

- More Hispanics. We consider this to be a great imponderable. High school completion rates for them (54 percent) are below those for blacks (64 percent) and whites (80 percent), and there is not the same traditional support for college attendance, particularly for females, as among blacks. Additionally, the prospect for continuing migration across the Mexican border is a great unknown. We also note the great variations among Hispanics— Cubans (6 percent) follow the national college attendance pattern, Chicanos (59 percent) tend gradually to catch up with it, Puerto Ricans (15 percent) to lag behind.[9] These variations have major regional implications for local attendance patterns (one-half of all Hispanics are in California and Texas, and they are largely Chicanos). Since Hispanics will become the largest minority population, the uncertainty about them is of major import in making national and, in particular, certain regional projections. A further factor is that, because Hispanics are not a separate race, they have not been separately identified in census population projections and so it is not possible, as it is for blacks, to project their historic participation levels. However, to the extent that their participation rates rise and to the extent that there will be more, even considerably more, of them, this will affect overall enrollment numbers favorably for both males and females.
- More retention. The dropout rate in four-year colleges historically has been about 50 percent with many dropouts for financial reasons. It has now fallen to 40 percent, with the major single reason being given as "boredom." We expect it to fall some more. We expect colleges to exert an all-out effort to increase the retention rate. We estimate that these efforts may add a 20 percent gain in time spent in college by those who in the past have not completed their four-year degrees and by academic transfer students enrolled in community colleges. Private colleges, in particular, have a great incentive to increase the number of their alumni with degrees since financial support comes proportionately more from them than from those who drop out. We note,

[9]Persons from Central and South America and "other Spanish" make up the remaining 20 percent. They may, perhaps, best be grouped with the Chicanos in terms of potential enrollment patterns.

however, that the recent retention experience in community colleges has been disappointing and so also has been the transfer rate to four-year colleges. Nevertheless, the internal market of students already on campus is both large and readily available for retention efforts.

- More part-time students. This will continue the current trend. It reduces to some extent, however, the level of full-time equivalent (FTE) enrollments. We expect that more students with good opportunities in the current labor market and prospective good returns on a college education will seek to combine work and education in the 1980s and 1990s. Interest in time-shortened degrees may also increase with the same effect on enrollments as students seek to enter the labor market on a full-time basis sooner and reduce the costs of college attendance to themselves and to their families in the course of doing so.
- More high school students (16- and 17-year olds) taking college level work in actual college classes on a part-time or full-time basis.
- More foreign students. The world population is rising rapidly, and some families in a number of developing countries are becoming increasingly affluent. Some Americans colleges are actively recruiting foreign students, and more may be expected to do so. Attendance has risen from 50,000 to 250,000 since 1960.[10]

These several considerations add up to an estimated increase of 10 percent (2 percent for blacks, 4 percent for majority women, and 4 percent for retention); offset by an estimated decline of about 5 percent for more part-time enrollment; for a net increase of 5 percent.

[10]Although we expect that the number of foreign students in this country will continue to grow, we have not included a specific calculation in the enrollment projection for several reasons: In recent years the U.S. share of students studying in foreign countries has been decreasing relative to other countries (although we continue to receive the greatest numbers). Over one-fourth of our foreign student population is from OPEC countries and could be afffected by foreign policy developments. Exchange programs with China and other countries are expected to expand, but the numbers of new students will be very small relative to our present enrollment of over 11 million. Finally, although only half as many Americans go abroad to study as students from other countries who come here, the rate of increase has been about twice as great as the increase in foreign student enrollments in this country.

We do not make calculations on Hispanics, 16- and 17-year-olds, and foreign students, although increases in these groupings would add to the 5 percent. Applied to a -10 percent (item 3 above) this results in -5 percent (C in Table 3 and the high end of our range); and applied to the -15 percent (item 4 above) comes to -10 percent (D in Table 3 and the mid-point of our range.)

A decline of 15 percent would result in 1997 FTE under-graduate enrollments at the same level as 1971; of 10 percent, 1973; and 5 percent, 1974 (see Figure 10).

We have concentrated on 1997, the expected low point for undergraduate enrollments. If enrollments were to fall by 15 percent, this would amount to an average decrease of less than 1 percent a year. We note that in the 1970s about 15 percent of all institutions experienced an enrollment decline of 20 percent or more and sur-vived the decade.

The decline will not come, however, at an even pace. Under-graduate enrollments are likely to remain fairly even through the academic year starting in the fall of 1982, even rising some. Then there will be:

Slide I: From fall 1983 through the academic year starting in the fall of 1988 (followed by a possible rise in 1989 and 1990); and then

Slide II: From the fall of 1991 through the academic year starting in the fall of 1997.

The first slide will carry enrollments down about 40 percent of the total decline and the second slide, the remaining 60 percent—this second slide will be the more precipitous of the two. (See Figure 11.)

This all adds up to four years on a plateau of enrollments (the academic years starting in 1979, 1980, 1981, and 1982), six years in the first slide and another six in the second slide for a total of twelve, with two years of a plateau or slight recovery in between and then followed by three years of recovery at the end from 1998 to 2000. Thus, there will be twelve really difficult years in the course of the next two decades; with six better years scattered at the start and the end and in the middle of this period.

Colleges will do what they can to smooth out the secondary impacts of this changing enrollment pattern on faculty hiring and

retention, and on their financial expenditures. Many of the repercussions will be subdued by adaptions within the system.

Colleges in general have about three more full academic years to
prepare themselves for the onslaught of Slide I.

Enrollments of 18-year olds will, of course, fluctuate much
more than all enrollments, and some colleges heavily dependent
upon them will be on a real roller coaster.

In a much more tentative way, we have tried to look ahead to the
year 2010. We expect the future fertility rate to be higher than the 1.8
rate of the last few years.

**Figure 10. Potential declines in FTE undergraduate enrollments as related to
enrollments in prior years**

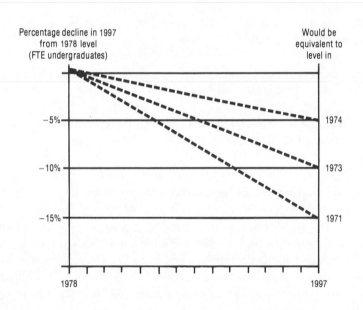

Sources: Carnegie Council estimates; 1974, 1973, and 1971 comparisons from U.S.
NCES, *Fall Enrollment. .* , appropriate years.

Figure 11. Generalized view of enrollments, 1979-2010

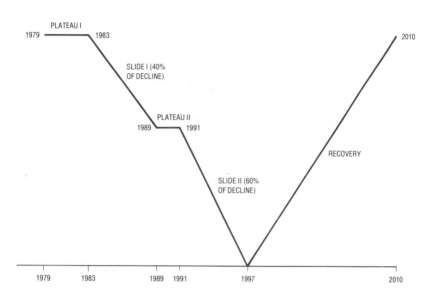

Source: Carnegie Council estimates.

We use the maintenance rate (2.1) for the period 1997 to 2010. We do this because the fertility rate might rise, but, more importantly, because rising levels of immigration are likely to have the same effect on enrollments. We do not expect that the United States, given its economic, political, and military positions in the world, and given the pressures for entry by aliens, will accept the possiblity of a declining total population or a long-run decline in the college population.

If undergraduate enrollments should decline by 10 percent by 1997, we would expect them to rise to about 1979 levels by the year 2010. This will be the period when the grandchildren of the GI's start attending college—a period of a new bulge.

The period of 2000 to 2010 will be a time of movement for other reasons than increasing enrollments. Faculty members recruited in the 1960s and 1970s—more than one-half of all faculty members—

will be retiring during this period. This will create many opportunities for new hires, including of women and minorities; it will lower the average age and average real salary levels of faculty members; and it will permit many adjustments to new fields of teaching and scholarship. The building space created in the 1960s and 1970s—one-half of all such space—will need to be remodelled or rebuilt, creating possibilities for better use of energy, improved use of new instructional media, more pleasing architecture. The conditions of the times are likely to draw into the leadership of higher education more persons interested in building institutions and undertaking innovations than was the case under the conditions of the prior two decades.

Notation: The new and preliminary enrollment figures for fall 1979 (as released by the National Center for Education Statistics in November 1979) are in all respects consistent with the above analysis; for example, that we are on an enrollment plateau, that there is a comparative increase in women, that part-time enrollment is growing. These figures were not available when the above analysis of potential trends was made.

Graduate Enrollments

We expect graduate enrollments to rise slightly between 1980 and 2000 in relation to undergraduate enrollments, despite the gloomy predictions about the value of the Ph.D. Too much has been made out of too little, in our judgment, based on prospects in too small a segment of the total. We have heard mostly about the less than 10 percent of graduate work that is in deep trouble (the academic Ph.D.) and less about the other more than 90 percent that has been moving along unimpaired or has even prospered. If graduate enrollments rise slightly relative to undergraduate enrollments, this would mean that they might (on the assumption of undergraduate declines in the range of -5 to -15 percent) remain roughly stable or fall roughly 10 percent.

Our anticipations for graduate enrollments take into account the following considerations:

There has been a secular rise in graduate enrollments starting from 0 percent of all enrollments in 1870 and rising to 7 percent

(FTE basis) in 1960 and 11 percent in 1977.[11]

Graduate enrollments relate to a longer age span than under-graduate enrollments, which concentrate on the years 18 to 21. Low years for the 18-21 and even the 18-24 age cohort will not have as much impact upon them.

More and more professions are encouraging, for entrance oppor-tunities, some work beyond the four-year undergraduate degree, as in engineering and business administration.

Some old professions are still expanding, as are law, theology, and health care specialties, including doctors of medicine and dentistry.

New professions are being created.[12]

Promotions and increased pay in more and more fields, as in teaching, social work, and other civil service occupations, de-pend upon additional graduate work. This is also true in private employment fields such as engineering and computer program-ming. Teacher education, which has declined at the under-graduate level—down in enrollments by one-quarter since the middle sixties, still prospers at the graduate level—up by one-quarter.

Many women and minorities are catching up with their ex-panding opportunities in new careers or with promotional as well as pay prospects in their current employment.

Competition in the bulge group of adults is fierce, and graduate education is one way of getting ahead of the competition; it is also a way of changing jobs; and it is also a way of adding to quality of life whatever the degree of success in the competition.

Some areas are negatively affected already in terms of enroll-ment, however, by the decline in the hiring of college teachers. These are in the academic Ph.D. categories, where all, or nearly all,

[11]Graduate enrollments constituted 14 percent of all enrollments in 1977 on a headcount basis, while graduate degrees were 25 percent of all degrees awarded in that year and were 31 percent of bachelors' and higher degrees.

[12]The number of occupational titles in both the "professional" and the "managerial" categories increased by 20 percent between 1960 and 1970.

employment is in college teaching, as in the humanities but also physics and botany. The academic-professional areas, such as chemistry and economics, find declines in college positions offset by increases in government and industry. Professional areas, like business administration, are doing well.

Our anticipations include:

Possible continuing increases at the M.A. level and further increases in some advanced professional fields

A decline of 50 percent by 1990 in what is now the academic half of Ph.D. graduates (the half now largely devoted to preparation for academic occupations),[13] with the other half holding constant. This academic half now accounts for only one-twelfth of total graduate enrollments. It is on this one-twelfth that many conceptions have been formed about the sad fate of graduate education in general.

The important phenomenon at the graduate level, as we see it, is internal redistribution rather than any major overall rise or decline. Graduate education has become a volatile element within total enrollments. It is volatile by level—first the Ph.D. level was up and now the M.A. It is volatile by field—for example, with science yielding popularity to business administration and theology. This volatility affects greatly the destinies of some colleges and universities and many fields. Graduate education has become the plaything of the labor market, of changing public policies in supporting graduate fellowships, of shifting social and intellectual concerns. The graduate division was once an enclave of sobriety and stability, and now it shows more instability than do undergraduate enrollments. Consequently, we make no specific projections about graduate enrollments, only noting that we expect them, over the two decades as a whole, to rise somewhat compared to whatever may happen to undergraduate enrollments.

[13]New doctorates employed by colleges have already gone down from their peak levels by two-thirds.

Uncertainties

We have discussed in our sessions, but are uncertain about, some other possible impacts on enrollments:

Military manpower policy—how many youths will be needed and what inducements will be offered to them, including educational subsidies? If absolute numbers in the armed services remain constant, then about 9 percent of all males 18-24 will be required in 1990 as against 7 percent now.

Youth policy—to what extent may public policy turn toward subsidy of the less advantaged youth and away from subsidy of the generally more advantaged youth who go to college; and to what extent might public policy start subsidizing entry into the labor market when youth will be in short supply rather than into college as it did when youth was in over-supply in the 1960s and 1970s? Changing public youth policy could have significant consequences.

Alternatives to college attendance—how many students will be drawn into what we have earlier called the Third Sector of educational activities by noneducational institutions, such as corporations; into use of new electronic media for instruction off campus; into credit-by-examination and credit-for-work experience managed by the First, or collegiate, Sector?

Application of the great "vacuum cleaner"—how many enrollments will colleges add by seeking out students wherever they may be found in places of work, in the military, in prison, in retirement; among housewives, among new immigrants, among high school students?

Affluence—how much will affluence increase, and will increasing affluence in the future, as in the past, lead to greater parental expenditures on college attendance by their children?

Inflation—if it continues, how much effect may it have on directing the attention of young persons and their parents to getting current income and reducing current expenditures, as against seeking a possible higher future income; or choosing a public instead of a private institution and, among public institutions, one within commuting distance?

More young people who are children of persons who went to college—will participation rates for this group continue to be comparatively high as in the past? Will college attendance come to be more and more the normal thing for young people to do?

Federal largesse in the form of student aid—were some current proposals to increase student aid dramatically carried into full effect, then young persons might pour into colleges, as seems to have happened already to a minor extent as a result of the Middle-Income Student Assistance Act of 1978. This could particularly be the case if such dramatic increases come at a time of prolonged and massive youth unemployment —young persons would have an offer they could not refuse.

We present our projections, at both the undergraduate and graduate levels, as a general estimate of what the future may hold. We think they suggest, at a minimum, that higher education faces neither a disaster nor a continuation of a Golden Age. They suggest moderate specific preparations for the future, not overall crash programs or just more of the same by everybody.

We do not present our projections year by year because they might create an impression of too great certainty and specificity; they would be an instance of misplaced concreteness in the midst of many uncertainties. Nor do we present a model based on two or three statistical inputs. We present instead a judgment call based on many considerations.

We end this discussion of potential enrollments with a caution. Earlier projections by the Carnegie Commission and the Carnegie Council have turned out to be on the high side.[14] In particular, the number of low-income students attracted by new student financial

---

[14]See *The Open Door Colleges: Policies for Community Colleges,* A Special Report and Recommendations by the Carnegie Commission on Higher Education (1970a); *New Students and New Places: Policies for the Future Growth and Development of American Higher Education,* A Report and Recommendations by the Carnegie Commission on Higher Education (1971); *Priorities for Action: Final Report of the Carnegie Commission on Higher Education* (1973a); *More Than Survival: Prospects for Higher Education in a Period of Uncertainty,* A commentary with recommendations of The Carnegie Foundation for the Advancement of Teaching (1975). Some other estimates of enrollment made earlier were also overly optimistic. Lewis Mayhew (1962, p. 93), for example, suggested in the 1960s that, "If the American ideology continues to evolve in its present direction of insisting that large numbers of young people receive college education, over 80% of the age group may well be enrolled in institutions of higher learning."

aid programs was overestimated.[15] In comparison with most persons and groups looking ahead to the future of higher education, we are once again clearly at the optimistic end of the spectrum.

Implications of the Demographic Depression for Students

Recent developments and the changes we project for the remainder of the century will give us a dramatically different composition of the national student body than we have had traditionally (Figure 12). In 1960 it was composed predominantly of young majority males attending full-time. By 2000, there will be more women than men, as many people over 21 as 21 and under, nearly as many part-time as full-time attendees, and one-quarter of all students will be minorities. Roughly one-half of the students in the classroom of 2000 would not have been there if the composition of 1960 had been continued. This is a fundamental, almost radical change in higher education.

We expect that students will be more nearly the center of attention on campus during the next 20 years than in the past 10. They will be recruited more actively, admitted more readily, retained more assiduously, counselled more attentively, graded more considerately, financed more adequately, taught more conscientiously, placed in jobs more insistently, and the curriculum will be more tailored to their tastes.

The demographic depression may cause difficulties for institutions, and for actual, and particularly for prospective, faculty members, but it may seem more like high prosperity for the students. They will seldom, if ever, have had it so good on campus. The difficulties of others can only redound to their advantage. This may well become their Golden Age.

[15]See Figure 17 for data showing no improvement in the ratio of lower income to higher income students for 1970 to 1977. This contrasts with our expectation of improvement (see, in particular, The Carnegie Foundation for the Advancement of Teaching, 1975).

Figure 12. Undergraduate student characteristics in 1960 and 2000 (projected)

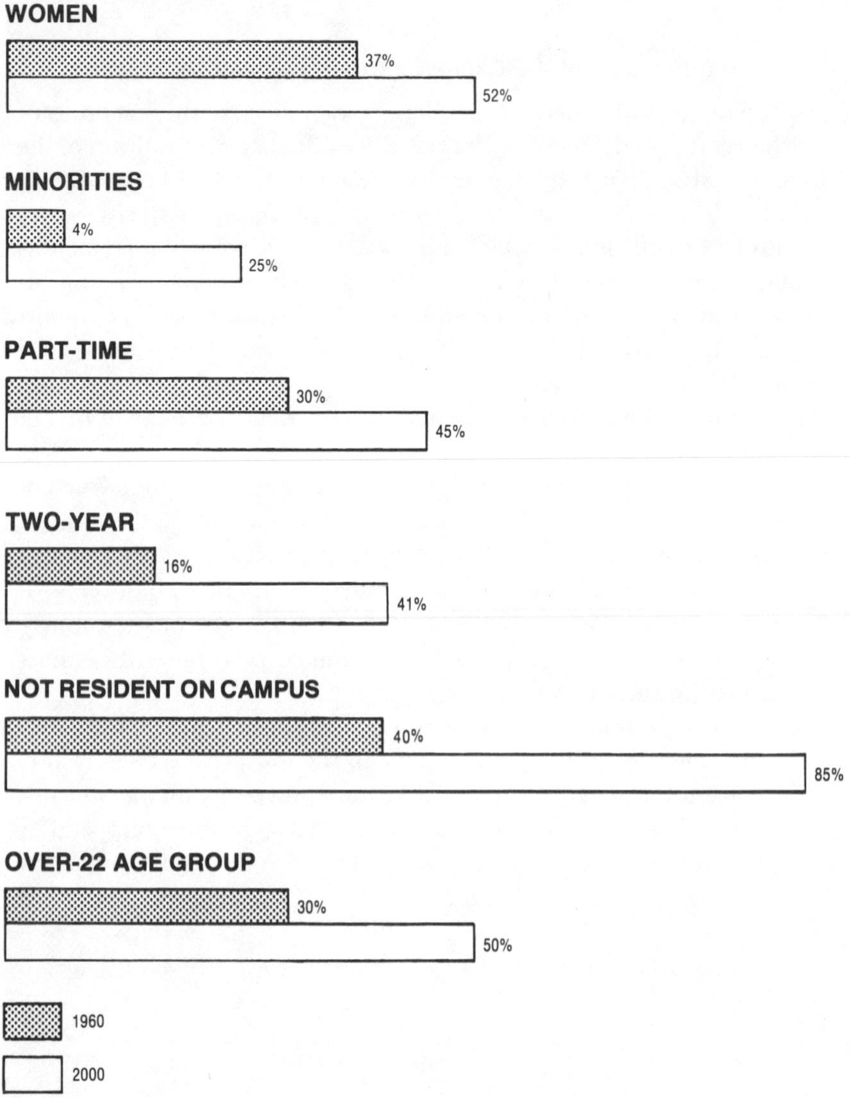

WOMEN

37%

52%

MINORITIES

4%

25%

PART-TIME

30%

45%

TWO-YEAR

16%

41%

NOT RESIDENT ON CAMPUS

40%

85%

OVER-22 AGE GROUP

30%

50%

1960

2000

Sources: U.S. Bureau of the Census (1964); U.S. NCES (1972); and Carnegie Council estimates.

4

A Disaggregative Approach to Enrollments

No demographic disease of epidemic proportions will sweep over all of higher education during the next 20 years. The demographic disease, rather, will be selective; some institutions will die from it; nearly all will be affected by it in one way or another; and all will need to take some precautions. But institutions must be looked at one at a time, case by case. Although we cannot make this examination, only the individual institutions can do that, we can indicate how an individual institution may be affected as part of the category within which it falls, by the region and locality where it is located, by its size and institutional identification, and by the presence of close competition.

We shall refer first to the Carnegie classification of institutions.[1] Table 4 shows the number of institutions and the total number of enrollments in each classification.

[1]For a full definition of these classifications and for other data looking at institutions of higher education in a disaggregative way, see Supplement D, *Gainers and Losers Among Institutions of Higher Education.* A brief listing of these classifications follows:

Research Universities: Among the 100 leading institutions in federal funding and awarding at least 50 doctorates.

Doctorate-granting Universities: Other universities awarding substantial numbers of doctorates.

Comprehensive Universities and Colleges: Institutions offering a liberal arts program in addition to professional or occupational programs, many offering the master's degree, but with very limited or entirely absent doctorate programs.

We see as falling in the least vulnerable category, in terms of negative enrollment changes, by and large, the following types of institutions:

Research Universities. They generally have high admission standards that can be lowered (with exceptions such as the University of California under the Master Plan), and they recruit on a regional or national basis. Their research and service functions should be in good demand. Their medical and other professional schools should be generally unaffected. Their only serious difficulties will be in the academic doctorate areas, some of which will be severely affected.

Selective Liberal Arts Colleges. These also have high admission requirements that are subject to downward adjustments, and they also are not limited to a single recruitment area. Generally, they have substantial endowments per student and strong alumni support. With less future pressure from the labor market directing students toward vocational subjects and with good prospects for their students in professional graduate fields, which recruit heavily from these colleges, their emphasis on the liberal arts can be more of an asset than it has been during the past decade.

We note generally that, among the research universities and the selective liberal arts colleges, the best may become comparatively better and the not-quite-the-best may become comparatively worse in the average academic precollegiate quality of their students, as the former fully maintain the selectivity of their students while the latter must make some concessions because the already small size of the pool of the ablest (and also well-to-do) students will have declined.[2]

Liberal Arts Colleges I: Highly selective four-year colleges offering a liberal arts program.
Liberal Arts Colleges II: All other four-year liberal arts colleges.
Two-Year Colleges and Institutes.
Professional Schools and Other Specialized Institutions: Institutions that have only a professional or specialized curriculum and do not have a liberal arts program.
Institutions for Nontraditional Study.

[2]See Doermann, 1978. He found that only 10 percent of high school graduates scored 450 or better on the verbal section of the Scholastic Aptitude Test (SAT) and came from families in the top quartile of the income range.

Table 4. Institutions of higher education by Carnegie classification and control, with full-time equivalent enrollment, 1977

Carnegie Classification	Number	Percentage of total institutions	Full-time equivalent enrollment	Percentage of full-time equivalent enrollment
Research Universities	98	3.1	1,657,148	19.4
Public	62	2.0	1,321,088	15.5
Private	36	1.2	336,060	3.9
Doctorate-granting Universities	86	2.8	929,362	10.9
Public	57	1.8	708,692	8.3
Private	29	0.9	220,670	2.6
Comprehensive Colleges and Universities	593	19.0	2,554,277	29.9
Public	354	11.3	1,901,274	22.3
Private	239	7.7	653,003	7.7
Highly Selective Liberal Arts Colleges	123	3.9	147,399	1.7
Public	0	0	0	0
Private	123	3.9	147,399	1.7
Other Liberal Arts Colleges	468	15.0	342,698	4.0
Public	11	0.4	15,816	0.2
Private	457	14.6	326,882	3.8
Two-Year Colleges	1,178	37.7	2,527,588	29.6
Public	923	29.5	2,376,129	27.8
Private	255	8.2	151,459	1.8
Other Specialized Institutions	578	18.5	376,936	4.4
Public	75	2.4	129,212	1.5
Private	503	16.1	247,724	2.9
Total	3,124	100.0	8,535,408	100.0

Sources: Carnegie Council Classification (1976); U.S. Center for Education Statistics (1978c).

Public Community Colleges. They have constituted the fastest growing segment of higher education over the past two decades. They enjoy strong local support and appeal to what we expect to be enlarging categories of students: minorities newly entering the stream of higher education, adults, and part-time students. They also are still adding to their functions (traditionally the offering of academic transfer, technical, and terminal general programs) new areas of activities designated as "community service" (instruction in nonvocational and nonacademic areas, such as swimming, physical fitness, and target practice) and "community based" (noninstructional cultural, recreational, social, and professional programs, such as local conventions and conferences). They may add more responsibilities for service to local youth, as we have recommended elsewhere.[3] Additionally, their approaches fit the new styles of many young people: easy-in, easy-out; part-time studies; low levels of pressure; vocational and recreational courses; opportunities to live at home or in a noncollegiate community; great leeway for individual patterns of behavior. In California, at least, many community college students are transfers *from* four-year institutions.

They are, however, vulnerable in certain ways: to Proposition 13 type actions when they are substantially funded from local sources, as in California where enrollments have recently decreased by 10 percent; to restrictions on gasoline supplies available

---

[3]See Carnegie Council on Higher Education (1979c). In Section 10 of that report, we recommend that colleges and universities (1) seek opportunities for partnerships with secondary schools, as in Boston, (2) establish offices of community service, (3) take decisive steps to reform teacher training, and (4) give special attention to improving the training of school administrators. Community colleges (and in some cases comprehensive colleges) should (1) cooperate with Comprehensive Employment and Training Act (CETA) and school authorities in the development of training and work-experience programs (as many are already doing), (2) experiment with admitting students at age 16 and with the development of middle colleges that combine the last year of high school with the first year of college, (3) open their occupational programs to high school students, and (4) develop more opportunities for cooperative education and apprenticeship. The federal government should support these changes by (1) increasing appropriations for FIPSE (especially for projects of colleges and universities designed to serve disadvantaged youth), (2) increasing funding of the Trio programs, and (3) increasing funding of the Teacher Corps program.

to students since they are commuter institutions[4]; to competitive intrusions from comprehensive colleges and universities in their areas eagerly searching for students; to the new electronic means of instruction; to the diversion of second-generation students to four-year institutions; to low retention rates as students stop out as well as in.

We note that community colleges may be classified as comprehensive or as specialized. The foregoing remarks relate primarily to the former. The latter can be greatly affected by the nature of their specialty; for example, some two-year institutions in Wisconsin were primarily concentrated on teacher training (12 of them have been closed) and some in North Carolina on one or a few technical specializations. About 10 percent of all public two-year colleges are specialized (and usually quite small); one-half of these (about 50) are academic only (most of them branch campuses of universities) and one-half of them (also about 50) are vocational only.

Community colleges also are under political attack from black colleges in the South, which operate in the same recruitment areas, and from social analysts on the political left who consider them to be part of a capitalist conspiracy to keep down the poor and the minorities.

The in-between category of average or above average vulnerability, but with many individual variations, includes:

Doctorate-granting Universities. Their academic Ph.D. programs will be especially hard hit. With few placements of such Ph.D. recipients in total, those who are placed will come mostly from the more prestigious research universities. With generally lower admission requirements already at the undergraduate level, these institutions have less flexibility in the way of downward adjustments than do the research universities. They are also more tied to demographic trends in their immediate regions, and this will hurt some much more than others.

---

[4]Which suggests a need for smaller and more widely distributed campuses and the introduction of bus services.

Comprehensive Colleges and Universities. These institutions also are tied more to their localities and more restricted in lowering admissions than are the research universities. Some of them are better situated, nevertheless, to draw on the traditional junior college market than are doctorate-granting institutions; and intense competition between many of these institutions and some community colleges is already beginning. Many of them are also aggressively pursuing the new M.A. market. This type of institution often pushed hard in an upward academic direction toward research and the Ph.D. in the 1960s, and many will push hard downward in the 1980s. They are well situated to move now in one and now in another direction as circumstances change. Along with the community colleges, they have demonstrated in the past unusual resiliency in adjusting to new circumstances.

Again, there are many variations within this category. Institutions that still concentrate on teacher education have already been hard hit; those that moved early and far into other occupational programs are much better situated, particularly if they have strong offerings in areas such as paramedical training and mineral technology. Generally, the public institutions have better assured futures than the private. However, some public institutions in this classification are very small and located in depopulating areas, and some private institutions are large and situated in metropolitan areas with many opportunities for adult, M.A., and other expanding programs.

The most vulnerable category, with enormous variations among individual institutions, includes:

Less-Selective Liberal Arts Colleges. It is not generally possible for them to greatly lower their admission requirements, and they usually recruit in their localities. For the latter reason, they can be badly affected if they are in a small town or rural area that is losing population or in a state that is losing population; and many of them are located in the East and Midwest, which are losing population. They can also be vulnerable if they are in large metropolitan areas with a vast range of low-tuition public institutions. They are particularly vulnerable if they are single sex, and very small in size—with heavy fixed costs per student and unable to offer the range of programs, particularly technical ones, that students have recently been demanding. If they have concentrated on teacher education and/or first-generation ethnic students, they are additionally affected. Teacher education at the undergraduate level has generally been cut by one-quarter. Second-generation students are likely to explore college opportunities more widely than is possible in the local, and often religious, institutions with which non-college attending parents have generally felt more comfortable as places for their children.[5]

For several of these reasons, less-selective Catholic institutions have been and will continue to be facing trouble.

Many of the colleges in this overall category feel particularly threatened by neighboring public comprehensive colleges and universities with low tuition and a broader variety of courses.[6]

There are many exceptions within this general category but particularly fundamentalist Protestant colleges in the South and colleges in expanding regions such as the Southwest, which are doing well with their enrollments.

Private Two-Year Colleges. They generally face the same handicaps as the less selective liberal arts colleges and have been, in any event, a declining group for some years. They are, however, a very heterogeneous group, and it is difficult to generalize about them. The more academic among them are more threatened than the more vocational, some of which are expanding their enrollments.

Only about 10 of the over 700 institutions in the most vulnerable categories are public; the remainder are private.

The first group of institutions will be more concerned with internal adjustments than with total decline of enrollments; the

---

[5]Second-generation students (currently half of the total) show greater preference than first-generation students for private institutions, and for research universities and selective liberal arts colleges. First-generation students are more likely to go to public community colleges and comprehensive colleges and universities, and to private less-selective liberal arts colleges. The generational effect on choice of institutions is substantial (see Table 5), and there will be comparatively more second-generation students in the future.

[6]See the discussion in Carnegie Council on Policy Studies in Higher Education (1977, pp. 21-22).

**Table 5. College attendance patterns among first- and
second-generation[a] undergraduates, 1975**

	Percentage Enrollment	
Carnegie Classification	*First-generation*	*Second-generation*
Total	53	47
Public	56	44
Private	42	58
Research Universities	33	67
Public	35	65
Private	24	76
Doctorate-granting Universities	42	58
Public	43	57
Private	38	62
Comprehensive Colleges and Universities	53	47
Public	55	45
Private	49	51
Liberal Arts I Colleges	23	77
Public	0	0
Private	23	77
Liberal Arts II Colleges	53	47
Public	65	35
Private	50	50
Two-Year Colleges	67	33
Public	67	33
Private	53	47

[a] As measured by father's education: First-generation = father's education less than
"some college"; Second-generation = father's education that is "some college" or
higher.

Source: Carnegie Council Survey of Undergraduates, 1975.

second with both; and the third with total decline, including, in some instances, the possibility of mergers, extinction, or fundamental restructuring. Few institutions in the first group are likely to disappear (no research universities and only two selective liberal arts colleges totally disappeared in the 1970s, although two of the latter merged with other institutions and one went under public control); some in the second; but possibly many in the third, particularly among the two-year private colleges. Assuming that the first group loses less than the average in total enrollments and the second loses about the average or a little more, then heavy losses must be sustained within the third category. Table 6 shows the number of institutions and their current enrollments in each of these categories. It shows the small size, in terms of enrollment, of the category that may have to absorb the heaviest blows.

We consider it very problematical to set forth estimates of the number of private colleges that will close. Recent estimates have suggested that 200 might close or that 200 might survive.[7] Too much depends on private actions and public policies that are as yet undetermined to make such estimates anything more than a wild guess. However, in our survey of institutions, 8 percent of the presidents saw the possibility of some major institutional change in the future including closing, merger, and shift in control from private to public sponsorship (Table 7). This is actually a slight decrease from the 10 percent shown in a similar survey in 1974.[8] There is, in any event, a modest attrition rate for institutions. From 1940 to 1970, 0.5 percent of all institutions closed or merged each year. This rate rose to 0.8 percent in the 1970s. Thus, the abnormality of the 1970s was not the total of 0.8 percent but the excess of 0.3 percent over the prior average. The prior number of closures and mergers amounts to 15 per year or 150 per decade, or an estimated 300 from 1980 to 2000. The questions then are: Will mergers and closures exceed 300 by 2000, and what types of institutions will be most affected?

[7]For the estimate of 200 closures see Behn (1979). For the estimate of 200 survivors (specifically 170) by 2007 "unless remedial action is taken soon," see Pyke (1977).

[8]Glenny and others (1976, p. 56). There has been an internal shift, however, with doctorate-granting universities now comparatively more uncertain about their futures.

**Table 6. Classification of institutions of higher education
by apparent degree of vulnerability, 1978[a]**

	Institutions		Enrollment
	Number	Percentage	Percentage of full-time equivalent enrollment
Less vulnerable	1,144	45	51
Research universities	98	4	20
Selective liberal arts colleges	123	5	2
Public two-year colleges	923	36	29
Vulnerable	679	27	43
Doctorate-granting universities	86	3	12
Comprehensive colleges and universities	593	23	31
More vulnerable	723	28	6
Less selective liberal arts colleges	468	18	4
Private two-year colleges	255	10	2

[a]Excluding specialized institutions.

Source: U.S. NCES (1979d) data adapted by Carnegie Council.

Table 7. Expectations of college and university presidents who say their institutions are likely to undergo major change, such as merger, consolidation, change in control, or closure by 1985–1986

Change	Research universities I		Research universities II		Doctorate-granting universities I		Doctorate-granting universities II		Comprehensive universities & colleges I		Comprehensive universities & colleges II		Liberal arts colleges I		Liberal arts colleges II		Two-year colleges		Total	Percentage of total
	Pub	Priv	Pub	Priv	Pub	Priv	Pub	Priv	Pub	Priv	Pub	Priv	Pub	Priv	Pub	Priv	Pub	Priv		
Weighted N (sample) =	32	22	33	14	38	18	19	11	247	128	101	106	0	123	11	457	905	132	2,397	—
Merge with another institution without change in control	0	0	3	0	0	1	0	2	6	4	6	2	0	0	2	18	24	7	75	
Become part of a multicampus system[a]	0	0	0	0	1	0	1	0	6	0	4	0	0	0	0	0	36	0	48	
Private institution will become public	—	0	—	0	—	0	—	0	—	2	—	0	—	0	—	0	—	14	16	
Possibly will close	0	0	0	0	0	0	0	0	0	0	0	2	0	0	1	18	12	14	47	
Total changes	0	0	3	0	1	1	1	2	12	6	10	4	0	0	3	36	72	35	186	7.8%

[a] Includes respondents expected to join an existing system, as well as those expecting a new system to be created.

Note: Five presidents mentioned "increased cooperation" with another institution as a possible major change. Under an "other" category not tabulated above, five institutions in Massachusetts indicated they were expecting major changes as a result of a reorganization of higher education in their state. Three others also expected a revision of state systems. Several mentioned expectation of more state control, although their status will not be changed nominally.

Source: Carnegie Council Survey, 1978.

Regional Variations

The states are in quite different situations, some losing and some
gaining population, some with lower and some with higher fertility
rates, some with lower and some with already higher high school
graduation and college attendance rates, some exporting and some
importing students, some gaining and some losing in comparative
per capita income. Table 8 shows the variations among states. Figure
13 converts the information in Table 8 into a judgment of whether
enrollments in each state will exceed, approximately equal, or fall
below the changing national average. The Southwest and the West
seem to be most favored. The South is generally in an advantageous
position, but there are great variations there (Spence, 1977, p. 28,
Mingle, 1978, p. 9). West Virginia is in quite a different situation
from Florida, for example. The Northern Tier of states is less favored.
Painting with a very broad brush, it appears that *comparative shares*
of college enrollments will change about as follows:

East:	-10 percent
Midwest:	-10 percent
South:	+ 5 percent
Southwest and West:	+10 percent or more.

Some institutions in the South and West that are now in the second
rank academically will make it into the first rank by the end of the
century.

Private and public institutions are somewhat differently affected by these geographical variations (see Figure 14). Nearly 60 percent
of private full-time equivalent enrollment is in states rated as "worse
than average" or "much worse than average," but only about 40
percent of public enrollment is in such states.

Specific locations are more important for some institutions than
for others. For those dependent on local recruiting, it is better to be in
a viable downtown area, such as Minneapolis or Denver, than in St.
Louis or Newark, which are currently much less viable; in a growing
suburb than in a depopulating rural area.

Table 8. State variations from the national average in youthful population, birthrates, high school graduation, college attendance, private enrollment, student migration, population changes, net migration of the population, per capita income, tax capacity, and tax effort, selected years.

	(1) Percentage change in 15–24 year old population, 1980–1990	(2) Percentage change in 15–24 year old population, 1980–1995	(3) Birthrate per 1000, 1977	(4) High school graduation rate, 1977	(5) Attendance rate in college, full-time equivalent enrollment/state population, 1977	(6) Private full-time equivalent enrollment as percentage of total full-time equivalent enrollment, 1976–1977	(7) Home-state students as percentage of enrolled students	(8) Percentage change in population, 1970–1977	(9) Percentage net migration of population, 1970–1977	(10) Percentage increase in per capita income, 1969–1978 (current $)	(11) Tax Capacity Index, 1975	(12) Tax Effort Index, 1975
UNITED STATES The national average	−16.4	−18.5	15.4	75.3	3.9	23.6	.83	6.4	3.4	100*	100	100
	ALL STATE FIGURES ARE DIFFERENCES FROM THE NATIONAL AVERAGE*											
NEW ENGLAND												
Connecticut	−7.3	−11.6	−3.7	+ 2.0	−0.4	+15.6	−.02	−3.9	−4.6	−19	+13	− 6
Maine	+2.6	+ 2.7	−1.0	+ 8.1	−0.9	+ 5.1	−.10	+3.2	+1.2	− 3	−26	+25
Massachusetts	−3.8	− 7.0	−3.4	+ 5.3	+1.2	+32.8	−.09	−4.8	−4.6	−14	− 6	+30
New Hampshire	+4.5	+ 4.4	−1.1	+20.3	+0.3	+19.4	−.30	+8.6	+6.8	− 5	− 3	−20
Rhode Island	+2.9	+ 1.6	−2.6	− 2.8	+1.4	+29.1	−.13	−8.0	−1.5	− 8	−14	+15
Vermont	+0.8	+ 0.1	−1.4	+12.4	+1.3	+20.0	−.32	+2.3	−0.1	−10	−16	+21
MIDDLE ATLANTIC												
New Jersey	−2.0	− 4.6	−3.0	+ 3.6	−1.0	+ 2.3	+.07	−4.2	−4.4	−11	+11	− 1
New York	−5.1	− 9.8	−1.9	− 1.6	+0.2	+18.9	+.06	−8.1	−8.5	−21	+ 2	+52
Pennsylvania	−8.1	−11.7	−2.3	+ 6.2	−0.7	+17.1	+.02	−6.5	−6.4	− 1	− 6	− 4
EAST NORTH CENTRAL												
Illinois	−4.6	− 6.1	+0.1	− 3.2	−0.1	+ 4.3	+.05	−5.2	−7.5	− 2	+14	− 8
Indiana	−4.2	− 6.1	+0.6	− 1.1	−0.6	+ 2.9	−.06	−3.8	−6.3	0	− 2	−18
Michigan	−4.8	− 6.9	−0.4	+ 1.4	−0.1	− 8.9	+.04	−3.6	−6.6	0	+ 1	+ 1
Ohio	−6.9	− 9.5	−0.3	+ 2.1	−0.6	+ 1.0	+.03	−6.0	−8.4	− 5	+ 2	−20
Wisconsin	−6.3	− 8.6	−0.7	+ 7.1	+0.2	− 9.7	+.04	−1.1	−3.2	+ 1	− 7	+20

(continued on next page)

Table 8 (continued)

	(1) Percentage change in 15–24 year old population, 1980–1990	(2) Percentage change in 15–24 year old population, 1980–1995	(3) Birthrate per 1000, 1977	(4) High school graduation rate, 1977	(5) Attendance rate in college, full-time equivalent enrollment/state population, 1977	(6) Private full-time equivalent enrollment as percentage of total full-time equivalent enrollment, 1976–1977	(7) Home-state students as percentage of enrolled students	(8) Percentage change in population, 1970–1977	(9) Percentage migration of population, 1970–1977	(10) Percentage increase in per capita income, 1969–1978 (current $)	(11) Tax Capacity Index, 1975	(12) Tax Effort Index, 1975
WEST NORTH CENTRAL												
Iowa	− 7.5	−10.2	+ 0.4	+ 5.4	−0.1	+ 7.5	−0.06	− 4.5	− 5.4	+17	+ 3	− 8
Kansas	− 4.9	− 5.3	− 0.4	+ 2.3	+0.3	−10.5	−0.01	− 3.0	− 4.5	+12	+ 5	−15
Minnesota	− 8.0	−10.2	− 0.1	+10.9	−0.1	+ 0.8	0	− 2.0	− 4.2	+ 8	+ 2	+15
Missouri	− 5.1	− 5.6	+ 0.4	+ 1.1	−0.3	+ 6.9	0	− 3.8	− 4.1	0	− 6	−15
Nebraska	− 3.7	− 3.3	+ 1.0	+ 8.9	+0.3	− 4.0	−0.03	− 1.3	− 4.1	+ 4	+ 3	−14
North Dakota	− 8.0	− 8.2	+ 3.3	+ 7.2	+0.6	−16.8	−0.02	− 0.6	− 4.9	+26	− 1	− 6
South Dakota	− 8.4	− 8.4	+ 1.8	+ 6.6	0	+ 6.0	−0.08	− 3.0	− 6.3	+21	− 9	−10
SOUTH ATLANTIC												
Delaware	− 4.1	− 5.2	− 0.3	+ 4.4	+0.3	− 8.6	−0.11	− 0.3	− 2.6	−12	+22	−14
District of Columbia	—	− 8.6	+14.6	−24.1	+5.0	+59.8	−0.55	−15.2	−16.4	+13	+20	+ 3
Florida	+13.1	+17.9	− 2.3	− 1.5	−0.7	− 3.7	0	+18.1	+18.9	+ 6	− 2	−20
Georgia	+ 9.2	+10.6	+ 1.7	− 6.8	−1.0	− 3.3	−0.04	+ 3.6	+ 0.2	+ 3	−12	−15
Maryland	+ 0.4	− 1.0	− 3.7	− 0.3	−0.3	+ 9.1	−0.02	+ 0.9	− 2.1	− 3	+ 2	+ 9
North Carolina	+ 5.8	+ 6.2	0	− 3.8	0	0	−0.02	+ 2.3	− 0.7	+ 5	−16	−12
South Carolina	+ 7.1	+ 8.8	+ 1.3	− 2.6	−0.3	− 0.2	+0.03	+ 4.6	+ 0.1	+13	−23	−13
Virginia	+ 3.3	+ 3.6	+ 1.5	− 1.2	−0.3	− 8.1	−0.06	+ 4.0	+ 1.3	+10	− 7	−12
West Virginia	+ 0.3	− 0.1	+ 1.0	− 1.7	−0.7	− 8.4	−0.06	+ 0.2	− 2.0	+25	−10	−15
EAST SOUTH CENTRAL												
Alabama	+ 0.4	+ 0.2	+ 1.2	− 6.6	−0.2	− 9.8	0	+ 0.7	− 2.2	+17	−22	−19
Kentucky	+ 2.7	+ 3.5	+ 1.9	− 6.7	−0.8	− 6.7	−0.01	+ 1.0	− 1.2	+15	−10	−16
Mississippi	+ 2.2	+ 2.3	+ 3.6	−12.4	−0.4	−13.1	+0.06	+ 1.4	− 3.5	+21	−30	− 5
Tennessee	+ 1.8	+ 1.7	+ 0.9	− 6.5	−0.4	+ 2.9	−0.04	+ 2.9	+ 0.2	+12	−18	−19

(continued on next page)

Table 8 (continued)

	(1) Percentage change in 15–24 year old population, 1980–1990	(2) Percentage change in 15–24 year old population, 1980–1995	(3) Birthrate per 1000, 1977	(4) High school graduation rate, 1977	(5) Attendance rate in college, full-time equivalent enrollment/ state population, 1977	(6) Private full-time equivalent enrollment as percentage of total full-time equivalent enrollment, 1976–1977	(7) Home-state students as percentage of enrolled students	(8) Percentage change in population, 1970–1977	(9) Percentage net migration of population, 1970–1977	(10) Percentage increase in per capita income, 1969–1978 (current $)	(11) Tax Capacity Index, 1975	(12) Tax Effort Index, 1975
WEST SOUTH CENTRAL												
Arkansas	+ 3.8	+ 4.7	+ 0.8	− 2.2	−1.2	− 8.1	0	+ 5.1	+ 2.9	+16	−22	−21
Louisiana	− 4.0	− 1.9	+ 3.9	+ 6.4	−0.6	− 9.5	+0.01	+ 1.2	+ 2.9	+20	+ 3	−19
Oklahoma	+ 3.5	+ 5.7	+ 0.2	+ 3.0	+0.3	− 8.3	−0.02	+ 3.4	− 1.5	+16	+ 2	−29
Texas	+ 7.7	+11.0	+ 2.9	− 3.9	0	− 9.7	+0.05	+ 8.2	+ 3.1	+20	+13	−32
MOUNTAIN												
Arizona	+15.4	+21.7	+ 2.8	− 0.6	+1.5	−19.9	−0.13	+22.9	+17.5	+ 8	− 7	+10
Colorado	+ 5.7	+ 8.7	+ 1.2	+ 6.3	+0.8	−13.8	−0.12	+12.9	+ 8.2	+14	+ 4	− 4
Idaho	+ 9.2	+12.8	+ 5.9	+ 8.3	−0.1	− 1.0	−0.15	+12.1	+ 6.8	+18	−13	− 5
Montana	− 2.3	− 0.7	+ 1.8	+ 6.2	−0.4	−14.1	−0.03	+13.9	+ 0.5	+ 2	− 2	− 4
Nevada	+12.1	+13.8	+ 0.5	+ 6.8	−1.0	−22.7	−0.03	+ 3.2	+19.8	+ 7	+51	−30
New Mexico	+ 2.8	+ 5.3	+ 3.6	+ 0.3	−0.3	−16.6	−0.06	+23.2	+ 4.1	+17	− 7	−12
Utah	+14.7	+21.1	+15.2	+ 7.3	+1.8	+13.8	−0.17	+13.3	0	+ 9	−14	− 9
Wyoming	+ 4.2	+ 5.9	+ 3.6	+ 6.3	−0.4	−23.6	−0.12	+15.8	+10.1	+35	+47	−27
PACIFIC												
Alaska	+12.7	+15.0	+ 5.0	−10.7	−1.0	−19.2	+0.11	+28.2	+23.7	+41	+43	+ 9
California	+ 2.0	+ 2.7	+ 0.5	− 2.4	+1.1	−11.1	+0.03	+ 3.2	+ 0.9	− 1	+10	+21
Hawaii	+ 6.8	+ 9.0	+ 3.6	+ 8.2	+0.5	−14.8	−0.08	+ 9.8	+ 1.1	−10	+ 9	+20
Oregon	+ 3.3	+ 4.9	+ 0.8	+ 2.2	+0.6	−10.4	−0.04	+ 7.2	+ 5.5	+17	− 2	− 1
Washington	− 0.3	− 0.7	+ 0.2	+ 2.1	+0.9	−11.6	+0.04	+ 0.8	− 0.2	+ 3	0	+ 1

*For example, the percentage change in Connecticut in the 15–24 year old population between 1980 and 1990 is −23.7. Since the change for the U.S. is −16.4%, the figure for Connecticut in column (1) is calculated as (−23.7) less (−16.4) = −7.3. For New Hampshire, the percentage change in the 15–24 year old population between 1980 and 1990 is −11.9. The figure in column (1) is calculated as (−11.9) less (−16.4%) = +4.5. In column (10) the U.S. increase in per capita income is an index to which state changes are related. The actual increase for the nation over this period was 114 percent.

(continued on next page)

Table 8 *(continued)*

Sources and Notes: Columns (1) and (2): Population estimates of the U.S. Bureau of Census (1979). Column (3): U.S. Department of Health, Education, and Welfare (1979). Columns (4) and (7): U.S. National Center for Education Statistics (1978b). Column (5): U.S. National Center for Education Statistics (1978c; 1978d). Columns (6), (8), and (9): U.S. Bureau of Census (1978). Percentage net migration of population is estimated as those coming in minus those leaving as percentage of the 1970 population. Column (10): U.S. Department of Commerce (1979). Columns (11) and (12): Tax Capacity is a measure of the total taxable resources per capita in the state under a uniform representative tax system. The Tax Effort index is a measure of the taxes raised per capita relative to the capacity. Positive numbers in column (11) indicate a larger than average fiscal capacity under the uniform representation tax system. Positive numbers in column (12) indicate a larger than average effort, given the capacity of the state. See Halstead (1978).

Explanations: Positive figures in columns 1, 2, 3, 8, 9, 10, 11 and indicate demographic and financial trends that would be expected to have a positive effect on enrollment trends, i.e., lessen the decline relative to the average for the U.S. as a whole. In columns 4 and 5, negative figures would have a positive effect on enrollment trends, because it was assumed that high school graduation and attendance rates were likely to rise if the present rates are below the national averages. Positive figures in column 6 were also considered a negative influence unless a significant proportion of the private enrollment is in elite institutions, as in Massachusetts. Column 7 measures the percentages of those enrolled who are studying in their home state. The lower this figure, the less important are the specific trend factors for this state in determining the group in which this state is likely to fall. A positive figure in column 12, indicating that the state is already making a strong tax effort, suggests a poor outlook for still higher taxes in the future.

Figure 13. Carnegie Council Projected Enrollment Trends in the 1990s Relative to the National Average

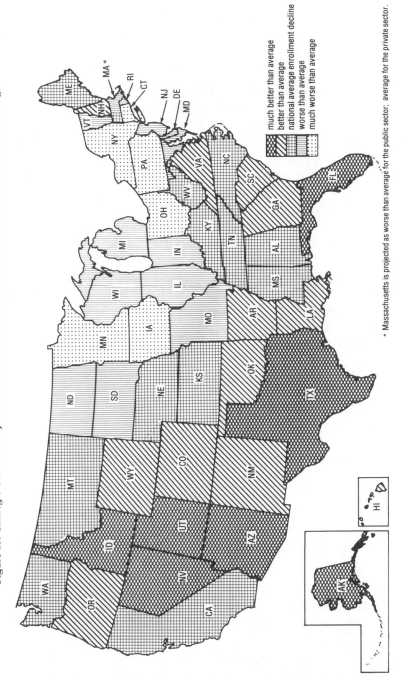

much better than average
better than average
national average enrollment decline
worse than average
much worse than average

* Massachusetts is projected as worse than average for the public sector; average for the private sector.

Source: Carnegie Council estimates.

Gainers and Losers

Future enrollment patterns will vary widely from campus to campus as they have during the past decade. Among institutions reporting figures for both 1970 and 1978[9], we found both gainers and losers: 59 percent registered increases, 12 percent remained stable (shifts in the range of -5 to +5 percent), and 29 percent lost FTE enrollment. Most of the enrollment gains were substantial, with over one-half of the 1,250 gainers reporting FTE increases in the 20 to 100 percent range and another 15 percent showing gains of more than 100 percent. The public two-year colleges were heavy gainers. The less selective liberal arts colleges, the two-year private colleges, and the public doctorate-granting institutions were among the more frequent losers. The research universities were the most stable. An overview of institutional gainers and losers and other changes during the 1970s is presented in Tables 9 and 10.[10]

The significant enrollment growth of the 1970s was also evident in the 111 new collegiate institutions that appeared, mostly in the public sector.[11] Seventy-eight two-year institutions, 24 less-selective liberal arts campuses, and 9 comprehensive colleges and universities opened. Of the 33 four-year colleges opening their doors from 1970 to 1978, 11 were considered especially successful because they continued to exist in 1978 and enrolled more than 1,000 students in that year. Ten of what we have identified as new successes are comprehensive colleges and universities and one is a liberal arts college.[12]

[9]Note that institutions not reporting enrollments for both years (often because they opened or closed during the 1970-1978 period) could not be included.

[10]These developments are explored in more detail in Supplement D, *Gainers and Losers Among Institutions of Higher Education.*

[11]There were also increased numbers of specialized and nontraditional institutions, mostly private, which are not included in the overall number of institutions reported here. These numbered 423 in 1970, increasing to 566 in the 1976 Carnegie Classification .

[12]The list includes Texas Eastern University, University of Houston campuses at Clear Lake City and Downtown, and Corpus Christi University; Liberty Baptist College (private) in Virginia; Francis Marion College in South Carolina; Metropolitan State University in Minnesota; the University of Maine—Portland-Gorham; the University of Alaska-Anchorage; National University (private) in California; and the only liberal arts college, Touro College (private) in New York. National University is counted as a "new success" here and in Supplement D but is not included in the count of 9 newly opened comprehensive colleges because it was founded as a specialized institution, moving into the comprehensive category only in 1978.

Figure 14. **Percentage distribution of private, public, and total full-time equivalent enrollment in states classified by relative enrollment changes in the 1990s (as in Figure 13)**

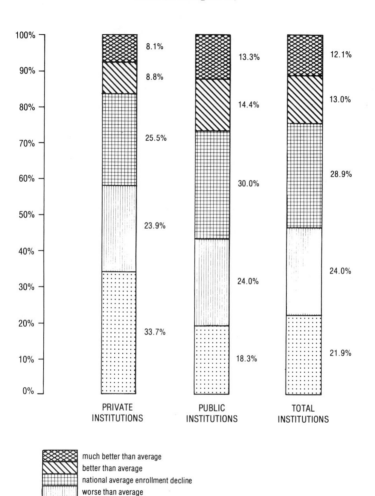

Source: Carnegie Council estimates.

Table 9. Summary of institutional gains, losses, and other changes, 1970-1978

	Total		Public		Private	
	Number	*(Percent)*	*Number*	*(Percent)*	*Number*	*(Percent)*
FTE enrollment changes[a]						
Gainers	1256	(59)	771	(68)	485	(48)
Losers	630	(29)	236	(21)	394	(39)
Stable[b]	259	(12)	129	(11)	130	(13)
Institutional changes						
Openings	111		80		31	
New successes[c]	11		8		3	
Closures	107		15		92	
Mergers	68		41		27	
Shifts in control	11					
Private to public					11	

[a] Enrollment changes could be analyzed only for those 2,145 institutions that reported enrollment in 1970 and 1978, so that 249 institutions that opened, closed, or otherwise did not report for both years are not included.

[b] Stable enrollment was defined as changes no greater than plus or minus 5 percent.

[c] New successes are defined as four-year institutions opening in 1970 or later and reporting headcount enrollment of 1,000 or more in 1978.

Sources: Carnegie Council staff analysis based on (U.S. National Center for Education Statistics) NCES, *Education Directory, Colleges and Universities*, 1970—1971 to 1978—1979 and NCES, *Opening Fall Enrollment*, 1970 and 1978.

Table 10. Institutional changes, **1970–1978**
(**Institutions as classified in the Carnegie Classification of 1970**)

Carnegie Classification (Number in 1970)	Percentage of Institutions				
	FTE enrollment changes[a]			Openings[b]	Closures, mergers, and shifts in control[b]
	Gainers	Losers	Stable		
Total (2,394)	58.6	29.4	12.1	4.6	7.9
Public (1,250)	67.9	20.8	11.4	6.4	4.6
Private (1,144)	48.1	39.0	12.9	2.8	11.4
Research Universities (92)	54.9	19.8	25.3	0	0
Public (57)	57.1	16.1	26.8		
Private (35)	51.4	25.7	22.9		
Doctorate-granting Universities (81)	48.8	35.0	16.3	0	0
Public (52)	44.0	40.0	16.0		
Private (29)	56.7	26.7	16.7		
Comprehensive Universities and Colleges (449)	45.2	37.8	17.0	2.0	1.8
Public (304)	47.5	36.9	15.6	2.6	2.0
Private (145)	40.4	39.7	19.9	0.7	1.4
Liberal Arts Colleges I (145)	51.8	29.5	18.7	0	3.4
Public (2)	50.0	0	50.0		0
Private (143)	51.8	29.9	18.2		3.4
Liberal Arts Colleges II (573)	48.6	41.2	10.2	4.4	12.2
Public (30)	82.6	8.7	8.7	10.0	6.7
Private (543)	47.0	42.7	10.3	4.0	11.3
Two-Year Colleges (1,054)	73.1	18.9	8.0	7.4	11.5
Public (805)	78.5	13.5	8.0	8.6	7.1
Private (249)	52.0	40.2	7.8	3.6	23.9

[a] Enrollment changes could be analyzed only for those 2,145 institutions which reported enrollment in 1970 and 1978, so that 249 institutions which opened, closed, or otherwise did not report for both years are not included.

[b] Percentages calculated from the number of institutions in each category in 1970.

Source: Carnegie Council calculations from U.S. NCES (1970; 1979d) data.

The boom years of the 1960s also gave rise to many new institutions, 66 of which were four-year institutions still drawing over 1,000 students each in 1978. This number includes campuses added to expanding state systems, particularly in California, Alabama, Florida, Texas, and New York, as well as notable new successes in the private sector, such as Oral Roberts University. Not included in this number are separate medical centers, law schools, other specialized campuses, and nontraditional institutions, such as SUNY's Empire State College. In addition, some 400 public community colleges were started in the 1960s with more than 1,000 students in 1978.

The number of institutions that ceased to exist in the 1970s in their original form was substantial; 107 closed, 68 merged, and 11 changed from private to public control. Only 15 of the closed institutions were under public control, all at the two- year level, and 12 of these were two-year teachers' colleges in Wisconsin, which were closed in 1971-1973 because state licensing requirements were increased. Of the remaining three public colleges that closed, one was a two-year branch campus that lost enrollment when a new community college opened nearby with lower tuition; the second was totally funded by local revenues and the limited local tax base was unable to continue support for the institution. The third burned down. All of the remaining closures were under private control, about equally divided between less-selective liberal arts and two-year colleges. Mergers, although less frequent, were a substantial source of change. Forty-one public institutions, mostly two-year colleges, including several two-year branches of four-year institutions, merged. The 27 private schools merging were mostly less-selective liberal arts campuses. Catholic colleges were hard hit: 48 closed or merged, and only 3 opened. Among similar Protestant colleges, 18 closed or merged, and 4 opened. Whether religiously affiliated or not, closed or merged institutions were more prevalent in urban areas than in rural, by 2 to 1. The smaller urban colleges were the more vulnerable, perhaps because they were less competitive with the wide range of low-cost educational options in the cities.

Many institutions have undergone changes sufficient to warrant reclassification under the Carnegie typology. Of the 2,394 colleges and universities that were classified in 1970, excluding outlying areas, 278 (11.6 percent) were classified differently in 1976. As

Table 11. Shifts in Carnegie Classifications, 1970–1976

Classification in 1970 (Number)	Number changing by 1976	Classification in 1976										
		Research Universities I	Research Universities II	Doctorate-granting Universities I	Doctorate-granting Universities II	Comprehensive Universities and Colleges I	Comprehensive Universities and Colleges II	Liberal Arts Colleges I	Liberal Arts Colleges II	Two-Year Colleges	Theological Seminaries	Other Specialized[a]
Private Institutions												
Research Universities I (22)	1	—	1	—	—	—	—	—	—	—	—	—
Research Universities II (13)	3	1	—	2	—	—	—	—	—	—	—	—
Doctorate-granting Universities I (19)	5	—	3	—	1	1	—	—	—	—	—	—
Doctorate-granting Universities II (10)	3	—	—	1	—	2	—	—	—	—	—	—
Comprehensive Universities and Colleges I (98)	9	—	—	—	3	—	6	—	—	—	—	—
Comprehensive Universities and Colleges II (47)	14	—	—	1	—	5	—	—	6	—	—	2
Liberal Arts Colleges I (143)	38	—	—	—	—	5	14	—	17	—	1	1
Liberal Arts Colleges II (544)	122	—	—	—	—	16	49	27	—	1	20	9
Two-Year Colleges (249)	15	—	—	—	—	—	—	—	9	—	3	3
Public Institutions												
Research Universities I (30)	3	—	3	—	—	—	—	—	—	—	—	—
Research Universities II (27)	2	2	—	—	—	—	—	—	—	—	—	—
Doctorate-granting Universities I (34)	8	—	5	—	3	—	—	—	—	—	—	—
Doctorate-granting Universities II (18)	7	—	—	7	—	—	—	—	—	—	—	—
Comprehensive Universities and Colleges I (220)	22	—	—	2	6	—	14	—	—	—	—	—

(continued on next page)

Table 11 (continued)

Public Institutions (continued)

Classification in 1976

Classification in 1970 (Number)	Number changing by 1976	Research Universities I	Research Universities II	Doctorate-granting Universities I	Doctorate-granting Universities II	Comprehensive Universities and Colleges I	Comprehensive Universities and Colleges II	Liberal Arts Colleges I	Liberal Arts Colleges II	Two-Year Colleges	Theological Seminaries	Other[a] Specialized
Comprehensive Universities and Colleges II (85)	1	—	—	—	—	1	—	—	—	—		
Liberal Arts Colleges I (2)	2	—	—	1	—	—	1	—	—	—		
Liberal Art Colleges II (30)	6	—	—	—	—	2	4	—	—	—		
Two-Year Colleges (805)	6	—	—	—	—	1	2	—	2	—		

Changes from Private to Public Control

Public Classification in 1976

Private Classification in 1970 (Number)	Number changing by 1976	Research Universities I	Research Universities II	Doctorate-granting Universities I	Doctorate-granting Universities II	Comprehensive Universities and Colleges I	Comprehensive Universities and Colleges II	Liberal Arts Colleges I	Liberal Arts Colleges II	Two-Year Colleges	Theological Seminaries	Other[a] Specialized
Comprehensive Universities and Colleges I (98)	1	—	—	—	1M	1	—	—	—	—		
Liberal Arts Colleges I (143)	1	—	—	—	1M	—	—	—	—	—		
Liberal Arts Colleges II (544)	3	—	—	1M	—	—	—	—	1	—		
Two-Year Colleges (249)	6	—	—	—	—	—	—	—	—	5		

[a] This group includes medical schools and medical centers; other separate health professional schools; schools of engineering and technology; business and management; art, music and design; law; teachers' colleges; and other specialized institutions.

M = Merger of private institution with public institution. (In these cases, the private institution's Carnegie type changes to the Carnegie type of the public institution with which it merges.)

Source: Carnegie Council calculations from U.S. NCES (1970; 1978a).

shown in Table 11, nearly 80 percent of the changes occurred among private institutions. Private liberal arts II colleges were most affected with 122 shifting classification; 3 out of 4 moving to the liberal arts I or comprehensive categories, and the rest shifting to two-year or specialized categories. Among the private liberal arts I colleges, 38 changes were recorded—19 became comprehensive colleges and universities, 17 changed to the less-selective liberal arts category, and 2 were reclassified as specialized schools.

Among public institutions, the comprehensive colleges and universities I were the most frequently affected by reclassification: 22 shifts occurred—8 into the doctorate-granting universities classification, and 14 became Comprehensive Universities and Colleges II.

Eleven private institutions changed to public control from 1970 to 1978 (6 two-year, 3 highly selective liberal arts, 1 less-selective liberal arts, and 1 comprehensive college), representing a small but important loss to the private sector.

Summary. At least 95 percent of all campuses underwent some significant change in the 1970s: they gained or lost enrollment, or opened or closed, or merged, or shifted to public control, or changed classification. Alteration of condition or status was almost universal; continuation of the status quo almost nonexistent. Campuses moved up and down, in and out, and sideways. Transformation was the rule; uniformity of condition the exception. The totality of shifts was generally most favorable for the public community colleges; and least favorable for the private less-selective four-year liberal arts colleges and private two-year colleges; but there were many exceptions. Each campus has had its own individual recent history; and is likely to have its own individual near future. Institutions of higher education have been riding off in all directions and will probably continue to do so: 3,000 different institutions face 3,000 different futures.[13]

---

[13]We use the figure 3,000 here to cover the total universe of institutions, including theological seminaries and other specialized institutions and nontraditional institutions (about 600), because changing conditions affect them as they do the approximately 2,400 institutions which we have analyzed above.

Implications of the Demographic Depression for Faculty

The situation of faculty members has generally been deteriorating for at least the past five years and may continue to do so in important regards for another decade or more.

Faculty compensation rose in real terms for the first 70 years of the twentieth century.[14] It has dropped now for the past decade. Faculty compensation in the 1960s not only gained on the cost of living but also on the average compensation of all civilian full-time employees. For the past few years, faculty members have been losing both relatively and absolutely in terms of their real compensation.

The labor market for faculty members has virtually collapsed in all but a few still active fields. At the peak of its activity, additions to the professoriate were being made at the rate of 20,000 and more per year. The current level of net additions is about zero and will remain at that level or below it for much of the rest of this century. If student-to-faculty ratios should keep on rising (say by 10 percent) on top of the rise of more than 10 percent in recent years, then the size of net reductions of the professoriate may become quite substantial. There will, of course, be some replacement needs for faculty members retiring, dying, or quitting the profession, but retirement rates will be low until the end of the century, given the age structure of the faculty.

The labor market consequences are most intense for young persons looking for their first jobs, for junior faculty seeking tenure, for temporary faculty kept in temporary status at college after college, for faculty members who would like to move from one institution to another but find no openings. Women and minorities were entering faculty status in significant but still insufficient numbers in the 1970s, and their prospects are diminished for most of the next two decades. Some faculty members with tenure now face dismissal; some colleges will close.

The tenured professoriate in four-year colleges will keep on aging with the ages of the modal group rising from 36 to 45 in 1980 to 56 to 65 in 2000 (see Figure 5). This will increase the age gap between students and faculty, raise the average cost of faculty salaries, and make it hard to introduce new fields, new courses, new subject

---

[14]For these and other data, see Supplement H, *Faculty Development Present and Future*. See also Figure 15.

Figure 15. Selected developments and projections affecting faculties

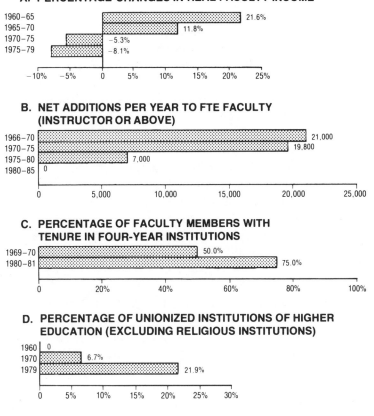

A. PERCENTAGE CHANGES IN REAL FACULTY INCOME

1960–65 · 21.6%
1965–70 · 11.8%
1970–75 · –5.3%
1975–79 · –8.1%

B. NET ADDITIONS PER YEAR TO FTE FACULTY (INSTRUCTOR OR ABOVE)

1966–70 · 21,000
1970–75 · 19,800
1975–80 · 7,000
1980–85 · 0

C. PERCENTAGE OF FACULTY MEMBERS WITH TENURE IN FOUR-YEAR INSTITUTIONS

1969–70 · 50.0%
1980–81 · 75.0%

D. PERCENTAGE OF UNIONIZED INSTITUTIONS OF HIGHER EDUCATION (EXCLUDING RELIGIOUS INSTITUTIONS)

1960 · 0
1970 · 6.7%
1979 · 21.9%

E. CHANGES IN SHARES OF SENIOR FACULTY BY CARNEGIE CLASSIFICATION AND REGION, 1963–1977

SUBSTANTIAL LOSS IN SHARE	SUBSTANTIAL GAIN IN SHARE
Research Universities: North and East	Comprehensive Universities and Colleges: South and West
Liberal Arts Colleges I and II: Nationwide	Two-Year Colleges: Nationwide
Other Doctorate-Granting Universities: Nationwide	

Sources: A: Bowen (1979). B: U.S. NCES (1978, p. 68) and Carnegie Council staff projections. C: Carnegie Council Survey of Faculty, 1969, and Carnegie Council staff projections cited in source B, above. D: Garbarino (forthcoming). E: Estimates prepared by the Carnegie Council staff based on NCES data on enrollment, faculty-student ratios, and number of employees of institutions of higher education.

matter. Tenure ratios, which were 50 percent as recently as 1969, have now risen to 75 percent; and colleges encounter new rigidities in redeploying their resources.

One consequence of all this has been a rise in collective bargaining. It was almost nonexistent in 1960. Its introduction was largely confined to two-year colleges during the 1960s, but, in the 1970s, it was extended significantly to four-year institutions also. Now, about one-fifth of all institutions are covered, and 24 states support in their laws collective bargaining by faculty members in public institutions. Collective bargaining, with potentially substantial impacts on traditional forms of academic governance, is encouraged by falling real income, threats of reductions in personnel, and the pressure for affirmative action.

The changes in the location of faculty members are startling. In 1963, 1 faculty member in 10 was in a two-year college; now it is 1 in 5. Faculty members of liberal arts colleges accounted for about 1 in 6 of all faculty members in 1963, and now for only 1 in 12.

Some faculty members are potentially much more affected than are others:

In the East and North more than in the South and West
In comprehensive colleges more than in community colleges; in less-selective more than in more-selective four-year liberal arts colleges; in doctorate-granting universities more than in research universities
In the humanities more than in the professions
In nontenured more than in tenured ranks
In closing and merging institutions more than in continuing ones.

The fate of faculties is intimately tied to the fate of their current institutions, since so few faculty members will have the opportunity to move elsewhere.

While students are likely to be advantaged, faculty members, by and large, can only be disadvantaged by the demographic depression. But the impacts will be quite varied, from some loss of real income to total loss of employment.

5

Anticipating the Next Two Decades

The next two decades will bring many changes. They will differ, as we have just noted, institution by institution. How might an institution think about its future?

The future is not fully determined in advance. It will be substantially affected by what institutions and individuals decide to do. Thus, it is important to have goals to achieve. What contributions can higher education make over the next two decades?

The nation, as a whole, may move in substantially new directions. What may be the roles of higher education as the nation itself changes?

Thinking About the Future

Looking ahead is a risky endeavor. Speculations about the future, however, can be useful. They can encourage others, particularly at the levels of the states and of systems of higher education and of individual institutions to:

Think about what is already largely determined, as for example:
  The sizes of the age cohorts that contribute to enrollments
  The faculty
  The buildings
  The universe of competitive institutions
  The methods of governance
  The accumulated heritage of the centuries.

Think about what is likely but not certain to change, as for example:
  A more favorable labor market for young persons and a higher rate
  of return on their investments in a college education
  The further professionalization of American society
  Greater family affluence and more second-generation college
  students
  Tougher competition from the military to get youth into service
  Greater competition for the public funds that now support higher
  education.
Think about what might happen, both for the better and the worse,
that is now unknown, as for example:
  Great new technological advances
  A major war
  A major depression
  Continuing high-level inflation.
Think about the tools at hand, such as:
  Policies
  Leadership.
And think how individual institutions may react to these devel-
opments and possibilities:
  What is threatened that is worth preserving, and what is possible
  that is new and worth developing? What are the comparative
  advantages of the institution? What can it do best?
  To what extent can the future be planned? What are the areas of
  self-determination? What contingency planning should be under-
  taken?
  What new institutional policies should be developed?
  What public policies should be supported?

Looking ahead is not just a matter of curiosity. It is also a matter
of effective adaptation—Hegel once wrote that "Hell is truth seen too
late." Looking ahead is also a matter of leadership, of trying to seize
hold of the future and to guide it, and not just to react to what
otherwise will happen.

Two decades quite different from the two just past now
confront higher education. They appear to offer fewer dramatic
possibilities for constructive action. But, like the last two decades,
what happens will be the result of external forces and internal
choices.

The great external forces in the last two decades were the

domestic consequences of Sputnik, the "tidal wave" of students that followed on the "baby boom" after World War II, the new affluence, the civil rights revolution, the war in Vietnam, and the student movement reflecting the impact of the latter two. Only one of these — the tidal wave of students—was seen in advance.

Only one great new force in the forthcoming two decades can now be identified: the demographic depression for higher education. But we can be certain that there will be others. Possible candidates are substantial inflation,[1] a full depression, another war, a deepening energy crisis, rising internal political unrest—all "bad." Or perhaps there will be a new era of "good feeling" consequent upon a new and more buoyant generation of youth,[2] a great wave of technical inventions and innovations, and there may be other "good" surprises. The one certainty, however, is uncertainty.

Higher education in the last period was not just a plaything of the external environment. Nor need it be in the next. Decisions[3] were made the last time around that were very consequential, including:

The move toward open-access higher education, particularly through expansion of community colleges

The continued concentration of new basic science programs in the universities

The shift of teachers' colleges to comprehensive colleges and universities

The introduction of vast new student aid programs at the federal level

---

[1]For the unfavorable impacts of inflation on colleges, see Harris (1970, chap. 54).

[2]See Easterlin (1978). See also his discussion of "demographic waves" in *Population, Labor Force and Long Swings in Economic Growth* (1968). Easterlin argues that, because of a declining birth rate since about 1960, the U.S. is entering a new period of growing scarcity of young adults, similar to that of the 1940-1960 period. Consequently, the 1980s should see a turnaround of some of the social, political, and economic conditions, for example, rising unemployment, increased divorce and crime rates, that have been results of demographic patterns rather than of a hardening social malaise, as is often asserted.

[3]We contrast decisions made by authorities within higher education and outside it but with responsibility for its welfare—including coordinating councils, governors, federal agencies, legislatures, the federal Congress, and The President—with broad external forces outside the control of these decision makers. We contrast human choice with implacable necessity.

The introduction of affirmative action for minorities and women
The predominantly ad hoc response to the student movement, containing it and channeling it rather than confronting it or embracing it
The clarification and preservation of differentiation of functions among different types of institutions
The perpetuation of the private college in general and of colleges founded for blacks in particular
The continuation of a system of higher education with major reliance on state support and control.

Other choices were available and even considered, and some-times strongly argued in each case—as was federal support for institutions as such rather than for students. None of these choices was enforced by the external environment. Other societies, faced by somewhat similar problems, usually, in fact, made different choices.

No other nation so embraced open-access higher education. Only Norway and Yugoslavia chose to expand enrollments via their versions of community colleges. The United Kingdom more aban-doned than converted its teachers' colleges. Most national govern-ments chose to aid institutions as such rather than to concentrate financial support on students as our federal government decided to do. Other nations often either put down the student movement (Japan) or embraced it into academic governance through uniform laws (Germany and Holland) or some of both (France). Several nations, Italy and Sweden (the U68 reforms) in particular, responded to enrollment increases by opening their elite institutions to mass enrollments rather than by choosing the route of differentiation of functions.

Choices will need to be made again.

In the United States last time, there were some surprises along the way with great specific impacts on higher education: the war in Vietnam and the rapid decline in the fertility rate (not generally apparent and recognized until about 1965 or later)[4] were among them. Now there are some wild cards that may or may not be played and, if they are played, we do not know when they will be played or how:

[4]The rates changed as follows: 1955-1959—3.7 percent; 1960-1964—3.5 percent; 1965-1969—2.6 percent; 1970-1974—2.1 percent; 1975-1979—1.8 percent.

- Will there be a major new student movement? When may it arise? What may be its themes? What directions may it pursue? It seems possible, looking at recurrent student movements (particularly since 1900), that there might be another such movement between 1980 and 2000 but, again looking at past history, its form and purpose are likely to be quite different from the last.

- How far will the new electronic technology develop? How much will it affect higher education? How much will it take place outside higher education? Video discs and cassettes are now becoming available. The Carnegie Commission (1972) once predicted that electronic presentations would penetrate significantly into lower division instruction and into the operation of libraries as learning resource centers, and substantially into extension courses by 2000.[5] The "Fourth Revolution" thus far is less spectacular than the Commission expected it to be. It is occurring unevenly in different institutions and in departments within institutions. It is taking place, but it does so with little fanfare and has not been closely monitored. To a large extent it has remained experimental. But it may now be ready for its "take-off" period. A study by the Corporation for Public Broadcasting and the National Center for Education Statistics, for example, showed that 86 percent of the state and land-grant colleges and universities, 64 percent of the two-year colleges, and 50 percent of the private colleges responding to the survey reported that they used television for on- and off-campus instruction ("Colleges make Big Use of Television, Study Shows," 1979, p. 3).

- Will there be further internal enrollment shifts, such as the recent shift of student majors to vocational and professional subjects, and what impacts will this have on the composition of faculties?

- What will be the new military recruitment policy? Eligible youths will be in scarce supply. Will the military turn to the draft, and, if so, who will be exempted? Will it rely on inducements for volunteers, and, if so, how large a role will educational benefits play? Military recruitment policy, whatever it may be, will have a major impact on the distribution and conduct of youths.

- To what extent will other organizations—museums, government

[5]See also the suggestion of Mood (1973) for utilization of video cassettes, national broadcasting of standard courses, and the like.

agencies, the military services, corporations—offer higher education? We have identified these organizations as the Third Sector that is opening up in postsecondary education. Corporate activity at the graduate level, in particular, is expanding rapidly.

- What will national and local policies be on taxation and on expenditure patterns? Will the Proposition 13 mentality and the tax limitation movement spread geographically and deepen their roots? What will be the priorities for expenditures? Where will higher education rate among them?

- What will happen to private rates of return on a college education to opportunities in the labor market, and to levels of employment; and how will these affect attendance in higher education and the types of programs followed within higher education?

- What changes may there be in the directions of national youth policy?

We cannot know in advance what the great external uncertainties will be, only that there will be some. We also cannot know how and when the above and other possible wild cards will be played. We do know, however, that higher education and the agencies directly responsible for its welfare will have choices to make. We discuss some of these choices in Section 6.

Setting Goals for the Future

We need to have some idea of where we would like to be 20 years from now in higher education if we are to guide our own future. Twenty years ago, in 1960, views were forming about where higher education should aim during the next 20 years:[6] at greater strength in science after Sputnik; at accommodating the "tidal wave" of students after

---

[6]See, for example, McConnell (1962). McConnell thought that planning for the future should be based on the assumption that there would be a much larger, more diverse, and less selective group of students than had previously been accommodated by higher education. Planning, too, should be based on the proposition "that a democratic, industrialized society needs many types and levels of talent and education" (p.46); he urged a "more rationally differentiated" higher education system (p. 51). He saw state coordination of public systems as "inescapable" and believed that: "When the motivation is positive and forward looking, when the purpose is to plan and support a diversified educational system of high quality and to use financial resources efficiently, and when the greatest possible degree of freedom is left to individual institutions, the result should be constructive" (pp. 143-144).

the rise of the birthrate subsequent to World War II; at creating a nationwide network of open-access institutions as was then being done on a statewide basis in California and Florida; at greater equality of opportunity for young persons to attend college regardless of family income, race, or sex; at reforms to meet the needs of the new students; at preparing more medical care personnel to meet the rising expectations for health care. These aims have all been substantially or at least significantly achieved. Their achievement has set the tone of the recent period, made it a Golden Age for higher education. What contributions should higher education be prepared to make in the next two decades?

At least the following contributions by higher education, it now appears, will be needed by the nation in 2000, and generally also in the years in between:

1. *Places to accommodate by 2010 approximately the same number of students as were enrolled in 1978.* It will not make sense in the meantime to substantially reduce capacity only to have to recreate it again in the near future. It will be better to find temporary alternative uses for any excess capacity.

2. *Institutions representing at least the degree of diversity we have today.* The United States is an intricate mosaic of races, ethnic groups, religions, occupational pursuits, styles of life; and is becoming ever more so, at least in occupational pursuits and styles of life. Institutions that pay attention to these diversities will be at least equally needed in the future as in the past.[7] Also, many students like to go to institutions that have their own personalities and distinctive reputations, that are out of the ordinary. Moreover, distinctiveness is one source of private funds, particularly from alumni—distinctiveness pays.

3. *Resources to impart higher levels of skill attainment than ever before.* The technologies of society keep on advancing, as do the complications in the interconnections of individuals and institutions. In particular, the professional and technical, and the managerial occupational groupings are the fastest growing in the nation. They are dependent for their staffing largely on college-

---

[7]See Stadtman (forthcoming) for a discussion of changing diversity in higher education.

trained personnel. They now employ one-quarter of the employed labor force, and college gradutes are also finding employment as technical sales personnel and in other high-qualifications fields as well. Society will need all the high-level talent it can find, trained to ever-higher levels of competence.

4. *Capabilities for more advanced scientific research.* Deeper scientific knowledge is essential to better health, to new sources of energy, to more productive technology, to more assured national defense. Research is still the "endless frontier" (Bush, 1945). Today it is knowledge that "is the field in which evolution takes place. It is the only thing that can really change. . . . Changes in knowledge are the basic source of all other changes. . ." (Boulding, 1978, p. 224). In the United States, the university has been the "Home of Science" (Wolfle, 1972) and, by all odds, the most effective home of science anywhere in the world. The place of the United States among the nations of the world will depend at least as much on the scientific advances within its universities as it did after Sputnik. Knowledge must now be ranked, along with land, labor, and capital, as a basic factor of production.

Productivity is dependent both on high skills and also on new technology through research, and each relates to the level and quality of education. Higher productivity will be necessary not only to advancing standards of living, but also to eliminating poverty, to supporting an aging population—one-fifth of the people will be 65 or over in 2025—and to using increasingly scarce raw materials more efficiently.

5. *Capabilities to educate a more active, better-informed, more humanely oriented citizenry.* Our democracy is experiencing a sad decline in the percentage of citizens who vote, just at a time when more issues of grave national concern confront us than at any other time since World War II. Those citizens who have attended college participate more actively in democratic public life,[8] are better informed about public issues, and are more concerned for

---

[8]The means now exist to control the lives of most people, the possibility that George Orwell (1949) described in *1984*. But an "enlightened citizenry" can provide a bulwark against tyranny. Thomas Jefferson, for example, wrote, "It is an axiom in my mind that our liberty can never be safe but in the hands of the people themselves, and that too of the people with a certain degree of instruction" (Letter to George Washington, Jan. 4, 1786). This is still our national conviction.

the welfare of and more tolerant about the inherent characteristics of their fellow human beings. They are also more efficient consumers, invest more of their income and more wisely, and take better care of their health. Overall, college attendance leads to better decision making in many areas of life at a time when better decisions about public and private matters are sorely needed.[9] (See Figure 16 for selected factors associated with attendance in college.)

6. *Capabilities to offer greater equality of opportunity and the possibility of a greater equality of earned income.* Attendance in college is clearly associated with higher income and more prestigious occupations. Higher education in the past decade, in particular, has substantially increased the opportunities for women, members of minority groups, and persons from low-income families. This is what the Japanese call "social rebirth"— persons are able to break away from the confines of inherited status and prior social restraints. Should present trends continue, which we hope and expect they will, there will be even more achieved equality of opportunity by the year 2000 for both minorities and for women. This is highly essential. Much progress has already been made by women and by blacks, compared to white males but none by young persons in the lower half of the income ranges compared to those in the upper half. (See Figure 17.)

Minority youth (including Hispanics) will increase in numbers, comprising nearly 30 percent of all youth by 2000. (Nonwhites will be 19 percent, and Hispanics are already 6 percent.) The nation will greatly need, as never before, the skills, the conviction that they have had a reasonable measure of equality of opportunity, the willingness to participate in the work and governance of the society of this one-quarter and more of the next generation. To accomplish this will require affirmative action in all aspects of American life.

Earned income may become more equalized as more people obtain more education, reducing the number of persons competing for manual positions and increasing the number competing

[9]For a discussion of these and other consequences of college education on the behavior of graduates, see Bowen (1977, chaps. 3-8) and Supplement E, *Higher Education and Human Performance.*

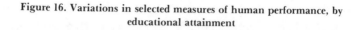

Figure 16. Variations in selected measures of human performance, by educational attainment

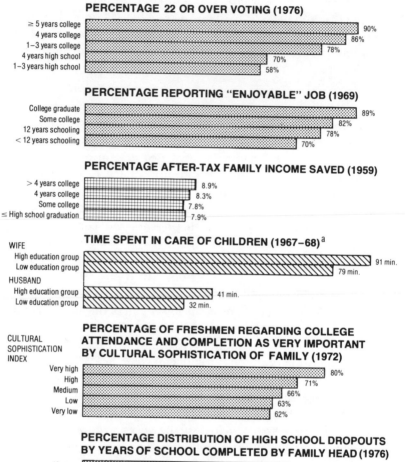

PERCENTAGE 22 OR OVER VOTING (1976)

≥ 5 years college	90%
4 years college	86%
1–3 years college	78%
4 years high school	70%
1–3 years high school	58%

PERCENTAGE REPORTING "ENJOYABLE" JOB (1969)

College graduate	89%
Some college	82%
12 years schooling	78%
< 12 years schooling	70%

PERCENTAGE AFTER-TAX FAMILY INCOME SAVED (1959)

> 4 years college	8.9%
4 years college	8.3%
Some college	7.8%
≤ High school graduation	7.9%

TIME SPENT IN CARE OF CHILDREN (1967–68)[a]

WIFE
High education group	91 min.
Low education group	79 min.

HUSBAND
High education group	41 min.
Low education group	32 min.

PERCENTAGE OF FRESHMEN REGARDING COLLEGE ATTENDANCE AND COMPLETION AS VERY IMPORTANT BY CULTURAL SOPHISTICATION OF FAMILY (1972)

CULTURAL SOPHISTICATION INDEX
Very high	80%
High	71%
Medium	66%
Low	63%
Very low	62%

PERCENTAGE DISTRIBUTION OF HIGH SCHOOL DROPOUTS BY YEARS OF SCHOOL COMPLETED BY FAMILY HEAD (1976)

< 12 years	68%
12 years	21%
> 12 years	11%

[a] Minutes in 48-hour period; other than physical care.

Source: Supplement E.

Figure 17. Progress toward equality of opportunity for college undergraduates, 1960 to 2000

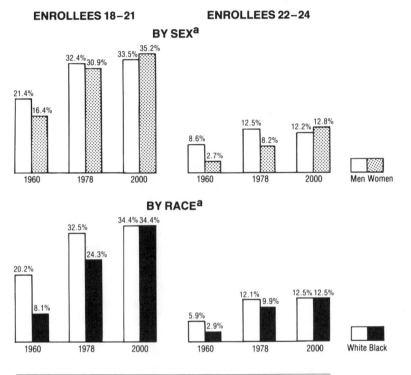

ENROLLEES 18–21   **ENROLLEES 22–24**

BY SEX[a]

BY RACE[a]

BY FAMILY INCOME

Ratio of enrollment rate of young persons from families with income above median to that of persons from families with income below median

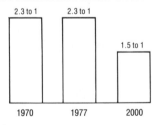

[a] Percentage of age group enrolled.

Sources: U.S. Bureau of the Census (1964; 1971; 1979b). Projections of enrollment rates of persons from high- and low-income groups are consistent with expectations discussed in *More than Survival* (The Carnegie Foundation for the Advancement of Teaching, 1975, pp. 113-125).

for nonmanual work. Within a few years after 1969, the rate of return on a college as against a high school education went down by over one-third, as many more college-educated persons entered the labor market during a period of intermittent recessions. This was not true, however, for the prior two decades, when the demand for college graduates was very high for teachers, for researchers, and for participants in many other professional and managerial occupations, and when the increased supply had not yet appeared on the market. Nor may it be true for the next 20 years when college graduates are likely to be in short supply because of the reduced size of the age cohort. However, in the long run, this is the tendency over long periods of time in a single nation, including the United States, and among nations at different stages of economic and educational development—the more advanced are the more equal in general. This equalizing impact of additional education, however, is reduced in a society like the United States where there is an open border between it and a much less advanced nation economically (Mexico).[10]

7. *Abilities to provide ever more constructive evaluation for national self-renewal.* The campus, today, is a major source of informed criticism of society and of proposals for improvement. This is true, in part, because the churches generally and the organizations of farmers and workers are less a source of social criticism than they have been historically in the United States. The campus in recent times has been a major source of re-evaluation in areas such as racial justice, the conduct of the Vietnam war, the preservation of the environment. This capacity for self-renewal through informed evaluation is as important as it ever has been in our national history as we face some totally new circumstances. The public apparently highly values informed criticism as seen by the response to investigative reporting on TV and in the press.

8. *Capacities to provide more services to the surrounding community.* College campuses are increasingly becoming centers for cultural, recreational, and social activities; this is particularly true for the public community colleges, but not for them alone. The Grange, the Union Hall, downtown, and even the churches are less and the

---

[10]See Supplement F, *Equality of Opportunity and Equality of Earned Income* for a discussion of the factual situation.

campuses more the centers of community life than they once were.

9. *Capability to maintain a network of contact and communication.* Institutions of higher education, professional organizations associated with them, and individuals within them provide a major means of communication among groups and individuals within the United States, and with foreign cultures. They are a major source for reporting, interpreting, and commenting upon single events and major developments alike. The university and its many parts comprise a key communications link in the modern world.

Preservation and enhancement of these nine capabilities are of importance to the nation as we approach and reach 2000. To preserve and enhance them will require the continuation of some institutions that might otherwise disappear because of the immediate circumstances of the next two decades, the employment of young scientists on campus whose talents might not otherwise be so well utilized, and the adequate financing of all institutions. To do this will not cost much, if any, additional money, as we shall note later. In fact, the total cost of higher education for most of the period to 2000 will be a smaller percentage of the GNP than it is today. The purposes to be served are great; the costs are modest.

Higher education needs a mood of anticipation and a sense of great purpose almost as much as it needs anything else: anticipation, at a minimum, of survival but also anticipation of an even more useful future, of much that ought to be done that can be done; anticipation of a revival of enrollments around the year 2000. Yet, dread is now the dominant mood. What is required, instead, is a forward thrust of plans, energy, and determination.

Prospects for Participation in an American Renewal

American society might change drastically, for the better or for the worse, over the next two decades, although we doubt this. If it should change drastically for the worse, perchance, the capabilities of higher education for solving problems would be even more needed by society, and, if there were a series of severe recessions or depressions, for absorbing youth that would otherwise be unemployed. Probably the least favorable situation for higher education would be a continuation of a national drift in no clear direction. We see, instead, possibilities for national and individual self-renewal within the context of present institutional arrangements as a result of:

America's view of itself as a nation of progress, as on the cutting edge of civilization, as a power in the world. This view has been challenged recently, and we expect the nation to rise to the challenge. Specifically, we appear to be facing a new confrontation with Russia, as after Sputnik, in many spheres of activity. Also, Americans have an expectation of growth and improvement internally and will not give up easily on these expectations. All this calls for a renewed effort to advance skills and technology, for more investment in human as well as physical capital. We may well experience a new burst of national vitality, as has happened repeatedly in our national history—for example, at the time of the New Deal, of our entry into World War II, of our period of postwar recovery, and of the early 1960s and the New Frontier.

The search for a way out of limited resources. We face a substantially steady state, at least for the short run, in sources of raw materials, energy, air, and water. Only new knowledge is still apparently limitless, the last frontier to explore, the one best remaining source of human advancement. The research university is the only place where knowledge in all its forms and aspects is brought together, where it is advanced the fastest and farthest. New knowledge will be needed as never before to preserve and enhance the use of physical resources.

The heightening of expectations of millions of Americans, particularly women, members of minority groups, and older persons. They want improved jobs and more fulfilling lives and better health. Education is one route to each of these goals. There is more concern generally for investment in self. People live longer, and they come to realize increasingly that (1) it consequently pays to invest more in their skills and in their capacities for using their lives, and (2) it is more worth looking around to determine how one may wish to use his or her life. Both realizations lead to more emphasis on additional years of education. Also, longer lives and more occupations from among which choices can be made encourage more midlife changes of jobs, often with an educational input in the process.

We expect that America will seek to maintain its place in a competitive world, that the search for an escape route from the current confines of fixed resources will go on, that Americans will not lower easily their individual expectations, and that the size of the American population will not be allowed to decline after 2000 almost regardless of fertility rates. Thus, we do not anticipate a fast or slow fade-out for American higher education. We expect it to continue to move forward in response to both national and individual aspirations.

Higher education is, of course, highly dependent on the national mood. It has advanced most rapidly when there has been a convergence between national aspirations and the capabilities of higher education. Such a period occurred in the decades after the Civil War when the land-grant movement contributed to agricultural and industrial advances. Another such period came in the 1960s, with higher education contributing to the responses to Sputnik and to the civil rights revolt. The vitality of higher education depends greatly on its opportunities to respond to the needs of the nation as expressed through the political process. A new period of national self-renewal may be ahead with favorable repercussions on higher education which could participate in the self-regeneration and self-revitalization process.

Our general approach in this report is to be aggressive about the future, not just defensive; to be determined to preserve a very valuable national resource, but to be flexible in how to accomplish this.

We agree with an editorial published in the *Washington Post*. It said: "Taken together, the universities are probably the strongest of all institutional influences on the American future" (December 21, 1977).

6

Choices to be Made

There is much that should be done, and much that can be accomplished. To maximize achievements, some hard choices must be made.

1. *Quality*. The quality of the academic product as measured by scores on tests taken before entering graduate work has deteriorated significantly.[1] The deterioration largely takes place prior to entry into college, since test scores out of high school have gone down similarly. That does not mean, however, that colleges can do nothing about it. They can make up for deficiencies accumulated in the high school. They can work with the high schools, as does the College of Letters and Science at Berkeley, to improve the quality of their instruction. They can also make efforts to improve the qualifications of their graduates who enter the teaching profession. Too many institutions of higher education have abdicated their responsibilities toward the primary and secondary schools.

What can and will be done depends on the individual college. We consider a desirable goal for the year 2000 to be a return to the academic quality level of 1960 in the achievement capacities of its

---

[1] The proportion of test-takers attaining scores above a critical level (the "high-ability" group) dropped from about 19 percent to 13 percent for arts and sciences graduate school applicants between 1966 and 1979, and from 18 percent to below 15 percent for graduate business school applicants. (Data supplied by Educational Testing Service, Princeton, N.J.)

graduates. Each institution should have this as its goal.[2] Our 1978 Survey of Institutional Adaptations to the 1970s found that 80 percent of institutions now do have "comprehensive basic skills programs."

Qualitative growth should replace quantitative growth, using the thought and energy that have previously gone into the latter: growth in the quality of teaching, research, and service.

2. *Balance.* Five mainstreams of intellectual activity constitute the central agenda of higher education: teaching and scholarly work in the sciences, the social sciences, the humanities, the creative and performing arts, and the professions. In recent times, great enrollment gains have been made by the professions and great losses sustained particularly by the humanities (The Carnegie Foundation for the Advancement of Teaching, 1977, p. 103). No single definition of "balance" can be set for American higher education. We do suggest, however, that each institution should define and seek to achieve its own chosen "balance" and not just let ad hoc actions yield some unplanned result. Balance involves both the composition of the faculty and the totality of courses offered; and the balance in how students actually spend their time. Recently, more time has been spent on electives and less on general education. We see a great need for rethinking the undergraduate curriculum along the lines we have suggested in *Missions of the College Curriculum* (1977).

Overall, we have two main concerns: (1) that the humanities are often being unduly neglected, and (2) that the creative and performing arts, given the new interests of students in the qualities of their lives, may still be subject to further expansion. We note, in connection with the humanities, that alumni most frequently state they wish they had taken more work in the humanities (Spaeth and

---

[2]In spite of the overall decline in the average Scholastic Aptitude Test (SAT) scores of entering freshmen, a group of high schools exists whose graduates' scores have maintained pre-decline levels or have risen (Thomson and DeLeonibus, 1978). It is difficult to determine if there are, similarly, colleges whose students' scores on examinations for entrance into graduate schools have also remained at prior levels or risen. Since some departments within colleges and universities are more effective than others, even within the same institution, overall institutional comparisons of student achievement tend to blur or wash out these important interdepartmental differences. (See Hartnett and Centra, 1977, pp. 491-507.) However, the experience at the high school level implies that individual colleges and departments within them can maintain or raise scores by their own special efforts.

Greeley, 1970, p. 69). The vocational emphasis of today may pass, and student interests may again shift back to the liberal arts. Thus, it would be wise for institutions to maintain a reasonable level of capacity to adjust to such a possible shift. We also note that colleges have a responsibility to preserve contact with all major aspects of the cultural heritage.

The greatest responsibility to preserve balance will probably fall on the research universities, in particular for maintaining graduate fields with low numbers of Ph.D. candidates, and on selective liberal arts colleges. Fortunately, they are in the least vulnerable category of institutions. Private and federal funds will be essential to their efforts, as state funds mainly follow the student market.

3. *Integrity.* We have elsewhere expressed concern for the deterioration of integrity on campuses.[3] In particular, we have noted: grade inflation, reduced academic requirements, low-quality off-campus programs, false promises by institutions, cheating, vandalism, and student defaults on loans. Higher education, which should set standards for other elements of society to emulate, now stands at the higher end of the range of "fraud, error, and abuse" in federal programs.[4] The morality of this disturbs us. So also do the potential political consequences. Public confidence in higher education was greatly shaken by the occasional resort to violence and mass pressure in institutions historically respected for reliance on reason and persuasion, during the student movement from 1968 to 1970. Erosion of respect for the integrity of higher education could have similar

---

[3]See our report on *Fair Practices in Higher Education* (1978). See also Bailey (1979b); and his discussion of "galloping shoddiness" in some programs (1979a).

[4]In 1978 the Comptroller General said that: "No one knows the magnitude of fraud against the Government....However, all indications are that fraud is a problem of critical proportion. Department of Justice officials believe the incidence of fraud in federal programs ranges anywhere from 1 to 10 percent of the programs' expenditures" (U.S. General Accounting Office, 1978). A report a few months earlier by the U.S. Department of Health, Education and Welfare's Inspector General (1978, Appendix 1) placed certain postsecondary education programs near the very top of the Department of Justice statistics. Of $3.6 billion disbursed for the five major student financial aid programs, $356 million (9.9 percent of the total) was lost through fraud and abuse. Since the issuance of these reports there has been some improvement, but the problem still remains a visible and public mark of deterioration in campus integrity.

consequences in the 1980s and 1990s. Each institution needs to examine its own conduct, as, for example, the University of Delaware has done. It will be a tragedy if the following prediction were to come true: "The competition for students in the next decade will become more and more rapacious with many of us abashed at the used-car huckstering techniques employed to proselytize students" (Glenny, 1978). The theme should be, instead, "moral responsibility."[5]

4. *Adaptations compatible with the academic standards and community character of each college.* Each institution will decide, and some have already, what adjustments will be made to the demographic depression. A few, such as medical schools and schools of mineral technology, need to make no adjustments. Others will need to make major adjustments, perhaps particularly the less selective liberal arts colleges and the comprehensive colleges and universities. Main areas for adaptation are the following:

Admission. How far, if at all, will academic entrance requirements be reduced? What arrangements will be made for part-time students, for transfers, for adults?

Recruitment. How much more effort will be put into recruitment? To what extent will student aid funds be used for purposes of recruitment in contrast to meeting actual financial needs?

Retention. What additional assistance will be given to students to encourage them to stay in college by way of academic, occupational, and personal counselling and by way of financial aids? To what extent, if any, will grading standards be further relaxed, will academic requirements be reduced, will disciplinary actions be eased?

Programs. What new programs will be added? Many new vocational programs have already been introduced. A corollary is: What old programs will be dropped?

New schedules. The conditions of the 1980s will make it particularly attractive for young persons both to go to college (to realize a higher prospective ratio of returns on a college education) and to work (to obtain current higher rates of pay). At the same time, the labor market will make possible more "split-level weeks" because more people in the labor market are on a part-time basis and absenteeism has risen in some industries,

[5]See the discussion in Hesburgh (1979, particularly pp. 155-157).

particularly on Mondays and Fridays, creating more opportunities for students to fill part-time vacancies. We still have a 40-hour work week with much of the labor force on actual schedules of less than 40 hours. This suggests a whole series of possible schedules for higher education with programs that can be completed only in the morning, or only in the afternoon, or only in the evening; or only on Tuesday, Wednesday, Thursday; or only on Monday, Tuesday, Wednesday; and so forth.[6] The possible introduction of the four-day week will enhance such possibilities. What new schedules will be adopted?

There are many possibilities in these and other adjustments, but dangers also. The dangers are threats to quality, to balance, and to integrity, and to the internal life of the campus which we discuss below. Each of these could be sacrificed in major ways; they could become the great casualties of the next two decades, unless individual institutions keep their importance constantly in mind.

5. *Dynamism.* The effective "management of decline" is extraordinarily difficult.[7] One tendency is to preserve the status quo in the short run, thus sometimes encouraging even further decline in the long run. Higher education has very special problems in this regard. Decisions on campus are mostly made on a consensus basis and involve several veto groups. Preservation of the status quo may be the only possible rallying point for a consensus. Also, historically, change has been a product of growth; has come by way of add-ons— higher education has been better at addition than at subtraction. It is not by chance that the two greatest periods of programmatic advancement have been the two periods of greatest growth:

1870-1890 when enrollments tripled (52,000 to 157,000 headcount); and the land-grant movement got started; science was greatly emphasized for the first time; service activities were added; the neoclassical college was replaced by the modern college and university; electives were widely introduced; the department was

---

[6]See Supplement G, *Academic Schedules and the Split-level Week.*

[7]"Education is likely to be the first major segment of the economy to suffer a relative decline, and management of this decline may very well set the tone for management of the general slowdown" (Boulding, 1975).

created as the basic unit of administration; graduate work was introduced; and much else.

1960-1980 when enrollments more than tripled (3,500,000 to 12,400,000 headcount); science efforts were greatly enhanced; universal-access higher education was introduced; the community college movement was extended nationwide; equality of opportunity was advanced as never before; and much more.

The absence of growth will be keenly felt. Governmental controls at the state and federal level, however well intended, are also reducing possibilities for dynamic change, making it harder to achieve, making it more costly in time and resources, tying up efforts in reporting and accounting. The aging faculties, the emergence of new veto groups, and the spread of collective bargaining add new rigidities. In higher education, contrary to the situation in American industry in the organizing decade of the 1930s, collective bargaining is a defensive, not an aggressive, act aimed mostly at holding on to as many of the advantages of the past as possible. Many of the pressures of the developing situation will encourage the spread of collective bargaining, particularly the erosion of the real incomes of faculty members, the emphasis on affirmative action, and the attacks on tenure.[8]

There are ways to encourage dynamism:

- Institutions can set a policy to reduce existing programs, perhaps by 1 to 3 percent a year, in order to start new programs; as Case Western Reserve did so successfully.
- The federal government can increase support for the Fund for Improvement of Post-Secondary Education (FIPSE), and the states can follow suit, as a few (including California and Florida) have done already, to encourage experimentation.
- State financing formulas can provide leeway for new endeavors.
- Private foundations can establish presidential discretionary endowment grants for innovation as the Hewlett and Mellon Foundations are jointly doing.
- Colleges can hold some percentage, for example, 10, of their faculty positions in temporary or short-term appointments.

[8]See Supplement H, *Faculty Development Present and Future.*

- Colleges can keep tenure ratios for faculty members at reasonable levels, for example, two-thirds of the total.

And there are major new areas for initiatives, including advancing the use of the new electronic technology,[9] enriching programs in the creative and performing arts, making more campuses serve as the cultural centers for their communities, adding new facilities and programs to aid youths to enter the world of work, introducing more global perspective into courses,[10] making better use of libraries as learning centers.

6. *Effective use of financial resources.* The financial resources of many institutions will be under pressure as seldom before. Lower enrollments will reduce total income from tuition and state support alike. Fixed costs per student will rise as these costs are spread over fewer students. Also, an aging faculty costs extra money—salaries of senior faculty members are generally twice the level of those of junior faculty members. Rapid inflation is particularly harmful to colleges since their prices are "sticky"—subject to change only once a year and set in the face of organized consumers. The rate of growth of the real national product of goods and services has been slowing down and is likely to continue to do so, and there are many competitive claimants for these goods and services.

Institutions of higher education, by and large, will need to be more concerned with the effective use of their resources. But the more effective use of resources does not come easily. Major constituencies—faculty and students—are not traditionally highly cost-conscious. Productivity is difficult to increase—it has remained virtually constant for the past half century. Two of the short-term ways to reduce costs (by cutting down on maintenance and by reducing expenditures on new library holdings) are both self-defeating in the long run.

[9]Eight years ago, Perkins (1972, p. 5) stressed the importance of educators collaborating closely in developing the applications of technology to the learning process. He warned that, "If such collaboration does not take place, then we must face the prospect of an educational business that is organized, its materials distributed, and its standards set completely outside the formal educational structure."

[10]See Burn (1980). The introduction reflects the Council's views on ways to reverse the erosive trends in international education of the past decade. See also the recent report of The President's Commission on Foreign Languages and International Studies (1979).

A major method of reducing costs, by increasing the student-to-faculty ratio, has drawbacks: it is limited by tenure rules; it reduces the variety of courses available, which can impair the attractiveness of the academic programs in small and middle-sized institutions; and it can reduce the attention given to the individual student. Also, the higher the student-to-faculty ratio, the fewer new jobs are available for potential faculty members. We expect, however, that student-to-faculty ratios might rise by as much as an additional 10 percent, which would reduce costs by about 5 percent. These ratios overall have already risen by 10 to 20 percent over the past two and one-half decades.[11] Some of this rise is caused by the shift of students from smaller to larger institutions and from private to public colleges. Heavy costs in the reduced quality of academic programs because of rising ratios, however, are borne by colleges with already restricted offerings. The impact on large, comprehensive institutions is less evident. Increases are easier in lecture courses in all types of institutions than in laboratory sections and tutorials, so that the way in which ratios are raised is of great importance. If they are raised by cutting out very low enrollment courses or by adding enrollments to medium-sized lecture courses, little may be lost. If, however, the ratios are raised by overloading laboratory sections or tutorials or by cutting out essential courses, then much can be lost.

The pressure on this ratio will be great. The two major ways to reduce costs are either by lowering the real levels of faculty salaries or by raising the student-to-faculty ratio. Either way has disadvantages. As between them, however, a judicious increase in ratios, at least in large institutions, may be both preferable and more politic; and, in any event, this has been the more common choice over the past decade. We note that the quality of teaching depends generally more on the approach of the teachers than the size of the class.[12].

[11]See Supplement I, *Instructional Costs and Productivity, 1930-1977.*

[12]One study found no clear correlation between student-faculty ratios and quality of instruction at the undergraduate level (Radner and Miller, 1975). A review of 40 years of research on methods of teaching (discussion groups versus lectures or independent study) concluded that "no particular method of teaching is measurably to be preferred over another when evaluated by student examination performances" (Dubin and Taveggia, 1968, p. 31).

We know of no novel ways to reduce costs, but we do urge consideration of more consortia,[13] of more nearly year-round use of resources, of discontinuation of unnecessary Ph.D. programs—many of which should never have been started—and of policies by states which allow institutions to keep the results of their cost-saving efforts to use on new programs. None of these will save much money, but each has other advantages. There are many other cost reduction methods that deserve consideration.[14]

[13]Both the costs and the benefits of interinstitutional programs were recently investigated in great detail. Thirty-seven cases of cooperative activities in the areas of cross registration, library and media cooperation, student services, group purchasing, nontraditional programs, and academic programs were carefully analyzed. It was concluded that such cooperative arrangements offered many advantages, including (1) avoiding costly and unnecessary duplication, (2) increasing quality of offerings and services, and (3) expanding the diversity and breadth of the educational experiences of the students. See Council for Interinstitutional Leadership (1979).

[14]See Bowen and Douglas (1971), who examined the cost and educational effectiveness of six different modes of instruction. The study was confined to undergraduate instruction in small, independent liberal arts colleges, but the results are suggestive for large institutions as well. They concluded that ". . .liberal arts colleges might cut costs and at the same time improve instruction by simplifying their curricula and adopting a judicious mixture of educational methods. . . an eclectic plan" (p. 73). In the eclectic plan, some courses would be taught using large classes and the lecture hall, while others would use programmed independent study, tutorial sessions, or small classes in a more conventional mode. Their detailed cost estimates of one eclectic plan suggest that considerable savings, without sacrificing educational quality, might be possible for many colleges through careful planning of the mixture of instructional modes (pp. 78-79).

Frederick Balderston (1974, chap. 7) has also suggested how cost analysis might be used in internal operations, management, and planning to improve the allocation of resources and secure increased educational benefits from a given expenditure of funds. A recent evaluation of such innovations as management information systems and management by objectives concluded that the benefits of these systems are worth their costs when they are properly developed and carried through in colleges and universities (Baldridge and Tierney, 1979, chap. 1).

319 Ways Colleges and Universities are Meeting the Financial Pinch (Academy for Educational Development, 1971) is a list of money-saving practices instituted by campuses to meet the increased financial pressures of the early seventies. Presidents, vice-presidents, and business managers supplied the detailed list which ranges from the fairly straightforward, noncontroversial suggestion (number 27): "At a state institution: Picking up monthly subsidy payments by messenger at state treasurer's office to save days in transit and make remittances available earlier for short-term investment," to significant policy changes: raising tuition, freezing salaries, for example. The list has been reproduced as an appendix in Mayhew (1979, pp. 306-320). Section 10 of this volume is a detailed discussion of how to control program and faculty costs in a period of retrenchment.

The suggestions in the text have also been discussed in considerable detail in

7. *Financing.* Higher education probably needs to reconcile itself to the possibility that there are not likely to be any massive new federal programs, although we make several suggestions in the next section about federal financing; and we see only one major area for expansion of state support. This places great emphasis on private support, which, over the long run, has been a falling component of support, even as the households of the nation have become more affluent. Private support carries with it not only money but, quite beyond the possibilities in public support, autonomy in its use and protection for the more strictly academic concerns of higher education for quality and balance. The Carnegie Commission (1973b, p. 9) once suggested that it was reasonable to expect that tuition in public institutions be about one-third of instructional costs offset by tuition scholarships on the basis of need. The exception would be community colleges, which should have comparatively low tuition (similar programs in comprehensive colleges and universities might also be included). The Council considers this to be a proposal worthy of consideration. Several states now approximate these levels. Tax policies should encourage private gifts to colleges. And states should consider all private gifts as over and above their own contributions. All institutions should seek to maximize their private sources of funds. A corollary of this is to encourage policies that make public funds act as nearly like private funds as possible. This means public foundations with the autonomy to act like the bes. of the private foundations. It also means channeling funds through private individuals as do the federal BEOG program and state tuition scholarship programs.[15]

8. *Leadership.* The call for leadership is a call to handle such problems as those just listed, none of them easy and several of them

---

Carnegie Commission and Carnegie Council publications. *The More Effective Use of Resources* (1972b) suggests modification of budgetary procedures that tend to discourage innovations and cost savings (pp. 107-110), recommends specific policies for increasing the flexibility of a campus in handling faculty problems related to changing enrollments (pp. 111-117), and points out many changes in degree structures that would achieve considerable economies (pp. 49-58). In addition, the training and development of a middle-level administrative staff is recommended, particularly for larger institutions (pp. 130-132). See also *More Than Survival* (1975a, chap. 6); and Mood and others (1974).

[15]See the discussion in Kramer (forthcoming).

contradictory in their implications for action; and a call to create conditions for progress in the absence of enrollment growth. Yet a period such as that ahead does not readily attract the ablest leadership—the tasks are grinding ones, the victories too often take the form of greater losses avoided, the internal constituencies are more likely to be united around doing nothing than doing something. "The problem of administration becomes more difficult and the quality of administration is apt to decline;" and the new skills required call for an "all too rare mixture of compassion and realism" (Boulding, 1975).

Additionally, it is difficult for new administrative talent to arise and be recognized. There are few successes along the line to lead to greater visibility and greater opportunities; there are no successes without costs; and the now-existing communications network, and the veto groups who use it, can turn the costs into guillotines. Aggressive leaders are often eliminated in the process.

Once in office, many presidents are caught in Catch-22 situations. Their boards ask for certain results, but getting those results antagonizes one or more constituencies (usually the faculty), and losing that constituency calls for replacement. Yet there are many able presidents still around, and their average years of experience on the job is now five. (Their predecessors had a median average of 6.5 years total tenure.)

We believe that the future period requires even more able leadership than that just past. In particular, we see the necessity for longer terms of, say, 10 years normal minimum, for presidents, because the problems are long-term and can be made worse by short-term presidents avoiding them or seeking short-term expedient solutions. We also see the need for more authority in the hands of the president,[16] which means more active support from his or her board.

---

[16]Our surveys and field visits indicate some tendency in this direction already due to the nature of the most insistent problems on campuses (finances and enrollments) and due to more governmental controls, since each of these problems concentrates attention on the president. An exception may be the campus head in a highly centralized multi-campus system. In the Carnegie Council Surveys of 1978, 44 percent of the presidents said their authority had increased and 88 percent thought they now had enough authority; although the authority of the president and the academic distinction of the faculty seem to move in opposite directions. The specific power we think it most important for presidents to have, facing the situation of the future, is the power to reallocate or discontinue faculty positions that become open.

We suggest:

- Better search methods assisted by the American Council on Education and by such organizations as the new Presidential Search Consultation Service established by the Association of American Colleges and the Association of Governing Boards.
- We also call attention to the good suggestions in the Nason report for the AGB (Nason, 1979).
- More concentration by boards of trustees on looking for leaders rather than survival managers—as they seem to have been doing of late. The challenges of the future require leadership, and good day-to-day management can be supplied at the vice-presidential level.
- Procedures for an early informal review of a president (say, after 2 years) with the understanding that following such a review the total term of office will be about 10 years in the absence of very strong reasons to the contrary.[17]
- Determination by boards to stand behind presidents who do well what the board has asked them to do. The costs should be estimated in advance, and boards should indicate their willingness to help bear them.[18]

We are also concerned that the membership of boards of trustees be strengthened.[19] Trustees, above all others, must assume the burden for the long-run and overall welfare of their institutions.

9. *Preservation of private colleges.* The preservation of these colleges is of almost equal value to the public institutions since the autonomy of the private colleges helps to protect the autonomy of the public colleges, their academic freedom, their ability to experiment, and their opportunity to grant attention to the individual student. The public at large is also well served by having their capacity to adjust to constituencies, for example, fundamentalist Protestants,

---

[17]For a discussion of reviews of presidential performance, see Nason (forthcoming).

[18]For a discussion of how presidents currently look upon their situations, see Stadtman (forthcoming). They generally are most worried about inflation and financial support (all institutions), about enrollments (especially private colleges), and government controls (especially public institutions).

[19]See Mortimer (forthcoming); and Nason (1974).

that cannot be equally served by public institutions. One test of the performance of leaders of the public segment is their willingness and ability to defend the survival of the private segment.

We call attention to the recommendations we have made elsewhere[20] for state support of private institutions, particularly through tuition scholarships based on student need. We oppose bailouts because they reduce the sense of self-dependence, but we do favor assistance with mergers. We also oppose tax credits for tuition, both because such a program is very costly and because it is very regressive in its incidence. We also oppose take-overs of private institutions by public authorities, as a general policy, because we believe the private segment should be continued under private governance. We favor experimentation with hybrid types such as the state-related colleges in Pennsylvania and New College in Florida, which preserve the private character of institutions while making public funds available to them. The tuition scholarships that we support make the competition with public institutions more fair and more based on the performance of the institution. Moreover, they can reduce the need for bailouts and help assure the autonomy of the private colleges.

We expect major political battles over these matters in states where there are many less-selective liberal arts colleges—particularly where these colleges have connections with religious institutions, and especially in states where enrollments will go down more than the average. This concentrates attention on the states in the Northeast and several of the Midwest states including Ohio, Indiana, and Illinois. Senators and representatives from those states may often favor, in particular, special federal subsidies for small colleges via tuition tax credits or in other ways; and they have many votes.

We do not wish to suggest that private colleges are an endangered species. Certain factors may be working in their favor:

- More affluence—which makes it easier for parents to afford private tuition
- Fewer children per family—which also makes it easier for parents to afford private colleges
- More second-generation students who are more likely to attend

[20]See *The States and Private Higher Education: Problems and Policies in a New Era,* (1977).

private colleges—the percentage of first-generation students may have peaked already

- Less labor market pressure for vocational subjects and more leeway for a liberal arts emphasis
- More emphasis on "quality-of-life" considerations that can be advanced by the collegiate atmosphere, which particularly marks many private colleges (and some public also)
- Strong alumni and community support as shown in resistance to the closings that have occurred or been attempted.

Nevertheless, private colleges meet many handicaps because of comparatively higher tuition (nearly $2,000 higher in private than in public institutions), predominant location in the Northeast and Midwest, intensified competition from public institutions, and frequent small size and location in small towns.

10. *Basic research.* Over the past half-century (1930–1980) the United States has become pre-eminent in the world in most areas of scientific research.[21] This has been of great benefit to the nation in peace and war. For a time, American standards of living were the highest in the world. World War II might have turned out quite differently if, at that time, the United States had not moved into the forefront of research in physics. Now this is changing. Some other countries surpass the United States in per capita income; Germany and Russia, in particular, are spending more of their resources on research and development than does the United States. The United States has been lagging in productivity growth for many reasons, one being less rapid rates of technological advance.[22]

A major reason for the historic American advantage has been the concentration of basic research in its universities as against government agencies or industrial laboratories as is the policy in many other nations. Several other nations, including Japan, Russia, and China, have been increasingly following the successful Ameri-

[21]See Ben-David and Zloczower (1962, pp. 45-84) for a comparative view of the systems of scientific research in the United States, England, Germany, France, and the U.S.S.R. The authors conclude that "the American university system, with its constantly expanding and heterogeneous functions, is now the most influential system of higher education and research" (p. 76).

[22]Supplement J, *A Comparative Review of Scholarly, Scientific, and Technological Progress in the United States.*

can practice. Some of the important aspects of the American experiment with concentrating basic science research in its universities have been:

- The contact of scholars across several fields of knowledge on the same campus
- The contact of researchers with the inquiring minds of graduate students
- The competitive search by universities for the best talent to be found within all segments of American society
- The training of the next generation of young scientists in the course of conducting current research
- The opportunity given young faculty members to conduct their own research, as against dependence on the head of the laboratory in other systems
- The provision of reasonably adequate funds from a variety of sources—several federal agencies, the states, industry, and private foundations
- The access to these funds on the basis of merit as judged by scientific peers, and keen competition to obtain funds by many scholars in many institutions of higher education where their promotions depend in part on their success
- The interest of many American universities in serving industry, agriculture, and the professions.

After a decade (1967–1977) of declining financial support from the federal government in real terms, federal support for university research once again is reaching what appear to be reasonable levels. State support, however, often tied to enrollments, is likely to go down, and this tendency should be offset, as we shall note later.

We have another major concern: the flow of young scholars into certain fields, such as physics, mathematics, and plant genetics.[23] This flow is prospectively not so much determined by the decline in enrollments, since the leading research universities will not be affected greatly if at all. Rather it is determined by the low faculty retirement rates for the next 10 to 20 years. There will be relatively few replacements, given the age profile of present faculty members. This

---

[23]See Supplement K, *Smoothing Out the Flow of Young Scientists into Universities.*

will deny opportunities to the ablest potential young scientists, including women and minorities, to find university employment and may discourage them from getting the Ph.D. at all. It will also, as a consequence, deny society the contribution of their services. Also, it is more productive to have a reasonable age spread within scientific departments. What we now have is a predominantly middle-aged group to be followed later by a bimodal distribution of older faculty members and younger faculty members coming in during the 1990s without many faculty members in the in-between years. Policies leading to a more uniform age distribution would both encourage the aspirations of young scientists of high potential who may feel that all doors are closed against them, and would result in departments which are more productive in both research and teaching. By 2000, American society could be seriously weakened in competition with other nations and also in its own capacity to respond to new scientific opportunities if modest policy actions are not taken, and we support a proposal set forth later in this report (Section 7 and Supplement K).

We have, as a further concern, the support of research libraries as overall institutional income declines with falling enrollments. Here, also, we will make a proposal later in this report.

The Internal Life of the Campus

We have an overall concern about higher education that transcends individual aspects. This is what may happen to the "private life" of the campus.[24] This life consists of the many personal relations among individuals and groups on campus, and the spirit and tone of the campus.

This life is threatened by the cessation of growth. Growth is the American way of life, even in academic enterprises. When enrollment growth stops and the flow of additional financial resources that goes with it slows down, and particularly when decline sets in, there is

[24]"The private life of education is what actually happens in the classroom, the libraries, the laboratories, at the desks, and in the offices—the moment-by-moment, day-to-day activities, and interactions of teachers and students engaged in teaching and learning" (Trow, 1975, pp. 113-127).

often a sense of failure and stultification that is self-confirming.[25] It also has other effects:

- It sets department against department, urgently competing for students and resources.
- It sets academic against vocational areas of the campus as, for example, the humanities against business administration—the former with low enrollment courses, the latter with high.
- It sets nontenured against tenured members of the faculty, and particularly nontenured female and minority members against male and majority members with tenure.
- It sets administrators and board against faculty and students in cutting back on programs.
- It creates a gulf between an aging faculty and students.
- It induces more time servers within the faculty. There is less competition to advance internally or get offers externally.
- It puts students in a position to dominate campus decisions and conduct in a manner that may unbalance traditional roles.
- It stifles opportunities for innovation.
- It sets purists arguing standards against pragmatists arguing survival.

Advancing the retirement age to 70 adds to the force of several of these developments.

Some of the adaptations we have noted earlier can weaken the sense of community and common experience on campus: the introduction of more part-time students, alternative schedules that keep people moving in and out like customers in a supermarket, less well-prepared students, more adult students, and efforts to retain reluctant students. They may well aid the college in other ways, but personal bonds among people can be weakened.

This can be particularly true where these bonds have been strong in the past, as in research universities and liberal arts colleges.

---

[25]We distinguish between the cessation of growth after a long period of growth and a continuing steady state condition. It is the former, not the latter, that gives rise to many tensions. The latter state, once achieved, can be a quite satisfactory one within the institution. The former state involves expectations denied and many uncertainties about the future.

The less-selective liberal arts colleges, in particular, may have to undertake adaptations that weaken their sense of community, as many have already, although others have done the opposite by returning to their roots in a religious faith or a local community. Less affected are the community colleges and many comprehensive colleges which, in the past, have been accustomed to making quick adjustments in response to the student market. Doctorate-granting institutions may be strongly affected as they have to give up some of their Ph.D. programs and their aspirations for academic excellence that stood so high in the 1960s; and many faculty dreams will be unrealized.

The institutions best able to preserve their strong internal community life are likely to be the research universities and selective liberal arts colleges. They are not so vulnerable to enrollment pressures, have traditions of strong faculty participation in the governance of the institution, have far more than average sources of financial support, have strong alumni encouragement for preserving the character of the institution, and have an on-campus style of life. They are in the best position to preserve not only their community life but also their academic quality, their balance among fields of study, their moral integrity—traditional concerns of the academic guild of professors.

The internal life of many institutions has already been weakened. There are several harsh realities: Students are often more self-seeking than in the 1960s in their vocational emphases and self-serving in their neglect of concern for campus and societal welfare. Faculty members are sometimes demoralized by declining real income, by loss of control of academic life to students and to external interference, by disappointed expectations for institutional improvements that are dear to them, by doubts about the social importance of their contributions, and, among young faculty members, by increased difficulty in attaining tenure. Administrators often feel blocked by interior and exterior barriers from significant improvements they would like to make. Institutions are frozen by the fear of fundamental change, including closure.

The internal life of the campus is threatened from another direction. This is the rise of external forces and authorities that increasingly dominate campus life: the implacable forces of inflation and demography and the competitive market for students, and of the authority of the state, the federal government, and the courts. This reduces the sense of autonomy and the spirit of independence, and encourages a sense of helplessness and alienation. It encourages collective bargaining aimed mostly at external threats. The campus no longer controls its own life to the extent it once did. It becomes less of a community and more of a self-interested professional organization as a result, more just another economic pressure group. Decision making is moving up and out. A principal potential of 1970 was more intense internal participatory democracy. In 1980, a principal potential is more external participation in the internal life of the campus as the federal government, in particular, has gone from being an investor in to a controller of the campuses. The combination of more participatory democracy from within and more participation from without can, together, greatly complicate the processes of governance and reduce the assumption of responsibility by anyone.

Within higher education as a whole, there is less a sense of common enterprise and more of a sense of campus against campus, segment against segment. Fights among organized constituencies within higher education are becoming more intense at the federal level and in some states. Instead of a united front, there is fragmentation and internecine warfare except when it comes to seeking large new sums of money for everybody. Excessive fears about the future add to the already strained relations in Washington, D.C., and in many states between public and private institutions.

Decline of enrollments and increasing external controls can sadly affect the internal life of the campus. We can only suggest that their potential effects be recognized early in the process and that efforts be made, campus by campus and higher education altogether, to offset them: to fight for community versus divisiveness; to fight for autonomy versus external domination.

Summary

The future holds many unknowns, and it also holds a range of already known choices that can be made by those making decisions about higher education. We have identified selected areas where something should be done and also can be done to affect the welfare of higher education. In many cases, no choice is the worst choice of all because it means either a downward drift in response to immediate pressures or a failure to seize upon constructive possibilities. We believe that the problems in each of these areas should be confronted head on and that explicit policies should be adopted in each of them. External, particularly market, pressures will not alone lead to the best results. Internal thought, resolution, and determination are needed to assure that higher education as a whole and institutions individually reach 2000 with capacity to perform undiminished or minimally diminished by the demographic depression. The surrounding environment in the next 20 years will create some special problems that we can already see. It does not, however, determine in advance how well these problems will be solved or how inadequately; human choice, or absence of choice, will settle that. A downward drift in quality, balance, integrity, dynamism, diversity, private initiative, research capability is not only possible—it is quite likely. But it is not required by external events. It is a matter of choice and not just fate. The emphasis should be on "managing for excellence."[26]

We conclude this section by noting how much of what needs to be done and can be done is subject to achievement at the institutional level. We have only suggested state and federal action in connection with the preservation of the private colleges and the enhancement of research efforts. All other goals can be achieved mostly, even only, by the action of institutions themselves. This places great responsibility on teachers, administrators, faculty leadership, and trustees; and on private financial support. Institutional action with private support is the single best key to unlock future possibilities.

---

[26]Balderston (1974) distinguishes among "managing for survival," "managing for stability," and "managing for excellence."

7

Courses of Action

Institutions

We urge all institutions of higher education to contemplate carefully their prospective futures and to determine the policies that will favorably affect, in particular:

- Improvement of the quality of teaching, research, and service
- The preservation of an essential balance among the main intellectual streams of academic endeavors against the pulls of the market
- The enhancement of integrity of conduct on campus
- Effective adaptations that do least damage to the internal life of the campus
- The continuation of dynamic adjustments to new possibilities without any compensating increase in resources
- The more effective use of resources and their better allocation internally
- The creation of conditions that encourage effective leadership
- The maximization of private funds to support higher education
- The preservation, with the cooperation of all of higher education, of the private sector of higher education with its autonomy intact and its diversity maintained
- The enhancement of the research capabilities of higher education
- The maintenance of the quality of internal campus life.

We have discussed each of these areas of policy determination in Section 6. Colleges and universities vary so enormously in their characteristics that these determinations can only take place institution by institution.

We believe that accreditation needs to be greatly improved as a backup to institutional efforts. There are suggestions that both the federal government and the states may abandon reliance on the mechanisms of accreditation developed by higher education. The federal government—in 60 programs administered by at least eight agencies and most of the states—has accepted private accreditation as an indication of institutional quality. Traditionally, also, within higher education, accreditation has been used to distinguish the marginal and less than marginal from the adequate programs in acceptance of credits and degrees. Now, additionally, there is a need to set some limits on the accepted forms of competition among the adequate and the more than adequate institutions; otherwise the whole level of competitive practices may decline. Both to persuade governments to accept higher-education-based accreditation and to police unfair competitive practices among accredited institutions of higher education, the associations with responsibility in these matters need to start using full-time staff, more meaningful standards in academic areas, and also to add consideration of competitive practices that reduce academic integrity. Better performance by the accrediting associations is the best defense against establishment of more direct governmental controls. In the meantime, the federal government and the states should continue to rely on private accreditation.

The States

Generally, as we see it, the period ahead will be a state period in terms of new initiatives and responsibilities for the welfare of higher education—as the prior 20 years were a federal period in terms of new initiatives. Fortunately, the states are now in better financial condition than they were five or ten years ago. The states generally have given good support to their systems of public higher education.[1] They need now to render substantial aid also to private higher education, wherever they have not already done so. We consider this to be a major challenge before them for the next 20 years. This can be done and should be done, given the prospect for declining student

[1]For a detailed study of state financial support in each state in recent years, see Ruyle and Glenny (1978).

enrollments, without in any way reducing the per student support in public institutions. The states with the most private enrollments subject to support tend also to be the states with the greater prospective decline in public student enrollments and thus with more potential leeway to support the private sector. We continue to advise that, in providing support, major reliance be placed on tuition scholarships based on need, with shared support from the federal government.[2]

We have two great fears about state conduct. One is that some state financial planners will underestimate potential enrollments and will promise to their governors and their legislative committees more in the way of savings than can be realized if higher education is not to be greatly harmed. The other is that some educational and financial planners will see an opportunity to "rationalize," to seize control of systems of higher education, to make higher education an agency of state government, to do so in the name of saving money while cutting less those institutions that go along with the process. Higher education performs as a largely autonomous segment of society so much better than it would as just another government bureau. We caution against:

Overeager promises to save money on higher education, and
Plans to place systems of higher education under increased state control.

We believe that the states generally should be prepared to maintain real per capita contributions to higher education at current levels. Such a policy will both create some leeway, as public enrollments go down, to give more aid to private colleges and to offset the higher cost per student for overhead as campus enrollments decrease, and also reduce burdens on taxpayers as per capita real income rises.[3] A few states should raise their per capita contributions in real terms; several may want to consider adding additional community colleges or equivalent programs in comprehensive colleges and universities to make open access available on a

[2]See our report *Next Steps for the 1980s in Student Financial Aid: A Fourth Alternative* (1979b).

[3]See Supplement L, *State Support of Higher Education.*

nationwide basis; and a number, we believe, should establish Area Health Education Centers.[4]

We also advise states to:

- Prepare financing formulas that will encourage diversity and new initiatives, that make allowance for rising overhead costs per student as enrollments go down, and that permit institutions to keep the private funds they raise. The Foundations in several Big Ten universities are a good model for the latter purpose. On formulas, we specifically suggest that reductions be less than the reductions in student numbers, for example, a range of 0.6 to 0.8 reduction for each 1.0 decline in FTE[5]

[4]One of the influential recommendations in the Carnegie Commission's report, *Higher Education and the Nation's Health* (1970b) was for the development of Area Health Education Centers (AHECs), which would be affiliated with university health science centers, but would be located in communities at some distance from those centers and would conduct programs of decentralized education in the health professions. Among the many AHEC programs developed in the 1970s were those of 11 universities (in as many states) which were selected in 1972 for the first contracts with the federal government under the provisions of the Comprehensive Health Manpower Training Act of 1971. Recently, Charles Odegaard, president emeritus of the University of Washington, completed an evaluation of these 11 programs for the Carnegie Council in a report entitled *Area Health Education Centers: The Pioneering Years, 1972-1978* (1979), in which he provides much evidence, if not hard statistical data, that the projects are making a significant contribution to overcoming geographical maldistribution of health manpower and overspecialization in the medical profession.

[5]This will take into account rising overhead costs; the rising salary costs for an increasingly older and thus higher-paid faculty; costs of new and improved and experimental programs; costs of providing renovations of facilities and special programs for physically handicapped and deaf and blind students; costs of more and better programs in basic learning skills; costs of new and better laboratory and instructional equipment; costs of meeting added reporting requirements by state and federal governments; costs of some gradual increase in quality and variety of academic programs; and costs associated with having more part-time students to register, counsel, finance, feed, park, provide with library places and services, provide with health services, etc. For a discussion of some of these considerations, see Academy for Educational Development (1979).

We say a range of 0.6 to 0.8 percent with the expectation that the higher end of the range might apply to community colleges and the lower end of the range to research universities, with the other types of institutions spread in between, but closer to the 0.8 end of the range. We make this distinction because community colleges are heavily oriented toward current services. They will be affected by rising overhead costs per student, rising level of salaries with an aging faculty, etc. However, they do not have

- Introduce state equivalents of the Fund for Improvement of Post-Secondary Education (FIPSE)
- Stop preaudit controls over expenditures, and emphasize instead postaudit measurements of managerial performance
- Ease the possibility of transfers of funds within institutions, preferably through lump-sum appropriations
- Provide for portability of state financial aid to students
- Step in, as necessary, to assist mergers of institutions,[6] which can be costly, and to help with close-outs—particularly the preservation of past records.

The states together, through regional associations and the Education Commission of the States nationally, may wish to:

- Encourage more sophisticated advance estimates of enrollments

---

the same responsibilities to the past and to the future that the research universities have. Research universities must serve the past in maintenance of research library collections, of museums, and of courses of study that reflect the heritage of the history of civilization (like departments of the classics) regardless of current enrollment fluctuations. They must also serve the future with the development of new research areas, of new scientific fields of teaching, of new specialties in established fields, particularly at the graduate level, before federal research funds and FTE enrollments support them. Thus, they need more financial leeway than do community colleges that more nearly follow current enrollments. Effective service to the present, the past, and the future, when enrollments are declining, all require some reasonable adjustments of financial formulas established in a period of enrollment growth.

We consider a range of 0.6 to 0.8 to be reasonable based on current knowledge. We suggest, however, careful study of this suggested range. In particular, it may turn out to be wise to lower the 0.6 figure.

[6]Millett (1976) describes the process of merger as "laborious" and almost certain to bring conflict and disagreement that may not subside for a decade or more. He warns against the expectation that mergers will have advantages for everyone involved or that mergers will accomplish miracles. Millett studied carefully the background, process, objectives, and consequences of 10 separate mergers that have occurred since the early sixties. Financial stress was clearly evident at the time of the merger in about half of the cases, and anticipated financial difficulties may have acted as a prod in most of the other instances. Financial aid from a state government can soften some of the economic blows of the merger, he suggests, but notes that only New York State has shown any disposition to offer that aid. Where public institutions are involved, the leadership of state officials can be crucial to a successful merger process. Given the expected financial stringencies of the eighties, the importance of public monies and public leadership in smoothing the process of merger will be greatly increased.

than many states now have—bad data give rise to bad plans[7]
- Assist interstate consortia and cooperative use of facilities, as has been done particularly under the auspices of the Southern Regional Education Board.

We should like to comment, additionally and briefly, on the state planning process. In a period of growth, when many new proposals are being made to the states, they act through their administrative officers and legislatures somewhat like a private foundation accepting this program and rejecting that. The institutions make the proposals. In a period of contraction, the process can be reversed. Then the state makes the proposals to cut back here and close out there. This is an enormous difference. The initiative shifts from the institution to the state. The process of cutting back and closing out by state action is politically more difficult, as experience in several states indicates, than that of exercising restraint on growth.

We recognize the need for states to insist in a period of contraction on the closing or merging of some institutions and the reduction of duplication among others. However, we suggest that reliance for contraction be placed mainly on the student market, letting the students decide which colleges and major programs within colleges will lose enrollments. We emphasize again, nevertheless, as we have done before, that colleges should maintain some reasonable balance among essential programs and not rely on student choices alone. Students, particularly as they get good advice

---

[7]We have examined all of the available state projections and plans, and nearly all states have one or both. We found the projections often to be inadequate and frequently, we believe, unduly pessimistic about enrollments. Also the plans, we believe, concentrate too heavily on the use of direct controls. On projections, we suggest in particular, where this has not already been done: attention to both public and private institutions, consideration of a range of data at least as comprehensive as that set forth in our Table 8, consideration of different subgroups as we do in Section 3, calculation of enrollments on an FTE (not headcount) basis, looking ahead at least 10 years. On plans, we suggest in particular, again where this has not already been done, consideration of both the public and private sectors, of the respective roles of the student market and direct government action in adjusting to declines, of the handling of mergers and close-outs, of support for interinstitutional cooperation and consortia, of statewide coverage by open-access institutions and by Area Health Education Centers (AHECS), of differentiation of functions among institutions, of minimum standards of fair academic practices.

from counseling agencies[8] (and we believe these agencies should be greatly strengthened) can probably make as good decisions, by and large, as can planners. And the process is so much easier politically— it is easier for the students to make the hard decisions one by one. For this process to work well, there need to be not only well-informed consumers but also fair competition among institutions based on the quality of their services. It is to assure more fair competition that we support tuition scholarships to students; these allow student choices to be made more on the basis of quality.

Thus, we suggest maximum constructive use of the student market to guide contraction.

We are doubtful about state-mandated review of academic programs. We believe that such review is better conducted by the institutions themselves, by the accrediting agencies, and by the students making their choices; and we question the wisdom of this great an intrusion into academic affairs. While we are against any fine-tuning of academic programs by state action, we recognize that the state may need to step in where there are very expensive large programs (like medical schools) in severe duplication of each other.

We recognize that states vary greatly in the prospective decline of their enrollments. There is more of a case to be made for full reliance on the student market where the decline is modest than where it is severe. Where it is severe, it may be better for the state to close, or better, merge some campuses than to have them all deteriorate. Public institutions are unlikely to merge on their own account. We say "merge" because it is easier to merge than to close, as evidenced by the experience related in Section 4 of almost no recent closures of public institutions except under very exceptional circumstances. By contrast, there was a substantial number of mergers. Where enrollment declines are severe, we see the need for a plan on mergers and on

---

[8]The Educational Testing Service, for example, operates a program for the College Entrance Examination Board which helps match up students and colleges. The Student Search Service provides colleges with names of students who have requested participation, and institutions then contact candidates who possess characteristics they consider desirable. Students are afforded the opportunity to learn about institutions they may otherwise never hear of, thus extending the range of realistic choices available to them. A 1979 survey indicated that 34 percent of high school seniors who participated in the search the previous year were applying to at least one college they learned of through the Student Search Service (College Entrance Examination Board, 1979, p. 6).

preservation of records. We believe less of a case can be made for reductions of academic programs within institutions by state action since this impinges upon their autonomy, involves very detailed review, and institutions, in any event, will be under great pressure to drop high-cost, low-enrollment programs. States should also plan to preserve the records of private institutions that close, leaving their closures, however, to the student market and the decisions of their trustees. There are circumstances, but we think somewhat limited ones, where there is a "need to plan" (Connecticut Board of Higher Education, 1979, p. 54). While supporting the need to plan for mergers and close-outs, we question the advisability of setting enrollment quotas for individual continuing institutions to spread out enrollments among them, preferring instead that they be allowed to compete in the student market.

The Federal Government.

In addition to providing financial aid to students, the federal government has a major role in maintaining the research capacity of higher education—"the indispensable partnership for excellence" (The Ford Foundation, 1978, p. 3).[9]

We suggest:

- Continuation of the present level of support for research in colleges and universities at approximately 12 to 13 percent of total federal support of research and development (R&D), while raising total federal support of R&D to about 1.8 percent of the GNP, which it averaged in the 1960s; it has been around 1.3 percent in the 1970s, rising recently. This would help offset any decline at the state level as enrollment-driven financing goes down in real terms. It would also make possible urgently needed improvements in the quality of laboratory equipment and other facilities.
- Establishment of a Fund for the Encouragement of Young Scientists. The fund would be used over a twenty-year period to assist the flow of young scientists into faculty positions in selected fields in universities either directly or through absorption of all or

[9]The "special responsibility" of the federal government in this area has been urged by the Council in many other publications. See, for example, *The Federal Role in Postsecondary Education* (1975c).

part of the costs of existing tenure positions. It would be administered by the National Science Foundation (NSF) upon recommendations as to fields and means of distribution by the National Academy of Sciences and the National Academy of Engineering. We consider this to be a very important investment in the future. We are impressed by the carefully developed proposal of the Committee on Continuity in Academic Research Performance, sponsored by the Commission on Human Resources of the National Research Council.[10] Recognizing that the shortage of positions for young scientists in research universities will become more acute until about 1991 and then will become less serious as retirement and mortality rates of existing faculty members rise, the committee recommended a program of five-year awards to particularly able scientists (some middle-aged and some relatively young) whose universities would undertake to open up new faculty tenure-track positions to recent Ph.D.s, with the number of awards gradually rising to a peak in 1991 and then declining. The costs of the recommended program would increase from $2.1 million in 1981-82 to $39 million in 1991-92 and then decline to the year 2000, and would be met partly by existing NSF funds and partly by increased appropriations. Emphasis would be placed on opening up some of the positions for women and members of minority groups. We suggest a similar but somewhat more flexible program, with provision for some awards directly to recent Ph.D.s and with ten-year awards to established scholars during the first decade of the program (the duration of awards to be reduced after that, as the shortages of positions become less serious). We, therefore, propose added appropriations in excess of the sums just listed, but not exceeding $100 million in any one year.[11]

- Encouragement, through appropriate tax policies, to industry and foundations to grant research funds to universities.
- Introduction of a policy to support research libraries and other

---

[10]See Supplement K, *Smoothing Out the Flow of Young Scientists into Universities.*

[11]We also suggest augmentation of funds for the National Endowment for the Humanities and National Endowment for the Arts for the same purposes. We suggest that private foundations may also wish to assist young humanists and artists beyond what they now do.

research resources, including computers, by including within overhead on research contracts a standard 5 percent allowance for this purpose; the current level is 1 to 3 percent varying among institutions. This policy should be adopted as a supplement rather than as an alternative to existing programs, particularly Title II, Part C of the 1976 Education Amendments. Title II, Part C remains an important element in preserving the nation's research libraries and should be fully funded at its 1979 authorization level of $20 million. Also necessary is the passage of legislation for a national periodicals center. Supplement J sets forth other policies to aid libraries.

We suggest that the federal government also consider:

- Policies to reallocate funds for student financial assistance to target them more on lower-income students, to create a more viable loan program, to place more emphasis upon student self-help, including through the College Work-Study program, and to assist the states with tuition scholarships (SSIG); all within existing total sums in constant dollars (Carnegie Council on Policy Studies in Higher Education, 1979b).
- Gradual increases in the funds allocated to the Fund for the Improvement of Post-Secondary Education.

We are disturbed not with the purposes of federal control over higher education but with their execution. We particularly support the purposes of the affirmative action policy. We make four proposals:

- Regulations should be issued only after improved advance consultation with representatives of higher education, including students and faculty members when they are affected.
- Regulations should not go beyond the purposes for which the money is appropriated; they should not have irrelevant requirements added on to them.
- A "Regulatory Impact Statement" should be required in connection with each set of regulations, modeled on Environmental Impact Statements, showing purposes to be achieved, costs of compliance including side effects, processes of advance consultation, consideration given to alternative methods to achieve the

same purposes, an indication of their appropriateness to higher education as distinct from other types of institutions, a date for full review and possible termination, and a provision for periodic reporting to Congress on their effectiveness.

• The zeal of bureaucrats pushing their own programs beyond the intent of the law and of lawyers trying in advance to cover every possibility of evasion and every potential case of litigation should be curbed.

Costs and benefits. The costs of the suggestions made above for new state and federal action are modest. They are more than offset by prospective declines in costs because of lower enrollments; these declines are both in current operating costs and in construction.[12] The consequence is that support of higher education will be a declining percentage of the GNP. (See Table 12.) More can be done for higher education and through it for the nation at substantially reduced shares of total federal and state revenues.[13] The benefits of our proposals will be particularly:

The maintenance of a strong private sector of higher education
The continuation of a high capability for basic research
Improved student financial assistance programs.

More important, however, than state and federal action is action by the institutions themselves. Their futures are mostly in their own hands. There is not one set of decisions to be made by the federal

---

[12]There will be need for construction funds, however, even with declining enrollments. Old buildings need to be renovated. Even new buildings must be adapted for handicapped students, must meet mandated regulations on earthquake and fire safety, and so on. Some buildings are totally obsolete.

[13]Note that expenditures will decline more sharply as a percentage of real GNP if the rate of growth of GNP is 3.5 percent per annum than if it is 2.5 percent. During the 1980s, the labor force is projected to grow at an annual average rate of 1.1 percent. Therefore, a 3.5 percent rate of growth in real GNP implies a 2.4 percent rate of increase in productivity, while a 2.5 percent rate of growth in GNP implies a 1.4 percent rate of increase in productivity. If the rate of growth of GNP were as low as 2.0 percent (not shown in Table 12), the implied rate of increase in productivity would be 0.9 percent. The annual average rate of increase in productivity in nonfarm business from 1970 to 1978 was about 1.5 percent (computed from data in The President, 1979, p. 226).

**Table 12. Current-funds expenditures and construction expenditures of
institutions of higher education as percentage of gross national
product, estimated, fiscal year 1979, and projected on the basis of several
assumptions, fiscal year 1998**

Year and assumptions	Current-funds expenditures	Percentage of GNP Construction expenditures	Total expend-itures
Estimated, 1978–79	2.10%	0.29%	2.39%
Projected, 1997–98 (in constant 1978 dollars) I. Annual average rate of growth of real GNP, 1978–79 to 1997–98 = 2.5%			
Undergraduate FTE enrollment declines by 5 percent; postbaccalaureate enrollment remains constant	1.62	0.18	1.80
Undergraduate FTE enrollment declines by 10 percent; postbaccalaureate enrollment remains constant	1.59	0.17	1.76
Undergraduate FTE enrollment declines by 15 percent; postbaccalaureate enrollment remains constant	1.57	0.16	1.73
II. Annual average rate of growth of real GNP, 1978–79 to 1997–98 = 3.5%			
Undergraduate FTE enrollment declines by 5 percent; postbaccalaureate enrollment remains constant	1.39	0.15	1.54
Undergraduate FTE enrollment declines by 10 percent; postbaccalaureate enrollment remains constant	1.36	0.14	1.50
Undergraduate FTE enrollment declines by 15 percent; postbaccalaureate enrollment remains constant	1.34	0.13	1.47

Sources: Estimated expenditures for 1978–79 adapted from data in U.S. National
Center for Education Statistics (1978d, tables 32 to 34). Projections by Carnegie
Council. Note that some components of current-funds expenditures do not vary
with enrollment; we have made reasonable estimates of increases in those components and have assumed that research expenditures increase along with GNP, as we
recommend. Construction expenditures will be largely for replacement, which will
be needed to some extent in a period of stable enrollment and to a lesser extent in a
period of declining enrollment. Reductions in FTE enrollment result in reductions
of 60 to 80 percent in expenditures for each FTE student below prior levels.

government. There are not 51 sets of decisions to be made by the federal government and the 50 states. There are 3,051 sets of decisions by the federal government, the 50 states and the 3,000 institutions. The future course of events depends upon all 3,051 sets of decisions.

We strongly urge that institutions, states, and the federal government, where they have not already done so, analyze what actions they should take and then take action.

Meeting the Problems of the Next Two Decades

1. A Checklist of Imperatives for Colleges and Universities

1. *Analyze All Factors Likely to Affect Future Enrollments*
   Demography • Changing population mix • Labor market changes • Type of institution • State population and fiscal trends
2. *Insist on Institutionwide or Systemwide Planning*
   Anticipate future problems • Avoid moving from crisis to crisis • Consider prospects for each campus in multicampus institutions
3. *Encourage Strong Leadership by Chief Executive Officer*
   Give him/her ample authority and assurance of reasonable length of term of service
4. *Intensify Recruitment Efforts and Reduce Attrition*
   Rely on methods appropriate to academic life • Avoid deceptive advertising
5. *Give High Priority to Maintenance of Quality*
   Maintain high standards for faculty • Insist on quality in teaching • Maintain distinctive characteristics of institution • Protect internal life of institution • Improve achievement capacity of graduates • Emphasize high standards of scholarship—and of research in research-oriented institutions • Preserve institutional integrity
6. *Encourage Innovation and Flexibility*
   Develop curriculum that is sensitive to change but also to emphasis on general education • Establish fund for innovation • Avoid too high a proportion of tenured-in faculty. Encourage new programs and instructional techniques
7. *Strive for Most Effective Use of Resources*
   Avoid excessive number of courses and proliferation of degrees • Review student-faculty ratios by department • Maintain adequate

support personnel • Avoid excessive cuts in plant maintenance and library acquisitions

8. *Seek Support from Private Sources of Funds*
Devise imaginative ways of approaching alumni and other donors

9. *Concentrate on proposals to federal and state governments that will result in better programs at no increase in the real levels of federal and state expenditures; that acknowlege the likelihood of some reductions but not proportionately to reduced enrollments.*

II. A Checklist of Imperatives for States

1. *Maintain At Least the Current Level of Per Capita Funding of Higher Education in Constant Dollars*
This principle should release funds for support of private higher education in a period of declining enrollment • States below national average in per capita funding should consider increasing it

2. *Provide Need-based Tuition Scholarships for All Needy Students*
Require reasonable self-help from students • Consolidate needs test with that of federal government to eliminate inequities • Provide for portability of scholarships

3. *Support Private Higher Education While Maintaining Its Autonomy*
Emphasize student aid as chief means of support • Contract for services of private institutions where appropriate • Maintain state tax policies that encourage private giving to both private and public institutions

4. *Assist in Developing Plans for Adaption of Higher Education to Changing Needs*
Encourage elimination of weak or overly specialized programs • Develop plans for mergers of institutions facing deficient enrollments • Avoid bailing out institutions • Encourage adaptation of programs where this will forestall closures

5. *Avoid Excessive Regulation of Higher Education*
Consult with representatives of higher education before adopting new regulations • Avoid preaudit controls over expenditures. Provide for easy internal transfer of funds

6. *Use Flexible Funding Formulas*
Encourage diversity among institutions and within institutions • Establish a fund for innovation modeled after FIPSE • Use

funding formulas that adjust for high-cost programs and rising overhead costs per student

7. *Encourage Institutional Consortia and Interstate Cooperation*
Support consortia that will permit greater diversity as well as economies • Seek interstate cooperation to provide for highly specialized and expensive programs and to develop improved enrollment and financing projections

8. *Ensure statewide coverage by open-access institutions and by Area Health Education Centers*

9. *Expend public funds, as far as possible, as though they were private funds*
Provide substantial autonomy for all institutions in their use of funds subject to competition in getting results and, wherever possible, make expenditures via private individuals as in state tuition scholarships.

III. A Checklist of Imperatives
for the Federal Government

1. *Improve Federal Student Aid Provisions Without Increasing Their Cost*
Target more aid to low-income students through revisions of the needs test and through a special BEOG override and modifications in SEOG • Require self-help from all students except in hardship cases • Replace the existing inadequate, costly, and inequitable loan programs by a National Student Loan Bank • Increase SSIG funding substantially so as to encourage fully developed state scholarship programs in all states • Avoid tuition tax credits, which are regressive and self-defeating

2. *Restore Policy of Adequate Support of Research*
Increase R&D appropriations as a percentage of GNP to levels of the 1960s and maintain that level thereafter • Adopt special program to maintain flow of young scholars along the lines of the proposal of the Commission on Human Resources • Avoid stop-and-go research financing • Increase funds to support scholarship in the arts and humanities • Provide higher and stable support for research libraries • Finance improvements in research facilities and equipment

3. *Encourage Private Giving to All of Higher Education*
   Maintain existing tax incentives for contributions
4. *Avoid Excessive Regulation of Higher Education*
   Consult with representatives of higher education and adopt impact statements for new regulations • Review existing regulations to eliminate unnecessary reporting and other burdensome requirements • Consolidate enforcement in a single agency, where many are involved, as in affirmative action • Avoid infringements on admissions policies, as in the case of medical schools, and other encroachments on autonomy
5. *Continue Health Manpower Policies Aimed at Overcoming Geographical Maldistribution and Overspecialization*
   Maintain stable support of medical and dental education, but discourage establishment of new medical schools • Continue support of National Health Service Corps and encourage new AHEC programs in lagging states
6. *Gradually Increase Support for FIPSE*
7. *Expend public funds, as far as possible, as though they were private funds*
   This includes substantial autonomy for the public foundations; and expenditures via private individuals, as in the BEOG program.

8

Higher Education
and the World
of the Future

The Carnegie Council has had an opportunity over the past six years to survey important aspects of American higher education and to meet with leaders in many parts of the nation and to hear about their experiences.

We end our review of the past and our efforts to preview the future with certain convictions—some of them we started with and they remain unchanged, others have been intensified, still others modified:

Higher education adds greatly to the quality of many individual lives through higher incomes but, beyond income and what income can buy, through the better use of the gift of time.

It leads to better-informed and more active citizens, and this is increasingly essential in a modern democracy.

Equality of opportunity has been substantially increased for minorities and for women and for low-income young persons generally. More of each are now entering the more prestigious and higher-paid professions and occupations. Yet we have been disappointed. Removing or reducing financial obstacles to higher education has not led to the increased attendance we anticipated, particularly for low-income persons. The home,

the local community, the nature of the elementary and secondary schools are such strong influences that provision of minimum financial opportunity to participate in higher education has a decisive influence in advancing fewer lives than we once expected. We have also discovered that fewer young persons (particularly majority males), given freedom of choice, seem to want to go to college than we once expected. Yet we remain convinced that higher education has the major responsibility in the nation to find high talent and to develop advanced skills among all elements of the population.

Scientific and technological advance is highly dependent on our research universities. The decline in their support over the past decade and more has injured the nation. Yet we again remain of the opinion that higher education has the greatest possibility of any institution for advancing knowledge.

The United States has the most adequate all-around system of higher education in the world. It offers access to more of the population and finds talent more adequately in all parts of society than in any other nation, and it offers students more range of choice. Its research contributions since about 1930 have been preeminent. It has avoided the decline into anarchy of Italy, the subservience to state ideology and stifling bureaucracy of Eastern Europe, the imposition of costly new forms of governance as in France, Holland, and West Germany, the submergence in a cultural revolution as in China from 1966 to 1976, the denigrating hierarchical system of institutions of Japan, the exploitation of institutions for political purposes endemic in several Latin American countries, and the debasement of the academic currency as in so many institutions in India.

We may underestimate the current strengths and ability of American higher education to adapt, survive, and advance. We have been greatly impressed by the boundless variety among and within institutions, and by the pervasive dynamism that animates the system—much more than we realized in advance. And we are increasingly convinced of the importance of both of these characteristics.

Our pluralistic system of governance gives a large and effective role to competition within and between institutions: com-

petition for students, for research funds, in service to society, in the advancement of scholarship. We should preserve
the pluralism and enhance the fiar competition that it en-
genders.

Our system has the capacity to improve the quality of its performance even as it declines quantitatively in enrollments.

Higher education in the United States is a great national resource that has been preserved by the generally thoughtful
care of the surrounding society and the devotion of many
of its participants. In our tendency to criticize and even berate,
we sometimes forget how fortunate we are.

Much has been accomplished for individual Americans and for
American society, yet there is still some unfinished business:

We have not yet spread universal access, defined as availability of
attendance at a postsecondary institution within commuting
distance on the basis of a high school diploma, to all populated
parts of the nation.

We have a long way to go to make possible the participation at the
highest levels of academic life of the ablest persons regardless of
race, sex, and family income.

These goals should be met by the year 2000.

We also have some new business, and in particular:

Introducing a more global perspective into higher education and
through it to other levels of the educational system

Guiding the use of the new electronic technology to assure that the
programs are of high quality and are not used for the purpose of
economic or political exploitation

Identifying the most productive areas for new research, such as
sources of energy and preservation of the environment, shifting
resources to them, and prosecuting them actively.

While we have a sense of great pride in what has been
accomplished and great faith in the capacity of higher education for
future contribution, we still have concerns:

That the competition for students over the next two decades may
be managed in ways that lead to a decline in academic quality,
in integrity of conduct, in the balance among the many

intellectual fields that constitute the universe of knowledge

That, in the absence of growth, institutions may lose their dynamism and flexibility, may succumb to counterproductive defensive reactions, may become a focus of dissatisfied expectations; that the tone of the internal life of many institutions may degenerate toward mutual suspicion and resignation to harsh fate

That diversity among institutions may be reduced; and that the heavy hand of government may tend to a homogenization of policies and practices that will stifle new efforts at distinctive styles and approaches

That equality of results by regulation may gradually come to replace equality of opportunity in fair competition; the former reducing and the latter elevating average performance

That some of the effectiveness and creativity of students and scholars associated with high morale and a belief in high purpose may be eroding.

Yet, despite these concerns, we believe that higher education will make essential contributions to the world of the future:

To a more participative society of a higher quality; to more people taking active charge of their lives; to more people taking part in the affairs of their community, state, and nation; to more people escaping the ancient shackles of ignorance and domination by others

To a more universal society as higher education adds to knowledge about and concern for the whole world, creates expanding communities of colleagues and friends, intensifies and improves the networks of communication

To societies more capable of self-renewal, not subject to decay and decline, through the influence of new knowledge, critical self-evaluation, constructive suggestions for the future.

Few other institutions have such capacity for the "improvement of the welfare of mankind around the world." The further cultivation of "man's unconquerable mind" may be the one best hope for a future greatly enhanced over the present we now know.

Supplement A

Sources of Funds
for Higher Education

Sources of funds for higher education can be classified in a number of different ways, depending on the purpose of the inquiry, with quite different results in terms of the relative importance of public versus private funds and in terms of other important distinctions. Probably the three most important systems of classification are according to (1) sources of current-funds income of institutions of higher education, (2) sources of total monetary outlays for higher education, and (3) sources of total economic costs of higher education, including forgone earnings of students.

Income for Educational and General Purposes

We begin with sources of current-funds income of institutions of higher education, because changes in the relative importance of these sources is of special concern to administrators of institutions. We also consider only *income for educational and general purposes,* excluding income of auxiliary enterprises (chiefly dormitories and cafeterias), sales and services of educational activities, and other similar items, because these items are usually managed so that income equals outgo. It is changes in the income of colleges and universities for educational and general purposes that primarily give rise to concern over the health of the educational enterprise.[1]

This supplement was prepared by Margaret S. Gordon, Associate Director, and Charlotte Alhadeff, Research Specialist.

[1]There are some exceptions to this generalization. In the late 1960s and early 1970s,

CENTER FOR HIGHER EDUCATION
3301 COLLEGE AVENUE
FORT LAUDERDALE, FLA. 33314

Table A-1 shows the changes in the sources of income of all institutions of higher education from 1929-30 to 1976-77.

Table A-1. Changes in sources of current income of all institutions of higher education for educational and general purposes, 1929-30 to 1976-77

Source	1929-30	1939-40	1959-60	1969-70	1976-77
Total (in $ millions)	$410.2	$527.1	$4,337.1	$16,200.0	$32,280.7
Percentage	100.0%	100.0%	100.0%	100.0%	100.0%
All public sources	41.8	40.7	59.6	63.9	63.1
Federal government	5.0	7.4	24.1	22.5	16.4
Research, etc.			19.1	14.0	9.4
Other			5.0	8.5	7.0
State governments	36.8	28.7	32.0	36.6	41.6
Local governments		4.6	3.5	4.8	5.1
All private sources	58.2	59.3	40.4	36.1	36.9
Tuition and fees[a]	35.1	38.1	26.8	26.8	28.2
Endowment income	16.7	13.5	4.8	2.8	2.3
Private gifts and grants	6.4	7.7	8.8	6.5	6.4

[a]Gross tuition, including student aid income.

Sources: 1929-30 to 1959-60 from O'Neill (1973, table A-1); 1969-70 from Carnegie Commission on Higher Education (1973, table A-13); 1976-77 from U.S. National Center for Education Statistics (1979, table 1).

(Comprehensive data were not collected before 1929-30.) The most noticeable feature of the table is the rise in the relative importance of public versus private financing of colleges and universities in the period since World War II. As we shall see, however, this reflects in large part the influence of two developments: (1) the relatively rapid growth of the public sector of higher education, and (2) the sizable increase in appropriations of federal funds for higher education after World War II. Within the public and private sectors, changes in sources of financing were much less pronounced, especially if federal funds are excluded.

---

for example, a number of leading universities, especially in the private sector, were incurring sizable deficits because of insufficient income from their teaching hospitals.

Tables A-2 and A-3 show the changes in the sources of institutional income for educational and general purposes of pub-

Table A-2. Changes in sources of current income of all public institutions of higher education for educational and general purposes, 1929-30 to 1976-77

Source	1929-30	1939-40	1959-60	1969-70	1976-77
Total (in $ millions)	$205.7	$271.0	$2,485.1	$10,750.0	$22,879.5
Percentage	100.0%	100.0%	100.0%	100.0%	100.0%
All public sources	79.8	75.3	82.4	81.0	79.7
Federal government		13.5	22.0	19.7	15.7
State governments	79.8	53.0	54.5	54.5	57.4
Local governments		8.9	5.9	6.8	6.6
All private sources	20.2	24.7	17.6	19.0	20.3
Tuition and fees[a]	15.8	20.3	13.4	15.3	16.9
Endowment income	3.1	2.5	0.8	0.4	0.4
Private gifts and grants	1.3	1.9	3.4	3.3	3.0

[a]Gross tuition, including student aid income.

Sources: 1929-30 to 1959-60 from O'Neill (1973, table A-2); 1969-70 from Carnegie Commission on Higher Education (1973, table A-13); 1976-77 from Carnegie Council estimates based on data in U.S. National Center for Education Statistics (1979, table 1).

lic and private institutions of higher education separately for the same time period. In the public sector, the shift from private to public sources was minor—public sources were predominant throughout the nearly 50-year period. The chief changes were the growth in the relative importance of federal funds and the reversal of that trend after the mid-1960s. The percentage of funds provided by state governments has been remarkably stable, and there has been no long-run tendency to rely relatively more heavily on tuition, although Table A-2 shows a slight increase in the share of tuition from 1959-60 to 1976-77. (It is important to keep in mind, however, that the data relate to gross tuition—approximately 3 percent of the income of public institutions in 1976-77 consisted of student aid grants, and thus net tuition income was about 14 percent in that year [17 percent minus 3 percent].) Although private philanthropy is a relatively unimportant source of income for public institutions

Table A-3. Changes in sources of current income of all private institutions of higher education for educational and general purposes, 1929-30 to 1976-77

Source	1929-30	1939-40	1959-60	1969-70	1976-77
Total (in $ millions)	$204.5	$256.1	$1,851.9	$5,450.0	$9,408.9
Percentage	100.0%	100.0%	100.0%	100.0%	100.0%
All public sources	3.5	4.0	29.0	30.4	22.1
Federal government		0.9	26.9	27.9	17.7
State governments	3.5	3.0	1.9	1.8	3.2
Local governments		0.1	0.2	0.7	1.2
All private sources	96.5	96.0	71.0	69.6	77.9
Tuition and fees[a]	54.6	57.0	44.8	49.5	55.7
Endowment income	30.5	25.2	10.1	7.3	7.1
Private gifts and grants	11.4	13.8	16.1	12.8	15.1

[a]Gross tuition, including student aid income.

Sources: 1929-30 to 1959-60 from O'Neill (1973, table A-3); 1969-70 from Carnegie Commission on Higher Education (1973, table A-13); 1976-77 from Carnegie Council estimates based on data in U.S. National Center for Education Statistics (1979, table 1).

as a whole (it is considerably more significant for some of the leading public research universities), the declining relative importance of endowment income and the increasing relative importance of gifts appears in the accounts for public institutions as well as for higher education as a whole.

Sources of income of private institutions have shown much more pronounced changes over the five decades than have those of public institutions. The decline in the share of endowment income has been marked, and, although the share of private gifts has increased somewhat, it has by no means offset the drop in relative income from endowments. All in all, private philanthropy accounted for about 42 percent of the income of private institutions in 1929-30, compared with 22 percent in 1976-77. The increased reliance on private gifts means that income is more uncertain and more dependent on continuous fund-raising efforts. The second major shift was the growth in the share of the federal government after World War II, followed by a decline from the mid-1960s on. (Unrevealed in Table A-3 is the fact that the federal share of the institutional income of private institutions reached its peak of about 35 percent in the early 1960s.) The fall in the federal share has been accompanied by a rise in the share of tuition, which is now back to approximately its prewar level. However, as we showed in *The States and Private Higher Education* (1977, pp. 78-79), reliance on tuition as a source of revenue varies enormously among private institutions, with the research universities receiving much smaller percentages of their income from tuition than other types of institutions do. Private comprehensive universities and colleges, on the other hand, tend to be heavily dependent on tuition.

In Tables A-4 and A-5, we show the changes in sources of funds for educational and general purposes of public and private

Table A-4. Changes in sources of current income of all public institutions of higher education for educational and general purposes, excluding federal funds, 1939-40 to 1976-77

Source	1939-40	1959-60	1969-70	1976-77
Total (in $ millions)	$234.5	$1,937.6	$8,630.0	$19,297.0
Percentage	100.0%	100.0%	100.0%	100.0%
Public sources	71.5	77.5	76.2	76.0
State governments	61.2	69.9	67.7	68.1
Local governments	10.3	7.6	8.5	7.9
Private sources	28.5	22.5	23.8	24.0
Tuition and fees[a]	23.5	17.1	19.0	20.0
Endowment income	2.8	1.0	0.6	0.5
Private gifts and grants	2.2	4.4	4.2	3.5

[a]Gross tuition, including student aid income.

Sources: 1939-40 to 1959-60 from O'Neill (1973, table A-2); 1969-70 from Carnegie Commission on Higher Education (1973, table A-13); 1976-77 from Carnegie Council estimates based on data in U.S. National Center for Education Statistics (1979, table 1).

institutions, *excluding* federal funds. This way of classifying the data is of special interest, because it shows quite substantial stability in sources of funds for both sectors, if federal funds are eliminated. Even so, it indicates that the decline in the relative importance of endowment income is not an artifact of the

Table A-5. Changes in sources of current income of all private
institutions of higher education for educational and general purposes,
excluding federal funds, 1939-40 to 1976-77

Source	1939-40	1959-60	1969-70	1976-77
Total (in $ millions)	$253.7	$1,354.7	$3,930.0	$7,733.8
Percentage	100.0%	100.0%	100.0%	100.0%
Public sources	3.1	3.0	3.5	5.4
State governments	3.0	2.7	2.5	3.9
Local governments	0.1	0.3	1.0	1.5
Private sources	96.9	97.0	96.5	94.6
Tuition and fees[a]	57.5	61.2	68.5	67.6
Endowment income	25.5	13.8	10.2	8.6
Private gifts and grants	13.9	22.0	17.8	18.4

[a]Gross tuition, including student aid income.

Sources: 1939-40 to 1959-60 from O'Neill (1973, table A-3); 1969-70 from Carnegie
Commission on Higher Education (1973, table A-13); 1976-77 from Carnegie Council
estimates based on data in U.S. National Center for Education Statistics (1979, table
1).

growth of federal funds. It is a very significant trend, even when
federal funds are eliminated, especially for the private sector.

In fact, however, endowment income in the private sector
is a significant source only for the more selective private institutions and has probably never been an important source for the
less-selective private colleges and universities. As we showed in
our report (1977, p. 80), endowment income accounted for 13
percent of revenue for educational and general purposes of
selective liberal arts colleges, versus only 4 percent for the less-
selective liberal arts colleges, in 1974-75. Within the private university sector, also, although endowment funds were relatively
more important than for most private four-year or two-year colleges, accounting for 9 percent of private university income for
educational and general purposes, there was enormous variation
from the more-selective to the less-selective private universities.
In a particularly affluent group of private universities, accounting for 8 percent of these institutions, endowment funds (in

capital rather than in income terms) amounted to $40,000 or more per full-time equivalent (FTE) student. These were all highly selective private universities. Nearly one-half of all private universities, on the other hand, had endowment funds amounting to less than $5,000 per FTE student, and a particularly poorly funded group (nearly 12 percent of all private universities) had endowment funds of less than $1,000 per FTE student.

It seems probable, in fact, that the decline over the decades in the relative importance of endowment income as a source of funding of private institutions of higher education reflects at least in part the relative growth of enrollment in less-selective private institutions. This is a somewhat speculative statement, however, because historical data appropriately classified do not exist. That the less-selective private institutions have increased their share of total private enrollment is clear.

Another point that needs to be made about the data in Tables A-1 to A-5 is that they understate the decline in the relative importance of tuition paid by students and their families, because they do not deduct from tuition income the tuition payments made by students from public and private student aid funds.

Examination of changes in sources of income also fails to reveal changes in the relationship between current income and current expenditures of institutions. In the early 1970s, current expenditures exceeded current income for a number of institutions, especially in the private sector, giving rise to a deficit on current account. Several studies showed that these deficits were primarily attributable to "student aid deficits," that is, institutions were dipping into endowment and other sources of funds to meet rising student aid expenditures. Over the course of the next several years, most private institutions managed to overcome these deficits through a combination of belt-tightening and special fund-raising efforts. Then, in 1974-75, largely because of the increased rate of inflation associated with the oil crisis, deficits reappeared and tended to persist—in varying degrees in the several types of private institutions—during the following two years (Carnegie Council, 1977, p. 185).

Sources of Monetary Outlays

Data on sources of monetary outlays for higher education (as shown in Figure 2 [p. 18] and Table A-6) provide more complete information on the financing of higher education than data on institutional funds, because they include amounts spent by students, particularly on subsistence, that do not flow through the accounts of higher education institutions. They also show separately all amounts allocated for student aid, even though—especially in the case of Basic Grants, veterans' educational benefits, and social security educational benefits—some student aid funds do not flow through institutional accounts but are spent on subsistence or on such items as books and supplies purchased from noninstitutional suppliers.

During the postwar period there was a steady and pronounced decline in the proportion of monetary outlays met by students and their families. On the other hand, the proportion met by the state and federal governments has increased substantially. The rise in the share of the states is explained chiefly by the increase in relative enrollment in public institutions and also, to a minor extent, by the increase in state scholarship funds. The rise in the federal share in the 1950s and the first half of the 1960s was explained in large part by funds for research, but since the mid-1960s the proportion represented by federal research funds has declined, while federal student aid expenditures and miscellaneous forms of federal support (such as the developing institutions program) have become relatively more important.

Total Economic Costs of Higher Education

The total economic costs of higher education include forgone earnings of students, as well as the other components that we have been considering. However, since subsistence costs would be met from earnings if the individuals concerned were not enrolled, subsistence costs are not included as a separate item in allocating economic costs.

As many economists have pointed out, when forgone earnings are included, the share of the costs of higher education borne by students and their parents is considerably higher than

Table A-6. Changes in sources of monetary outlays for higher education, including research expenditures, 1929-30 to 1976-77
(amounts in $ millions)

Source	1929-30		1939-40		1959-60		1969-70		1976-77	
	Amount	Percentage	Amount	Percentage	Amount	Percentage	Amount	Percentage	Amount	Percentage
Total[a]	$770.1	100.0%	$922.5	100.0%	$7,377.0	100.0%	$24,969.0	100.0%	$50,358.3	100.0%
Students and families										
Gross tuition payments	144.1	18.7	200.9	21.8	1,161.2	15.7	4,330.0	17.3	9,101.0	18.1
Subsistence	367.0	47.7	409.2	44.4	3,044.0[b]	41.3	8,769.0[b]	35.1	18,078.0	35.9
Less total student aid	-13.0	-1.7	-22.4	-2.4	-445.4	-6.0	-2,309.4	-9.3	-8,081.0	-16.1
Net expenditures	498.1	64.7	587.7	63.7	3,759.8	51.0	10,789.6	43.1	19,098.0	37.9
State governments (not including student aid)	150.8	19.6	151.2	16.4	1,389.2	18.8	5,950.0	23.8	13,426.0	26.7
Local governments			24.4	2.6	151.8	2.1	770.0	3.1	1,631.5	3.2
Federal government	20.6	2.7	38.9	4.2	1,040.9	14.1	3,640.0	14.6	5,249.4	10.4
Research					828.7	11.2	2,270.0	9.1	2,717.0	5.4
Other (not including student aid)					212.2	2.9	1,370.0	5.5	2,532.4	5.0

(continued on next page)

Table A-6 *(continued)*

Source	1929-30 Amount	Percent-age	1939-40 Amount	Percent-age	1959-60 Amount	Percent-age	1969-70 Amount	Percent-age	1976-77 Amount	Percent-age
Student aid (including institutional funds)[c]	$ 13.0	1.7%	$ 22.4	2.4%	$ 445.4	6.0%	$ 2,309.4	9.2%	$ 8,081.0	16.0%
Federal	—	—	—	—	233.1	3.2	1,536.1	6.2	6,482.0	12.9
State	1.0	0.1	1.2	0.1	15.0	0.2	200.0	0.8	589.3	1.2
Private	5.9	0.8	7.4	0.8	77.9	1.1	273.3	1.1	350.0[d]	0.7
Philanthropy (less private student aid)	94.7	12.3	111.7	12.1	589.9	8.0	1,510.0	6.1	2,872.4	5.7

[a]Items may not add to totals because of rounding.

[b]Subsistence payments are based on recently revised estimates by the Carnegie Council staff.

[c]Institutional student aid expenditures, which may come from private and public sources, are not shown separately, but are included in total student aid.

[d]Estimated.

Sources: Carnegie Commission on Higher Education (1973, tables A-1 to A-13); U.S. National Center for Education Statistics (1979, table 1). For student aid data, Carnegie Council on Higher Education (1975, table 4); selected federal budget documents; and Carnegie Council (1979, tables 6, 7, and 8).

when no account is taken of the earnings that students sacrifice because of the time spent on their studies. Moreover, the decline in the share of students and families when estimated on this basis (Figure A-1) has been quite moderate, because there have been several conflicting tendencies at work. Although the share of the taxpayer has been rising in the past few decades because of the increase in the proportion of enrollment in public institutions and because of the growth of student aid, wage rates have also been rising substantially. On the other hand, the rise in the labor force participation rate of students has meant that we must now make a larger allowance for their part-time earnings during term time in estimating forgone earnings. This trend has been enhanced by the growth of enrollment in public community colleges, where students tend to be older and are particularly likely to be working part-time. And on this basis, as in our previous estimates, the share of philanthropy has declined.

There is room for debate about the justification for aggregating forgone earnings. Undoubtedly, forgone earnings represent a sacrifice for the individual student, and this is particularly true, as we have pointed out in our reports on student aid, for students from low-income families. If all students were suddenly to drop out of college, however, the unemployment rate of young persons of college age would undoubtedly rise sharply for a time, and our estimate of forgone earnings would have to be revised sharply downward. Nevertheless, estimates of the total economic costs of higher education are clearly inadequate if no account is taken of forgone earnings.

References

Carnegie Commission on Higher Education. *Higher Education: Who Pays? Who Benefits? Who Should Pay?* New York: McGraw-Hill, 1973.

Carnegie Council on Policy Studies in Higher Education. *The Federal Role in Postsecondary Education: Unfinished Business 1975-1980.* San Francisco: Jossey-Bass, 1975.

Carnegie Council on Policy Studies in Higher Education. *The States and Private Higher Education: Problems and Policies in a New Era.* San Francisco: Jossey-Bass, 1977.

Carnegie Council on Policy Studies in Higher Education. *Next Steps for*

Figure A-1. Percentage of economic costs of higher education met by students and families, taxpayers, and philanthropy, 1929-30 to 1976-77

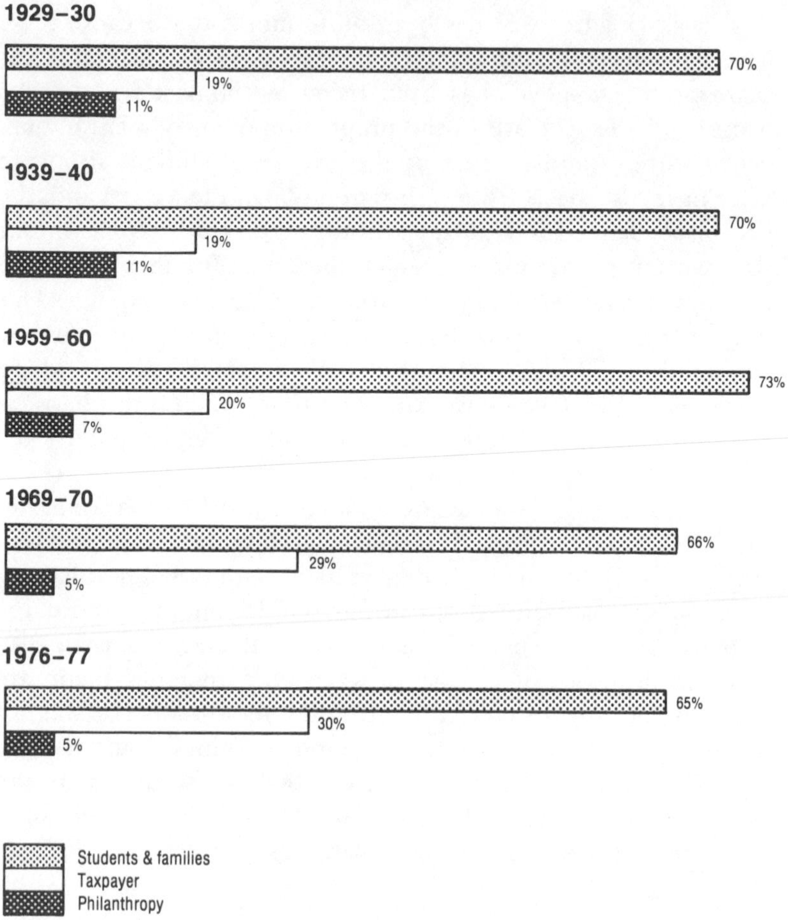

1929–30

70%

19%

11%

1939–40

70%

19%

11%

1959–60

73%

20%

7%

1969–70

66%

29%

5%

1976–77

65%

30%

5%

Students & families
Taxpayer
Philanthropy

Sources: 1929-30 to 1969-70 from Carnegie Commission on Higher Education (1973, tables A-1 to A-13; see pp. 49-50 for discussion of method of estimating forgone earnings); estimates for 1976-77 by Carnegie Council staff.

the 1980s in Student Financial Aid: A Fourth Alternative. San Francisco: Jossey-Bass, 1979.

O'Neill, J. A. *Sources of Funds to Colleges and Universities.* Carnegie Commission on Higher Education. Berkeley, Calif.: 1973.

U.S. National Center for Education Statistics. *Financial Statistics of Institutions of Higher Education, Current-Funds Revenues and Expenditures, Fiscal Year 1977.* Washington, D.C.: 1979.

Carnegie Enrollment Projections

The Carnegie Council's enrollment projections are less optimistic than those of some analysts and much less pessimistic than those of others. They predict a moderate decline in undergraduate FTE enrollment—ranging from 5 to 15 percent—from 1978 to 1997. In developing our projections, we have taken into consideration: (1) demographic trends, (2) the rising trend of adult and part-time enrollment, (3) enrollment trends for majority men and women, (4) the prospect for enrollment of blacks, (5) the difficult problems of predicting enrollment trends for other minority groups, especially Hispanics, (6) the probability of increased retention rates in an era when colleges will be struggling to retain their enrollments, (7) the likelihood of earlier college entrance for a modest number of 16- and 17-year olds, and (8) probable trends in postbaccalaureate enrollment. We have made no specific projections of enrollment of Hispanics, for reasons discussed below.

Demographic Trends

The only factor influencing future enrollment trends that is virtually certain is the coming decline in the size of the college-age population, resulting from the falling birthrates of the last two

This supplement was prepared by C. E. Christian, Research Fellow, and Margaret S. Gordon, Associate Director, with the assistance of Ruth Goto, Postgraduate Researcher.

decades. The young people who will be entering college from 1980 to 1997 are already born, and the number of persons of college age can be predicted with reasonable accuracy for this period (barring a catastrophe, such as an epidemic). The 18-year-old population, which reached a peak in 1979, will decline 26 percent by 1992. The broader 18- to 21-year-old group will follow much the same pattern, dropping 24 percent by 1994. If we consider the entire traditional college-age group, which now includes all of those aged 18 to 24, we find that it will continue to rise until 1981, after which there will be a decline of 23 percent by 1997.

We cannot, however, infer that college enrollments will change in precisely the same way as the size of the 18- to 24-year-old population, because of the changing ethnic and racial composition of the college-age population; changing enrollment rates among age, sex, and racial groups; and especially the rise in relative enrollment rates of persons in the 25 and older age bracket. In 1965, 80 percent of enrollment was accounted for by students aged 18 to 24, but by 1975 this group represented only 66 percent of the total. Among undergraduates, students aged 25 and older accounted for 28 percent of total headcount and nearly 20 percent of FTE enrollment in 1978. Educational planners must increasingly take into account the needs of older students, especially as their numbers as well as their enrollment rates are increasing rapidly. As Table B-1 shows, the most pronounced population increase in the period from 1978 to 1997 will occur among those aged 35 to 54. The postwar babies—born chiefly in the decade from 1945 to 1955—are now aged 25 to 35 and will be moving into the 35 and older bracket in the 1980s.

For the purpose of estimating trends in the size of the youthful population in the last few years of the present century and the first decade of the 21st century, we have adjusted Bureau of the Census enrollment projections somewhat. Census population projection Series II assumes that the fertility rate (the average number of lifetime births per woman of childbearing age) moves toward 2.1, while Series III assumes that it moves toward 1.7. We have developed an adjusted projection of

Table B-1. Population changes by age and race, 1978 to 2010

Age group	Number (thousands)			Percentage change		
	1978	*1997*	*2010*	*1978-1997*	*1978-2010*	*1997-2010*
18 years						
Total	4,229	3,143	3,457	−25.7%	−18.3%	+10.0%
White	3,578	2,530	2,849	−29.3	−20.4	+12.6
Black	573	478	479	−16.6	−16.4	+ 0.2
18-21 years						
Total	17,106	12,733	14,255	−25.6	−16.7	+12.0
White	14,519	10,259	11,719	−29.3	−19.3	+14.2
Black	2,262	1,914	2,002	−15.4	−11.5	+ 4.6
18-24 years						
Total	28,980	22,239	25,294	−23.3	−12.7	+13.7
White	24,670	17,884	20,774	−27.5	−15.8	+16.2
Black	3,733	3,341	3,590	−10.5	− 3.8	+ 7.5
25-34 years	33,949	36,841	36,246	+ 8.5	+ 6.8	− 1.6
35-54 years	47,564	74,094	75,236	+55.8	+58.2	+ 1.5
55 years and over	44,619	52,936	67,762	+18.6	+51.9	+28.0

Sources: U.S. Bureau of the Census (1977); and Carnegie Council estimates of the youthful population to 2010.

the college-age population, assuming that the fertility rate moves toward 2.1—from its present level of about 1.8—between now and 1997 and remains at that level thereafter. We have several reasons for assuming a rise in the fertility rate:

1. Quite recently the birthrate has turned upward, after declining almost steadily since the late 1950s. From a low point of 14.8 live births per 1,000 population in 1975 and 1976, the birthrate averaged 15.6 in the first eight months of 1979. Particularly significant is the fact that first-order births rose sharply among mothers aged 30 to 34 from 1976 to 1977 and somewhat less sharply among mothers aged 25 to 29, suggesting delayed decisions to bear children in these age

groups. This is a particularly interesting development, because these are the age groups that were born during the period of high birthrates from the end of World War II to the mid-1950s and who had been expected to produce a population explosion when they reached child-bearing age—an explosion that did not occur.[1]

2. The increase in the proportion of minority group members, with their relatively high fertility rates, in the youthful population can be expected to result in an increase in the fertility rate in the future.

3. Continued immigration, especially of Mexican-Americans, can be expected to affect overall population growth, as well as the fertility rate.

These assumptions, of course, do not affect the size of the college-age population until about 1998, when the children born in the coming years will begin to reach age 18.

Although the college-age population will be smaller in 2010 than it was in 1978, the population aged 25 to 34 will be somewhat larger, while that aged 35 to 54 will be immensely larger than in 1978. The number of potential enrollees in these older age groups will be very large even if their enrollment rate does not rise markedly, and we predict that it *will* rise somewhat. In addition, of course, we project higher enrollment rates for women, for blacks, and possibly for Hispanics, although Hispanics are not specifically incorporated into our projections.

In developing our projections we experimented with several models. The first of these, which was based entirely on demographic changes, simply applied the present enrollment rate for each age-sex-race group to the projected numbers in the group in each future year. The resulting "constant rate" projection was useful in providing a base-line set of numbers, which could then be adjusted to reflect the changes in enrollment rates of the various population groups that we anticipated would be likely to occur.

[1]Data on first-order births are from U.S. National Center for Health Statistics (Feb. 1979). Other, more recent data on the birthrate are from later issues of the same report.

Our second model was based on long-term historical trends in enrollment rates of age-sex cohorts since the 1940s, and on trends since about 1967 for age-sex groups classified by race (racial breakdowns were not regularly published in the census bureau's *Current Population Reports* until 1967). Trends in enrollment rates for each group were studied, and past trends provided a basis for estimating future changes in rates.

The projection that we have actually used involves judgmental adjustments in the "constant rate" projection, reflecting not only analysis of past trends but also incorporation of our best estimates of enrollment changes that are likely to occur under the conditions prevailing in the next several decades, for example, enhanced efforts of colleges to improve their retention rates. We have not, however, attempted to take explicit account of certain factors that might have a profound influence on future enrollment changes—such as economic conditions, military policy, and energy shortages—because of the great uncertainties associated with the possible impact of such changes. Our projections should be viewed as an estimate of the future changes in college enrollment that are likely to occur under conditions that evolve from past trends in political and economic developments, but that do not represent the impact of radical abrupt changes in these influences.

Majority Men and Women

Enrollment rates of majority males have dropped sharply since about 1969. There are a number of reasons why the future behavior of enrollment rates for this group is difficult to predict. However, if we consider changes in enrollment rates of youthful males in the 1960s, as well as in the 1970s, we note that there was a pronounced rise in the later half of the 1960s during the Vietnam conflict, when student draft deferments reached peak levels (Figure 9, p. 41). When the period from about 1964 to 1973 is removed from the chart, as in Figure 8 (p. 40), we see that enrollment rates of youthful male age groups in recent years have returned to approximately their pre-Vietnam levels. However, the recent decline in enrollment rates of those aged 22 to 24—and also in the broader 18- to 24-year age group—

since 1975 is undoubtedly explained largely by reduced enrollment of veterans. The fall in enrollment rates of those aged 18
to 21 is more difficult to explain. We will return to this question later.

Enrollment of veterans has been falling off as Vietnam-era
veterans exhaust their eligibility for GI educational benefits,
which lasts for ten years after leaving the service. From a high
point of 1.3 million in fall 1975, the number of veterans enrolled had fallen to about 600,000 by fall 1978 (U.S. Veterans
Administration, quarterly), and a continued decline in enrollment of Vietnam-era veterans can be expected. During the
1980s, however, veterans who have completed service in the
volunteer army and who have earned educational benefits under
the Post-Vietnam Veterans' Educational Assistance Act of 1976
can be expected to enroll.[2]

It is too early to develop reliable estimates of the number
of veterans who will use educational benefits earned under the
new legislation, but it seems certain that total enrollment of
veterans during the 1980s will be considerably below the peak
level reached in the mid-1970s.

High school graduation rates of majority males also
reached a peak toward the end of the 1960s and have since declined somewhat. Probably the threat of being drafted induced
some male high school students to continue in school during the
later half of the 1960s. Continuation of the recent decline in
high school graduation rates could further deplete the pool of
potential college students.

Unfortunately, the two major sources of high school completion data reveal somewhat different trends and are not precisely comparable. Data reported by the U.S. National Center
for Education Statistics (NCES) show the actual number of high
school graduates (as reported by schools) divided by the average
(i.e., one-half) of the 17- to 18-year-old population (Figure
B-1). They indicate that the graduation rate for boys has de-

---

[2]Under the provisions of that act, each person entering military service has a right to
enroll in an educational benefits program, in which case the individual must agree to
monthly pay deductions of $50 to $75, which are matched on a $2 to $1 basis by the
Veterans Administration.

Figure B-1. High school graduates as a percentage of the average 17- to 18-year-old civilian population, by sex, 1900 to 1978

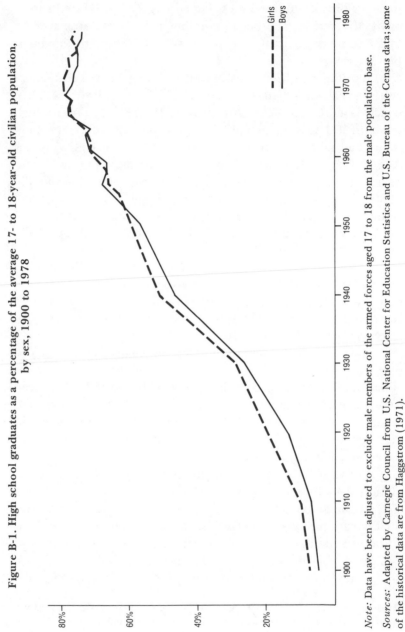

Note: Data have been adjusted to exclude male members of the armed forces aged 17 to 18 from the male population base.

Sources: Adapted by Carnegie Council from U.S. National Center for Education Statistics and U.S. Bureau of the Census data; some of the historical data are from Haggstrom (1971).

clined appreciably since the late 1960s, while that for girls has also declined, but more moderately. Unfortunately, no racial or ethnic breakdown is available in the case of these data. The U.S. Bureau of the Census also provides data on high school completion rates, based on its *Current Population Reports* (a household sample survey). These data, shown in Table B-2 for whites,

Table B-2. High school completion rates for 18- to 21-year olds, by race and Spanish origin, 1967 to 1978

	All races	White	Black	Spanish origin
1967	74.8%	77.3%	55.6%	—
1968	75.9	78.4	57.6	—
1969	77.0	79.8	56.8	—
1970	77.4	80.1	58.4	—
1971	77.3	80.0	59.2	—
1972	78.0	80.2	63.2	51.1%
1973	78.4	80.9	61.9	51.1
1974	78.2	80.6	63.3	56.3
1975	78.0	80.6	60.4	57.2
1976	77.7	79.7	64.1	52.0
1977	77.9	80.1	63.2	55.5
1978	78.2	80.4	63.7	53.9

Source: U.S. Bureau of the Census, *Current Population Reports: School Enrollment,* selected issues.

blacks, and young persons of Spanish origin aged 18 to 21, indicate little change for whites during the 1970s; an increase for blacks in the early 1970s but no net changes since then; and, among the Hispanics, a rise to 1975 followed by a decline. They also suggest a slightly higher high school graduation rate than the NCES figures. Differences in the published figures are actually larger than our comparisons show, because we have eliminated male members of the armed forces (who include a slightly higher percentage of dropouts than the civilian population) from the NCES data for boys. The census data, which relate to the civilian noninstitutional population, exclude not only members of the armed forces, but also young persons in institutions, who are unlikely to be high school graduates.[3] In view of the increase in the proportion of blacks and Hispanics, with their lower high school completion rates, in the youthful population, a decline in overall high school graduation rates in the coming years might seem likely. However, the high school graduation rate in the South, which has historically been relatively low, has been rising in recent years for both blacks and whites.[4]

Some analysts, notably Dresch (1975), have predicted that the unfavorable job market for college graduates will depress majority male enrollment rates in the future. We discuss this issue in Supplement C and point out that an improvement in the job market for college graduates is likely to occur in the later half of the 1980s, when the number of graduates will probably decline.

All things considered, we believe that the most reasonable estimate of the future behavior of the enrollment rate of majority males involves no change from 1978 to 2000. This estimate is reflected in Table B-3, which shows our projections of enrollment rates for various groups that received separate consideration.

As for majority women, their enrollment rates—once very much below those of men—have displayed a long history of upward movement (Figure B-2). In fact, women have comprised a majority of the freshman classes for the past two years, are continuing on to graduate school in greater numbers, and are increasingly aspiring to educational and career goals previously considered the province of men. With continuing affirmative action efforts in government, industry, business, and education, we expect that women will be attracted by expanded opportunities for high-level entrance and advancement in the labor market. Thus, we anticipate their enrollments will not only catch up to male rates, but surpass them by 5 percent in the year 2000.

---

[3]For additional discussion of these differences, see the Council's recent report, *Giving Youth a Better Chance* (1979), Section 2.

[4]Mingle (1978).

Table B-3. Undergraduate enrollment rates, actual 1978
and projected 2000

Population group	Enrollment rate	
	1978	2000
16-17 years	.033	.033
18-21 years		
White men	.335	.335
Black men	.231	.335
White women	.315	.352
Black women	.253	.352
22-24 years		
White men	.122	.122
Black men	.120	.122
White women	.078	.128
Black women	.110	.128
25-34		
Men, college-experienced	.079	.079
Men, non-college-experienced	.024	.024
Women, college-experienced	.063	.063
Women, non-college experienced	.025	.025
35 and over		
Men and women, college-experienced	.045	.045

Sources: U.S. Bureau of the Census, *Current Population Reports: School Enrollment* (1979a); and Carnegie Council projections.

Black Enrollment

Future enrollment of black men and women cannot be discussed in the aggregate because of the widely divergent patterns of college participation within the black population. We expect the children of more affluent blacks, many of whom will be second-generation attenders, to continue to be attracted to higher education by the expanding opportunities to fulfill their high educational and career goals. However, those at the bottom of the income distribution appear to compose an "underclass"

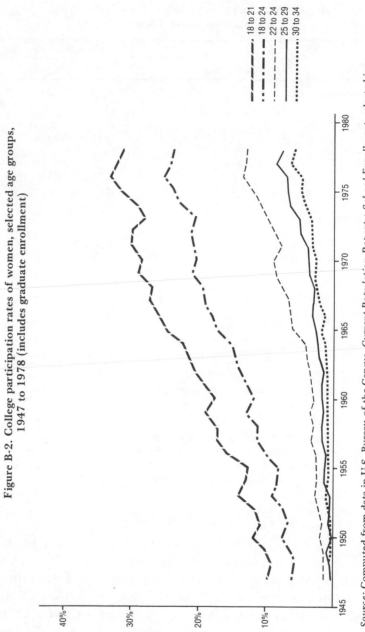

Figure B-2. College participation rates of women, selected age groups, 1947 to 1978 (includes graduate enrollment)

18 to 21
18 to 24
22 to 24
25 to 29
30 to 34

Source: Computed from data in U.S. Bureau of the Census, *Current Population Reports: School Enrollment,* selected issues.

of blacks, caught in a complex web of social, economic, cultural, and educational disadvantages for which we foresee no quick cures. Their plight is likely to get worse before it gets better and will be in stark contrast to the expanding progress of the more affluent blacks. Our assumption that black enrollment rates will reach parity with whites by the year 2000 reflects our view that the rise in enrollment rates of the more affluent blacks will push the overall black participation rate upward.

Recent trends in enrollment rates of whites and blacks by family income quartile are shown in Figures B-3 and B-4. Among white men, there was a declining tendency in the enrollment rate for all income groups in the early years of the decade, followed by a leveling off in recent years. Among white women, the increases have occurred chiefly in the upper-income groups. Among blacks, enrollment rates controlled for family income status now generally exceed those of whites, but the fact that a much larger proportion of blacks comes from low-income families holds down the overall enrollment rate for blacks. Only among black men in the lowest family income quartile does the enrollment rate lag behind that of the corresponding group of white men, and among this group of black men increases in the enrollment are likely to be slow and difficult because of the social and economic problems of black ghetto families.

Hispanic Enrollment

Hispanics present particularly difficult projection problems because of the ethnic and cultural variety within the Hispanic population, and because of the fact that separate data on Hispanics are available only for very recent years. Nearly 60 percent of Hispanics are of Mexican origin (Table B-4), and 60 percent of the Hispanic population is in the Southwest—the five states of Arizona, California, Colorado, New Mexico, and Texas (Figure B-5). New York's Hispanic population, which makes up 13 percent of the total, is predominantly Puerto Rican, while a substantial proportion of the relatively affluent Cubans lives in Florida.

The proportion of low-income families among Hispanics is considerably higher than in the total white population, but

Figure B-3. Enrollment rates of male primary family members aged
18 to 24 by race and family income quartile, 1970 to 1976

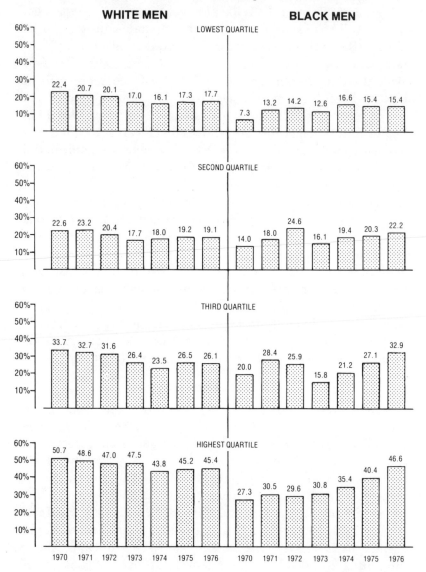

Source: Adapted by Carnegie Council from data in U.S. Bureau of the Census, *Current Population Reports: School Enrollment,* selected issues.

Figure B-4. Enrollment rates of female primary family members aged 18 to 24 by race and family income quartile, 1970 to 1976

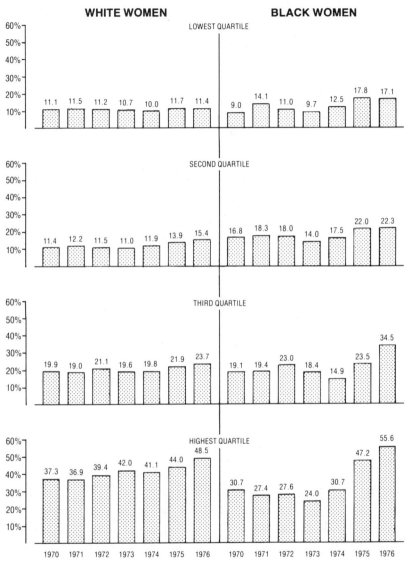

Source: Adapted by Carnegie Council from data in U.S. Bureau of the Census, *Current Population Reports: School Enrollment,* selected issues.

Table B-4. Distribution of the Hispanic population
by country or area of origin, 1978

Type of Spanish origin	Number	Percentage
Mexican	7,151,000	59.4%
Puerto Rican	1,823,000	15.1
Cuban	689,000	5.7
Central or South American	863,000	7.2
Other Spanish origin	1,519,000	12.6

Source: U.S. Bureau of the Census (1979b).

**Figure B-5. Distribution of the Hispanic population by
state of residence, 1978**

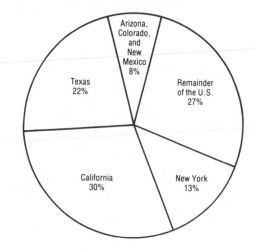

Source: U.S. Bureau of the Census (1979b).

slightly lower than among the blacks.[5] However, high school completion rates are appreciably lower among Hispanics than among blacks, as we have seen, and in some urban ghetto areas, the school dropout rate among Hispanics has been estimated at 85 percent. Cultural mores among some groups of Hispanics do not encourage aspirations for higher education or for profes-

[5] For recent data, see U.S. Bureau of the Census (1979c, table 37).

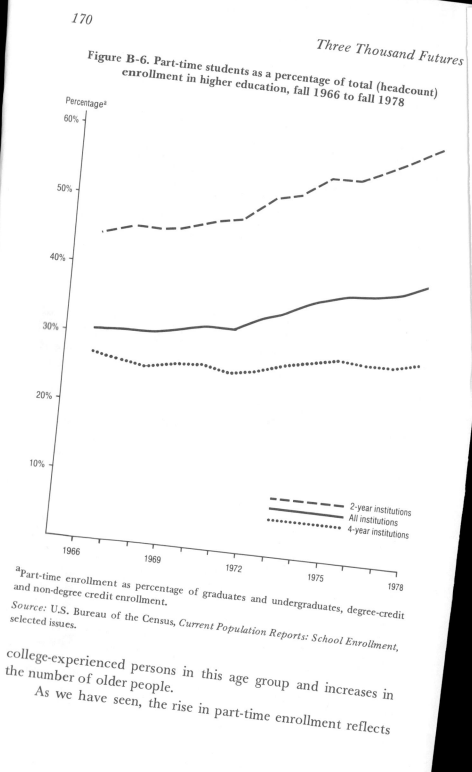

Figure B-6. Part-time students as a percentage of total (headcount) enrollment in higher education, fall 1966 to fall 1978

Percentage[a]

60%

50%

40%

30%

20%

10%

- - - - 2-year institutions
——— All institutions
·········· 4-year institutions

1966   1969   1972   1975   1978

[a]Part-time enrollment as percentage of graduates and undergraduates, degree-credit and non-degree credit enrollment.

Source: U.S. Bureau of the Census, *Current Population Reports: School Enrollment,* selected issues.

college-experienced persons in this age group and increases in the number of older people.

As we have seen, the rise in part-time enrollment reflects

sional career goals among women, and poor English-speaking ability is a handicap for many Hispanics. Cubans tend to attain higher educational levels than other Hispanics.

It is generally agreed that Hispanics were significantly undercounted in the 1970 census for several reasons. No Spanish language forms were used, and few enumerators were bilingual. Many Hispanics live in isolated rural areas, where enumerator access is difficult, or in urban ghetto areas which may appear threatening, especially to non-Spanish-speaking census workers. These conditions are thought to have led to some degree of data estimation based on observation without interviewing. Further, the definition of Spanish origin was broad and was applied inconsistently in different regions. Another significant problem is the large illegal alien Hispanic population that could be expected to avoid being counted. For the 1980 census, bilingual forms and enumerators will be used in conjunction with better identification techniques and extensive public relations programs in the Hispanic community.

We were not able to develop separate enrollment projections for Hispanics, because the Bureau of the Census does not project the Hispanic population separately but includes them in the racial categories of white, black, and other—with 91 to 93 percent of Hispanics counted as white. We do know, however, from 1976 U.S. Office of Civil Rights data, that Hispanics are 4.8 percent of all undergraduate students, and that 59 percent of them are attending two-year institutions compared to only 45 percent of white students. Hispanics received 2.8 percent of baccalaureate degrees awarded during the 1975-76 academic year, 2 percent of masters degrees, 2.6 percent law, 2.3 percent medicine, and less than 1 percent of all doctorates. Enrollment data for Hispanics are also available in Bureau of the Census reports from 1972 on, but the period since 1972 is too short to provide a reliable basis for establishing trends.

Adult and Part-Time Enrollment

In recent years there has been a pronounced increase in adult enrollment and in part-time enrollment. The two trends are clearly interrelated, because the older a student, the more likely he or she is to be enrolled on a part-time basis. However, the growth of part-time enrollment is not entirely explained by the increased enrollment of adults. It is also partly attributable to such developments as the growth of urban institutions, the development of open-door community colleges, and, within community colleges, the relatively rapid growth of occupational programs in the 1970s.

Differences among the enrollment projections of various analysts are frequently attributable to a considerable extent to differing assumptions about future adult enrollment trends. The more optimistic projections assume pronounced increases in adult enrollment. On the other hand, projections based on traditional methods (estimating the future size of the 18-year-old population, the high school graduation rate, the percentage of high school graduates who will enroll in college, and their retention rates through the undergraduate and graduate years) tend to ignore the phenomenon of adult enrollment.

Our projection assumes a moderate increase in adult enrollment rates and in part-time enrollment rates in the future. We have a number of reasons for anticipating an increase in adult enrollment:

1. The more flexible patterns of participation in higher education that have become apparent in the last decade or so. Students stop in and stop out, and thus do not conform to the earlier pattern of entry at age 18 and participation in full-time study until graduation.
2. The impact of technological changes in the economy on occupational needs. Increasingly, it is recognized that many adults will experience occupational shifts during the course of their working lives, and that retraining may be necessary to accomplish those shifts successfully.
3. The fact that future cohorts of adults are more likely to have had some college experience than the typical older adult today. Studies of participation in adult education show that persons with some college experience are much more likely to enroll as adults than those who have not been to college at all. We have taken explicit account of this tendency in

developing our projections of enrollment rates among those aged 25 and older.

In spite of all of these considerations, however, we have had to take into account the fact that the increase in undergraduate enrollment rates of those aged 25 and older—and also of those in the 22- to 24-year-old group—reflected in part the sharp rise in enrollment of Vietnam-era veterans in the first half of the 1970s. Enrollment of veterans, as we have seen, reached a peak in 1975, followed by a decline that is likely to continue for some years to come.

Figure B-6 shows that the most pronounced increase in part-time enrollment has occurred in two-year institutions—from 44 percent of the total in 1966 to 61 percent in 1978. The increase in the percentage of part-time enrollees in four-year institutions has been much more moderate. Overall, part-time students accounted for 41 percent of all students in 1978.

In developing our projection of adult enrollment, we estimated enrollment among those aged 25 to 29 for those with college experience and those with no college experience, finding that enrollment rates were much higher for the former than for the latter group. We then assumed that the percentage with college experience in this age group would remain relatively constant in the future and that the aging adult population would gradually include a larger proportion of persons with college experience rates comparable to those of the present population aged 25 to 29. Thus, this factor would tend to induce higher enrollment rates among aging cohorts in the future. Table B presents these estimates only in summary form. It indicates, for example, that 7.9 percent of college-experienced men aged to 34 were enrolled in 1978, compared with 2.4 percent of men with no college experience. In the 35 and older group it shows an enrollment rate of 4.5 percent, which relates only to those with some college experience (we assume that enrollment is negligible among those with no college experience). This enrollment rate is assumed to remain constant to 2000, but it must be kept in mind that the enrollment numbers involved (on an basis) will tend to rise because of increases in the percentage not only the increased enrollment rates of older persons, but other factors as well. We estimate, in developing our projections, that the proportion of all students enrolled on a part-time basis will increase 10 percent by the year 2000.

The 16- to 17-Year-Old Group

We anticipate some increase in the enrollment rate of those aged 16 to 17, as a result of programs encouraging high school seniors to enroll in nearby colleges, lowering of the age of admission to community colleges, and the like. However, we make no explicit adjustment for this increase in our projections, because the impact is expected to be a one-time event (though spread over a period of several years) and not a continuing source of increasing enrollment rates. Enrollment rates of 16- and 17-year olds, in any case, are so small that a modest increase would have little effect on total undergraduate enrollment.

As we suggested earlier, we believe that many colleges will make serious efforts to increase student retention rates in the coming period of increased competition for students. In fact, many institutions are already developing improved retention programs. The colleges that we consider most vulnerable to declining enrollment—less-selective private colleges—are in a particularly good position to develop counseling and remedial programs aimed at improved retention in the more personal environment of private colleges, many of which are small. In the community college sector, we anticipate little change in retention rates for students not enrolled in transfer programs, but we believe that those aiming at transfer to a four-year school will find opportunities for transfer improved and will also be better qualified for transfer because of improved retention programs in two-year colleges, some of which are now providing three rather than two years of study preparing for transfer. For these reasons, we anticipate that students who, under present circumstances, would be likely to drop out will, by the year 2000, increase the time spent enrolled in college by about 20 percent. This assumption is used for 18- to 24-year olds, because they are considered to be more responsive to retention programs of institutions, whereas enrollment decisions of older persons are more likely to be influenced by factors external to the institution, especially those related to job opportunities.

A review of recent changes in dropout rates also lends some support to our assumption that retention will be improved in the future (see the discussion in Section 3).

Postbaccalaureate Enrollment

Historical data on graduate enrollment include, for the most part, only persons enrolled for master's and doctor's degrees. They do not include first-professional students (enrolled for such degrees as M.D., D.D.S., and J.D.), who were lumped with undergraduates. Only for recent years are separate data readily available on first-professional enrollment, although data on first-professional degrees conferred are available for earlier periods.

Figure B-7 shows the pronounced rise in the proportion of total headcount enrollment accounted for by graduate enrollment from 1890 on. The share represented by graduate enrollment fell somewhat in the 1950s, experienced a sharp recovery in the early 1960s, and then tended to level off.[6] The behavior of the graduate share of FTE enrollment—available only for recent years—has been similar.

Although the growth of graduate enrollment has slowed down somewhat in the 1970s, along with the growth of undergraduate enrollment, the overall changes mask a pronounced shift in the composition of graduate enrollment. As the job market for Ph.D.'s has worsened—a trend that began in 1969—there has been a decided decline in enrollment in the more academically oriented Ph.D. programs, and a pronounced rise in enrollment in professional fields, such as architecture, business administration, health professions, and public affairs and services.[7] The increase in some of the professional fields has

[6]Prior to 1976, all unclassified enrollment was included in undergraduate enrollment, but in the last few years it has been allocated to undergraduate and to graduate enrollment as appropriate. We have adjusted the figures for 1970 to 1975 for consistency with later data.

[7]For a detailed analysis of these changes, along with projections to 1989, see von Rothkirch (1978).

sional career goals among women, and poor English-speaking ability is a handicap for many Hispanics. Cubans tend to attain higher educational levels than other Hispanics.

It is generally agreed that Hispanics were significantly undercounted in the 1970 census for several reasons. No Spanish language forms were used, and few enumerators were bilingual. Many Hispanics live in isolated rural areas, where enumerator access is difficult, or in urban ghetto areas which may appear threatening, especially to non-Spanish-speaking census workers. These conditions are thought to have led to some degree of data estimation based on observation without interviewing. Further, the definition of Spanish origin was broad and was applied inconsistently in different regions. Another significant problem is the large illegal alien Hispanic population that could be expected to avoid being counted. For the 1980 census, bilingual forms and enumerators will be used in conjunction with better identification techniques and extensive public relations programs in the Hispanic community.

We were not able to develop separate enrollment projections for Hispanics, because the Bureau of the Census does not project the Hispanic population separately but includes them in the racial categories of white, black, and other—with 91 to 93 percent of Hispanics counted as white. We do know, however, from 1976 U.S. Office of Civil Rights data, that Hispanics are 4.8 percent of all undergraduate students, and that 59 percent of them are attending two-year institutions compared to only 45 percent of white students. Hispanics received 2.8 percent of baccalaureate degrees awarded during the 1975-76 academic year, 2 percent of masters degrees, 2.6 percent law, 2.3 percent medicine, and less than 1 percent of all doctorates. Enrollment data for Hispanics are also available in Bureau of the Census reports from 1972 on, but the period since 1972 is too short to provide a reliable basis for establishing trends.

Adult and Part-Time Enrollment

In recent years there has been a pronounced increase in adult enrollment and in part-time enrollment. The two trends are clearly interrelated, because the older a student, the more likely he or she is to be enrolled on a part-time basis. However, the growth of part-time enrollment is not entirely explained by the increased enrollment of adults. It is also partly attributable to such developments as the growth of urban institutions, the development of open-door community colleges, and, within community colleges, the relatively rapid growth of occupational programs in the 1970s.

Differences among the enrollment projections of various analysts are frequently attributable to a considerable extent to differing assumptions about future adult enrollment trends. The more optimistic projections assume pronounced increases in adult enrollment. On the other hand, projections based on traditional methods (estimating the future size of the 18-year-old population, the high school graduation rate, the percentage of high school graduates who will enroll in college, and their retention rates through the undergraduate and graduate years) tend to ignore the phenomenon of adult enrollment.

Our projection assumes a moderate increase in adult enrollment rates and in part-time enrollment rates in the future. We have a number of reasons for anticipating an increase in adult enrollment:

1. The more flexible patterns of participation in higher education that have become apparent in the last decade or so. Students stop in and stop out, and thus do not conform to the earlier pattern of entry at age 18 and participation in full-time study until graduation.
2. The impact of technological changes in the economy on occupational needs. Increasingly, it is recognized that many adults will experience occupational shifts during the course of their working lives, and that retraining may be necessary to accomplish those shifts successfully.
3. The fact that future cohorts of adults are more likely to have had some college experience than the typical older adult today. Studies of participation in adult education show that persons with some college experience are much more likely to enroll as adults than those who have not been to college at all. We have taken explicit account of this tendency in

developing our projections of enrollment rates among those aged 25 and older.

In spite of all of these considerations, however, we have had to take into account the fact that the increase in undergraduate enrollment rates of those aged 25 and older—and also of those in the 22- to 24-year-old group—reflected in part the sharp rise in enrollment of Vietnam-era veterans in the first half of the 1970s. Enrollment of veterans, as we have seen, reached a peak in 1975, followed by a decline that is likely to continue for some years to come.

Figure B-6 shows that the most pronounced increase in part-time enrollment has occurred in two-year institutions—from 44 percent of the total in 1966 to 61 percent in 1978. The increase in the percentage of part-time enrollees in four-year institutions has been much more moderate. Overall, part-time students accounted for 41 percent of all students in 1978.

In developing our projection of adult enrollment, we estimated enrollment among those aged 25 to 29 for those with college experience and those with no college experience, finding that enrollment rates were much higher for the former than for the latter group. We then assumed that the percentage with college experience in this age group would remain relatively constant in the future and that the aging adult population would gradually include a larger proportion of persons with college experience rates comparable to those of the present population aged 25 to 29. Thus, this factor would tend to induce higher enrollment rates among aging cohorts in the future. Table B-3 presents these estimates only in summary form. It indicates, for example, that 7.9 percent of college-experienced men aged 25 to 34 were enrolled in 1978, compared with 2.4 percent of men with no college experience. In the 35 and older group it shows an enrollment rate of 4.5 percent, which relates only to those with some college experience (we assume that enrollment is negligible among those with no college experience). This enrollment rate is assumed to remain constant to 2000, but it must be kept in mind that the enrollment numbers involved (on an FTE basis) will tend to rise because of increases in the percentage of

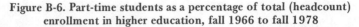

Figure B-6. Part-time students as a percentage of total (headcount) enrollment in higher education, fall 1966 to fall 1978

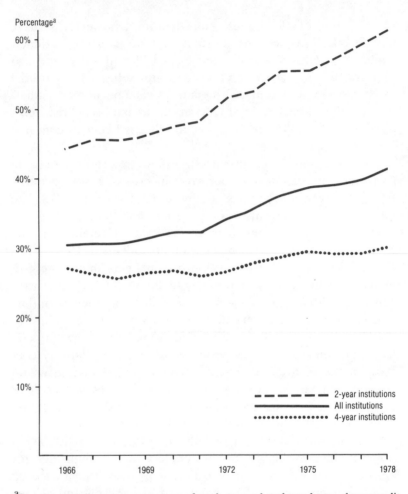

^aPart-time enrollment as percentage of graduates and undergraduates, degree-credit and non-degree credit enrollment.

Source: U.S. Bureau of the Census, *Current Population Reports: School Enrollment,* selected issues.

college-experienced persons in this age group and increases in the number of older people.

As we have seen, the rise in part-time enrollment reflects

not only the increased enrollment rates of older persons, but other factors as well. We estimate, in developing our projections, that the proportion of all students enrolled on a part-time basis will increase 10 percent by the year 2000.

The 16- to 17-Year-Old Group

We anticipate some increase in the enrollment rate of those aged 16 to 17, as a result of programs encouraging high school seniors to enroll in nearby colleges, lowering of the age of admission to community colleges, and the like. However, we make no explicit adjustment for this increase in our projections, because the impact is expected to be a one-time event (though spread over a period of several years) and not a continuing source of increasing enrollment rates. Enrollment rates of 16- and 17-year olds, in any case, are so small that a modest increase would have little effect on total undergraduate enrollment.

As we suggested earlier, we believe that many colleges will make serious efforts to increase student retention rates in the coming period of increased competition for students. In fact, many institutions are already developing improved retention programs. The colleges that we consider most vulnerable to declining enrollment—less-selective private colleges—are in a particularly good position to develop counseling and remedial programs aimed at improved retention in the more personal environment of private colleges, many of which are small. In the community college sector, we anticipate little change in retention rates for students not enrolled in transfer programs, but we believe that those aiming at transfer to a four-year school will find opportunities for transfer improved and will also be better qualified for transfer because of improved retention programs in two-year colleges, some of which are now providing three rather than two years of study preparing for transfer. For these reasons, we anticipate that students who, under present circumstances, would be likely to drop out will, by the year 2000, increase the time spent enrolled in college by about 20 percent. This assumption is used for 18- to 24-year olds, because they are considered to be more responsive to retention programs of institutions, whereas enrollment decisions of older persons are more likely to be influenced by factors external to the institution, especially those related to job opportunities.

A review of recent changes in dropout rates also lends some support to our assumption that retention will be improved in the future (see the discussion in Section 3).

Postbaccalaureate Enrollment

Historical data on graduate enrollment include, for the most part, only persons enrolled for master's and doctor's degrees. They do not include first-professional students (enrolled for such degrees as M.D., D.D.S., and J.D.), who were lumped with undergraduates. Only for recent years are separate data readily available on first-professional enrollment, although data on first-professional degrees conferred are available for earlier periods.

Figure B-7 shows the pronounced rise in the proportion of total headcount enrollment accounted for by graduate enrollment from 1890 on. The share represented by graduate enrollment fell somewhat in the 1950s, experienced a sharp recovery in the early 1960s, and then tended to level off.[6] The behavior of the graduate share of FTE enrollment—available only for recent years—has been similar.

Although the growth of graduate enrollment has slowed down somewhat in the 1970s, along with the growth of undergraduate enrollment, the overall changes mask a pronounced shift in the composition of graduate enrollment. As the job market for Ph.D.'s has worsened—a trend that began in 1969—there has been a decided decline in enrollment in the more academically oriented Ph.D. programs, and a pronounced rise in enrollment in professional fields, such as architecture, business administration, health professions, and public affairs and services.[7] The increase in some of the professional fields has

[6]Prior to 1976, all unclassified enrollment was included in undergraduate enrollment, but in the last few years it has been allocated to undergraduate and to graduate enrollment as appropriate. We have adjusted the figures for 1970 to 1975 for consistency with later data.

[7]For a detailed analysis of these changes, along with projections to 1989, see von Rothkirch (1978).

Figure B-7. Graduate enrollment as percentage of total headcount enrollment, 1890 to 1978, and as percentage of total FTE enrollment, 1963 to 1978

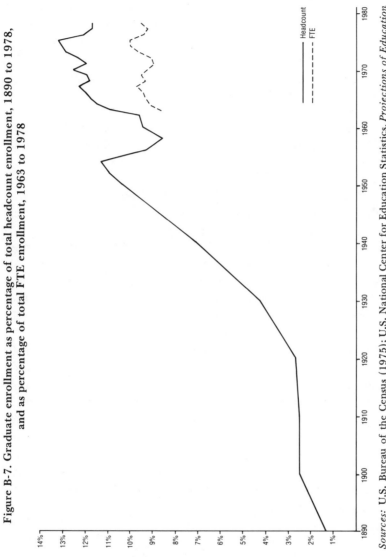

Sources: U.S. Bureau of the Census (1975); U.S. National Center for Education Statistics, *Projections of Education Statistics*, selected issues.

been dramatic. Moreover, since the standard graduate degree in many of these professional fields is the M.A. rather than the Ph.D., the number of master's degrees awarded has displayed a fairly steady upward trend, whereas the number of doctor's degrees earned leveled off in the mid-1970s and, more recently, has been declining. Interestingly, however, the decline in the number of doctorates awarded has occurred only among men, whereas the number of doctor's degrees awarded to women has steadily increased during the 1970s. Between 1972 and 1978, the number of doctor's degrees awarded to men fell from 27,757 to 22,537, or 19 percent, while the number awarded to women rose from 5,287 to 8,313, or 57 percent (National Research Council, 1979, p. 3).

The number of first-professional students rose from about 170,000 in 1970 to about 240,000 in 1976, or about 43 percent. Although first-professional enrollment will probably continue to increase somewhat, the rate of increase may well slow down, because the pronounced expansion of medical schools that began in the late 1960s will soon have run its course, the outlook in the job market for lawyers is uncertain, and other first-professional programs tend to have relatively small enrollment.

Adding first-professional enrollment to graduate enrollment, we find that total postbaccalaureate enrollment increased from about 1.2 million in 1970 to 1.6 million in 1976, or about 33 percent. The rate of increase of postbaccalaureate enrollment is likely to slow down somewhat in the 1980s, as the number of recipients of B.A. degrees declines, but we anticipate that postbaccalaureate enrollment will not decline as much as undergraduate enrollment. The long-run upward trend in the percentage of students going on for advanced degrees and the tendency of adults to come back for graduate or professional study after several years of employment are likely to continue. These trends have their roots in the long-run rise in the demand for persons with highly specialized, advanced training.

References

Carnegie Council on Policy Studies in Higher Education. *Giving Youth a Better Chance: Options for Education, Work, and Service.* San Francisco: Jossey-Bass, 1979.

Dresch, S. P. "Educational Saturation: A Demographic-Economic Model." *AAUP Bulletin*, Autumn 1975, *61* (3), 239-247.

Haggstrom, G. "The Growth of Enrollment in Higher Education in the United States." Berkeley, Calif.: Carnegie Commission on Higher Education, unpublished paper, 1971.

Mingle, J. R. *Black Enrollment in Higher Education: Trends in the Nation and the South.* Atlanta: Southern Regional Education Board, 1978.

National Research Council, Commission on Human Resources. *Summary Report 1978: Doctorate Recipients from United States Universities.* Washington, D.C.: National Academy of Sciences, 1979.

U.S. Bureau of the Census. *Historical Statistics of the United States, Colonial Times to 1970.* Bicentennial Edition. Part 2. Washington, D.C.: 1975.

U.S. Bureau of the Census. *Current Population Reports: Projections of the Population of the United States, 1977 to 2050.* Series P-25, No. 704. Washington, D.C.: 1977.

U.S. Bureau of the Census. *Current Population Reports: School Enrollment—Social and Economic Characteristics of Students: October 1978 (Advance Report).* An annual series. Series P-20, No. 335. Washington, D.C.: 1979a, and selected issues.

U.S. Bureau of the Census. *Current Population Reports: Persons of Spanish Origin in the United States: March 1978.* Series P-20, No. 339. Washington, D.C.: 1979b.

U.S. Bureau of the Census. *Current Population Reports: Money Income in 1977 of Families and Persons in the United States.* Series P-60, No. 118. Washington, D.C.: 1979c.

U.S. National Center for Education Statistics. *Digest of Education Statistics, 1977-78.* Washington, D.C.: 1978, and selected issues.

U.S. National Center for Education Statistics. *Projections of Education Statistics.* An annual series. Washington, D.C.: selected issues.

U.S. National Center for Health Statistics. *Monthly Vital Statistics Report.* A monthly series. Washington, D.C.: Feb. 1979, *27* (11), and selected issues.

U.S. Veterans Administration. *Veterans Benefits Under Current Educational Programs: Information.* A quarterly series. Washington, D.C.: selected issues.

von Rothkirch, C. *Field Disaggregated Analysis and Projections of Graduate Enrollment and Higher Degree Projection.* Technical Report No. 5. Berkeley, Calif.: Carnegie Council on Policy Studies in Higher Education, 1978.

The Labor Market and Higher Education

Throughout most of American history, the value of a college degree in opening the door to high-status and well-paid jobs has been taken for granted. Never was the confidence in a high rate of economic return from investment in a college education greater than in the 1960s, when young people and their parents became familiar with estimates indicating that the average lifetime incomes of college graduates were nearly $200,000 more than those of high school graduates. To be sure, the gains were not nearly so impressive as this for women or for blacks, but the situation began to improve even for these less-favored groups in the labor force under the impetus of the civil rights movement from the mid-1960s onward.

All of this changed in the 1970s. College graduates encountered much stiffer competition in the labor market and frequently had to settle for jobs that would have been regarded as unsuitable in the halcyon 1960s—jobs that were not in the favored professional or managerial categories but lower down on the occupational ladder. Relative incomes of college graduates also became less favorable, at least for younger age groups. The extent of the change, however, was exaggerated by some analysts—most notably by Freeman in *The Over-Educated American* (1976) who compared the relative incomes of college

This supplement was prepared by Margaret S. Gordon, Associate Director, and Charlotte Alhadeff, Research Specialist.

graduates in the early 1970s with their relative position around 1968, when the ratio of the average income of college graduates to that of high school graduates was exceptionally high by historical standards. As we will show, if changes over a longer period than the above are taken into account, the comparative position of college graduates, income-wise and in terms of types of jobs obtained, altered to a much more moderate extent than Freeman's data show.

We believe that the relative position of college graduates in the labor market will become more favorable in the later part of the 1980s when the supply of new recipients of bachelor's degrees will level off or decline. The reasons for this prediction are made clearer by considering the historical changes in the labor market for college graduates.

Historical Trends

The first seven decades of the present century were characterized by a steady (or practically steady) gain in the educational attainment of the population. In 1900, only about 6 percent of the relevant age group graduated from high school, and only about 4 percent were enrolled in college. By 1940, almost one-half of the age group graduated from high school, and undergraduate enrollment in college amounted to about 15 percent of the 18-21 year age group. Since 1940, the gains in educational attainment can be traced (on the basis of more detailed data) for a relatively youthful age group, for which, of course, the increases show up much more quickly than they do for the entire population (Figure C-1). A number of striking points are revealed by these data:

1. In terms of gains in percentage points, progress has accelerated since 1940, for example, about 47 percentage points in the proportion with four years of high school or more in the 37 years from 1940 to 1977 compared with about 33 percentage points in the 40 years from 1900 to 1940. The acceleration is even more pronounced for the percentage with four years of college or more.
2. Somewhat surprisingly, the percentage reporting four years of high school or more ("or more" signifies some post-high

Figure C-1. Percentage of persons aged 25 to 29 who had completed
four years of high school or more and who had completed four years
of college or more, by race, 1940 to 1977

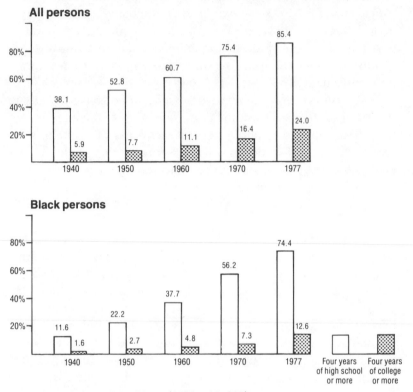

Source: U.S. Bureau of the Census (1978, table 225).

school education) increased by 10 percentage points between
1970 and 1977, even though the high school graduation rate
(the annual number of high school graduates reported by
schools divided by the 17-year-old population) leveled off at
about 75 percent from the late 1960s on. The gain in the percentage of 25-29 year olds reporting four years of high school
or more probably reflects, at least in part, the widening availability of high school equivalency certificates and the increasing availability of community college or postsecondary technical education to young people who are not high school

graduates. It may also, however, reflect the reluctance of some respondents in a household survey to admit that they (or members of their households for whom they are reporting) are not high school graduates.

3. The percentage reporting four years of college or more has also risen sharply in the 1970s, in spite of the decline in the college enrollment rate of youthful white males (noted in Supplement B). When the figures are broken down by sex, moreover, they show very little difference between the gains of men and those of women.

4. The gap in educational attainment of blacks and whites has narrowed markedly since 1940—probably reflecting the urbanization of the black population more than any other single factor—and this narrowing occurred at a particularly pronounced rate between 1970 and 1977. (Here, however, it is important to note that the percentage of blacks reporting four years of college or more reached 13.0 percent in 1976 and fell slightly from 1976 to 1977.)

The demand for college graduates has historically risen along with the increase in supply. The surplus in the supply of college graduates that developed in the 1970s was largely unprecedented. Only in the Great Depression of the 1930s had a comparable situation been experienced. The chief explanation of the rising demand for college graduates has been the long-run upward trend in the proportion of the labor force engaged in professional and managerial occupations (Figure C-2). Here again, however, we note a pronounced acceleration of the rate of change from 1940 on, at least in the case of men. Thus, the sharp rise in the percentage of young people graduating from college after 1940 occurred in an environment in which the demand for college graduates was increasing sharply. In the case of women, the increase was delayed, but after 1970 the percentage of women employed in professional and managerial occupations rose considerably more in percentage points than did that of men.

What accounted for the pronounced increase in demand for college graduates in recent decades? Here we must distin-

Figure C-2. Professional and managerial workers as a percentage
of all workers, by sex, 1900 to 1978

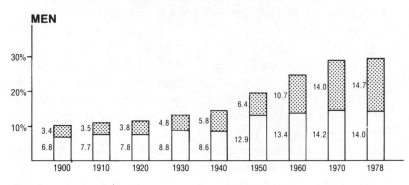

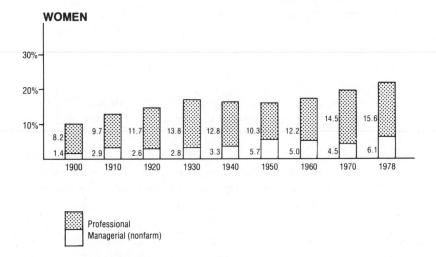

Sources: Carnegie Commission on Higher Education (1973, p. 26); U.S. Bureau of
Labor Statistics (1979a, table 22).

guish between the change in the 1940s, which reflected a partially temporary set of influences, and the gains of the 1950s
and 1960s. The percentage of men employed in managerial
occupations increased sharply from 1940 to 1950, in considerable part because of the many World War II veterans who
started their own small businesses after the war, assisted by low-

interest loans under the GI bill and some state programs. By and large, these small businesses flourished under the favorable conditions prevailing after the war, but in the mid-1950s the failure rate increased, and a drop in self-employment, which persisted for more than 10 years, occurred (Carnegie Commission, 1973, p. 28). Many of the men who went into small businesses, of course, were not college graduates—Figure C-2 relates to all professional and managerial workers as a percentage of all workers, not just to college graduates—but a good many of them had some college education.

The primary factors responsible for the particularly favorable job market for college graduates in the 1950s and 1960s were: (1) the sharp rise in the percentage of the Gross National Product (GNP) spent on research and development (R&D) from about 1952 to the mid-1960s; (2) the related expansion of the aerospace industries; and (3) the progress of the huge cohorts of postwar babies through the school system and on up into college, creating a greatly increased demand for teachers at each level of schooling as they proceeded. Moreover, during the 1960s, despite the enormous increase in the number of recipients of bachelor's degrees, the impact on the supply of graduates seeking jobs was held down by the greatly increased propensity of graduates to go on to graduate and professional training—motivated for many of the men by the prospect of draft deferral, like the decision of many to enroll in college in the first place.

All of this changed quite drastically toward the end of the 1960s. Federal expenditures on research and development declined as a percentage of GNP; the aerospace industries moved into a period of dwindling employment; and the drop in the absolute number of live births from the mid-1960s on led to a decline in the number of children entering elementary school by the end of the 1960s. Moreover, sharp cutbacks in federal fellowships and new restrictions on draft deferrals for graduate students in the late 1960s reduced the propensity to go on to graduate work and led to unprecedented numbers of college seniors seeking jobs each spring.

The most lasting impact of these changes has been in the

job market for teachers and for college faculty members—although the full severity of the impact on the market for faculty members will not be felt until the early 1980s, when the shrinking cohorts of young people born in the mid-1960s and later reach college age. It is for this reason that the fields most severely affected are those in which graduates depend primarily on schools and colleges for job opportunities.

Analysts, like Freeman, who have tended to concentrate on comparisons between the 1970s and the exceptionally favorable 1960s, have created an exaggerated impression of the shift in the job market for college graduates. Whether we consider the relative incomes of college graduates or the percentages who are employed in occupations below professional and managerial levels, we find that the situation in the 1970s is not greatly different from that of the 1950s—although clearly inferior to that of the 1960s.

- Starting salaries for recipients of bachelor's degrees are indeed lower in relation to those of employees in all industries than they were in the 1960s, but they continue to be well above their relative levels of the early 1950s (Endicott, 1976). Moreover, relative starting salaries for women have approached those for men and in 1979 actually exceeded those for men in engineering and in finance/economics (College Placement Council, 1979b, p. 5).
- The ratio of the median income of male college graduates to that of male high school graduates declined somewhat between 1969 and 1977 but in 1977 was almost equal to its level of 1959 and well above the ratio for 1949. For women, the ratio in 1977 was equal to that of 1959 and far above its 1949 level (Figure C-3).
- The change in the job market, of course, has affected younger graduates primarily, and thus we might expect incomes of young college graduates to have shown a particularly sharp drop in relation to those of high school graduates of comparable age. In fact, a substantial drop did occur between 1970 and 1977 for both men and women aged 25 to 34, but here again the ratio for men remained higher than in 1949

Figure C-3. Ratio of median income of college graduates to
median income of high school graduates, persons aged 25 and over,
by sex, 1949 to 1977

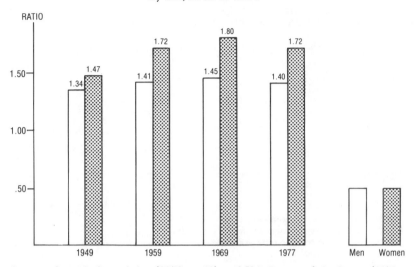

Sources: Carnegie Commission (1973, p. 50); and U.S. Bureau of the Census (1979, table 47).

and for women was far above its 1949 level (Figure C-4). The data for men suggest that the trough may have passed, but for women the comparative income of college graduates has continued to decline in recent years. The ratios for women who are year-round full-time workers are considerably lower than those for all women with income, reflecting the fact that, among all women with income, the higher incomes of college graduates are partly explained by the fact that they are more likely to be year-round full-time workers. But, even for year-round full-time workers, the ratios for women have dropped sharply. It is not much of an exaggeration to attribute the sharp swing in the ratios for women to the changes in the job market for teachers, which employed approximately one-half of all female college graduates who were in the labor force in the 1960s. Not only did the percentage of women graduates going into teaching increase in the 1950s and 1960s, but the relative incomes of teachers rose. In the 1970s, the sharp decline in the demand for teachers has forced a rising propor-

Figure C-4. Selected ratios of average incomes of college graduates
to those of high school graduates, for persons aged 25 to 34, by sex,
1949 to 1977

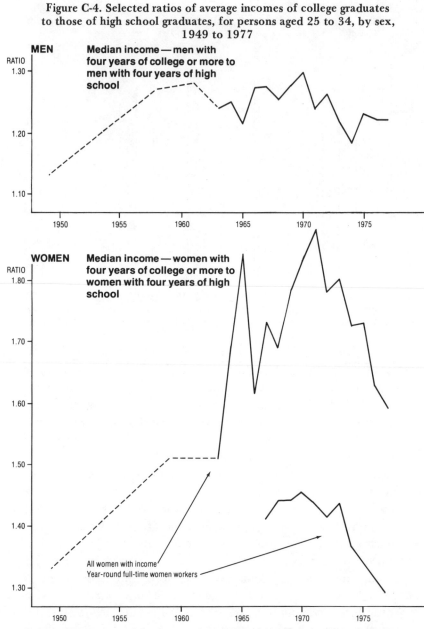

Sources: U.S. Bureau of the Census, *Current Population Reports,* Series P-60, appropriate years.

tion of female college graduates to accept lower-paid jobs, such as clerical and sales positions.

• In a more intensive analysis of the comparative income of recent male college graduates, Smith and Welch (1978) computed ratios of earnings of college graduates aged 25 to 34 to those of high school graduates aged 20 to 29, arguing that a high school graduate who has not gone on to college has been in the labor market longer and therefore has benefited more from experience than a college graduate of the same age. Their data, which are shown in Table C-1, indicate greater

Table C-1. Ratios of earnings of college graduates aged 25 to 34
to those of high school graduates aged 20 to 29, 1967 to 1975

	Weekly wages	*Annual earnings*
1967	1.52	1.56
1968	1.54	1.55
1969	1.55	1.57
1970	1.57	1.62
1971	1.54	1.64
1972	1.51	1.61
1973	1.51	1.61
1974	1.47	1.58
1975	1.48	1.69

Source: Smith and Welch (1978).

stability in the ratios over the entire period from 1967 to 1975, especially in terms of annual earnings, when the college graduates are paired with the younger age group of high school graduates than when the comparisons are made for the 25-to-34 age group alone. In fact, in terms of annual earnings, the relative position of college graduates in 1975 was superior to that of 1967. The higher ratios in terms of annual earnings than in terms of weekly wages are explained by the fact that college graduates are much less likely than high school graduates to experience unemployment.

• Smith and Welch (1978) also compare the behavior of earnings of men in their peak earnings years—ages 35 to 49 in the case of high school graduates and ages 40 to 54 in the case of college graduates—with those of young men with the same number of years of educational attainment (Table C-2). These tables show, in the words of the authors, that "for both annual earnings and weekly wages and for *both high school and college graduates,* the fall in the relative incomes of new entrants dwarfs any changes examined in the relative wages across schooling groups." They concluded that "it is a story of the overcrowded new entrant and not the overeducated American." (We show only annual earnings in Table C-2.)

Table C-2. Ratios of annual earnings of high school graduates and college graduates in peak earnings years to those of new entrants to the labor force, 1967 to 1975

	High school graduates aged 35 to 49 to those aged 20 to 24	College graduates aged 40 to 54 to those aged 25 to 29
1967	1.56	1.63
1968	1.66	1.52
1969	1.64	1.55
1970	1.73	1.54
1971	1.81	1.67
1972	1.84	1.73
1973	1.86	1.71
1974	1.86	1.79
1975	1.93	1.91

Source: Smith and Welch (1978).

· The reports of college graduates accepting blue-collar and service jobs are supported by occupational data, which show that the percentages of college graduates employed in professional occupations fell substantially between 1970 and 1977 for both men and women, whereas the proportions in occupations below professional and managerial levels rose significantly (Figure C-5). Yet the situation in 1977 somewhat resembled that of 1950, and, in fact, the percentages employed

Figure C-5. Changes in the occupational distribution of college graduates, by sex, 1950, 1970, and 1977

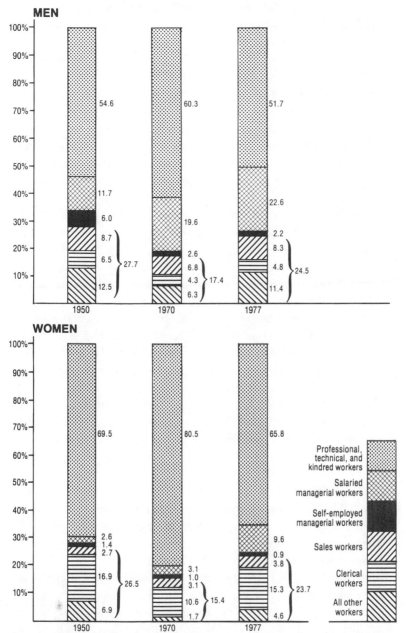

Sources: Computed from data in U.S. Bureau of the Census (1956, pp. 107-109; 1973); U.S. Bureau of Labor Statistics (1977).

below professional and managerial levels were smaller than in 1950. The proportions employed above these levels were held up by a rise in the percentages employed in salaried managerial positions—particularly pronounced for women after 1970, reflecting in large part the impact of the civil rights movement on job opportunities for women.

The thoughtful reader will immediately recognize that, since the increase in employment of college graduates in lower-level jobs must have occurred chiefly among the young, the proportion of young graduates forced to accept jobs below the professional or managerial level must have been exceedingly high to bring about so substantial a change in the occupational distribution of college graduates between 1970 and 1977. The Bureau of Labor Statistics has very recently (1979b, pp. 18-19) published data indicating the contrasts between the types of jobs recent college graduates obtained in the period from 1969 to 1976 compared with those they obtained from 1962 to 1969. All in all, 65 percent entered professional or managerial positions in the more recent period, compared with 90 percent in the earlier period. The decline occurred entirely in the professional fields—from 73 percent in 1962-1969 to 46 percent in 1969-1976—whereas the percentage entering managerial positions increased slightly from 17 to 19 percent. Data are not available for the two sexes separately, but Figure C-5 suggests that the drop in the percentage getting professional jobs was much more severe for women than for men, whereas the percentage getting salaried managerial positions rose more markedly for women. In fact, although the overall position of women college graduates in the 1970s has been unfavorable, the large gain in the proportion going into managerial positions has been a bright spot in the picture, as has the improvement in entering salaries for women in such positions, noted earlier.

· Historically, job opportunities for black male college graduates have been inferior, and a relatively large proportion of them have been employed as clergymen and schoolteachers—traditionally low-paid occupations. This helps to explain why incomes of nonwhite male college graduates compared even

more unfavorably with those of whites with comparable educational attainment in 1949 than did the incomes of nonwhite men with lower levels of education (Figure C-6). Rela-

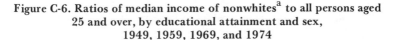

Figure C-6. Ratios of median income of nonwhites[a] to all persons aged
25 and over, by educational attainment and sex,
1949, 1959, 1969, and 1974

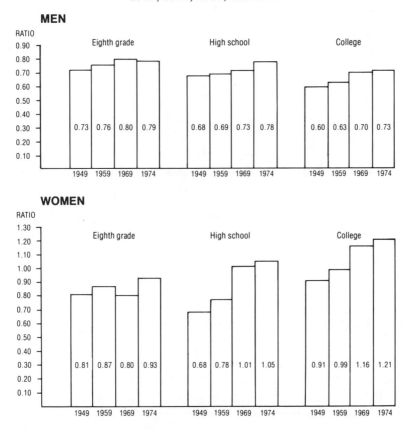

[a]Data for 1969 and 1974 relate to blacks only; for earlier years, to nonwhites.

Sources: U.S. Bureau of the Census, *Current Population Reports,* Series P-60, appropriate years.

tive incomes of black male college graduates continued far
below those of white male graduates as recently as 1974, but
the comparisons for men of all ages fail to reveal the striking

improvement in the relative position of recent black male college graduates so thoroughly documented by Freeman (1977) and indicated in Figure C-7.

Figure C-7. Ratio of mean income of black male to white male high school and college graduates, aged 25 to 29, 1959, 1969, and 1973

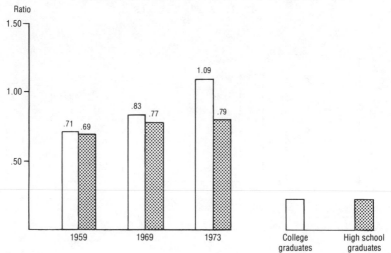

Sources: Freeman (1977, p. 34); figures for 1973 are from unpublished data.

Rates of Return

The human capital school within the economics profession regards studying for a college degree as a decision to invest in enlarging one's human capital. Through the accumulation of knowledge, one develops embodied human capital which later yields an annual return from the investment in the form of higher income, much as investment in physical capital yields an annual return. The rate of return is estimated by computing the annual additional after-tax earnings of, let us say, college graduates over high school graduates (discounting future earnings at an appropriate interest rate) as a percentage of the average cost to the individual of achieving a college degree. Included in the cost of achieving a degree are educational expenses plus forgone earnings. Estimates of the rates of return from investment in a college degree have consistently indicated that they are comparable to or even higher than the going rates of return from investment in physical capital, ranging from 10 percent upward.

Illustrative of many estimates of rates of return—selected because they permit comparisons over three decades and show results for women as well as men—are those in Figure C-8. Not

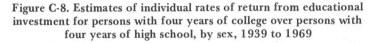

Figure C-8. Estimates of individual rates of return from educational investment for persons with four years of college over persons with four years of high school, by sex, 1939 to 1969

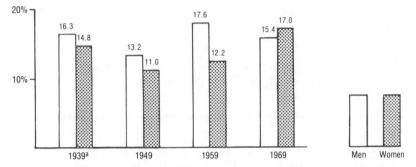

[a]1939 estimates are for persons with some income; this makes them more nearly comparable with estimates for later years, which relate to persons in the labor force, than alternative 1939 estimates, which include persons with no income.

Source: Carnoy and Marenbach (1975, p. 316).

surprisingly, more recent estimates by Freeman (1976, p. 26) show a decline of 2.5 to 3.5 percentage points in rates of return between 1968 and 1973. Since relative earnings of college graduates have not risen appreciably since 1973, rates of return have probably not changed much since then.

Estimates of the rate of return must be treated with caution. They express a relationship that prevails at a given point in time between average lifetime incomes of college graduates and average lifetime incomes of high school graduates. They do not tell us how the individual college graduate will fare—he may do much better than the average or much worse. They do not tell us how life cycles in earnings might change over time. The advantage of college graduates, moreover, can not be attributed entirely to longer education. A portion must be attributed to ability, since it is the more able students who are particularly likely to go to college. However, studies that have attempted to measure the comparative contribution of ability (for example, Taubman and Wales, 1974) indicate that differences in ability explain only a minor portion of the superior earnings of college graduates.

More basic objections have been raised, especially by writers affiliated with the "New Left," about the assumption of human capital theorists that earnings differences are explained by differences in productivity of workers. In fact, argue these writers (for example, Bowles and Gintis, 1975), earnings differentials are strongly influenced by differences in the bargaining power of various groups in the labor force, by the degree of monopoly or oligopoly in different industries, by the rate of growth or rate of decline of different industries (computers versus railroads, for example), and the like.

Another line of criticism emphasizes "credentialism," that is, the argument that employers use possession of the college degree as a convenient and economical screening device. This charge is frequently coupled with a contention that there is very little relationship between educational attainment and the productivity of a worker on the job (for example, Berg, 1970). In fact, in the 1950s and 1960s, most of the increased employment of college graduates resulted from occupational growth requirements rather than from educational upgrading within occupations. The reverse, however, has been true in the 1970s. Most of the increased employment has been attributable to a rise in the proportion of college graduates within broad professional and managerial occupation groups. This is entirely to be expected. Labor economists have long observed the tendency of employers to raise their selection standards in periods of an excess supply of job applicants.

The problem with the credentialism charges is not that they are without validity, but that they are frequently overstated. Most of the evidence discussed by Berg (1970), for example, of a lack of relationship (or of an actual inverse relationship) between educational attainment and productivity in employment, relates to blue-collar and relatively low-level white-collar jobs. Moreover, as Psacharopoulos (1973) has shown, rates of return from investment in education are nearly as high for those with some college (dropouts) on the basis of the estimates of most investigators as rates of return for those with a bachelor's degree. If the possession of the degree were really the critical requirement for higher earnings, one would expect the rate of return to be far lower for those with less than four years of college than for those achieving the degree.

Taking these objections and others into account, one may reasonably conclude that rate-of-return estimates provide a very rough indication of the contribution of education to differentials, but that other factors are also important in explaining variations in earnings.

The Impact on Enrollment

Some of the gloomier predictions of the behavior of enrollment in the next several decades, particularly those of Dresch (1975)—and, in a more qualified way, those of Freeman (1976)—are based on the assumption that decisions to enroll in college are inevitably adversely affected by a decline in the rate of return from investment in a college education. The assumption is plausible—and surely the decline in the enrollment rate of youthful white males in the 1970s is probably partly explained on this basis, as well as by the change in the draft situation—but we actually know very little about how far the rate of return would have to decline to depress the rate of enrollment or about how the relationship between the rate of return and enrollment might be affected by other influences. Dresch (1975) projected a drastic decline in college enrollment in the later part of the present century on the basis of an assumption that the "equilibrium ratio" of the average wage of college graduates to that of nongraduates is 1.45 (the average ratio over the period from 1960 to 1972), that the ratio will be below that level from 1979 to 2003, and that the impact on college enrollment will inevitably be strongly negative.

Over a long period of time, a continuous decline in the rate of return from investment in college might depress college enrollment rates, but we have almost no basis for predicting how far the rate of return would have to fall before its depressive effect became apparent. Adequate income data have been available only for the last few decades, and over most of this period the estimated rate of return has remained high.

In the short run, also, the effect of a depressed job market for college graduates is not easy to predict. First of all, we question the exclusive importance of economic motives in decisions to enroll. Second, even if one assumes that economic conditions play a crucial role at the margin (that is, for those whose attitudes toward enrolling are somewhat uncertain), one can well conceive of two streams of young people being affected in different ways. One stream would be discouraged from enrolling by the poor job prospects for college graduates, and perhaps also by the greater difficulty of financing college attendance in a recession, while the other stream would be encouraged to enroll because job prospects for high school graduates are also poor. The relative size of the two streams may well be influenced by changes in the relationship between unemployment rates of high school and college graduates (those of high school graduates being invariably somewhat higher). In fact, the unemployment rate of recent high school graduates was far higher in relation to that of recent college graduates in the spring of 1975 than it was in the spring of 1971. This difference could go far toward explaining the apparently contradictory fact that the percentage increase in college enrollment fell off in 1971 and rose sharply in 1975. When unemployment is widespread among high school graduates, the "opportunity cost" of attending college (the sacrificed earnings) becomes zero for all those who cannot find a job.[1] College is a good place to spend a few years while waiting for the situation to improve.

This phenomenon has appeared also in a number of countries of Western Europe in the last few years of higher unemployment. In one of the essays on youth in advanced industrial societies prepared for the Carnegie Council, Henri Janne, the

---

[1]Mincer (1966, p. 98) finds evidence of relative increases in school enrollment in recessions and characterizes this as "an interesting reflection of changing opportunity costs during the business cycle."

Belgian sociologist, refers to the "parking function" of Belgian universities that has developed in the last few years (Janne, 1979) while the unrest at the University of Rome has clearly been influenced by a large increase in enrollment that has occurred in a period of poor job prospects.

Other Job-Related Benefits

Before discussing the job outlook for college graduates in the next two decades, we need to consider certain other job-related advantages of college graduates. Particularly important is the greater stability of jobs held by college graduates. This is especially true for those who have been in the labor force a number of years, but, even among young workers, the unemployment rate tends, on the whole, to vary inversely with educational attainment (Figure C-9). Interestingly, however, in 1977 (although not invariably in earlier years) the unemployment rate of young white workers who had completed one to three years of college was slightly below that of those who had completed four years of college or more. This is probably explained by the fact that, in the 16-to-24 age group to which the data apply, relatively more college graduates are likely to be recent entrants to the labor force than among those with fewer years of college.

Another striking point brought out in Figure C-9 is the far higher unemployment rate of blacks, regardless of educational attainment. In earlier years, the corresponding data related to nonwhites and showed a comparatively low unemployment rate for nonwhite college graduates, a rate that was actually slightly lower than that for white college graduates. In 1977, for the first time, the data were published for blacks rather than for nonwhites and showed a sharply higher unemployment rate for black than for white college graduates. The difference appears to be explained by the fact that the most important nonwhite group other than blacks consists of Japanese- and Chinese-Americans, who have very low unemployment rates and very high rates of college graduation. Thus, they account for a much larger proportion of youthful nonwhite college graduates than of the general population. Even so, removal of the Asian-Americans may not fully explain the difference between the 1976 and

Figure C-9. Percentage of civilian labor force unemployed, by
educational attainment and race, persons aged 16 to 24 not
enrolled in school, October 1977

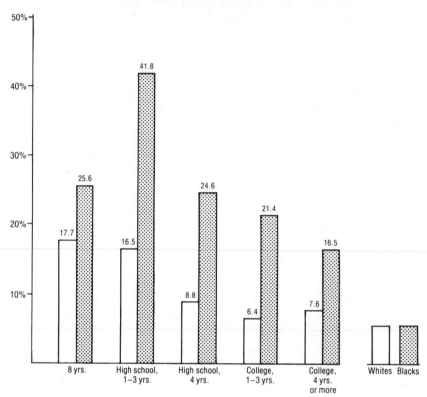

Source: U.S. Bureau of Labor Statistics (1978, table I).

1977 data. This new indication of a high unemployment rate
for black college graduates calls for some qualification of the
conclusions of Freeman (1977) and others with respect to the
pronounced improvement in the job market status of black college graduates, but the data need to be published on this basis
for several years to indicate whether the unemployment rate
continues to be high for young black college graduates.

The jobs held by college graduates are also safer (less prone
to industrial accidents and diseases) than those of persons with
less education, chiefly because they are in more sedentary occu-

pations. And, in the case of men, they offer more opportunities for advancement and are more secure in the later years of working life.

Also exceedingly important is the fact that professional and managerial jobs held by college graduates tend to be more interesting and challenging than the jobs held by persons with less education. One indication of this is the far higher percentage of workers in professional occupations than in average white-collar and manual occupations who "would choose similar work again" (Figure C-10).

The Outlook for the Future

We believe that the long-run upward trend in the percentage of workers in professional and managerial occupations will continue and may well occur at a more pronounced rate in the 1980s than has characterized the 1970s. Among other influences, the energy crisis is creating an increased demand for specialized engineering and scientific skills. The proliferation of specialties in the health field can also be expected to continue,. as well as the more widespread use of computerized techniques.

On the supply side, the number of college graduates entering the labor market can be expected to level off or decline by the mid-1980s, four years after the decline in the size of the college-age population gets under way. If our projections of postbaccalaureate enrollment are correct, another factor limiting the supply entering the labor market will be an increase in the proportion going on for postbaccalaureate training, especially in professional fields.

The impact of a long-run increase in demand and of a leveling off or actual decline in the supply of college graduates, therefore, should bring about an improvement in the job market for graduates in the later half of the 1980s.

For many years to come, however, graduates with special types of training sought by business and industry will do much better in the job market than those with nontechnical liberal arts training. This is the pattern that has developed very clearly in the 1970s, and the only years that have not been favorable for graduates with the types of professional and technical train-

**Figure C-10. Percentage of persons in selected occupational groups
who would choose similar work again**

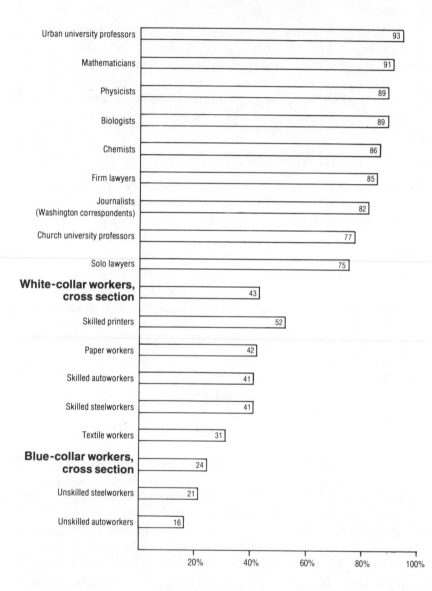

Source: U.S. Department of Health, Education, and Welfare (1973, p. 16).

ing sought by business firms have been recession years. The years from 1977 to 1979 were consistently favorable, and Table C-3 shows percentage increases in new hires from 1978 to 1979 by employers recruiting from college placement offices for graduates with particular types of training.

Table C-3. Percentage increases in hires by curricular groupings and degree levels, by employers recruiting through college placement offices, June 1978 to June 1979

Curricular groupings	Bachelor's level	Master's level	Doctoral level	All levels
Engineering (including engineering technologies)	22%	24%	31%	22%
Sciences, math, and technical (including computer science, etc.)	20	17	20	19
Business (including accounting, marketing, business management, etc.)	11	16	(a)	12
Nontechnical (including liberal arts, social science, home economics, etc.)	4	17	3	5
Total, excluding federal government	14	18	22	15
Total, including federal government	9	18	22	10

(a) Number of cases very small.

Source: College Placement Council (1979a).

Students have responded to the changes in the job market in the 1970s by shifting their fields of concentration out of the less-favored academic fields—especially the humanities—into professional fields, as we note elsewhere in this report. These shifts will undoubtedly continue, and some fields that now offer attractive prospects may be plagued by a surplus supply in the future—to be replaced in their turn by other fields in which demand is rising rapidly.

The generally optimistic tone of this assessment of the

future, however, must be tempered by the comment that a slow rate of economic growth could well mean a continuation of a relatively unfavorable job market for college-educated young people. Most economists anticipate somewhat slower growth in the next decade or so than was characteristic, say, of the 1960s. The real question is: How slow? With a rate of growth of 3 to 4 percent per annum, the prospects for college graduates would probably gradually improve. With a rate of growth of 2 percent or less, their prospects would probably be poor, and this in turn could well have a depressing effect on enrollment rates, especially of majority males.

References

Berg, I. *Education and Jobs: The Great Training Robbery.* New York: Praeger, 1970.

Bowles, S., and Gintis, H. *Schooling in Capitalist America: Educational Reform and the Contradictions of Economic Life.* New York: Basic Books, 1975.

Carnegie Commission on Higher Education. *College Graduates and Jobs: Adapting to a New Labor Market Situation.* New York: McGraw-Hill, 1973.

Carnoy, M., and Marenbach, D. "Return to Schooling in the U.S., 1939-69." *Journal of Human Resources,* Fall 1975, pp. 312-331.

College Placement Council. *Recruiting '79: A Special Report for CPC Members.* Bethlehem, Pa.: June 1979a.

College Placement Council. *Salary Survey: A Study of 1978-79 Beginning Offers.* Final Report. Bethlehem, Pa.: July 1979b.

Dresch, S. P. "Educational Saturation: A Demographic-Economic Model." *AAUP Bulletin* (American Association of University Professors), Autumn 1975, *61* (3), 239-247.

Endicott, F. S. *Trends in Employment of College and University Graduates in Business and Industry, 1972-1976.* Evanstown, Ill.: Northwestern University, 1976.

Freeman, R. B. *The Over-Educated American.* New York: Academic Press, 1976.

Freeman, R. B. *Black Elite: The New Market for Highly Educated Black Americans.* New York: McGraw-Hill, 1977.

Janne, H. *Education and Youth Employment in Belgium.* Berkeley, Calif.: Carnegie Council on Higher Education, 1979.

Mincer, J. "Labor Force Participation and Unemployment: A Review of Recent Evidence." In R. A. and M. S. Gordon (Eds.), *Prosperity and Unemployment.* New York: Wiley, 1966.

Psacharopoulos, G., and Hinchliffe, K. *Returns to Education.* New York: Elsevier, 1973.

Smith, J. P., and Welch, F. "The Over-Educated American? A Review Article." *The Rand Paper Series.* Santa Monica, Calif.: The Rand Corporation, Nov. 1978.

Taubman, P. and Wales, T. *Higher Education and Earnings: College as an Investment and a Screening Device.* New York: McGraw-Hill, 1974.

U.S. Bureau of the Census. *U.S. Census of the Population: 1950.* Special Report PE-5B. *Education.* Washington, D.C.: 1953.

U.S. Bureau of the Census. *U.S. Census of the Population: 1950.* Special Report PE-1B. *Occupational Statistics.* Washington, D.C.: 1956.

U.S. Bureau of the Census. *U.S. Census of the Population: 1960.* Vol. 1, part 1. *Characteristics of the Population: U.S. Summary.* Washington, D.C.: 1964.

U.S. Bureau of the Census. *U.S. Census of the Population: 1970. Subject Reports: Educational Attainment.* PC(2)-5B. Washington, D.C.: 1973.

U.S. Bureau of the Census. *Statistical Abstract of the United States, 1978.* Washington, D.C.: 1978.

U.S. Bureau of the Census. "Money Income in 1977 of Families and Persons in the United States." *Current Population Reports.* Series P-60, no. 118. Washington, D.C.: 1979 and annually.

U.S. Bureau of Labor Statistics. *Educational Attainment of Workers, March 1977.* Special Labor Report 209. Washington, D.C.: 1977.

U.S. Bureau of Labor Statistics. *Students, Graduates, and Dropouts in the Labor Market, October 1977.* Special Labor Force Report 215. Washington, D.C.: 1978.

U.S. Bureau of Labor Statistics. *Employment and Unemployment During 1978: An Analysis.* Special Labor Force Report 218. Washington, D.C.: 1979a.

U.S. Bureau of Labor Statistics. *Occupational Projections and Training Data.* Bulletin 2020. Washington, D.C.: 1979b.

U.S. Department of Health, Education, and Welfare. *Work in America.* Washington, D.C.: 1973.

Supplement D

Gainers and Losers
Among Institutions
of Higher Education

The American system of higher education includes about three thousand colleges and universities with particular missions, characteristics, and environments. To take a closer look at the dynamics of institutional life in the 1970s, we have gathered information on institutional openings, closures, mergers, changes from private to public control, and enrollment gains and losses. Being particularly interested in the less-selective private liberal arts and private two-year colleges which will be among the hardest pressed in the years ahead, we analyzed them in greater detail by enrollment size, location, and religious affiliation. Throughout we have analyzed changes by type of institution referring to the Carnegie typology.

Institutions of higher education were first classified by the Carnegie Commission in 1970 followed by a revision by the Carnegie Council, *A Classification of Institutions of Higher Education: Revised Edition* (1976), which describes the categories as follows:

This supplement was prepared by C. E. Christian, Research Fellow, with the assistance of Marian Gade, Postgraduate Researcher, Ruth Goto, Postgraduate Researcher, and Mitchell Zeftel, Research Assistant.

1. Doctorate-granting Institutions

1.1 Research Universities I. The 50 leading universities in terms of federal financial support of academic science in at least two of the three academic years, 1972-73, 1973-74, and 1974-75, provided they awarded at least 50 Ph.D's (plus M.D.'s if a medical school was on the same campus) in 1973-74. Rockefeller University was included because of the high quality of its research and doctoral training, even though it did not meet these criteria.

1.2 Research Universities II. These universities were on the list of the 100 leading institutions in terms of federal financial support in at least two out of the above three years and awarded at least 50 Ph.D's (plus M.D.'s if a medical school was on the same campus) in 1973-74. At least 25 of these degrees must have been Ph.D's. Alternatively, the institution was among the leading 60 institutions in terms of the total number of Ph.D.'s awarded during the years from 1965-66 to 1974-75. In addition, a few institutions that did not quite meet these criteria, but that have graduate programs of high quality and with impressive promise for future development, have been included in 1.2.

1.3 Doctorate-granting Universities I. These institutions awarded 40 or more Ph.D.'s in at least five fields in 1973-74 (plus M.D.'s if on the same campus) or received at least $3 million in total federal support in either 1973-74 or 1974-75. No institution is included that granted less than 20 Ph.D.'s (plus M.D.'s if on the same campus) in at least five fields regardless of the amount of federal financial support it received.

1.4 Doctorate-granting Universities II. These institutions awarded at least 20 Ph.D.'s in 1973-74 without regard to field, or 10 Ph.D.'s in at least three fields. In addition, we include a few doctorate-granting institutions that may be expected to increase the number of Ph.D's awarded within a few years.[1]

2. Comprehensive Universities and Colleges

2.1 Comprehensive Universities and Colleges I. This group includes institutions that offered a liberal arts program as well as several other programs, such as engineering and business administration. Many of them offered master's degrees, but all lacked a doctoral program or had an extremely limited doctoral program. All institutions in this group had at least two professional or occupational programs and enrolled at least 2,000 students in 1976. If an institution's enrollment was smaller than this, it was not considered very comprehensive.

2.2 Comprehensive Universities and Colleges II. This list includes state colleges and private colleges that offered a liberal arts program and at least one professional or occupational program, such as teacher training or nursing. Many of the institutions in this group are former teachers colleges that have broadened their programs to include a liberal arts curriculum. In general, private institutions with less than 1,500 students and public institutions with less than 1,000 students in 1976 were not included even though they offered a selection of programs, because they were not regarded as comprehensive with such small enrollments. Such institutions are classified as liberal arts colleges. The enrollment differentiation between private and public institutions was made because public colleges with small enrollments are usually new institutions that can be expected to grow rapidly. However, some predominantly teachers colleges, especially in sparsely populated states, have been losing enrollment in re-

[1]In all cases the term *Ph.D.* also includes the Ed.D. and other doctor's degrees.

cent years, and in such cases we have continued to classify them in the 2.2 group, even when their enrollment has fallen below the usual minimum.

3. Liberal Arts Colleges

3.1 Liberal Arts Colleges I. These colleges scored 1030 or more on a selectivity index developed by Alexander W. Astin[2] or they were included among the 200 leading baccalaureate-granting institutions in terms of numbers of their graduates receiving Ph.D.'s at 40 leading doctorate-granting institutions from 1920 to 1966 (National Academy of Sciences, *Doctorate Recipients from United States Universities, 1958-1966,* Washington, D.C.: 1967, Appendix B).

The distinction between a liberal arts college and a comprehensive institution is not always clear-cut. Some of the institutions in this group have modest occupational programs but a strong liberal arts traditions. A good example is Oberlin, which we continue to classify as a liberal arts college. It awarded 76 Mus.B. degrees out of a total of 623 bachelor's degrees in 1974 and had an enrollment of 2,858 in 1976. Or, consider two Pennsylvania institutions, Lafayette and Swarthmore. Lafayette awarded 89 B.S. degrees in engineering in 1974 out of a total of 458 bachelor's degrees and has been included in our Comprehensive Universities and Colleges II group. Its enrollment in 1976 was 2,243. Swarthmore has an engineering program leading to a B.S. degree, but it awarded only 16 B.S. degrees out of a total of 280 bachelor's degrees in 1974 and had a 1976 enrollment of 1,223. Swarthmore has a strong liberal arts tradition and did not meet our minimum enrollment cri-

---

[2]The index has not been published but is available on tape from the Higher Education Research Institute, Los Angeles. It is based on average SAT scores (verbal and mathematical) of freshmen entering each institution, as reported in several institutional directories in the early 1970s.

terion for a private college to be classified as comprehensive, but our decisions in the cases of Oberlin and Lafayette had to be at least partly judgmental.

3.2 Liberal Arts Colleges II. These institutions include all the liberal arts colleges that did not meet our criteria for inclusion in the first group of liberal arts colleges. Again, the distinction between "liberal arts" and "comprehensive" is not clear-cut for some of the larger colleges in this group and is necessarily partly a matter of judgment.

4. Two-Year Colleges and Institutes

5. Professional Schools and Other Specialized Institutions

5.1 Theological seminaries, bible colleges, and other institutions offering degrees in religion. In general, we include in this category only those institutions that do not have a liberal arts program as well as a religious program of instruction. Colleges that combine liberal arts and religious instruction are generally classified in one of our two liberal arts categories. However, if the liberal arts program appears to be very minor, and the primary purpose of the institution is to train members of the clergy, we classify it in this category. Like the distinction between a comprehensive institution and a liberal arts college, this distinction is not always clear-cut and requires judgment.

5.2 Medical schools and medical centers. As indicated in our previous discussion, this category includes only those that are listed as separate campuses in the NCES directory. In some instances, the medical center includes other health professional schools, for example, dentistry, pharmacy, or nursing.

5.3 Other separate health professional schools

5.4 Schools of engineering and technology. Technical institutes are included only if they award a bachelor's degree and if their program is limited exclusively or almost exclusively to technical fields of study.

5.5 Schools of business and management. Business schools are included only if they award a bachelor's or higher degree and if their program is limited exclusively or almost exclusively to a business curriculum.

5.6 Schools of art, music, and design

5.7 Schools of law

5.8 Teachers colleges

5.9 Other specialized institutions. Includes graduate centers, maritime academies, military institutes (that do not have a liberal arts program), and miscellaneous.

New Institutions

From 1970 to 1978, 111 new collegiate institutions appeared, mostly public two-year and private liberal arts colleges. Table D-1 shows the distribution of these new institutions among the

Table D-1. Institutional openings, 1970-1978

Classification (number[a])	Institutional openings	
	Number	*Percentage*
Total (2,394)	111	4.6%
Public (1,250)	80	6.4
Private (1,144)	31	2.7
Research Universities (92)	0	0
Public (57)		
Private (35)		
Doctorate-granting (81)	0	0
Public (52)		
Private (29)		
Comprehensive (449)	9	2.0
Public (304)	8	2.6
Private (145)	1	0.7

(continued on next page)

Table D-1 *(continued)*

| | Institutional openings | |
Classification (number[a])	Number	Percentage
Liberal Arts I (145)	0	0
Public (2)		
Private (143)		
Liberal Arts II (573)	24	4.2
Public (30)	3	10.0
Private (543)	21	3.9
Two-Year Colleges (1,054)	78	7.4
Public (805)	69	8.6
Private (249)	9	3.6

[a]Number of institutions is based on the 1970 Carnegie classification and does not incorporate changes (openings and closings) during the 1970-78 period, nor specialized institutions and those outside the 50 states and D.C. National University opened as a specialized institution and therefore is not counted in Table D-1. In 1978 it moved into the comprehensive category and is included as a "new success" here and on page 72 of the report.

Source: Carnegie Council analysis of the U.S. National Center for Education Statistics data, *Fall Enrollment in Higher Education,* appropriate years.

Carnegie typologies. Table D-2 lists the 77 four-year institutions we term "new successes"—institutions opening during the past twenty years that had enrollments of over 1,000 students in 1978 (headcount). We do not name the some 550 community colleges established during the period.

Table D-2. Successful four-year institutions founded 1960-1978[a]

Carnegie Classification	Name of institution	Year founded
Research Universities		
Public:	CUNY, Graduate School and University Center	1961
Doctorate-granting		
Public:	University of California, Irvine	1960
Comprehensive Universities and Colleges		
Public:	California State College-Sonoma	1960
	Florida Atlantic University	1961

Table D-2 *(continued)*

Carnegie Classifica-tion	Name of institution	Year founded
Public:	Northeastern Illinois	1961
(continued)	University of South Alabama	1963
	Metropolitan State College (Colorado)	1963
	Florida Technological University	1963
	University of West Florida	1963
	Saginaw Valley State College (Michigan)	1963
	Southwest State University (Minnesota)	1963
	University of Missouri-St. Louis	1963
	Indiana University-Purdue University-Ft. Wayne	1964
	Cleveland State University (Ohio)	1964
	Wright State University-Main Campus (Ohio)	1964
	University of Colorado-Colorado Springs	1965
	Florida International University	1965
	University of North Florida	1965
	Southern Illinois University at Edwardsville	1965
	University of Illinois-Chicago Circle Campus	1965
	Indiana State University-Evansville	1965
	Louisiana State University-Shreveport	1965
	Missouri Southern State College	1965
	University of North Carolina-Charlotte	1965
	University of Wisconsin-Parkside	1965
	University of Wisconsin-Green Bay	1965
	University of Alabama at Birmingham	1966
	University of the District of Columbia-Mt. Vernon Square	1966
	SUNY-College of Utica-Rome (New York)	1966
	Pennsylvania State University-Capitol Campus	1966
	Northern Kentucky University	1968
	Governors State University (Illinois)	1969
	Indiana University-Purdue University-Indianapolis	1969
	Ramapo College of New Jersey	1969
	Stockton State College (New Jersey)	1969
	CUNY-Medgar Evers College (New York)	1969
	University of Texas at Dallas	1969

(continued on next page)

Table D-2 *(continued)*

Carnegie Classification	Name of institution	Year founded
Public:	University of Texas of the Permian Basin	1969
(continued)	University of Texas at San Antonio	1969
	University of Alaska-Anchorage	1970
	University of Southern Maine	1970
	Francis Marion College (South Carolina)	1970
	Metropolitan State University (Minnesota)	1971
	Corpus Christi State University (Texas)	1971
	Texas Eastern University	1971
	University of Houston at Clear Lake City (Texas)	1971
	University of Houston-Downtown College (Texas)	1974
Private:	Sacred Heart University (Connecticut)	1963
	Pace University, Pleasantville-Briarcliff Campus (New York)	1963
	Nova University (Florida)	1964
	Liberty Baptist College (Virginia)	1971
	National University (California)	1971
Liberal Arts I		
Public:	University of California, Santa Cruz	1962
Liberal Arts II		
Public:	California State College-San Bernardino	1960
	California State College-Dominguez Hills	1960
	University of Maryland-Baltimore County Campus	1963
	Troy State University of Dothan-Ft. Rucker (Alabama)	1965
	California State College-Bakersfield	1965
	University of Massachusetts-Boston Campus	1965
	Troy State University at Montgomery (Alabama)	1966
	Auburn University at Montgomery (Alabama)	1967
	SUNY-College at Purchase (New York)	1967
	Evergreen State College (Washington)	1967
	Sangamon State University (Illinois)	1969
Private:	Point Park College (Pennsylvania)	1960
	Baptist College at Charleston (South Carolina)	1960
	Biscayne College (Florida)	1962
	Nathaniel Hawthorne College (New Hampshire)	1962
	Long Island University-Southampton Center (New York)	1962

Table D-2 *(continued)*

Carnegie Classification	Name of institution	Year founded
Private:	John F. Kennedy University (California)	1964
(continued)	Mercer University in Atlanta (Georgia)	1964
	Hawaii Pacific College	1965
	Hampshire College (Massachusetts)	1965
	Bellevue College (Nebraska)	1965
	Oral Roberts University (Oklahoma)	1965
	Mid-America Nazarene College (Kansas)	1966
	Touro College (New York)	1970

a"Successful" is defined as having 1,000 headcount enrollment in 1978.

Institutional Closures and Mergers

Table D-3 shows the 107 closures of the 1970s, the 68 mergers, and the 11 changes from private to public control by Carnegie category.

Table D-3. Institutional closures, 1970-1978

Classification	Closings		Mergers		Changes to public control	
	Number	Percentage	Number	Percentage	Number	Percentage
Total	107	4.5%	68	2.8%		
Public	15	1.2	41	3.3		
Private	92	8.0	27	2.3	11	1.0%
Research Universities	0	0	0	0		
Public					0	0
Private						
Doctorate-granting	0	0	0	0		
Public					0	0
Private						
Comprehensive	0	0	7	1.6		
Public			6	2.0		
Private			1	0.7	1	0.7

(continued on next page)

Table D-3 *(continued)*

Classification	Closings		Mergers		Changes to public control	
	Number	Percent-age	Number	Percent-age	Number	Percent-age
Liberal Arts I	2	1.4	2	1.4		
Public	0	0	0	0		
Private	2	1.4	2	1.4	1	0.7
Liberal Arts II	42	7.3	19	3.3		
Public	0	0	2	6.7		
Private	42	7.7	17	3.1	3	0.6
Two-Year Colleges	63	6.0	40	3.8		
Public	15	1.9	33	4.1		
Private	48	19.3	7	2.8	6	2.4

Note: Percentages calculated from the number of institutions in each classification in 1970.

Source: Carnegie Council analysis of U.S. National Center for Education Statistics, *Education Directory, Colleges and Universities,* appropriate years.

Enrollment Changes

We investigated enrollment changes during the 1970s in terms of both headcount and FTE. The headcount figures are not presented because we judged them to be spuriously skewed by the significant recent increases in part-time attendance: gains were overcounted and losses were undercounted. An overview of enrollment changes is presented in Table D-4, showing the number of institutions in each category that gained or lost enrollment, or which remained stable within a range of plus or minus 5 percent.

The Most Vulnerable Colleges

Because the less-selective private liberal arts and two-year colleges are the most vulnerable to decline in the years ahead, we conducted more detailed analyses of their recent history. To determine to what extent the small college has been hurt by enrollment loss and closure, tabulations of major changes were made separating institutions by size of headcount enrollment as shown in Table D-5 and Figure D-1.

Table D-4. Full-time equivalent (FTE) enrollment changes, 1970-1978

	FTE enrollment																
	Gains								Stable[b]		Losses						
	Total		Less than 20%		20% to 100%		More than 100%				Total		Less than 20%		20% or more	
Classification (number)[a]	Number	Percentage	Number	Percentage	Number	Percentage	Number	Percentage	Number	Percentage	Number	Percentage	Number	Percentage	Number	Percentage
Total (2,145)	1,256	59	367	17	697	32	192	9	259	12	630	29	316	15	314	15
Public (1,136)	771	68	177	16	458	40	136	12	129	11	236	21	128	11	108	10
Private (1,009)	485	48	190	19	239	24	56	6	130	13	394	39	188	19	206	20
Research Universities (91)	50	55	36	40	13	14	1	1	23	25	18	20	15	16	3	3
Public (56)	32	57	22	39	9	16	1	2	15	27	9	16	8	14	1	2
Private (35)	18	51	14	40	4	11	0		8	23	9	26	7	20	2	6
Doctorate-granting (80)	39	49	21	26	18	23	0		13	16	28	35	20	25	8	10
Public (50)	22	44	12	24	10	20	0		8	16	20	40	14	28	6	12
Private (30)	17	57	9	30	8	27	0		5	17	8	27	6	20	2	7
Comprehensive (436)	197	45	77	18	106	24	14	3	74	17	165	38	78	18	87	20
Public (295)	140	47	56	19	70	24	14	5	46	16	109	37	47	16	62	21
Private (141)	57	40	21	15	36	26	0		28	20	56	40	31	22	25	18

(continued on next page)

Table D-4 (continued)

	FTE enrollment															
	Gains								Stable[b]		Losses					
	Total		Less than 20%		20% to 100%		More than 100%				Total		Less than 20%		20% or more	
Classification (number)[a]	Number	Percentage	Number	Percentage	Number	Percentage	Number	Percentage	Number	Percentage	Number	Percentage	Number	Percentage	Number	Percentage
Liberal Arts I (139)	72	52	46	33	24	17	2	1	26	19	41	29	25	18	16	12
Public (2)	1	50	0	0	1	50	0	0	1	50	0	0	0	0	0	0
Private (137)	71	52	46	34	23	17	2	1	25	18	41	30	25	18	16	12
Liberal Arts II (510)	248	49	78	15	129	25	41	8	52	10	210	41	97	19	113	22
Public (23)	19	83	2	9	10	43	7	30	2	9	2	9	1	4	1	4
Private (487)	229	47	76	16	119	24	34	7	50	10	208	43	96	20	112	23
Two-Year Colleges (889)	650	73	109	12	407	46	134	15	71	8	168	19	81	9	87	10
Public (710)	557	78	85	12	358	50	114	16	57	8	96	14	58	8	38	5
Private (179)	93	52	24	13	49	27	20	11	14	8	72	40	23	13	49	27

[a]Enrollment changes could be analyzed only for those 2,145 institutions that reported enrollment in 1970 and 1978, so that 249 institutions that opened, closed, or otherwise did not report for both years are not included.

[b]Stable enrollment was defined as changes less than plus or minus 5 percent.

Source: Carnegie Council analysis of U.S. National Center for Education Statistics, Opening Fall Enrollment, appropriate years.

Table D-5. Institutional changes in private less-selective Liberal Arts Colleges and private Two-Year Colleges, by size, 1970-1978

Carnegie Classification and headcount enrollment (number)[a]	Openings	Closings	Mergers	Changes to public control	FTE enrollment							
					Gains				Stable[b]	Losses		
					Total	Less than 20%	20% to 100%	More than 100%		Total	Less than 20%	20% or more
Private Liberal Arts II (544)	22	47	17	3	229	73	124	32	50	208	93	115
Under 500	17	32	7	2	53	8	28	17	8	35	12	23
500-1,000	2	13	8	1	106	35	61	10	26	97	49	48
Over 1,000	3	2	2	0	70	30	35	5	16	76	32	44
Private Two-Year (249)	9	51	7	6	93	23	51	19	14	72	22	50
Under 500	8	47	6	2	69	11	41	17	10	37	9	28
500-1,000	1	1	0	3	19	9	8	2	4	20	7	13
Over 1,000	0	3	1	1	5	3	2	0	0	15	6	9

[a]Number of institutions is based on 1970 data and does not incorporate changes (openings and closings) during the 1970-78 period, nor institutions in Puerto Rico and U.S. Territories.

[b]An enrollment was considered stable if it did not fluctuate more than plus or minus 5 percent from its 1970 level.

Source: U.S. National Center for Education Statistics, Fall Enrollment in Higher Education, appropriate years.

Figure D-1. Institutional changes by size of enrollment for
private Liberal Arts Colleges II and private Two-Year Colleges,
1970-1978

PRIVATE LIBERAL ARTS II COLLEGES

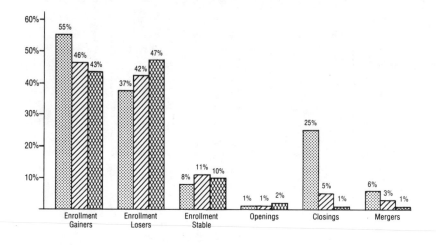

PRIVATE TWO-YEAR COLLEGES

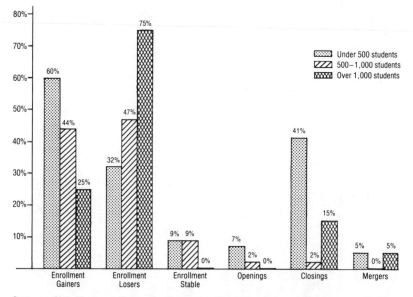

Sources: U.S. National Center for Education Statistics, *Education Directory, Colleges and Universities,* appropriate years; U.S. NCES, *Fall Enrollment in Higher Education,* appropriate years.

Campuses with fewer than 500 students tend to be very unstable. They were more likely to gain enrollment than were larger institutions, but they were also the most likely to close or to merge with other institutions.

Table D-6 shows closures and mergers among these vulnerable segments of higher education by size, location, sex of student body, and curricular offerings.

Table D-6. Private Liberal Arts Colleges II and private Two-Year Colleges that closed or merged, 1970-1978, by size, location, sex of student body, and curricular offerings

Type of institution and headcount size in 1970	Religious affiliation			Location		Sex of student body			Curricular offerings				
	Protestant	Catholic	Independent	Urban[a]	Rural[b]	Men	Women	Coed	Lib. Arts	Teach. Prep.	Voc.	Prof.	Grad.
Private Liberal Arts													
Colleges II	8	26	32	40	26	3	16	47	66	46	9	12	10
Under 500	5	16	19	27	13	2	12	26	40	25	6	8	4
500 plus	3	10	13	13	13	1	4	21	26	21	3	4	6
Private Two-Year													
Colleges	10	22	24	40	16	6	13	37	56	11	24	4	0
Under 500	10	20	21	35	16	6	12	33	51	10	21	4	0
500 plus	0	2	3	5	0	0	1	4	5	1	3	0	0

[a]Urban indicates location in a central city or urban fringe of a Standard Metropolitan Statistical Area as defined in 1974 by the U.S. Department of Commerce, National Bureau of Standards.

[b]Rural indicates locations outside of a Standard Metropolitan Statistical Area.

Note: This table includes eight institutions that closed in 1970 and do not appear in the 1970 *Education Directory*. They are not included in the count of closings in Table D-3 or in Table 1, p. 12.

Sources: U.S. National Center for Education Statistics, *Education Directory, Colleges and Universities*, appropriate years; U.S. NCES, *Fall Enrollment in Higher Education*, appropriate years.

Supplement E

Higher Education and
Human Performance

In much of the literature on the outcomes of higher education, especially in the writings of economists of the human capital school, the income effects of higher education are the focus of attention to the exclusion of other impacts of the college experience.[1] Yet college education affects cultural interests, political and community activities of graduates, consumption patterns, savings and investment patterns, the status and care of the individual's health, and, perhaps most important of all because its effects are passed on to the next generation, performance as parents. Moreover, society as a whole, and not just the individual college graduate, benefits from many of these impacts. When a college-educated individual heads a drive for funds for the symphony orchestra or chairs a committee appointed to revise the state constitution, the benefits of his or her college experience accrue to all music lovers in the community, in the first instance, and to all citizens of the state, in the second.

To be sure, the differences between college graduates and persons with less education that show up in surveys are average differences—not all college graduates will display the characteristics or attitudes indicated by the averages. Moreover, the fact that young people who enroll in college tend to be more able

This supplement was prepared by Charlotte Alhadeff, Research Specialist, and Margaret S. Gordon, Associate Director.

[1] For data on the income effects, see Supplement C.

than those who do not enroll helps to explain the differences in patterns of behavior between college and high school graduates. And yet, decided changes in attitudes occur during the course of a college education. Between freshman and senior year, most students become more tolerant of views that differ from those they accepted when they were younger; they also become less conventional, more capable of dealing with complexities, better informed, and less religious (Feldman and Newcomb, 1969; and Bowen, 1977).

Cultural Interests and the Quality of Life

There is abundant evidence that college graduates are more interested in art, literature, and music than those who have not attended college. For example, large percentages of both upperclassmen and alumni report "broadened literary acquaintance and appreciation" as one of the benefits received from college (Table E-1). College graduates are also much more likely to read

Table E-1. Percentages of upperclassmen and alumni mentioning various types of benefits received from college

	Upper-classmen	Alumni
Background and specialization for further education in some professional, scientific, or scholarly field	71%	64%
Awareness of different philosophies, cultures, and ways of life	69	64
Vocabulary, terminology, and facts in various fields of knowledge	69	79
Broadened literary acquaintance and appreciation	57	62
Science and technology—understanding and appreciation	43	54

Source: Pace (1974, pp. 52-53, 56-57).

periodicals than those who have not been to college, and far more of them read the more serious types of periodicals, such as the *New York Times Magazine, Time,* and the *National Geographic* (Robinson, 1971, p. 97).

Some of these differences are, however, not as striking as one might expect. In a study of contrasts between high school graduates who had attended college four years and those who had been employed consistently for four years, Trent and Medsker (1968, p. 143) found that the college group was more likely to browse in bookstores and attend concerts, lectures, art exhibits, and the like. But the shift in interest of the college group toward cultural magazines was relatively slight, whereas the difference between the college group and the noncollege group in interest in classical music was very pronounced. For example, in 1963, 37 percent of the male 1959 high school graduates who had attended college reported "a great liking for classical music," compared with only 14 percent of the employed group. Among the women, the contrast was even greater: 50 percent of the college group reported "a great liking for classical music," compared with 13 percent of the employed group.

Whether broadened cultural interests heighten life satisfaction and improve the quality of life is less clear, probably because "happiness" and general satisfaction with life are elusive concepts. In a recent study by Campbell, Converse, and Rodgers (1976), about 2,000 men and women were questioned about their general sense of well-being. One of the striking findings was that the relationship between income and "general sense of well-being" differed between those who had one or more college degrees and those who did not have a college degree. Among those without a degree, a sense of well-being was positively related to income level, whereas among those with one or more degrees there was little relationship between income and a sense of well-being. The authors develop an interesting interpretation of this difference, suggesting that, among the more highly educated, low income is less a reflection of lack of opportunity about career choices than of voluntary choices of occupations that yield relatively low incomes, e.g., the ministry. Highly educated people who choose occupations with comparatively low monetary rewards presumably place a high value on the nonpecuniary aspects of their occupations, such as service to society, more freedom at work, more leisure, and more self-fulfillment. On the other hand, the low incomes of those without a college degree probably reflect less freedom of choice about occupations and, thus, more of a feeling of frustration about a low material standard of living.

Although Campbell, Converse, and Rodgers (1976) found that college graduates expressed higher satisfaction with their health, educational level, and standard of living than those without a college degree, the relationships tended to be loose. Education, the authors suggested, curbs uncritical satisfaction and broadens awareness of alternatives (pp. 146-47). Other studies of personal happiness have found that more educated people tend to be relatively introspective and concerned with the personal and interpersonal aspects of their lives. As Withey put it, for example, "the data seem to point to education as broadening one's perspective and raising the aspiration level, which leads to problems and frustrations as well as challenges" (1971, p. 89).

Political and Community Activities

College graduates tend to be better informed about public affairs, more active politically, and more involved in volunteer community activities than persons with less education. This is one of the respects in which higher education yields social as well as individual benefits.

Recently a large-scale study (Hyman, Wright, and Reed, 1975) has shown that a knowledge of both domestic and foreign affairs is positively related to educational attainment (Figure E-1). The study took the form of a review and analysis of a large number of nationwide surveys of public opinion between 1949 and 1971. The data in Figure E-1 are based on surveys in the early 1960s, but similar results were obtained from surveys in other periods. The survey questions on domestic affairs involved such items as name recognition of political figures, characteristics of elected officials, or which party controlled Congress. Knowledge of major events affecting U.S. foreign policy was tested to indicate familiarity with foreign affairs.

Not only are college graduates better informed about public affairs, but they are also much more likely to vote and to

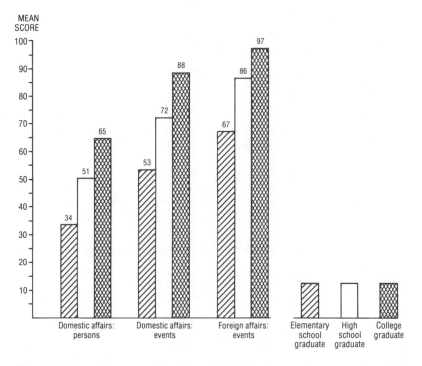

Figure E-1. Mean scores on knowledge of public affairs in the early 1960s, by level of educational attainment

Note: All age groups were combined (by weighting each group's mean score equally) in order to simplify the presentation.

Source: Hyman, Wright, and Reed (1975, tables 3.1, 3.2, 3.3, 3.4).

engage in other types of political activity. Although the voter turnout varies from one election to another, a positive relationship between educational attainment and propensity to vote shows up consistently. The difference between high school graduates and those with less than four years of high school in this respect is especially pronounced, while the data also show that individuals who have had five or more years of college education are even more likely to vote—although by a small margin—than those with just four years of college (Figure E-2).

Not surprisingly, along with more knowledge of political

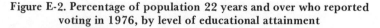

Figure E-2. Percentage of population 22 years and over who reported
voting in 1976, by level of educational attainment

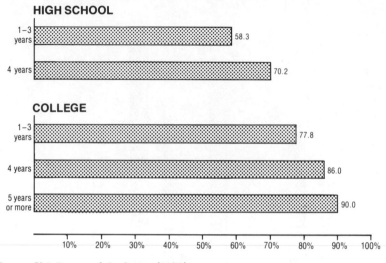

Source: U.S. Bureau of the Census (1978).

affairs and a greater propensity to vote goes a greater tendency
to participate in political activity. Many surveys have confirmed
the consistent, positive effect of education on such behavior as
trying to influence how others vote, writing to public officials,
or giving money to political campaigns or candidates (Withey,
1971, pp. 115-120).

Related to the greater propensity of highly educated people to engage in political activity is their greater tendency to
participate in volunteer community activity. They have a better
understanding of the roles and needs of community organizations and of the contributions of those organizations to community welfare than do less-educated people.

A study conducted in the mid-1960s showed that hours of
volunteer work contributed by both husbands and wives were
positively related to the educational attainment of the family
head (Figure E-3). Since the educational attainment of hus-

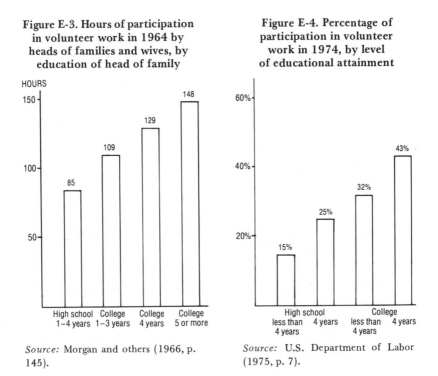

Figure E-3. Hours of participation in volunteer work in 1964 by heads of families and wives, by education of head of family

Figure E-4. Percentage of participation in volunteer work in 1974, by level of educational attainment

Source: Morgan and others (1966, p. 145).

Source: U.S. Department of Labor (1975, p. 7).

bands and wives tends to be highly correlated, it may be assumed that there was a positive relationship between the educational level of the wives as well as of the husbands and their participation in volunteer activity, even though the data were classified by the educational level of the family head. Another, more recent, study also showed a strong positive relationship between educational attainment and the percentage of respondents participating in volunteer activity (Figure E-4).

A significant aspect of the relationship between higher education and volunteer community activity is the extent to which colleges and universities have projects—organized by students themselves or by various campus organizations—that involve direct student participation in local activities. A survey conducted in 1974 indicated that about 450,000 students at approximately 1,900 colleges and 500 high schools served as part-time volunteers in local community service projects. The activities range from "working with young children to helping the elderly and include drug abuse prevention, tutoring, companionship and recreation projects, consumer education, corrections, and housing improvements" (U.S. Department of Labor, 1975, p. 13).

Tolerance of Nonconformity

One of the most striking impacts of a college education—and one that has an important bearing on the successful functioning of a democracy—has to do with the tolerance of nonconformity. We observed earlier that one of the differences between college freshmen and seniors is the greater tolerance of differing points of view among the seniors. Recently, a classic study of tolerance that was carried out in the mid-1950s (Stouffer, 1955) has been replicated by Nunn, Crockett, and Williams (1978). The results show a strong positive relationship between educational attainment and political tolerance (Table E-2). The authors suggest that tolerance is more than passive acceptance of what exists but is ideally "an active process that reflects an appreciation of free-flowing diversity of ideas and recognition that one's own free expression is made possible by such a climate of opinion" (ibid., p. 12).

Consumption, Savings, and Investment

Families headed by a college graduate tend to save a slightly larger share of their incomes, i.e., consume a slightly smaller share, than families with a less-educated head, as we showed in Figure 16 (p. 92). However, since college graduates tend to have higher incomes than those who have not graduated from college and since the percentage of income saved is positively related to income, this higher savings rate could be explained entirely by higher incomes. It requires more sophisticated treatment of the data to separate the effects of income and education on the propensity to save.

One of the few studies that has attempted such an analysis

Table E-2. Percentage distribution of Tolerance Scale scores,
by occupation and level of education, national cross-section,
1954 and 1973[a]

Level of education	Tolerance Scale Scores			
	Percentage less tolerant	*Percentage in-between*	*Percentage more tolerant*	*Number*
White collar[b]				
Less than high school	18%	52%	30%	335
High school	11	43	46	353
Some college	8	33	59	180
College graduate	4	27	69	235
Blue collar[b]				
Less than high school	23	57	20	968
High school	12	50	39	261
Some college	12	35	54	69
College graduate	8	23	69	13
White collar[c]				
Less than high school	13	47	40	143
High school	12	29	59	356
Some college	6	19	75	280
College graduate	3	12	85	431
Blue collar[c]				
Less than high school	25	43	32	566
High school	12	30	58	343
Some college	7	19	74	117
College graduate	10	11	79	19

[a]Percentages in tables are based on combining the results of the two surveys.

[b]Refers to present occupation of respondent only; persons retired or unemployed at time of interview, persons with farm occupations, and housewives are omitted.

[c]Refers to present occupation or most recent occupation for persons retired or un-employed at time of interview; persons with farm occupations and housewives omitted.

Source: Nunn, Crockett, and Williams (1978, p. 62).

was conducted for the Carnegie Commission on Higher Education by the National Bureau of Economic Research. The results indicated that "both the average and marginal propensity to save increase with the schooling attainment of the head of the household, after controlling for other important factors" (Solmon, 1975, p. 277).

Not only do families headed by a college graduate tend to consume somewhat smaller percentages of their incomes, but their patterns of consumption also differ from those of families headed by less-educated persons. For one thing, they tend to investigate the market availability of products more carefully before making major purchases of durable goods (Mueller, 1954). They are also much more likely to subscribe to consumer product-rating publications or to use them in libraries than families headed by less-educated persons (Morris, 1976, p. 117).

Although families with highly educated heads tend to have higher incomes than those with less-educated heads and therefore have consumption patterns that are consistent with higher-income status, Michael (1975) has shown that education has effects on consumption that are independent of the income effect. Families with relatively well-educated heads, for example, tend to spend less on food for home use, tobacco, alcoholic beverages, personal care, and automobiles, but more on food away from home, house operations, leisure, and education than families with less-educated heads, even after allowing for the effects of income.

Not only do families with relatively well-educated heads tend to save somewhat larger proportions of their incomes than families with less-educated heads, but they also display greater sophistication in the ways in which they respond to the threat of inflation. The more educated the family head, for example, the more likely would the response to anticipated inflation be to increase investments in common stock, real estate, and mutual funds. On the other hand, respondents from families with relatively uneducated heads were much more likely to give the "wrong" answer as to how they would respond to anticipated inflation—they would purchase fixed-dollar assets, shun debt, and practice austerity (Solmon, 1975, pp. 279-280).

Education also affects investment patterns. Families with relatively well-educated heads are more likely to invest in common stock and mutual funds, whereas families with less-educated heads are more likely to invest in savings accounts and United States savings bonds. These differences, of course, can be interpreted in several ways. Savings accounts are more accessible for families with only small amounts to invest, whereas, for families with larger incomes, stocks and mutual funds are relatively more accessible, and the favorable tax treatment of capital gains is an advantage. However, as Solmon (1975, p. 289) points out, a preference for common stocks also suggests a greater willingness to take risks and, on the basis of historical trends, a likelihood of higher private returns. He also suggests that "a society characterized by complete aversion to risk will be less progressive and dynamic than one characterized by a more even distribution of attitudes toward risk." This implies that the greater willingness of more educated persons to undertake risk may constitute a social benefit. Historical patterns, however, have been rudely shaken in the last year or so, and a preference for high-yield fixed-interest securities may currently (1980) appear more rational than it did five or six years ago.

Health

There is little question that more-educated people tend to enjoy better health and longer life expectancy than less-educated people, but part of the difference is clearly attributable to the fact that highly educated people are unlikely to be employed in hazardous or physically arduous occupations, and only a few studies have disentangled the effects of education and occupation on relative health status.

Even so, there is evidence that education has a positive effect on health, after holding other variables constant (Grossman, 1972, p. 81). One of the factors that apparently contributes to the better health of educated persons is greater knowledge of nutrition. In a study of the effect of educational attainment on the nutritive quality of the family's diet, the percentage of households with optimal diets increased with the level of education (U.S. Department of Health, Education, and Welfare, 1973, p. 47). In addition, the use of medical services tends to vary directly with the level of education. As Klarman

(1965, p. 29) put it, "The better-educated are more health-conscious and have a more positive attitude than the less-educated toward the early, and preventive, use of services." It follows that the rising educational level of the population must be a factor, along with increasing health insurance coverage, in explaining the increasing proportion of the Gross National Product (GNP) expended on health care.

Intergenerational Effects

One of the most important impacts of higher education is on the performance of college graduates as parents. There is growing evidence that the children of relatively educated parents not only enjoy better medical care and better diets, but that they tend to be better prepared for school and to show superior achievement levels in school. The quantity and quality of verbal interaction with adults, the motivation for achievement in school, and the richness of the physical environment are important factors in explaining the effectiveness of a given amount of school resources (Bowles, 1970).

Although the educational level of both parents is important in explaining impacts on children, there is evidence that the educational level of the mother is more important than that of the father. This is an old view—Marshall, the founding father of modern economics, long ago wrote: "General ability depends largely on the surroundings of childhood and growth. In this the first and far the most powerful influence is that of the mother" (1947, p. 207). A recent study by Leibowitz (1974) lends support to Marshall's view. Thus, the social impact of the higher education of women may be seriously underestimated if the effects on child raising are not explicitly taken into account.

Although highly educated married women are more likely to be in the labor force than married women with less education, they are as likely to take time out of the labor force when they have small children in the home. In fact, having children under 3 years of age is an equally forceful deterrent to labor force participation for married women, regardless of educational level, but college-educated women also tend to work less than women with lower levels of education when they have children aged 3 to 5 and somewhat less even when their children are 6 to 11 (Leibowitz, 1975, p. 186).

Furthermore, women who have had some college education spend more time on the care of their children than women with less education, and the difference applies to both physical care and other types of care of children, as Table E-3, which is

Table E-3. Time spent on household activities involving caring
for children, by education, 1967-1968
(Minutes spent in a 48-hour period)

Activity	High-education group[a]	Low-education group[a]	Average
Number of children	2.17	2.41	2.29
Physical care of children			
by wife	129.51	116.40	122.36
by husband	14.90	12.26	13.46
by others	5.67	4.41	4.98
Other care of children			
by wife	90.96	79.17	85.86
by husband	40.77	31.51	36.77
by others	44.74	36.38	41.12
Physical care per child			
by wife	59.6	48.3	53.4
by husband	6.9	5.1	5.9
by others	2.6	1.8	2.2
Other care per child			
by wife	41.9	32.9	37.5
by husband	18.8	13.1	16.1
by others	20.6	15.1	18.0

[a]Low-education group consisted of women who had not gone beyond high school; high-education group included women who had at least one year of college or training beyond high school.

Source: Leibowitz (1975).

based on a study of more than 1,000 families in 1967-68, shows. Highly educated husbands also spend more time on the care of children, although the differences between these men and those with less education are not as pronounced as in the case of the wives.

The differences in educational progress of young adults and children of various ages, by educational attainment of parents, are shown in Figure E-5. The positive relationship between educational progress and educational attainment of the parent, however, must be interpreted with some care. Highly educated parents are more likely to live in suburbs or in portions of cities with superior schools. Thus, the children benefit not only from the direct influence of educated parents, but also from the fact that relatively educated parents are in a position to see that their children attend comparatively better schools.

There was a time when it was argued that social investment in the higher education of women was not justified, because female college graduates would spend much of their time out of the labor force and would not "make use" of their education. This argument is no longer being used—and not only because the labor force participation rates of highly educated married women have been climbing rapidly. The evidence that their children benefit has come to be increasingly recognized. As Schultz (1972, pp. S21-S22), the leader of the human capital school of economists, has put it: "I would contend that a college graduate generates only a few externalities that accrue as benefits to other persons, with one major exception, namely, the important benefit the education of a woman gives her children in terms of preschool training and experience."

Social Mobility

The tendencies for college graduates to enjoy higher incomes and higher-status occupations than persons with lower levels of education are, of course, closely related. And yet, the benefits of higher income and higher social status are somewhat distinct. A relatively uneducated, self-employed businessman can achieve a high income without enjoying the access to influential social and community circles that a doctor or lawyer or architect may enjoy. There is no question that one of the major motives for attending college throughout American history has been the upward social mobility involved in access to higher-status occupations. As we saw in Supplement C, the probability that a college graduate will be employed in a professional or managerial occu-

Figure E-5. National assessment of educational progress in selected subjects, by age, and by parents' education,[a] 1972-1973

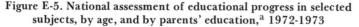

CITIZENSHIP

READING

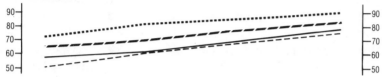

LITERATURE

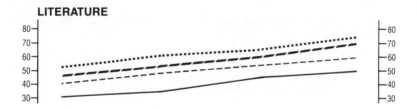

WRITING

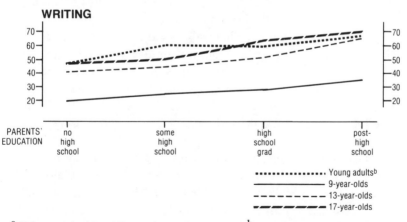

PARENTS' EDUCATION   no high school   some high school   high school grad   post-high school

```
·················· Young adultsb
───────────── 9-year-olds
────────── 13-year-olds
━━━━━━━━━━ 17-year-olds
```

[a]Highest attained by either parent.   [b]Ages 26-35.

Source: U.S. National Center for Education Statistics (1975, pp. 155-158). Scores are from material in the files of the National Assessment of Educational Progress, 1860 Lincoln St., Denver, Colo., Oct. 1972, Feb. and March, 1973.

pation has been considerably lower in the 1970s than it was in the 1960s, but not greatly different from what it was in the 1950s. We also expressed the view in Supplement C that the access of college graduates to professional and managerial occupations would improve in the later half of the 1980s.

There is another aspect, however, of the relationship between higher education and social mobility that is highly significant. Higher education has become a major vehicle for intergenerational upward social mobility for individuals born into families at lower socioeconomic levels. In one of the most important studies of social mobility ever conducted, Blau and Duncan (1964) found a high positive association between the educational attainment of a son and the extent to which that son was able to achieve an occupation that was substantially higher in the occupational hierarchy than that of his father (Figure E-6). The proportion of sons who experienced upward mobility increased steadily from a low of 12 percent for those reporting no schooling to a high of 76 percent for those with five or more years of college. As for those achieving "long distance" upward mobility, the corresponding percentages ranged from 8 percent for those with less than five years of schooling to 53 percent for those with some postgraduate work. Conversely, the percentages experiencing downward mobility varied inversely, in general, with the son's educational attainment.

Blau and Duncan (1964) also examined the question of whether education had become more important over time as a determinant of social mobility. Through an analysis of factors influencing the mobility of respondents in four age groups— from 25 to 34 to 55 to 64—they concluded that the influence of education on careers had become more pronounced over time.

Historically, black male college graduates have found higher education less effective as a path to upward social mobility than have their white brothers, and the Blau and Duncan study provides impressive evidence of the far less favorable mobility patterns of black than of white men. In part, this result was attributable to the fact that the only professional occupations that were widely accessible for black college graduates

Figure E-6. Percentage distribution by observed intergenerational mobility, for men in each category of educational attainment

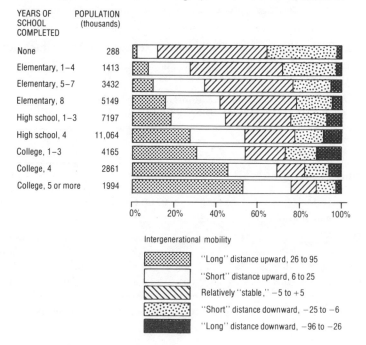

Source: Blau and Duncan (1964, p. 157).

historically were teaching (in segregated schools) and the ministry. However, as we noted in Supplement C, black college graduates have achieved greatly improved access to professional and managerial occupations since the mid-1960s. These issues are discussed more fully in Supplement F.

Striking evidence of the increasing role of higher education in relation to upward social mobility is provided by studies of the changing social origins of business leaders. In one of these studies,[2] by Newcomer (1955), data were developed on the social origins of the president and board chairman of a sample

[2]Other similar studies were conducted by Taussig and Joslyn (1932) and by Warner and Abegglen (1955).

of large corporations in each of three years—1900, 1925, and 1950—using such sources as *Who's Who in America*, contacts with living relatives of the executives, etc. Gould (1965) conducted a similar study, duplicating Newcomer's methods, in 1964. The results reveal a steady increase in the educational attainment of top business executives over time (Table E-4).

Table E-4. Educational attainment of big business executives, 1900, 1925, 1950, and 1964

Educational attainment	1900	1925	1950	1964
Number of executives	310	326	869	849
Percentage	100.0%	100.0%	100.0%	100.0%
Grammar school	23.2	22.1	4.3	0.2
High school	37.7	26.3	20.1	8.7
College, no degree	11.0	11.4	13.5	15.6
College, first degree	19.4	25.4	45.3	44.9
Graduate study	8.7	14.8	16.8	30.6

Sources: Computed from data in Newcomer (1955, p. 68); and Gould (1965, p. 34).

This evidence in itself would not necessarily show a rise in the role of higher education as an avenue to social mobility (it might simply show a rise in educational selection standards), but, when it is combined with other evidence, the conclusion is quite clear. Lipset (1979, pp. xiii-xiv), for example, showed—drawing on the Newcomer and Gould data—that 46 percent of the executives in 1900 were from wealthy families, but that in 1964 only 11 percent came from such families. On the other hand, the percentage from poor families rose from 12 percent in 1950 to 23 percent in 1964. Moreover, the Gould study shows that the percentage whose fathers were in ordinary or relatively low-level white-collar or blue-collar occupations rose from slightly over 10 percent in 1900 to about 20 percent in 1964. Even so, the sons of fathers in professional and managerial occupations continued to make up a large majority of big business executives in 1964. Thus, there is evidence both that higher education has encouraged upward social mobility and that those born into professional and managerial families continue to have an advantage, as critics like Bowles (1968) would argue.

Conclusions

The evidence discussed here suggests that increased access to higher education over time has impacts on society that go well beyond the higher incomes of college graduates or the rise in the proportion of the labor force engaged in professional and managerial occupations. The participation of college-educated adults in the cultural, political, and organizational aspects of community life are important assets in a democratic society, as is the tolerance of nonconformity displayed by college graduates. The fact that health is positively related to educational attainment, as are the propensities to consume more efficiently, to save a higher proportion of income, and to invest in a more sophisticated manner, also constitutes positive impacts of higher education. Of considerable importance, as well, is the evidence that college-educated parents tend to give more careful attention to the care and early learning of their children than do less-educated parents.

In this brief summary, we have not attempted to cover all aspects of the impact of higher education on human performance, which are considered more comprehensively in other studies.[3] Moreover, it must be recognized that not all of the results of studies conducted in the past are necessarily valid for all time. We do not as yet, for example, have a clear picture of the impact of the rising aspirations of women to follow traditionally male careers on their attitudes toward childbearing and childrearing. There is clearly a need for continuing research on many of these questions.

References

Blau, P. M., and Duncan, O. D. *The American Occupational Structure.* New York: Wiley, 1964.

[3]Both the Carnegie Council and its predecessor, the Carnegie Commission, sponsored several comprehensive studies of the impact of higher education, including both the pecuniary and nonpecuniary aspects (Withey, 1971; Juster, 1975; and Bowen, 1977).

Bowen, H. R. *Investment in Learning: The Individual and Social Value of American Higher Education.* Sponsored by the Carnegie Council on Policy Studies in Higher Education. San Francisco: Jossey-Bass, 1977.

Bowles, S. "Toward Equality of Educational Opportunity." *Harvard Educational Review,* Winter 1968, *38*, 89-99.

Bowles, S. "Towards an Educational Production Function." In W. F. Hansen (Ed.), *Education, Income, and Human Capital.* New York: National Bureau of Economic Research, 1970.

Campbell, A., Converse, P. E., and Rodgers, W. L. *The Quality of American Life.* New York: Russell Sage Foundation, 1976.

Feldman, K. A., and Newcomb, T. M. *The Impact of College on Students.* Vol. 1. San Francisco: Jossey-Bass, 1969.

Gould, J. M. "The Big Business Executive/1964: A Study of his Social and Educational Background." *Scientific American,* Special Edition. New York: 1965.

Grossman, M. *The Demand for Health: A Theoretical and Empirical Investigation.* New York: National Bureau of Economic Research, 1972.

Hyman, H., Wright, R., and Reed, J. S. *The Enduring Effects of Education.* Chicago: University of Chicago Press, 1975.

Juster, F. T. (Ed.). *Education, Income, and Human Behavior.* Sponsored by the Carnegie Commission on Higher Education. New York: McGraw-Hill, 1975.

Klarman, H. E. *The Economics of Health.* New York: Columbia University Press, 1965.

Leibowitz, A. "Home Investments in Children." *Journal of Political Economy,* March/April 1974.

Leibowitz, A. "Education and the Allocation of Women's Time." In F. T. Juster (Ed.), *Education, Income, and Human Behavior.* New York: McGraw-Hill, 1975.

Lipset, S. M. *The First New Nation.* Rev. ed. New York: Norton, 1979.

Marshall, A. *Principles of Economics.* 8th ed. New York: Macmillan, 1947.

Michael, R. "Education and Consumption." In F. T. Juster (Ed.), *Education, Income, and Human Behavior,* pp. 246-252. New York: McGraw-Hill, 1975.

Morgan, J., and others. *Productive Americans.* Ann Arbor, Mich.: Institute for Social Research, University of Michigan, 1966.

Morris, J. "Some Simple Tests of the Direct Effect of Education on Preference and on Nonmarket Productivity." *Review of Economics and Statistics,* Feb. 1976.

Mueller, E. "The Sample Survey." In L. H. Clark (Ed.), *Consumer Behavior,* pp. 36-87. New York: New York University Press, 1954.

Newcomer, M. *The Big Business Executive: The Factors That Made Him.* New York: Columbia University Press, 1955.

Nunn, C. Z., Crockett, H. J., Jr., and Williams, J. A., Jr. *Tolerance for Nonconformity: A National Survey of Americans' Changing Commitment to Civil Liberties.* San Francisco: Jossey-Bass, 1978.

Pace, C. R. *Evaluating Liberal Education: A Report Prepared for the Lilly Endowment.* Los Angeles: Graduate School of Education, University of California, 1974.

Robinson, J. P. "Mass Media Usage by the College Graduate." In S. B. Withey (Ed.), *A Degree and What Else?* New York: McGraw-Hill, 1971.

Schultz, T. W. "Optimal Investment in College Instruction: Equity and Efficiency." *Journal of Political Economy*, May/June 1972, *80* (3), Part II, S2-S30.

Solmon, L. C. "The Relation Between Schooling and Saving Behavior: An Example of the Indirect Effects of Education." In F. T. Juster (Ed.), *Education, Income, and Human Behavior.* New York: McGraw-Hill, 1975.

Stouffer, S. A. *Communism, Conformity, and Civil Liberties.* Garden City, N.Y.: Doubleday, 1955.

Taussig, F. W., and Joslyn, C. S. *American Business Leaders: A Study of Social Origins and Social Stratification.* New York: Macmillan, 1932.

Trent, J. W., and Medsker, L. *Beyond High School: A Psychosociological Study of 10,000 High School Graduates.* San Francisco: Jossey-Bass, 1968.

U.S. Bureau of the Census. *Current Population Reports: Voting and Registration in Election of November 1974.* Series P-20, No. 203. Washington, D.C.: 1976.

U.S. Bureau of the Census. *Current Population Reports: Voting and Registration in the Election of November 1976.* Series P-20, No. 322. Washington, D.C.: March 1978.

U.S. Department of Health, Education, and Welfare. *Indicators of Educational Outcomes, Fall 1972.* Washington, D.C.: 1973.

U.S. Department of Labor. *American Volunteers, 1974.* Washington, D.C.: 1975.

U.S. National Center for Education Statistics. *Digest of Education Statistics, 1974.* Washington, D.C.: 1975.

Warner, W. L., and Abegglen, J. C. *Occupational Mobility in American Business and Industry.* Minneapolis: University of Minnesota Press, 1955.

Withey, S. B. (Ed.). *A Degree and What Else? Correlates and Consequences of a College Education.* New York: McGraw-Hill, 1971.

Supplement F

Equality of Opportunity and Equality of Earned Income

Higher education is an investment in the future, and both private and public decisions concerning higher education reflect choices about what the future can and should be like. In the American context this has meant a perennial concern with whether arrangements for higher education tend to favor or impede a future in which there would be as much, or more, equality than in the past. Would it be a future in which individuals with relatively fewer advantages would be able to compete equally for the opportunities conferred by higher education? Would individuals—both advantaged and disadvantaged—use higher education opportunities in such a way as to reduce or increase the overall differences in outcomes among individuals?

These rather vague questions can be specified in many ways, yielding distinct answers and hypotheses. We here concentrate on two: (1) whether efforts to provide more equal opportunity to acquire higher education are reasonably well conceived and reasonably effective, and (2) whether the kind of system that provides equality of opportunity also tends to conduce to greater equality of earned income. The priority of these

This supplement was prepared by Martin Kramer, Senior Fellow, with the assistance of Thomas Phalen and William Carmichael, Research Assistants.

two questions lies in the fact that much of the public, which has supported higher education generously, would be profoundly disillusioned if the answer to either question was negative. Higher education would not stand well with the egalitarian commitments of the society if its equal opportunity strategy increased overall differences in income or if this strategy contributed to more equal incomes without giving individuals more equal opportunity for their talents and energies to count.

The American Strategy for Increasing Equality of Opportunity

For the past decade, at least, much of the discussion of equality of opportunity for higher education has been in terms of a somewhat different concept, that of "equal access," which can give rise to considerable confusion. One can think of an opportunity as a kind of offer and actual participation through enrollment as a kind of acceptance. The notion of "access" is used in a way which is taken to combine offer and acceptance, so that, for example, equal access is often considered to be denied if participation is unequal between members of two groups or if some students find it harder to make use of equal opportunities than do others.

It is bound to be easier, at least comparatively, for a society to devise an equal opportunity strategy than an equal access strategy—and also easier to evaluate whether it is well thought out and effective. It is one thing to make organized arrangements to offer opportunities and to equalize the terms of offers to individuals, and another thing to induce individuals to make equal use of them.

"Opportunity," therefore, seems the better concept to focus on. In general, an opportunity is a possibility of doing something desirable where circumstances do not prohibit doing it. This abstract definition already suggests some of the complexities of assessing equality of opportunity for higher education in American society. This complexity can best be seen in the context of highly specialized education. Only a limited number of people, for example, want to study music at a conservatory. For the others, the existence of the opportunity and the terms on which it is available are hypothetical (but still important, much as the freedom to start a newspaper is important to people who do not dream of doing it). For those who *do* want to attend a conservatory, there are different kinds of factors that affect whether they can. Native talent or the lack of it is one. Previous training—its objectives, resources, and success—is another. The scarcity or surplus of places in conservatories is yet another. The mechanics of competition, if any, for admission to places are also a factor. So is the ability to meet noncurricular but practically related requirements of attendance, like paying for tuition and for subsistence costs while attending. So may be—or at least have been—circumstances unrelated to either the course of study or practical arrangements for study, such as the race or sex of the prospective student.

The implicit American strategy for increasing equality of opportunity for higher education has had elements corresponding to all of these differences of circumstance that could prevent attendance by some students but not by others who have similar aspirations. The following are the main elements of that strategy:

1. *Legal prohibition of inequalities of opportunity based on factors like race or sex.* The adequacy of legal remedies for such discrimination when it exists is sometimes open to question, but it is hardly questionable that legal prohibition brings about much compliance without any need to invoke enforcement machinery.
2. *Eliminating or greatly reducing inequality in financial resources.* The vehicle has been public and private student aid. The terms on which student aid is available may increase equality of resources by some measures better than by others, but it is unquestionably a powerful lever.
3. *Increasing the number of student places.* This reduces competition for places and thereby reduces the importance of inequalities that might be judged relevant in such competition. Increasing the number of places can also be done in a way that reduces inequalities in dealing with practical problems, such as geographical distance and costs. The growth in com-

munity colleges has, for example, served all of these functions.

4. *Reducing, or compensating for, inequalities in preparation considered when students compete for places.* Programs to bring previously disadvantaged students to the same stage of preparation as their advantaged peers have often been disappointing. Much more effective has been the trend toward reducing admissions requirements—whether by dropping prerequisites, lowering test score cutoffs or introducing procedures for waiving requirements. Such moves have probably reduced the competitiveness of admissions generally, especially in those areas where good earlier schooling gave an important advantage.

5. *Reducing the importance of differences in academic talent by providing opportunities in higher education to develop many nonacademic talents in technical, manual, and esthetic areas.* Again, it is the community colleges that have taken the lead.

This implicit strategy addresses the major kinds of differences in circumstance that have traditionally resulted in inequalities of opportunity for higher education. Some countries have done more, or had more apparent success, on individual problems than has the United States. Some have, for example, mounted student aid programs that more effectively eliminate financial inequalities, at least among the academically gifted. Some countries have simply not had to deal at all with some problems of the American scene, for example, traditions of racial discrimination. But no other country has mounted programs dealing so comprehensively with so many of the sources of inequality of opportunity. And, as a result, in no other country has the option become so pervasively available of using at least some elements of the country's higher education system to pursue individual goals.

Data do not exist to measure the success of individual components of the American equal opportunity strategy or of the strategy as a whole. Fundamentally, there is no way to control for differences in desire or motivation for higher education. But we do have "access" data on the enrollment rates of different socioeconomic and demographic groups that permit control for conventional academic ability. These data tend to show narrow, or at least narrowing, differences (Tables F-1, F-2, F-3).

Table F-1. Percentage of students entering college from the high school classes of 1961 and 1972, by socioeconomic status (SES) and ability

	1961		1972	
Ability quartile	Above median SES	Below median SES	Above median SES	Below median SES
1 (low)	26%	12%	27%	14%
2	40	18	37	25
3	62	34	55	39
4 (high)	84	64	73	64

Source: Adapted from Peng (1977).

Table F-2. Percentage of students entering college from the high school classes of 1961 and 1972, by sex and ability

	1961		1972	
Ability quartile	Men	Women	Men	Women
1 (low)	22%	17%	21%	22%
2	34	25	33	30
3	53	43	53	47
4 (high)	78	71	72	74

Source: Adapted from Peng (1977).

Table F-3. Percentage of students entering college from the high school class of 1972, by race and ability

	1972		
Ability quartile	Black	White	Hispanic
1 (low)	26%	17%	29%
2	54	33	50
3	65	53	60
4 (high)	78	75	78

Source: Adapted from Peng (1977).

The measures in Tables F-1, F-2, and F-3 say something important and positive about the broadening of higher education opportunities, but there are important caveats. For example, the main reason why college entrance rates are so high for Hispanics—higher than for whites of comparable ability—probably has more to do with the low rates of high school completion in some Hispanic communities than with effective recruitment of Hispanics by the colleges. With high school completion rates so low, the persistence needed to finish high school must be so strong that it carries over and results in high college entrance rates for those Hispanic students who have it. The same is probably also true for black students. To generalize, it is perfectly possible—and perhaps a fact—that college opportunities for disadvantaged groups are fairly good, while their high school opportunities are poor. The result may be a combined secondary and higher education system that is not doing nearly as much as it should.

In any case, almost no one is entirely satisfied with the progress that has been made toward equal opportunity for higher education. There are several sources of dissatisfaction that are really quite distinct and that call for separate treatment:

1. Some feel that the various components of the equal opportunity strategy do the right things but do not do enough, e.g., that there should be stronger enforcement of anti-discrimination laws or that there should be more generous student aid.
2. Some find the strategy itself unsatisfactory or unacceptable because it does not result in as much equality of outcomes as they would like to see.
3. Some feel that the sorting of individuals into different kinds of institutions perpetuates undesirable traditions of elitism.
4. Some feel that the strategy is too costly.
5. Some find the difference in the resources invested in students in different fields and institutions unacceptable. Similarly, some find unacceptable the different level of educational investment in college students in general as compared with non-college youth and older groups.

6. Some are concerned that the present strategy does not do much about subtle interactive effects between opportunity and aspirations, family background and social stereotypes. That is, it does not equalize the use of opportunities and, in that sense, "access."

Should the strategy be carried further? The answer—and whether an objective answer is possible at all—must depend on which component of the strategy is in question. On some components, we may have gone about as far as we should go. There are certainly enough places in the system, and the system does quite well in reallocating them among students with different aspirations. (The system has, for example, reallocated places from liberal arts to occupational programs with a speed that has itself caused problems.) Programs for those with nonacademic talents have multiplied. There are also an increasing number of observers (including the Carnegie Council) who think that there is now almost enough student aid in the aggregate but that it should be better distributed.

Further, reducing admissions requirements has certainly been effective. Although it is easy to deride this component of the strategy, it should be considered against the background of other national systems of higher education, which sometimes have tracking systems so rigid that it is almost impossible for a student who has gone to the "wrong" schools to enter a university. Compared with these systems, our flexibility about entrance requirements can be seen to have much merit.

In contrast, efforts to reduce or compensate for inequalities of preparation have a long way to go. More resources for remedial programs would appear clearly warranted, except for the fact that the task has turned out to be so difficult. Too many of the occasional successes seem to have depended on inspired teaching, highly motivated students, and happy accidents. Present programs can be said only conditionally to represent an inadequate effort: *If* it becomes possible to make up for inadequate preparation through reliable programs easily replicated with more usual teachers and more usual students, *then* the present level of effort would seem grossly inadequate.

In the case of machinery for enforcing legal prohibitions of discrimination, it is not even possible to specify objectively what would be an adequate effort in given circumstances. In the nature of the case, regulations and remedies must impinge on the recruitment, hiring, and promotion procedures of colleges and universities. There must, therefore, be a tradeoff between the value of what can be done to prevent or remedy discrimination and the value of letting academic institutions conduct these procedures autonomously. What represents too much intervention to some is bound to represent too little to others. Competing values here are too fundamental to permit resolution of the issue by the expedient of spending more money, successful as that approach has been in enhancing equality of opportunity through creating more places and providing more student aid.

Should the strategy be faulted because it does not yield equality of results? It has become fashionable to discount the importance of equality of opportunity because it cannot reasonably be expected to lead directly to equality of results among individuals, that is, equalities of status and other rewards, such as income and wealth. The differences between individuals and their life histories will always mean different results, even with equality of educational opportunity. But, what higher education can do should not be slighted because it cannot overcome all the factors that lead to differences of outcome. The fashionable tendency to discount the importance of equality of opportunity ignores four major considerations:

1. It is immensely important to individuals that what they do with their talents should make a difference in outcomes and that irrelevant characteristics of race, sex, or origin should not.
2. Although equality of opportunity does not guarantee equality of results among individuals, it does tend to reduce inequality of results among members of *groups* sorted by irrelevant characteristics of race, sex, and origin. That is, if differences in educational opportunities between an advantaged and disadvantaged group are reduced, a substantial reduction in the difference between the earnings and other

rewards of average members of the two groups can be expected, even though differences in outcome among members of the same group will still be large and may even widen. Jencks, for example, has estimated that equalizing the amount of schooling, including higher education, received by black and white males would have reduced the average income difference between them by 25 to 30 percent.[1]

3. Equality of opportunity complements other egalitarian programs. For example, the prospects of poor children are probably far better if they are assured the benefits of an adequate health care program *and* educational opportunities than only one or the other.

4. Higher education opportunities may contribute to a long-term balance between the supply and demand for people with higher education qualifications; this balance would favor greater equality of earnings generally, as discussed later in this supplement.

Does the strategy perpetuate an undesirable elitism? A major component of the strategy has been the creation of open-access institutions with ample places. The strategy has left intact institutions, like the highly selective liberal arts colleges, which successfully prepare small numbers of students for admission to graduate and professional schools, which lead in turn to highly rewarding and influential career roles. However, to interpret this state of affairs as a failure of the equal opportunity strategy requires the acceptance of premises that are a good deal more radical than many of those who criticize the strategy on this ground seem to realize. There is, in fact, a great deal of educational and occupational mobility in the United States, certainly as compared to other countries. Table F-4 shows that the chances that a child from a low-status family will go to college are better in the United States than in many other Western industrialized countries and were better even before the recent rapid growth in open-access institutions. Available evidence suggests that the chances may be about five times as great as in the

---

[1]Jencks (1979); Jencks (1973) estimated 15 to 30 percent.

Table F-4. Relative chances of access to higher education for youth from professional and white collar families as compared with those from manual workers' families, in selected countries

	Ratios of enrollment probabilities	Reference year for Students	Reference year for Parental occupations
Austria	3.8	1970	1972
Belgium	4.6	1966	1961
Finland	3.4	1969	1970
France	5.0	1973	1968
Germany	3.3	1970	1971
Greece	2.2	1970	1971
Italy	5.8	1967	1969
Luxembourg	4.5	1972	1966
Netherlands	8.5	1970	1964
Norway	5.3	1970	1972
Spain	7.4	1970	1970
United Kingdom	1.4	1971	1971
United States	2.2	1965	1965
Yugoslavia	4.0	1969	1971

Source: Adapted from Busch (1975).

Soviet Union.[2] Figure F-1 shows that blacks—surely a bellwether group for the permeability of the American class system —no longer must contend with exclusionary policies in elite colleges. In 1972 low-ability blacks were only slightly more likely to attend nonselective four-year institutions than low-ability whites, and high-ability blacks were even more likely than high-ability whites to attend highly selective institutions. Table F-5 shows that a larger proportion of male Americans in elite occupations come from families where the father was a manual worker than in other industrialized noncommunist societies, although it must be borne in mind that a larger proportion of all jobs in the United States can be labeled "elite."

[2] Special tabulation of cumulative college entrance rates of the National Longitudinal Study of 1972 high school graduates; and data cited in Yanowich (1977).

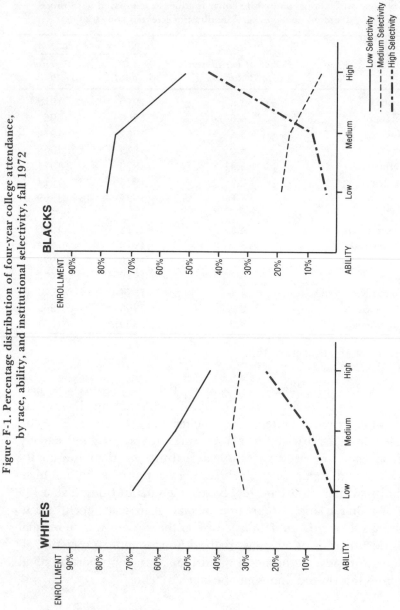

Figure F-1. Percentage distribution of four-year college attendance, by race, ability, and institutional selectivity, fall 1972

Source: Bailey and Collins (1977).

Table F-5. Percentages of men in elite occupations with fathers
in manual occupations, in selected countries

	Percentage of elite	*Elite as percentage of labor force*
Denmark	1.1%	3.3%
France	1.6	6.1
Germany (Fed. Rep.)	1.5	4.6
Italy	1.5	6.6
Japan	7.0	11.7
Netherlands	6.6	11.1
Sweden	3.5	6.7
United Kingdom	2.2	7.5
United States	7.8	16.0

Source: Miller (1960, p. 37).

But, if elite careers and elite colleges are not the preserves of an upper class, then it is a radical position to reject the American equal opportunity strategy because it allows selective institutions to continue alongside nonselective ones. In American circumstances, this position would require that one be prepared to argue that society as a whole, and not just its educational institutions, should be reorganized to provide fewer roles for persons with elite academic preparation. Otherwise, there would have to be other mechanisms than educational ones for selecting and training individuals for elite roles.

This is not to say that a stratified system of higher education poses no perils to equal opportunity. There probably are many students who wrongly assess the kind of academic work they can do and would like to do and who, for these reasons or because of family and peer relationships, choose institutions where their talents will be less developed than they would be at more selective institutions. But, in a system without open-admissions institutions, many such individuals might not enter higher education at all and would not have the opportunity, as many now do, to transfer to more academic or more selective specialized institutions later. And, without selective institutions, the system would be hard pressed to provide adequate support and challenge to gifted students.

Is the strategy too costly? In absolute terms the equal opportunity strategy is costly. Far more institutions and students need to be supported than would have been the case with an exclusionary system that assured places and support only for those students with great academic potential and strong motivation. In the lean years ahead, the costs of the strategy may leave less to invest in the most promising students than would appear desirable.

The issue here is the real wealth of the society and the value of investing some portion of that wealth in higher education for persons of only modest talent and motivation. There are countries so poor or at such a stage of development that it makes sense to invest in higher education only for the few whose talents are most needed, however such need is determined. The United States, however, has been rich enough that it could afford to do otherwise, and its economy has provided far more jobs requiring training and education beyond secondary school than an academically gifted elite could begin to fill. It may be that the society will be poorer in the future in real terms. One consequence may be much greater competition between highly academic and less academic institutions for available funds. But it would have to be a great deal poorer, and the American economy would have to be structured very differently, for the priority of equal opportunity expenditures to be seriously eroded.

Are the resources invested in individual students too unequal to afford adequate equality of opportunity? Inequalities of investment are, in fact, pronounced. Real costs per student (as distinct from student charges) at selective institutions run considerably higher, on the average, than at nonselective ones. Costs for students in some fields—the sciences and health professions, especially—are higher than those for students in the humanities and social sciences. Further, there is clearly more explicit investment in students in higher education, on the average, than in most people who have not gone to college. This difference is smaller when implicit investment through on-the-job training is taken into account. But, because employers intend to recoup most such on-the-job investment, the amount of net investment in individuals from which they can be expected to profit must still differ between those who have gone to college and those who have not.

Given these facts, there are certainly serious questions to be raised about resource allocation within higher education and within society generally. But they are not simply questions about equality of opportunity, but about the intersection of opportunities, individual choices, and resource allocation.

Three examples will illustrate the issues involved. Take, first, training in nuclear physics. Not everyone wants to be, or has much promise of being, a nuclear physicist. If the terms on which an individual can seek training to become one are reasonably equalized with respect to race, sex, and family resources, among other factors, then the large outlays on behalf of those who do seek such training successfully should not be put down as diminishing equality of opportunity. Rather, the high per-student outlays reflect the cost of extending the range of opportunities to include nuclear physics—a field in which training is very expensive.

For a contrasting case, take that of undergraduate liberal arts students. The largest item of per-student cost is instructional staff. There is a widely held pedagogical assumption that a smaller student-teacher ratio is advantageous to students. It is an easy step to suppose that students from otherwise disadvantaged backgrounds should attend institutions with equal or smaller ratios than otherwise more favored students. This would tend to produce equal or greater costs per student and, therefore, to suggest that equal or greater amounts of money should be spent *per* disadvantaged student. But, again, it is because specific educational goals and processes are envisioned, entailing specific inputs in specific quantities, that equal or greater investment in disadvantaged individuals seems desirable. The situation is unlike the nuclear physicist example only in assuming similar goals and processes, where that example assumed a distinguishing educational process, requiring special resources.

For a third case, take that of students with an auditory or visual handicap. Here, even if the goals of the educational program are the same, the processes, to be effective, must be somewhat different, and the modifications required are likely to result in greater per-student expense.

Together, the three cases suggest that relative equality of resource allocation is a good indicator of relative equality of opportunity only if the assumed goals and processes are the same. If goals are different, what is at issue is the range of opportunities to be provided, and not equality of opportunity. If goals are the same, but the processes are different, equality of opportunity is genuinely at issue in resource allocation, but differences in *per-student* resources, not equality, would ordinarily be most conducive to equality of opportunity.

Generally, equality of opportunity depends on equality of investment, *other things being equal,* but this *ceteris paribus* clause is too open to give much policy guidance. Other things not equal may include student preference for different courses of study, society's determination (on cost and other grounds) of the number of places to be provided in each course of study, and the objectives, processes, and resources-use efficiency of training in each. Substantial differences in investment—as between young people who go to college and those who do not— are a good indication of the relative neglect of a large group, but not an accurate measure of what should be done on its behalf.

A general principle mandating equality of investment would curtail privilege in a quite different way from the principle of equality of opportunity. The principle of equality of opportunity operates to reduce to the most relevant minimum the kinds of differences between individuals that count in competing for opportunities, or to reduce the differences themselves. It is most easily and completely satisfied when the need for competition can be avoided altogether, as it almost can be sometimes, for example, in the case of access to public libraries. The principle of equality of investment, on the other hand, suggests an upper cost limit on the range of opportunities to be provided. It also suggests some kind of compensatory payment to individuals who choose educational programs costing less than the limit. But the equal investment principle says nothing about nonfinancial barriers or the terms of competition for places. Historically, extreme inequality of investment has usually gone hand in hand with extreme inequality of opportunity. However, the one is not the other, and an equal opportunity strategy can go a long way—as has the American strategy —without coming close to equalizing investment. A principle of equalizing investment is a good guide for an equal opportunity strategy only in dealing with educational goals and processes held valid for all, and, then, only if modified to mandate *at least* equal resources for those whose opportunities are more restricted by circumstance.

Does the strategy deal effectively with the subtle interactive effects among opportunities, aspirations, family backgrounds, and social stereotypes? There is no component of the strategy that deals, in any systematic way, with such things as the discomfort of a ghetto youth on an ivy league campus or the set of inhibitions that tend to make many women avoid the natural sciences. One could frame a definition of opportunity that would relegate such problems to the status of factors that inhibit the seizing of opportunity, rather than viewing them as part of the structure of opportunities and, therefore, as relevant to equality of opportunity. They nonetheless constitute obstacles that some need to overcome, while others do not.

Can these problems be dealt with in a systematic way by public policy? There have been some notable attempts. The community colleges have made an effort to be "open door" institutions which has meant, among other things, an effort to reduce social discomfort. The College Entrance Examination Board has, for a good many years, suggested that colleges may wish to estimate the expected family financial contributions of very low income students not as zero, but as negative, so that compensatory student aid could be made systematically available to such students and so that they would not have to feel that they bring their poverty with them when they come to college. Less systematic have been federal, state, private, and group-sponsored programs for extra counseling and psychological support. Sometimes these programs seem to work, sometimes not. Symbolism and ideology tend to loom large in the premises of many of the programs and sometimes place their advocates in adversary positions vis-à-vis the institutions they seek to make more open.

What can be said generally about efforts to reduce inhibitions on motivation is perhaps cold comfort to those who see this as the central problem of an equal opportunity strategy. But it can nonetheless be said that the aspirations of members of groups formerly denied equal opportunities have changed greatly in the past two decades, with or without the benefits of explicit policy intervention. It can also be said that an educational system has come a long way whose main remaining problem in providing equality of opportunity is to strengthen the personal autonomy and broaden the horizons of those to whom opportunities are otherwise available. It is perhaps also worth saying that the persistence of such problems recalls education to the fact that it has never been simply a service industry, but an effort actively to discover talent and to develop autonomous personal commitments. This is what teachers thought they were doing (and knew they would have to do over again with each generation of college students) long before equality of opportunity attained its present place on the public agenda.

The Contribution of Equal Opportunity to Equality of Earned Income

Greater equality of opportunity does not necessarily lead to greater equality of earnings between individuals or in the society as a whole in the short run. For example, in today's conditions, those who benefit by equality of opportunity for medical education typically end up with earned incomes several times the median. But the interesting question from a policy perspective is whether the American equal opportunity strategy described in the previous section has a long-run tendency, in a society and economy such as ours, to reduce inequality of incomes. Unless incomes are highly regulated, there will be differences in earnings attributable to many factors other than education. Nonetheless, it may be that the economy's demand for skills is such and the supply of skilled individuals through the educational system is such that they work together in the direction of greater equality of earnings. Some of the conditions for this kind of development do seem to be approximated by American circumstances.

In general, whether workers receive more nearly equal rates of pay when more of them are obtaining college educations depends on the nature of the economic and educational institutions of their society and the stage of its history. S. Kuznets (1955) suggested that there is a pattern to the changes in the distribution of incomes that accompany industrialization. A traditional (usually agricultural) society may be characterized by either small or very large dispersion of incomes, but those groups with the lowest incomes will often receive a larger share of all income than in more affluent societies—for the simple reason that they must receive such a share to survive. With industrialization, Kuznets argued, a number of factors come into play that tend to increase income inequality. The migration of rural populations to industrial centers creates a pool of workers willing to compete for low-paying, unskilled jobs. The rewards to entrepreneurship and capital invested in hitherto unexploited natural resources, technologies, and opportunities for large-scale undertakings also tend to widen the income distribution. After the first phase of industrialization, however, unskilled migrants are a smaller proportion of the workforce. Their descendants seek and obtain higher-level skills. This maturing of an industrial society together with egalitarian government policies in the areas of taxation and income transfers tends to reduce income inequalities.

Cross-sectional data comparing the degree of income inequality in countries at different stages of industrial development appear consistent with this suggested pattern (Table F-6), although the situation in many countries would require special explanation. Kuznets' conjecture concerning the general trend of industrialization also seems confirmed by Psacharopoulous' finding (1973) of high but declining marginal returns to educational investment in the earlier stages of economic development. Although the rate of return to education may then rise with the adoption of advanced technologies, a tendency toward greater

Table F-6. Measures of dispersion of before-tax money wages and salaries
of full-time male workers in nonagricultural industries,
twenty-five countries, various years

| | Ratio of income received to median per capita income | | |
Country and year	By fifth percentile	By tenth percentile	Seventy-fifth percentile
Czechoslovakia, 1964	1.7	1.5	.9
New Zealand, 1960-61	1.8	1.5	.8
Hungary, 1964	1.8	1.6	.8
Australia, 1959-60	1.9	1.6	.8
Denmark, 1956	2.0	1.6	.8
United Kingdom, 1960-61	2.0	1.6	.8
Sweden, 1959	2.0	1.7	.8
Yugoslavia, 1963	2.0	1.7	.8
Poland, 1960	2.0	1.7	.8
Germany (F.R.), 1957	2.1	1.7	.8
Canada, 1960-61	2.1	1.7	.8
Belgium, 1964	2.1	1.6	.8
United States, 1959	2.1	1.7	.8
Austria, 1957	2.1	1.7	.8
Netherlands, 1959[a]	2.2	1.8	.7
Argentina, 1961	2.2	1.8	.8
Spain, 1964	2.2	1.8	.8
Finland, 1960	2.5	2.0	.7
France, 1963	2.8	2.1	.7
Japan, 1955	2.7	2.1	.6
Brazil, 1953	3.8	2.5	—
India, 1958-59[b]	4.0	3.0	.7
Ceylon, 1963	4.0	3.0	—
Chile, 1964[b]	4.0	3.0	—
Mexico, 1960	4.5	2.8	.7

[a]Married couples treated as single units.

[b]Rough estimates based on data for manual workers only.

Source: Adapted from Kravis (1973).

equality of earnings may persist because of an increasing ratio of the number of those with college education to the number of those with secondary education, and of those with secondary education to those with only primary education. Psacharopolous finds that those who complete higher education earn nearly 6.5 times as much as primary school graduates in poor countries compared to only 2.5 times as much in rich countries.

Coleman (1973) finds a remarkable *pari passu* convergence in both incomes and educational attainment in the United States over the past 50 years, taking the variation in schooling and incomes that existed in 1929 as the standard and dividing the coefficients of variation of education and income for several years by those for 1929 (Table F-7).

Table F-7. Dispersion of incomes and educational attainment, selected years relative to 1929

	1929	1935-36	1946	1960	1968	1970
Income	1.0	0.89	0.71	0.67	0.59	0.61
Education	1.0	0.88	0.71	0.67	0.60	0.55

Source: Coleman (1973).

It helps to see the role of higher education in increasing equality of earnings against the background of such patterns. With the progress of industrialization, more people perceive the returns of higher levels of education, and training and investment in human capital becomes more intensive. Returns to such investment eventually fall, however, as individuals with high levels of skill become relatively more plentiful and therefore cheaper to hire. Industrialization first generates unskilled jobs but also increases demand for people with higher skills. Greater inequality results. But then the capacity of the education and training system to provide people with higher level skills becomes more rationalized and responsive, reducing the likelihood of long-term skill shortages. Thus, the education and training system is first a factor in increasing social mobility and, then, a factor in reducing differences in rewards.

There is nothing that guarantees that this course of development will proceed smoothly and without painful anomalies. Migration can continue to occur, bringing into industrial centers people who do not meet the productivity expectations of an economic system that is already well advanced. Group inequalities created by custom and prejudice may persist. The role of the educational system, then, is not just to enable long-term benign trends to proceed. It is challenged to create a high degree of upward income and occupational mobility for recent entrants into the process even when it has reached the stage of narrowing the distances mobile individuals must traverse.

Anomalies aside, Tinbergen (1975) has pointed out that the supply of workers of each level of education could come to be so nearly equal to the demand that earnings could come to be approximately equal. For supply to bring about something close to equality of earned income requires that two conditions be met. First, the educational system needs to be so flexible and responsive that it can readily produce the number of workers with the qualifications required. Second, subsidies to education combined with the nonmonetary attractions of more educated occupations must be adequate to offset fully all of the individual's additional costs of education (including opportunity costs) over and above the consumption value of life as a student.

The American equal opportunity strategy has created circumstances closely approximating these two conditions. By creating an ample number of places in institutions competing with each other for students and by making many of these places available to students who are not academically gifted in traditional terms, the strategy has created circumstances in which institutions can be expected to be highly flexible and responsive to the economy's demands for trained and educated workers. Clearly, there is already much such flexibility and responsiveness. For example, the American higher education system has shown that it can quickly mount programs for training new categories of health professionals and recruit serious students for them without holding out the prospect of salaries much exceeding those of skilled manual craftsmen. It may be more realistic to foresee American society as one in which such adaptations become commonplace than as one in which large earnings differentials are the stimulus for a few highly motivated individuals to incur heavy personal investment burdens to qualify themselves for privileged occupational niches. An educational system producing individuals with highly differentiated levels of skills and productivity could nonetheless be one that makes major contributions to greater equality of earnings.

Other components of the equal opportunity strategy are highly supportive of this kind of development. Low tuition and student aid greatly reduce out-of-pocket costs of education. It therefore takes less of a difference in the earnings and non-monetary rewards of educated occupations compared to those of other occupations to induce a choice of additional schooling.

Tinbergen (1975) sees the role of higher education in achieving greater equality of earnings in terms of the outcomes —of a race between the changing supply and the changing demand for college-educated workers. If higher education is winning the race—producing individuals with higher education qualifications more rapidly than changing technology increases their productivity—then inequalities between the earnings of persons with different levels of schooling will decrease. If technology wins—creating more jobs in which higher education qualifications are productive or enhancing their productivity in existing jobs—then inequalities of earnings will increase. Tinbergen documents the case for viewing higher education as the apparent winner, given long-term trends over the first half of this century. If so, periods such as the 1960s, in which education and technology appear to have run neck-and-neck, would be something of an aberration.

Tinbergen suggests that, if education does not appear to be gaining fast enough on technology and if inequality of earnings is narrowing too slowly, public policy might wish to favor the side of education by deliberately increasing the supply of college-educated workers in order to make their relative earnings fall. Additionally, or alternatively, public policy might bias investments in technology in favor of industries and processes using less-educated workers more productively. But it may well be that the American priority on equality of opportunity has led to a higher education system so organized and subsidized that education stands to win the race handily without such additional public interventions to reduce the relative returns to higher education in the interest of greater earnings equality. An equal opportunity strategy, far from being the source of widening disparities of income it may appear to be in the short run, may in fact suffice to fill as large an egalitarian role as the society wants education, as opposed to other institutions, to play.

The role of nonmonetary rewards in choice of careers may be especially worth stressing in this context. If people now increasingly want jobs that provide variety, opportunities for self-expression, and attractive physical surroundings, then they will be willing to incur higher investment costs and to accept lower pay in order to have such jobs. It is easier to design jobs meeting these specifications that use the skills of those with higher education than other skills. Higher education, therefore, plays a role in the evolution of a society subscribing to the maxim, "to each according to the disagreeableness of his work." The result could be an inequality of earnings the reverse of the traditional one, with the higher educated earning less than those in many manual occupations.

Current Issues

The long-run relationships between higher education and equality discussed so far are somewhat tangential to the issues most discussed in recent years. The main such issues are four:

- Whether the overall distribution of income in the United States has stabilized in recent decades in ways that leave large and permanent inequalities of income
- Whether education plays a major role in reducing the intergenerational transmission of inequality, i.e., in bringing the incomes of offspring closer to the average than the incomes of the parents were
- Whether inequalities of educational opportunity between dif-

ferent groups, especially different ethnic groups, have been a major cause of income inequalities between them, such that reducing inequalities of opportunity can be a relatively effective way of reducing income inequalities between groups
• How demand in the labor market for persons with skills and/ or credentials transmitted by education actually interacts with supply to create more, or less, equality.

The first of these issues affects educational policy in a somewhat roundabout way. If the overall income distribution seems to change little, if at all, despite much economic and social change, including much more participation in higher education, then it becomes easy to despair of relatively mild and noncoercive egalitarian social policies, such as increasing equality of educational opportunity. It therefore adds importantly to the credibility of such policies to recognize that the income distribution has not been nearly so stable as it appears to have been at first sight: Kuznets (1974) has shown that when the types of family unit are taken into account—their size and the age of their members, in particular—a reduction of about one-tenth of the income inequality existing in 1947 had occurred by 1969. Education may, in fact, be regarded as one factor in making income inequality appear more persistent than it really is. As education qualifies a larger proportion of workers for occupations in which the ratio of peak earnings to earnings at entry is large—as is the case in many professions—the resulting differences in earnings will show up in cross-sectional data as increasing inequality of earned income, offsetting reductions in inequality among persons in the same stage of their careers (or over their lifetimes), including reductions resulting from more education. Kuznets points out that inequality of earnings between the newly trained and the established professional, captured by cross-sectional data, has altogether different implications for social policy than inequality between people at the same point in their lives with similar consumption needs, but unequal prospects.

The two Jencks books—*Inequality* (1972) and *Who Gets Ahead?* (1979)—deal with matters bearing on the second issue—

the role of education in reducing intergenerational inequalities in income. Looking at mature males (over age 25 [1972]; 25 to 64 [1979]), Jencks finds that getting more education is a good strategy for the individual seeking to improve his position, less effective for the society as a whole if it seeks to bring all incomes closer to equality, but by no means a strategy that cancels out the advantages or disadvantages of family background. We are left, in *Inequality*, with the view that an explicit policy of income redistribution is by far the most direct and promising way to reduce inequality and, in *Who Gets Ahead?*, with the view that greater equality of productivity, coupled with labor market institutions forcing recognition of their equality, might also work.

In the earlier book Jencks and his associates (1972) were hardly concerned at all with the third issue—the reduction of intergroup inequality—or the fourth—the receptivity of the labor market to persons with different amounts of education. The second book (1979) is concerned with both the third and fourth issues, but does not deal with the labor market's reception of young blacks and young whites entering adult careers for the first time in the late 1960s and early 1970s.

The events of those years showed three things quite dramatically: First, more equal opportunities for higher education can, in some conditions, lead rather quickly to more equal rates of pay between groups. Second, one such helpful condition is for the overall level of demand for the college-educated to increase and to postpone, at least, a situation of oversupply. Third, conditions really do change, raising doubts about the predictive value of an essentially retrospective analysis such as Jencks'. Different cohorts launching their work careers in different conditions may face altogether different prospects. For example, the decline (estimated by Jencks) in the value of a high school education for older blacks in the 1960s may never be redressed; the improvement in the same decade in the value of higher education to young blacks is, at the same time, enormously hopeful. As in Kuznets' sketch of the role of education in the process of economic development, outcomes depend on the consonance between educational opportunities and labor market conditions at a particular time, and this means for a particular generation.

The difference in educational attainment between black and white males just entering the labor force has narrowed greatly in recent decades (Table F-8). The increases in the

Table F-8. Years of school completed at estimated time of labor market entry, selected years, 1930-1970

	Year of labor market entry				
	1930	1940	1950	1960	1970
Mean schooling of blacks	5.9	8.0	9.9	11.1	11.4
Mean schooling of whites	9.6	11.1	12.0	12.6	12.6
Proportion of blacks with less than 9 years of school	.78	.58	.31	.15	.11
Proportion of whites with less than 9 years of school	.42	.22	.15	.10	.07
Proportion of blacks with more than 12 years of school	.03	.07	.13	.19	.19
Proportion of whites with more than 12 years of school	.08	.20	.32	.37	.38

Source: Smith and Welch (1978).

amount of schooling received by black males shown in Table F-8 (and probably also improvements in its quality) have in recent years been accompanied by an increase in the earnings advantage conferred by college (Table F-9).

The late 1960s boom in demand for the college-educated was even more of a boom for black men than for white men just entering the labor market. The recession in demand of the mid-1970s cancelled out some of the advantage of college-educated young black males, but left it much more comparable to that of whites than it had been before the boom.

Again, however, it must be stressed that it was not higher education alone, outside a specific historical context, that brought about greater equality of earnings. Favorable labor market conditions were also necessary. Technology, economic

Table F-9. Percentage increase in income associated with a year of college attendance for black and white males entering the labor market

	Blacks	Whites
1967	7%	14%
1968	12	15
1969	14	16
1970	24	15
1971	23	15
1972	18	12
1973	11	12
1974	12	12

Source: Adapted from Smith and Welch (1978).

organization, and the growth of service industries had created conditions in which the skills imparted by higher education commanded a premium. If this had not been so, the vastly increased number of white males with college education (let alone, blacks) would not have found jobs in which their skills and credentials could be translated into higher earnings. It was greatly in the interest of earnings equality for young blacks that technology was neck-and-neck with education in Tinbergen's "race" during the 1960s, but not, apparently, in the interest of older less-educated blacks.

How much of the improved earnings advantage of young black males is owed to affirmative action programs and how much to the more nearly equal productive skills of prospective black and white job candidates, as perceived by employers? It is hard to believe that employer acceptance of black credentials could have come so far so fast without the spur of affirmative action. Yet, affirmative action at its best tends to disguise its own long-run effectiveness. It tends to succeed by giving members of disadvantaged groups an incentive—better job prospects —to obtain training, which employers are then asked to recognize at its true value. Employers' motives are mixed. They want to avoid the sanctions of affirmative action programs, and they also want to hire productive workers. As they find that newly trained minority workers are in fact productive, the motive of compliance becomes of less importance and ordinary economic incentives of more importance. In retrospect it will be hard to say which motive carried the most weight. Freeman (1977) and Smith and Welch (1978) take opposite views of this controversy.

Quite apart from the role of affirmative action and other direct government interventions, the way in which the labor market translates education into earnings is a matter of continuing controversy. The simple view—which is not necessarily wrong for all that—is that investment in higher education creates an asset that yields a return to the possessor when an employer purchases his services. Accordingly, it seems possible to distribute such investments among individuals so that returns to their labor and skills are more equal. But are employers this rational? If so, only a rapid increase in the number of jobs in which the human capital of college graduates is productive can explain the continued earnings premium of college graduates through the 1960s. Otherwise, their rapid increase in numbers would have driven down or eliminated their earnings premium, with a resulting earnings equality or reversed inequality as envisioned by Tinbergen. This did not occur, and those who went to college in the 1960s seem to have made economically rational decisions, achieving returns in keeping with their investment (Nollen, 1974).

But other explanations for the maintenance of the earnings premium of college graduates have been advanced, premised in part on doubts that the demand for college-trained skills could really have grown so fast in the 1960s. One such explanation is that possession of a college degree is not even a rough measure of an increment of human capital that employers want to obtain, but is rather a measure of the individual's talent, initiative, and docility, which, together in some combination, have enabled him to stay in college for four years. Employers always need more workers who have these characteristics and fewer of those who do not, so on this "screening" hypothesis it is not necessary to explain a continued earnings premium for college graduates by a growth in the number of jobs in which higher education is a productive asset.

Although the behavior of some employers has probably always fitted the screening hypothesis (and that of many employers for brief periods), it is hard to believe that screening effects explain the earnings advantage of college graduates and its amount for long periods and in many societies.[3] First, if raw talent, initiative, and docility were all that employers seek from college graduates, someone in some industrial society, capitalist or socialist, would have found a better way to screen for these characteristics than that of placing young people in highly costly institutions for several years. Second, it cannot be solely the credential or diploma that confers the earnings premium of college graduates—as the screening hypothesis would seem to require—since those who drop out before receiving the credential also have a considerable earnings advantage. Third, the earnings advantage of college graduates continues as they grow older, that is, beyond the time needed for employers to substitute for the credential their own independent assessments of the talent, initiative, and docility of college graduates. But if, for these three reasons, the screening hypothesis is implausible as a full explanation of the maintenance of the earnings premium of college graduates through the 1960s, we are left with the view that there must have been a genuine—and large—increase in the demand for the skills of college graduates during that decade.[4]

The other case that well illustrates how the earnings impact of educational opportunities depends on other social factors is that of women. It is tautological, or nearly so, that educational opportunities will tend to equalize the earnings of men and women only if they use similar opportunities in similar proportions, and if they can and do use their educational qualifications similarly at each stage of job choice and job progression. It is, of course, well known that women have tended to enroll in college programs in different proportions than men, that they have traditionally tended to withdraw from the labor force for considerable periods, and that they have tended to go into predominantly "women's" careers, such as elementary and second-

[3]This paragraph summarizes arguments presented in Layard and Psacharopoulos (1974).

[4]For other perspectives on this question, see Supplement C in this report.

ary school teaching. All of these factors together, along with some out-and-out discrimination, has given rise to lifetime earnings profiles quite different for men and for women with given levels of education (Figure F-2). It is not possible to sort out

Figure F-2. Median annual income of full-time, year-round workers by age, for male and female high school and college graduates, 1971

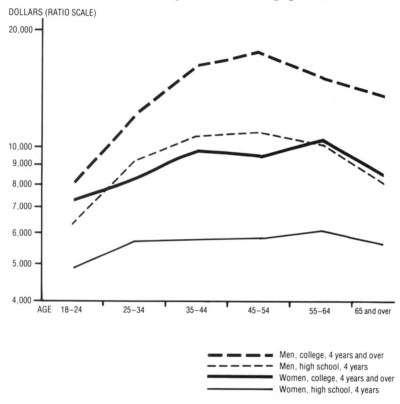

DOLLARS (RATIO SCALE)

- - - - Men, college, 4 years and over
- - - - - Men, high school, 4 years
———— Women, college, 4 years and over
———— Women, high school, 4 years

Source: The President (1973, p. 105).

the separate effects of choice of academic program, hiring practices, on-the-job training differences, promotion policies, and periods spent outside the labor force in generating these different profiles. Nor is it clear how much and how fast changes in these factors will reduce inequalities in earnings between men and women.

There are, however, a few items of information that tell part of the story of the interaction of women's educational participation and the labor market over the past two decades. There seems to have been a period in which the educational decisions of young women were increasingly in conflict with continuing discrimination in employment. Between 1962 and 1973 the effects of discrimination on women's earnings were changing hardly at all (Featherman and Hauser, 1976). But a comparison of 1955 and 1972 high school graduates shows significant convergence in the experiences, attitudes, and choices of young men and women over roughly the same period (Table F-10; a

Table F-10. The relationship between sex and college-related variables, 1955 and 1972

	Simple correlation with sex[a]	
Variables	1955	1972
Semesters, high school mathematics	−0.273*	−0.255*
Semesters, high school science	−0.250*	−0.223*
Parents highly influential on college attendance	−0.011	0.017
Attended college because college graduates earn more	−0.312*	−0.227*
Attended college because friends went to college	0.012	−0.033
Attended college to develop socially	0.137*	−0.083*
Attended college to marry well	0.168*	0.018
Attended college because of its academic reputation	0.113*	0.105*
Attended college because of its excellence in field of interest	0.052	0.069*
Attended college because of admission standards	−0.063	0.114*
Believes women can have career and children simultaneously	0.121*	0.045
Father's education (0 = none; 9 = Ph.D. or professional degree)	0.119*	0.006
Mother's education	0.107*	0.016

(continued on next page)

Table F-10 *(continued)*

| | Simple correlation with sex[a] | |
Variables	1955	1972
Major		
Humanities	0.099*	0.150*
Social science	−0.076	−0.027
Engineering, math, or physical science	−0.273*	−0.237*
Education	0.371*	0.233*
Business	−0.201*	−0.224*
Medical fields	0.202*	0.172*

[a]The correlations presented are between a dummy sex variable (male = 0 and female = 1) and the variables listed. A negative correlation coefficient implies a predominantly male characteristic, while a positive coefficient implies a predominantly female characteristic. A zero correlation implies that the characteristic predominates in neither group.

*Significant at .01 level.

Source: Polachek (1978).

change toward zero from either a positive or negative correlation with sex represents a convergence in the experience, attitudes, and choices of young men and women). Studies have found that women's decisions appear to take into account the lower return that will result from expected withdrawal from the labor market (Nollen, 1974). In particular, it appears that women take into account the relatively greater importance of on-the-job training in some careers than in others and are more likely to choose college majors leading to careers in which on-the-job learning is important if they expect to be employed for a greater part of their lives than if they expect to spend less of their lives in paid jobs (Polachek, 1978). So it seems likely from the changes in the college choices of young women that they were already, in the 1960s, beginning to envision spending more time in jobs than earlier generations of women and that they would increasingly seek to enter fields that had previously been predominantly male. They have, of course, done so, with a curious result: either because predominantly male fields have been the chief battleground or because of affirmative action, female-to-male starting salary ratios have become more favorable to women in traditionally male fields, such as engineering and finance, than in fields that have been more accessible to women historically, such as home economics and library work (Table F-11).

Table F-11. National average monthly salary offers to bachelor's degree candidates, by sex and functional area, 1976-77

Functional area	Men	Women	Ratio—women to men
Accounting/Auditing	$1,065	$1,060	.995
Business administration	940	849	.903
Communications	829	721	.870
Community and service organizations work	747	702	.940
EDP—programming/systems	1,115	1,090	.978
Engineering	1,279	1,328	1.038
Farm and natural resources management	895	941	1.051
Finance and economics	936	927	.990
Health (medical) services	937	864	.922
Home economics and dietetics	853	685	.803
Law enforcement services	933	798	.855
Library and related work	742	598	.806
Manufacturing and/or industrial operations	1,212	1,122	.926
Marketing—consumer product/services	931	890	.956
Marketing—industrial product/services	1,055	1,029	.975
Mathematics/statistics	1,016	1,016	1.000
Merchandising/sales promotion	883	812	.920
Personnel/employee relations	973	869	.893
Public administration	879	762	.867
Research—nonscientific	990	789	.797
Research—scientific	1,119	1,062	.949
Rotational training—technical	1,241	1,195	.963
Rotational training—nontechnical	911	866	.951

Source: College Placement Council, 1979.

It is important to note that these trends are in all probability self-reinforcing. If some young women in the 1960s were beginning to shift their sights, despite adverse labor market conditions, one can only expect that many more will do so as they see that careers in traditionally male fields are increasingly viable and carry, for the moment at least, an income advantage.

Conclusions

The two questions asked at the beginning of this note can be given positive, if qualified, answers: First, the nation's strategy for providing more nearly equal opportunity in the higher education system is an appropriate and effective one. Second, the system does tend to operate in ways that are conducive to greater equality of earned income. These are conclusions about tendencies, not about guaranteed results. The larger structure of social institutions within which the higher education system operates may or may not reinforce these tendencies or offset them at any one point in time. For example, the removal of financial barriers to attendance and the proliferation of opportunities for nontraditional students are striking evidence of a comprehensive and realistic equal opportunity strategy. But there is no guarantee that the culture in general or prior schooling in particular will motivate the same percentage of disadvantaged as of advantaged students to use the opportunities available. The outcome depends on other institutions as well.

Similarly, the great flexibility of the higher education system in training individuals to meet changing labor market demand for skills is a great resource for social mobility and, by limiting the intensity and duration of skill shortages, tends to reduce inequalities of income attributable to skill shortages. But, again, the behavior of other institutions codetermines outcomes. If, as in the 1960s, the demand for the skills of the college-educated races ahead, then even a highly adaptive system of higher education like the American one may not achieve much reduction in earnings differences in the short run, although it can still contribute much to social mobility.

Quite another way to look at the role of the higher education system in increasing greater equality of opportunity and of income is to chart the progress of specific previously disadvantaged groups in using the system. If it in fact serves them well, then we can have additional confidence that its flexibility and responsiveness are indeed working in the interest of greater equality. And, from this point of view, it does seem abundantly clear that the equal opportunity strategy has been accompanied by major changes in the actual use of the system by members of some important disadvantaged groups. Ability-controlled college entrance rates have, in fact, become more nearly equal between whites and blacks and men and women. Further, shifts in the proportions of students entering different fields have also occurred. The measure of group results does, of course, have problems of its own. We do not know, but can only guess, the extent to which remaining obstacles account for the decisions of those blacks and women who still do not go to college. What we can say, and emphatically, is that where a flexible and responsive higher education system has opened new paths there are those who take them. The equal opportunity strategy is clearly no mere rhetorical device. It consists of real and established institutional arrangements that have given lasting new directions to careers.

References

Bailey, J. P. and Collins, E. F. *Entry into Postsecondary Education.* Research Triangle Park, N.C.: Research Triangle Institute, 1977.

Busch, G. "Inequality of Educational Opportunity by Social Origin in Higher Education." In *Education, Inequality, and Life Chances.* Vol. 1. Paris: Organization for Economic Cooperation and Development, 1975.

Coleman, J. S. "Equality of Opportunity and Equality of Results." *Harvard Educational Review*, 1973, *43* (1).

College Placement Council. *Salary Survey: A Study of 1976-77 Beginning Offers.* Final Report. Bethlehem, Pa.: 1979.

Featherman, D. L., and Hauser, R. M. "Sexual Inequality and Socioeconomic Achievement in the U.S., 1962-1973." *American Sociological Review*, June 1976.

Freeman, R. B. *Black Elite: The New Market for Highly Educated Black Americans.* The Carnegie Commission on Higher Education. New York: McGraw-Hill, 1977.

Jencks, C. "Inequality in Retrospect." *Harvard Educational Review*, 1973, *43* (1).

Jencks, C., and others. *Inequality: A Reassessment of the Effect of Family and Schooling in America.* New York: Basic Books, 1972.

Jencks, C., and others. *Who Gets Ahead?* New York: Basic Books, 1979.

Kravis, I. "A World of Unequal Incomes." *Annals of the American Academy of Political and Social Science*, Sept. 1973.

Kuznets, S. "Economic Growth and Income Inequality." *American Economic Review*, March 1955, *45* (1).

Kuznets, S. "Demographic Aspects of the Distribution of Income Among Families: Recent Trends in the United States." In W. Sellekaerts, *Econometrics and Economic Theory: Essays in Honor of Jan Tinbergen.* White Plains, N.Y.: International Arts and Sciences Press, 1974.

Layard, R., and Psacharopoulos, G. "The Screening Hypothesis and the Returns to Education." *Journal of Political Economy*, Sept.-Oct. 1974, *82* (5).

Miller, S. M. "Comparative Social Mobility." *Current Sociology, 9* (1). Oxford: Basil Blackwell, 1960.

Nollen, S. D. "The Supply and Demand for College Educated Labor." Doctoral dissertation, Graduate School of Business, University of Chicago, 1974.

Peng, S. S. "Trends in the Entry to Higher Education: 1961-1972." *Educational Researcher*, Jan. 1977.

Polachek, S. W. "Sex Differences in College Majors." *Industrial and Labor Relations Review*, July 1978, *31* (4).

Psacharopoulos, G., and Hinchliffe, K. *Returns to Education.* New York: Elsevier, 1973.

Smith, J. P., and Welch, F. *Race Differences in Earnings: A Survey and New Evidence.* Santa Monica: The Rand Corporation, 1978.

The President. *Economic Report of the President, 1973.* Washington, D.C.: U.S. Government Printing Office, 1973.

Tinbergen, J. *Income Distribution: Analysis and Policies.* Amsterdam: North-Holland, 1975.

Yanowich, M. *Social and Economic Inequality in the Soviet Union.* New York: M. E. Sharpe, 1977.

Supplement G

Academic Schedules and the Split-Level Week

Preferences, Needs, and Opportunities

Academic schedules and off-campus centers are being examined at many institutions of higher education. The impetus comes from several quarters. Some colleges and universities are responding to the scheduling and location preferences of older adults. Some are adapting selected programs to serve clientele sponsored by public agencies, such as local welfare, vocational rehabilitation, or manpower offices.[1] Some are seeking to use physical facilities more efficiently or to reduce the costs of instruction, e.g., by greater use of part-time faculty.

The impetus for re-examination of academic schedules also comes from those young people who "vote with their feet" or otherwise express a desire for greater scheduling options. Just prior to their graduation, respondents in the National Longitudinal Study of the High School Class of 1972 were asked their "expected activity" following graduation. Over one-fourth expected to work while going to college (Table G-1), and increasing numbers of young persons do combine education and work (see Figure G-1).

This report was prepared by Marian L. Gade, Postgraduate Researcher, and John R. Shea, Senior Fellow.

[1] Because stipends, unemployment compensation, or welfare payments are involved, such agencies tend to seek the quickest route to self-sufficiency. This means short, intensive programs without waiting periods.

Table G-1. Expected activity following graduation of high school seniors, as reported in the National Longitudinal Study of the High School Class of 1972

Expected activity	Number	Percentage
Work full-time only	2,936	24.2%
College full-time only	2,459	20.3
Combine work and college	3,350	27.6
All other[a]	3,375	27.8
Total	12,120	100.0

[a]Includes (1) full-time vocational training only (3.3 percent); (2) full-time apprenticeship or on-the-job training only (1.8 percent); (3) full-time work plus part-time vocational training (3.3 percent); (4) full-time vocational training plus part-time work (6.9 percent); (5) full-time on-the-job training plus part-time vocational training (0.8 percent); (6) military only (4.0 percent); (7) full-time homemaker only (3.1 percent); and (8) full-time homemaker plus part-time vocational training (4.9 percent).

Note: Details may not add to totals due to rounding.

Source: Nolfi and others (1977), p. 111-135.

For older adults, the opportunity to attend college part-time, or to schedule classes around work and family responsibilities, may determine whether one gets a college education or not. In a survey undertaken in the early 1970s for the Commission on Non-Traditional Study (Gould Commission), adults interested in further learning opportunities were asked about desired time schedules. Far more adults preferred evening classes (49 percent) than any other option (Table G-2). Nevertheless, rather sizable percentages of would-be adult learners preferred "two or more mornings or afternoons a week" (11 percent), "two or more full days a week" (9 percent), or "one or two evenings a week plus occasional weekends" (8 percent).

Occasionally, the impetus for new schedules comes from employers, unions, or professional organizations. Over 200 community colleges offer off-the-job training for apprentices. Such work is often scheduled in the late afternoon or evening, or in the winter for apprentices in the construction trades. Nursing and police work are two large occupational categories where

Figure G-1. Civilian labor force participation rates[a] of young
adults enrolled in school, October 1948 to October 1976

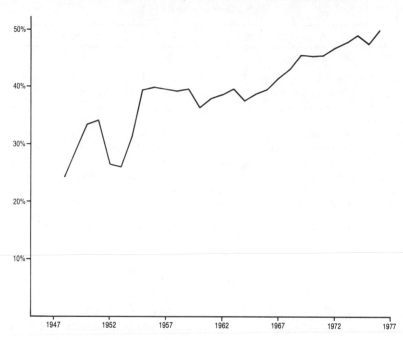

[a]Percentage of civilian noninstitutional population in the civilian labor force.

Source: The President (1978, p. 242).

shiftwork is common, and for this reason early morning, evening, and other scheduling formats are encountered in programs
for them. In-service training of teachers is the historic backbone
of intensive summer programs—a congruence between work and
academic schedules.

A number of employers around the country have asked for
modified schedules to facilitate collegiate training designed to
meet affirmative action or other goals. International Business
Machines arranged with Syracuse University, for example, to
provide the upper division component of a baccalaureate degree
in business administration in a series of three-month, intensive,
residential sessions on campus.

Table G-2. Desired time schedules of would-be adult learners, 1972

Schedule	Percentage
One evening a week	23
Two or more evenings a week	26
One morning or afternoon a week	6
Two or more mornings or afternoons a week	11
One full day a week	2
Two or more full days a week	9
One weekend day a week	2
Both weekend days a week	0
One or two evenings a week plus occasional weekends	8
One or two evenings a week plus one or two weeks during the summer	4
Two weeks to a month during the summer	2
Other time	4
No response	4

Source: Carp, Peterson, and Roelfs (1973, p. 94).

Labor Market Aspects

From the point of view of the labor market, there are some advantages in more flexible scheduling on the part of higher education institutions. Not only would such arrangements permit workers to fit in some higher education, but they would enable employers to fill current gaps in employee ranks and to respond to worker desires for fewer working hours or more flexible work schedules.

1. Partly because so many youths and older women are in the labor force, but reflecting other developments as well (affluence, changed preferences for working life), part-time employment has grown more rapidly than full-time. "Whereas in 1970 1 of every 8 workers was a part-timer compared with 1 of 10 in the early 1960s, estimates today are closer to 1 in

every 5½ workers, the large proportion voluntary" (Meier, 1979, p. 4).

2. Increased absenteeism, particularly at the beginning and end of the week, reflects the desire on the part of some workers to work fewer hours per week and poses a problem for the employer who is, for example, trying to keep a production line in operation. The Monday and Friday absence rate may be two or possibly three times that on the midweek days, although great differences will be found among industries, companies, geographical regions, and times of year.

One employer response has been to hire students to fill in on Mondays and Fridays; the automobile companies in Detroit have hired Wayne State University students for this purpose from time to time. But these students then need academic schedules that will permit them to go to school only on midweek days. Coordination on the part of students/employees, institutions, and employers could benefit all three groups, but the present arrangements are makeshift and unsatisfactory for all parties.

3. Flexitime arrangements are on the increase. These involve schedules under which employees can vary, within limits, the time they start and end work while working a contracted number of hours in a specified time period, for example, one week or a pay period. In 1977 it was estimated that about 13 percent of all nongovernmental organizations with 50 or more employees used flexitime and about 6 percent of all employees were on flexitime (about 3 million persons). The use of this option doubled between 1974 and 1977, according to some estimates, and is expected to continue to make rapid gains (Nollen and Martin, 1978, pp. 5-6).

The most common pattern has flexible starting and stopping times each day with one or two "core periods" during which all employees must be at work.

Flexitime arrangements are often used to provide a block of time for educational pursuits. A common usage is for a student in a night class to leave work early to provide time for preparation and travel to the class. In Europe, where flexible work schedules are much more common than in the United States (perhaps one-third of Swiss workers are on flexitime), many firms offer courses themselves, scheduling instruction during noncore periods of the day when employees can attend (Owen, 1979, 93, 100).

4. The "compressed workweek" may already have peaked after a rapid increase from about 1971 to 1975 (Nollen and Martin, 1978, p. 37). Over 50 percent of compressed workweeks are four-day weeks; the three-day and four and one-half day workweek each accounted for almost 20 percent of such schedules in 1976. These schedules compress the full number of working hours into a shorter time period, permitting long weekends without the loss of pay that results from absenteeism. However, results have been mixed, and expansion of the compressed workweek is not seen as likely, partly because of laws requiring overtime pay for hours over eight worked in a day and partly because many union contracts bar such arrangements.

Maklan (1977, p. 160) compared blue collar workers on a five-day, 40-hour workweek with a group on a compressed (four-day) work schedule and found no tendency for the day off to be used in educational pursuits, but other groups of workers may differ in the uses to which they put their extra time off from work.

5. More and more employees are engaged in shiftwork, and it has spread from traditional working-class occupations, such as mining and automobile production, to offices and the service sector. In some European countries, up to 25 percent of the workforce is engaged in shiftwork, and the International Labour Organization estimates a 100 percent increase in the number of shiftworkers (for nations where figures are available) between 1950 and 1974 (Bengtsson, 1979, p. 19).

Shiftwork makes it difficult for workers to schedule classes, especially if they rotate shifts, and the trend toward more shiftwork will work against increased participation in educational pursuits unless classes are scheduled carefully and flexibly.

Scheduling Options in Higher Education

Colleges and universities, especially public two-year campuses, are accommodating increasing numbers of part-time students (see Figure B-6). Four of every ten students are enrolled part-time, compared to three in ten 12 years ago. The number of Americans 25 years old or older enrolled in college increased by 48 percent between 1973 and 1978—from 2.616 million to 3.872 million. Over one-half of these older students are women, and about two-thirds are enrolled part-time (U.S. Bureau of the Census, *Current Population Reports,* Series P-20, appropriate years).

The 1960s witnessed considerable experimentation with the academic calendar, and calendar changes continue to occur. Eleven years ago, 83 percent of the nation's colleges and universities used a "traditional semester" calendar, with classes beginning in mid-September, a short break occurring in late January, and the second semester extending through the end of May. Now, less than 10 percent operate under this calendar (Coughlin, 1978, pp. 12-13). The most popular calendar today is "early semester," with fall classes beginning in August and ending before Christmas. Besides a longer midwinter break (which saves on fuel costs), the second semester typically ends in early May. Nearly 50 percent of the country's campuses follow the "early semester" pattern. The "quarter system" is used by 24 percent, and the "4-1-4" plan by 13 percent (Coughlin, 1978, pp. 12-13).

The 4-1-4 system, with its interim (typically one-month) term in January, offers opportunities for travel, employment, and "intensive" rather than longer-term, "concurrent" course patterns. In addition, such a calendar offers more potential entry and exit points for students (or trainees), some of whom wish to begin or end their studies at times other than the beginning or end of regular terms. In the Carnegie Council Surveys of Institutional Adaptations to the 1970s (henceforth cited as Carnegie Council Surveys, 1978), over a third of the institutions indicated that "some students may begin their studies [in degree-credit courses or programs] at times other than the beginning of an academic term (for example, open-entry, open-exit programs)."

In the same surveys, respondents were asked about what might be called "split-level schedules," wherein instructional programs are designed so that some students are able to complete all (or nearly all) work for a degree or certificate by attending classes:

- Only in the morning
- Only in the afternoon
- Only in the evening
- Only on weekends
- Only on selected days of the week, for example, Monday, Tuesday, and Wednesday.
- Only in the summer
- Only in special, intensive sessions, for example, two weeks, twice a year, plus independent study.

According to the Carnegie Council Surveys, 1978, 91 percent of institutions of higher education offer some degree-credit *courses* in the evening; two-fifths [40 percent] offer degree-credit courses on weekends. When it comes to *programs* (rather than individual courses), "split-level schedules" are somewhat less common, but impressive nonetheless. There are, as might be expected, important differences among institutions of various types. In this regard, the findings from the Council's Surveys, 1978, may be summarized as follows. (See Table G-3.)

1. Public colleges and universities (especially two-year campuses) are more likely than private to report that one or more programs are designed so that some students may complete all (or nearly all) work for a degree by attending classes: only in the morning; only in the afternoon; only in the evening; on selected days of the week; or in the summer.
2. Equal percentages of private and public institutions offer programs that can be completed only on weekends or in special,

Table G-3. Percentage of institutions with various split-level schedule options for one or more degree-credit programs, by Carnegie type and control

	Weighted N^a	Percentage offering program(s)[b]						
		Morning	Afternoon	Evening	Weekends	Selected days of the week	Summer	Intensive sessions
Public (Total N = 1,307)								
Research Universities I	26	33%	14%	39%	19%	19%	44%	29%
Research Universities II	30	26	20	55	10	27	45	16
Doctorate-granting Universities I	35	8	3	63	13	8	46	13
Doctorate-granting Universities II	18	39*	28*	67*	22*	39*	67*	17*
Comprehensive Universities and Colleges I	232	40	24	66	14	33	43	16
Comprehensive Universities and Colleges II	91	29	23	46	0	33	33	9
Liberal Arts Colleges II	8	40*	25*	55*	0*	36*	0*	0*
Two-Year Colleges	855	59	30	82	6	41	15	6
Average		50	28	74	8	37	24	9
Private (Total N = 1,047)								
Research Universities I	22	5*	5*	59*	14*	14*	23*	5*
Research Universities II	14	7*	21*	50*	0*	0*	29*	0*
Doctorate-granting Universities I	17	11*	11*	72*	11*	39*	39*	6*
Doctorate-granting Universities II	11	18*	0*	55*	0*	27*	0*	18*

Comprehensive Universities and Colleges I	122	29	12	82	25	27	36	22
Comprehensive Universities and Colleges II	100	25	10	53	9	20	24	14
Liberal Arts Colleges I	110	13	8	12	3	2	7	3
Liberal Arts Colleges II	430	24	18	32	6	20	12	10
Two-Year Colleges	208	38	17	23	6	17	13	3
Average		26	15	38	8	18	16	9

[a]Original sample respondents to the B questionnaire. Smallest N responding to any of the subitems in Q20c.

[b]*Respondents* were given the following statement, under the heading of "Degree-credit courses and programs," and asked: "Does this statement apply now?" The statement read: "One or more programs are designed so that some students may complete all (or nearly all) work for a degree by attending classes: (1) only in the morning; (2) only in the afternoon; (3) only in the evening; (4) only on weekends; (5) only Mon., Tues., Wed., only Thur., Fri., or Sat., or some similar combination; (6) only in the summer; (7) in special, intensive sessions (e.g., two weeks, twice a year, plus independent study)."

*Based on less than 20 sample cases.

Source: Carnegie Council Surveys, 1978.

intensive sessions, for example, two weeks, twice a year, plus independent study.

3. The most common split-level scheduling option involves the possibility of completing work for a degree in the evening: 74 percent of the public campuses and 38 percent of the private do this. The least common options in both the public and private sectors involve weekends and special, intensive sessions.

4. Among public institutions, two-year colleges are somewhat more likely than their four-year counterparts to offer morning, afternoon, evening, and selected-days-of-the-week options, but are somewhat less likely to offer weekend, summer, and special, intensive-session programs.

5. Among private institutions, two-year campuses are less likely than their four-year counterparts to offer any of the options except exclusively morning or afternoon schedules.

Analysis of replies to the Carnegie Council Surveys, 1978, indicates that there are other variables related to an institution's offering of scheduling options to complete (or almost complete) degree requirements. The most important of these are the needs of part-time students and the academic characteristics of entering freshmen.

1. Part-time students
   a. As might be expected, public institutions with part-time students accounting for more than one-third of total FTE enrollments tend to be above average in the number offering scheduling options. For example, well over 50 percent of these institutions have morning programs, over 80 percent have evening programs, and almost 50 percent have selected-day-of-the-week options.
   b. About two-thirds of the private institutions with part-time students constituting over one-third of FTE enrollments have evening programs, about one-third of these institutions have selected day programs, and almost one-third have morning programs.
2. Academic characteristics of entering freshmen

a. Institutions, both public and private, drawing mostly from the top 10 percent of high school graduates offer fewer scheduling options than do others, except that they are more likely to offer intensive sessions.
b. Institutions whose freshmen are of all ability levels or that have essentially "open-admission" policies are more likely than more selective schools to offer morning, afternoon, evening, and selected-day-of-the-week options.
c. Summer and weekend programs range across both selective and nonselective institutions.

Respondents were asked if there had been a change in emphasis in these scheduling options since 1969-70. Over 50 percent of the institutions indicated "little or no change." Only a few institutions had decreased options; among those that had increased options, there were increases in evening programs in all public categories, averaging over 50 percent of public institutions, less in private.

Weekend programs increased at 90 percent of the private institutions who responded to this question and at 84 percent of the public, by far the largest percentage increase of any of the options, although actual numbers were small.

Those institutions not presently offering scheduling options were asked whether they were planning or considering any of them for the future. Although the number of responding institutions was quite small, some of the results are striking (see Table G-4).

• Just as public institutions are more likely than private to offer these options at present, public institutions are also more likely to be considering their adoption in the future, except in the case of summer and intensive sessions, where the proportions are equal.
• The most dramatic result comes in the category of weekend programs. At present only 8 percent of all institutions offer such programs, but 43 percent of the public and 35 percent of the private institutions not now offering this option are considering such programs.

Table G-4. Percentage of institutions not now offering various split-level schedule options, who are considering or planning each option for the future, by Carnegie type and control

	Weighted N^a	Percentage considering or planning to offer program(s)^b						
		Morning	After-noon	Eve-ning	Week-ends	Selected days of the week	Sum-mer	Intensive sessions
Public (Total N = 330)								
Research Universities I	14	0%	5%	25%	25%	6%	7%	25%
Research Universities II	12	0	0	8*	23	6	0	18
Doctorate-granting Universities I	8	14	13	38*	32	16	8*	24
Doctorate-granting Universities II	5	0	0	40*	33	0	0*	15
Comprehensive Universities and Colleges I	74	9	7	43	26	16	4	13
Comprehensive Universities and Colleges II	50	14	13	52	42	14	14	15
Liberal Arts Colleges II	4	0*	0*	0*	50*	0*	0*	25*
Two-Year Colleges	161	21	26	54	49	26	15	22
Average		16	19	47	43	22	13	20
Private (Total N = 566)								
Research Universities I	9	0	0	0*	5	0	0	0
Research Universities II	6	0*	0*	50*	36*	9*	50*	33*
Doctorate-granting Universities I	4	8	8	0*	0	0*	11*	8
Doctorate-granting Universities II	5	0*	0*	0*	18*	0*	0*	0*

Comprehensive Universities and Colleges I	21	14	13	29	44	13	9	22
Comprehensive Universities and Colleges II	42	8	13	38	39	10	5	18
Liberal Arts Colleges I	73	0	4	13	16	4	10	12
Liberal Arts Colleges II	254	7	6	45	42	18	17	17
Two-Year Colleges	107	13	28	48	29	13	13	27
Average		8	11	39	35	13	14	19

[a]Original sample respondents to the B questionnaire. Smallest N responding to any of the subitems in Q20c(C).

[b]Respondents were presented with various split-level schedule options (see Table G-3) and asked, "Does this statement apply now?" Those who answered "No" were asked, "Are you considering or planning for this in the future?"

*Based on less than 10 sample cases. Because this table only counts those who presently do not have the option, the universe is very small in several categories.

Source: Carnegie Council Surveys, 1978.

- Since almost three-fourths of public institutions now offer evening programs, there are only a few left to adopt this option. However, almost 50 percent of those remaining public institutions (and 39 percent of the private) are considering evening programs. Comprehensive and two-year institutions are especially likely to be considering starting such a program.
- The public two-year colleges emerge as the most innovative of all categories with respect to planning new schedule options. In the case of every option except intensive sessions, they are the most likely of all public institutional categories to be considering adoption.
- The private Research Universities I and Liberal Arts Colleges I not now offering these options plan to cling most strongly to more traditional scheduling structures. These schools may enroll higher than average numbers of more "traditional" students, and they are the categories least likely to be affected by enrollment declines.

Nature and Use of New Schedules

From site visits by Carnegie Council staff (cited as Site Visits, 1979), it would appear that exclusively morning or afternoon schedules are rarely intentionally offered by the college. Rather, at larger institutions that cater to part-time as well as full-time students, many students arrange their courses (and laboratories) so as to have afternoons or mornings free for part-time work. As to selected-days-of-the-week schedules, Saturday morning classes (as part of a Tuesday, Thursday, and Saturday sequence) have gone out of style, and Wednesdays (or Fridays) are in some cases free for work or play. Again, the site visits seem to suggest few intentionally offered compressed week schedules.

With regard to evening and weekend programs, however, schedules seem to be explicitly geared, in most instances, to be attractive to persons with family or work responsibilities. Weekend college programs often involve classroom or seminar work from Friday afternoon through Saturday evening (an "intensive" format). Evening programs may involve one or two (or more) evenings of rather concentrated study.

The many "external degree programs" (EDPs) now offered

around the country often serve a clientele similar to that desiring flexible scheduling options, since the EDPs emphasize minimal classroom course work and individually designed, self-directed study. A 1976 study identified 244 EDPs at the undergraduate level, of which about three-fourths were bachelor-level programs and the others associate-level (Sosdian and Sharp, 1977).

A telephone survey of 25 selected institutions (18 private and 7 public) confirmed these findings. It revealed a large number of degree-credit programs catering to persons who might find it difficult to attend college under a more traditional schedule, especially working persons and women with family obligations: 18 of the 25 institutions offered programs through which a student could earn a degree by attending only in the evening or on weekends or, less commonly, for a concentrated period combined with off-campus, independent study.

Institutions have become ingenious in carrying instruction to students: Indiana University-Purdue University at Indianapolis offers a "Learn & Shop" series of courses utilizing department store meeting rooms in suburban shopping centers as well as a "Weekend College." Pace University teaches classes at 7:00 A.M., before working hours, as well as at lunchtime, in the evenings, and on weekends, in both urban and suburban locations. Adelphi University has rented railway cars and provides instruction in business administration to enrolled commuters on their way to and from work in New York City. George Washington University holds classes in federal office buildings throughout Washington, D.C., and the University of Northern Colorado provides day care for children of women attending its nontraditional program.

Some institutions, such as the California State University at Los Angeles and Wayne State University in Detroit, have offered evening courses for many years as a part of their regular curriculum, making little or no distinction between day and evening students, while other institutions consciously tailor programs to the working student who can only attend in the evening. Nova University is exclusively an evening college with over 90 percent of its students also holding full-time jobs; Memphis

State University has an evening program for full-time workers offering the same array of undergraduate and professional majors available to traditional students; Adelphi's "University College," Eastern Montana College's "College after Five," and the evening division of Syracuse University's "University College" all afford opportunities to obtain degrees through evening attendance.

Loyola University of Chicago has a combined evening and weekend program, while Mundelein College offers a weekend program in which students attend every other weekend from Friday evening through Sunday afternoon.

Enrollments in these nontraditional programs appear to be expanding, except where established evening programs share in overall institutional enrollment declines. Programs are offered in institutions representing a variety of Carnegie categories, but 5 of the 18 institutions offering new schedule options were in the Comprehensive Universities I category. Only 1 of the 5 liberal arts colleges contacted offered such programs.

Some combination of size, location, and curricular orientation appears to play a part in whether or not an institution undertakes programs designed to take advantage of populations not served by traditional weekday schedules. For example, only one of the colleges offering these programs has an enrollment below 3,000 and most are over 10,000. All of the institutions offering evening and weekend programs are located in Standard Metropolitan Statistical Areas. On the other hand, only one of the seven institutions not offering nontraditional scheduling is over 2,000 in enrollment (a state university campus located outside a metropolitan area). Three of the other institutions in this group are small liberal arts colleges located in small communities. Of the three located in metropolitan areas, two offer specialized programs that require full-time commitment, and the third is a traditional black college. None of the institutions surveyed purposely provides schedules with classes only on certain weekdays and not on others to facilitate split-week work schedules, although students may work out such schedules for themselves within the framework of the overall program.

More Flexible Schedules: Advantages and Disadvantages

It is not completely clear whether adding scheduling options is in the long-range interest of all institutions of higher education. Selective institutions in the research university and liberal arts categories may not wish to encourage part-time study along with part-time work—at least in fields where paid work or family duties add little to the learning process or take valuable time away from self-study and laboratory work. Even in this case, however, at least some adults who meet preestablished admissions standards would doubtless benefit from being able to take established courses. Chances are remote that such students would lower the quality of instruction.

Aside from opening existing courses to part-time students, a number of prestigious institutions, for example, Harvard, Johns Hopkins, do accommodate adults in part-time evening programs leading to degrees.

In many institutions that emphasize instruction rather than research, there are fewer reservations about "new academic schedules." Yet, even in these cases, the costs and benefits from the point of view of faculty and other campus leaders may not clearly favor expansion of scheduling options. Factors to be considered include: (1) unit costs of instruction if courses or sections are added; (2) need for program development, for example, remedial studies, staff development; (3) extension of child care, counseling, and academic support services; (4) change in hours and usage of libraries, bookstores, laboratories, equipment, etc.; (5) parking, transportation, and campus security; (6) opportunity (and implications) of hiring part-time faculty and altering the teaching schedules of full-time faculty; (7) changes in the frequency (and load) imposed on admissions offices, the Registrar, Bursar, and so forth; and (8) use of janitorial services, space, and energy savings (or costs).

Premium shift differentials for regular faculty employed in weekend or evening programs would, in most instances, result in higher unit costs of instruction than in regular daytime programs. The tradition in evening and nontraditional programs is to rely heavily on "overload" compensation of existing faculty and on greater use of part-time, adjunct faculty.

As in the case of time-shortened degree programs, scheduling options may be expected to reduce the *private* costs of a college education. Well over one-half the cost (to the individual and society) of full-time college attendance by young people of traditional college age takes the form of forgone earnings. For older adults, with greater earnings potential, the fraction is considerably higher. Whether a program is inferior to another in some absolute sense may not be critically important for the student. An evening or weekend program, because it accommodates work schedule constraints, may be superior from the student's point of view, all things considered.

From a public policy point of view, additional considerations include

- Established competitive relationships between public and private institutions in off-campus, weekend, and evening programs, and the advantages and disadvantages of various forms of support, e.g., institutional aid vs. student aid
- Probable changes in the nature and quality of programs and in the costs of instruction
- Diversity, access, and second-chance opportunities for a college degree, and the extent to which "new academic schedules" would further affirmative action goals
- Implications of new academic schedules for the draft, the youth labor market, tax policies, and student aid programs
- The potential of split-level schedules in helping to solve the problem of young scholars, by perhaps encouraging greater sharing of faculty workloads and new combinations of teaching and research
- Reducing social costs of traffic congestion, excessive energy use, absenteeism, and other factors that inhibit growth in economic productivity.

References

Bengtsson, J. "The Shape of Work to Come: Prospects." *Change*, July-Aug. 1979, *11* (5), 16-21.

Carp, A., Peterson, R., and Roelfs, P. *Learning Interests and Experiences of Adult Americans.* Berkeley, Calif.: Educational Testing Service, 1973.

Coughlin, E. K. "The Changing Academic Calendar." *Chronicle of Higher Education,* Jan. 16, 1978.

Maklan, D. *The Four-day Workweek: Blue Collar Adjustment to a Nonconventional Arrangement of Work and Leisure Time.* New York: Praeger, 1977.

Meier, G. S. *Job Sharing: A New Pattern for Quality of Work and Life.* Kalamazoo: W. E. Upjohn Institute for Employment Research, Feb. 1979.

Nolfi, G., Fuller, W. C., and Associates. *Experience of Recent High School Graduates: The Transition to Work or Postsecondary Education.* Report prepared for U.S. National Center for Education Statistics. Cambridge, Mass.: University Consultants, Inc., 1977.

Nollen, S. D., and Martin, V. H. *Alternative Work Schedules.* New York: AMACOM (Division of American Management Association), 1978.

Owen, J. D. *Working Hours.* Lexington, Mass.: Heath, 1979.

Sosdian, C. P., and Sharp, L. M. *Guide to Undergraduate External Degree Programs in the United States—Spring 1977.* Washington, D.C.: National Institute of Education, Dec. 1977.

The President. *Employment and Training Report of The President, 1978.* Washington, D.C.: 1978.

Supplement H

Faculty Development
Present and Future

The great influx of students into the nation's colleges and universities in the 1960s brought faculty members increasing affluence, an expanding job market that offered opportunities for wide choice among positions, and rapid advancement in rank and salary. In the decade of the 1970s, however, faculty found themselves in an increasingly insecure economic situation, caught between inflationary pressures, on the one hand, and greater competition for fewer openings, on the other.

Institutions, too, faced rapidly increasing costs as the prices of essential supplies, such as energy, rose dramatically. Confronted with erosion of the value of endowments in an inflationary period, resistance to tuition increases, and taxpayer reluctance to provide sharply increasing appropriations for public higher education, institutions tried to hold the line on increases in salaries—the largest component of institutional budgets. Faculty, in turn, joined together to bargain collectively in an attempt to do together what they could not do singly: maintain standards of living and ensure job security. The concept of the university as a collegial body made up of independent teachers and scholars began to be supplanted by views of faculty members and institutions as groups with differing economic interests along the lines of labor and management in other sectors of the economy.

This supplement was prepared by Marian Gade, Postgraduate Researcher, Charlotte Alhadeff, Research Specialist, and Margaret S. Gordon, Associate Director.

Faculty Compensation

The 1960s were a period of substantial increases in faculty incomes, both in monetary and real terms (Table H-1). The rate

Table H-1. Changes in salaries and compensation of faculty members, in current and constant (1967-68) dollars, and in Consumer Price Index 1959-60 to 1978-79 (1967 = 100.0)

	Salaries		Compensation[a]		Consumer Price Index
	Current dollars	Constant dollars	Current dollars	Constant dollars	
1959-60	65.7	76.2	63.9	74.2	88.0
1964-65	84.6	92.3	83.4	90.9	93.7
1967-68	100.0	100.0	100.0	100.0	102.1[b]
1969-70	114.5	103.1	116.0	104.4	111.1
1970-71	120.4	103.1	122.7	105.1	116.8
1971-72	125.3	103.6	128.7	106.4	121.0
1972-73	131.9	104.9	136.2	108.3	125.8
1973-74	140.1	102.2	145.8	106.4	137.1
1974-75	148.7	97.6	155.3	102.0	152.3
1975-76	158.2	97.0	166.1	101.8	163.1
1976-77	166.9	96.8	176.2	102.1	172.5
1977-78	171.3	93.1	179.8	97.7	184.1
1978-79	182.4	90.6	194.7	96.7	201.4

[a]Salaries plus fringe benefits.

[b]In the case of the consumer price index, 1967 = 100.0.

Sources: Computed from data in Bowen (1978, table A); "Nearly Keeping Up . . ." (1978); and "An Era of Continuing Decline" (1979).

of inflation was minimal in the early part of the decade, and, even during the Vietnam conflict in the later half of the decade, was not as high as in the later half of the 1970s. Meanwhile, the demand for faculty members was buoyant, and faculty bargaining power was strong. Bowen's historical data (1978, table A) indicate that the 41.2 percent advance in total faculty compensation in constant dollars from 1959-60 to 1969-70 exceeded that in any previous decade except for the 1920s, when faculty compensation overcame the sharp drop experienced during the inflationary years of World War I.

The experience of the 1970s has been very different. A high rate of inflation and a greatly reduced rate of faculty hiring have combined to reduce faculty bargaining power and the real incomes of faculty members. As Table H-1 shows, the rate of advance of faculty salaries in constant dollars slowed to a virtual halt in the early years of the decade, and, since 1972-73, faculty real salaries have been dropping—by 1978-79 reaching a level nearly 10 percent below that of 1967-68. Total faculty compensation has behaved somewhat less unfavorably than faculty salaries, as institutions liberalized fringe benefit packages, but by 1978-79 even total compensation was down more than 3 percent, compared with 1967-68.

In fact, the historical record shows that periods of sharp inflation have generally had an adverse impact on faculty real incomes. Bowen's data indicate that the only previous decades in the twentieth century when there was an actual decline in faculty real incomes were those of World War I and World War II. Harris's study of the economic position of Harvard from its beginnings in 1636 shows that inflationary periods have been bad, not only for faculty salaries, but also for the financial position of colleges and universities (Harris, 1970).

Aggregate data, however, understate the extent of the decline in faculty real incomes. Because there has been relatively little hiring in the 1970s, the percentage of lower-paid young faculty members has declined, and the proportion in the higher ranks has increased. This means that a portion of the overall increase in salaries reflects a shift of the faculty "mix" into higher ranks. The American Association of University Professors (AAUP) calculated that from 1967-68 to 1977-78, when there was a decline of 7.0 percent in real faculty salaries on the basis of the AAUP's published data, the actual decline was 10.6 percent after adjustment for the change in composition of faculty ("An Era of Continuing Decline," 1979, p. 5).

Faculty compensation has increased relatively more in current dollars in some types of institutions than in others, and, on the whole, the differences are related to differences revealed by data on the financial status of institutions. Faculty members in public universities and comprehensive colleges have had larger increases than those in most other types of institutions, except for the public two-year colleges with no faculty ranks, where the overall increase in compensation has been higher than in any other type of institution (Table H-2). Faculty members in private universities have done almost as well as their colleagues in public universities, while those in public liberal arts colleges fared only slightly less well than those in public universities and comprehensive colleges. In private liberal arts colleges, professors and associate professors have had much larger increases than their lower-ranked colleagues, while in private comprehensive colleges, increases have generally lagged, and those in private two-year colleges have been distinctly lower than in other groups of institutions. Full professors in public liberal arts colleges (a relatively small number of institutions) have also had exceptionally small increases.

One of the interesting points brought out by Table H-2—and already suggested above—is that rank by rank, the loss in real faculty compensation has been considerably more pronounced than the aggregative figures indicate. The overall loss in real faculty compensation between 1971-72 and 1978-79, according to AAUP data, was 9.1 percent. All of the percentage losses shown in Table H-2 were larger than this, and those in certain groups of institutions were much larger.

Bowen (1978, p. 9) has argued that the object of institutional policy should not be simply to keep up with compensation offered by other universities and colleges, nor even to keep up with the cost of living: "These goals are not adequate for the future soundness of American higher education. Instead, the goal should be to keep pace with the growth of compensation in the economy generally." Bowen concluded that, since 1970, "compensation in higher education . . . has clearly failed to keep pace with compensation in the rest of the economy." Total compensation for all civilian full-time employees increased at an annual average rate of 8.1 percent in current dollars between 1970 and 1975, while compensation for faculty increased only 6.1 percent in the same period (Bowen, 1978, table 7). Although faculty salaries are relatively high compared to those of the rank and file of American workers, they are con-

Table H-2. Percentage changes in faculty compensation by rank in public and private institutions of higher education, by AAUP category, 1971-72 to 1978-79 (in current and constant [1967] dollars)

Control and rank	Current dollars					Constant dollars				
	I^a	IIA^b	IIB^c	III^d	IVe	I	IIA	IIB	III	IV
Public										
Professor	47.1%	48.3%	44.3%	31.9%		−11.4%	10.9%	−13.3%	−20.8%	
Associate professor	47.6	50.2	46.6	41.6		−11.3	−9.8	−11.9	−14.9	
Assistant professor	46.4	46.6	45.8	38.0		−12.1	−11.9	−12.4	−17.1	
Instructor	49.8	46.2	41.6	48.1		−10.0	−12.2	−14.9	−11.0	
No rank					52.9%					−8.2%
Private (independent)										
Professor	46.4	39.2	43.1	30.0		−12.1	−16.4	−14.0	−21.9	
Associate professor	45.2	41.0	41.5	41.4		−12.8	−15.3	−15.0	−15.1	
Assistant professor	43.3	39.6	39.7	30.7		−13.9	−16.2	−16.1	−21.5	
Instructor	47.8	34.8	33.1	34.4		−11.2	−19.0	−20.1	−19.3	
No rank					27.8					−23.2

[a]Category I: includes institutions which offer the doctorate degree and which conferred an annual average of 15 or more earned doctorates in the most recent three years in at least three nonrelated disciplines (essentially universities).

[b]Category IIA: includes institutions awarding degrees above the baccalaureate but not included in Category I (similar to Carnegie classification of comprehensive universities and colleges).

[c]Category IIB: includes institutions awarding only the baccalaureate or equivalent degree (similar to Carnegie classification of liberal arts colleges).

[d]Category III: two-year institutions with academic ranks.

[e]Category IV: institutions without academic ranks (mostly two-year).

Sources: "Coping with Adversity" (1972, table 5); and "An Era of Continuing Decline" (1979, table 13).

siderably lower than salaries for business executives and somewhat lower than those in the federal government, and they have declined more rapidly in real terms than have salaries in business and government for employees with comparable qualifications. (See Table H-3.)

Whether viewed from the cost-of-living perspective or as compared with changes in compensation throughout the economy, higher education faculty salaries clearly fell in real terms during the 1970s. Indications are that salaries will rise again in 1979-80 between 6 and 7 percent in monetary terms, while prices rise perhaps twice that amount. The situation does not look hopeful for the future, for, as FTE enrollments decline, institutions will face increasing pressure to resist paying full cost-of-living increases to faculty.

Collective Bargaining

The increasing number of collective bargaining agreements in higher education institutions has been one response to falling real salaries, but wages and salaries are only one aspect of a general defensiveness that drives faculty to band together for what they view as collective survival in a difficult period. "Job security has become the major issue in collective bargaining between colleges and their faculty unions" (Semas, 1976). Yet, contrary to the expectations of some observers who expected unionization to spread rapidly throughout all of higher education in the 1970s in response to threatened cutbacks and financial stringency, "creeping unionism" seems better to describe the trend since 1966, when the first four-year colleges were organized (Garbarino, 1975, p. 57). The movement had begun somewhat earlier in public two-year colleges.

After fairly rapid growth in the late 1960s and early 1970s, spurred especially by the organization of CUNY in 1969 and of SUNY in 1971, there was a period of relatively slow growth of faculty unionism during 1973 and 1974. In 1975 unionization jumped, mainly because two multi-institutional systems were organized. In that year, also, five public institutions rejected unionization entirely, compared with only four previous instances of rejection in public institutions since the

Table H-3. Comparison of average annual rates of increase in real
salaries for individuals in different occupational groups

Occupational groups	1967-68 to 1977-78	1967-68 to 1972-73	1972-73 to 1977-78
Average academic salary	0.8%	0.9%	−2.4%
	1967-1977	1967-1972	1972-1977
Wage or salary income of male year-round workers			
Professional and Technical	0.1%	1.8%	−1.5%
Managers and Professional	0.5	2.2	−1.3
Clerical and Kindred	1.3	2.7	−0.1
Craft and Kindred	0.8	2.2	−0.6
Basic annual pay rates for professional and administrative federal employees			
Grade P4 or GS-11	1.0	1.9	a
Grade P6 or GS-13	1.1	2.1	0.2
Grade P8 or GS-15	0.9	2.1	−0.3
Average salaries in selected professional and administrative positions in private industry			
Auditor III	a	1.7	−1.8
Accountant IV	0.5	1.3	−0.3
Chief Accountant IV	0.7	2.3	−0.9
Attorney IV	1.7	5.4	−1.9
Attorney VI	1.8	5.4	−1.6
Chemist V	a	0.6	−0.5
Chemist VII	−0.1	0.5	−0.6
Engineer VI	−0.3	0.6	−1.1
Engineer VIII	−0.6	a	−1.2
Job Analyst IV	−0.4	0.1	−0.9
Buyer IV	2.1	4.8	−0.6
Director of Personnel III	0.5	1.0	0.0

[a]Figure is less than one-tenth of one percent, plus or minus.

Source: "An Era of Continuing Decline" (1979).

faculty bargaining movement began. Organization continued at about the same rate in 1976, again because of systemwide unit elections in Florida and Illinois. The Illinois election was the result of a voluntary agreement between the governing board of the regional universities and the faculty organization, drawn up in the absence of any legislative requirement for collective bargaining. Only Ohio, in addition to Illinois, has experienced substantial organization without supporting state legislation.

In 1977, four-year institutions experienced their lowest rate of organization since 1968, while the two-year colleges had considerably greater bargaining activity, almost all of it in California, where 21 institutions held elections. Organizing continued at a relatively low level in 1978, with about one out of every four elections resulting in a "no agent" vote; this has been the trend in recent years with the major research universities and private liberal arts colleges, in particular, resisting organization (see Table H-4).

The slow rate of unionization is also attributable to the fact that few states have passed supporting legislation since

Table H-4. Percentage of campuses in selected Carnegie categories with collective bargaining agreements, 1979

Category	Public	Private
Research Universities I	7%[a]	9%
Research Universities II	33[b]	0
Doctorate-granting Universities I	18	11
Doctorate-granting Universities II	21	27
Comprehensive Universities I	30	18
Comprehensive Universities II	38	9
Liberal Arts Colleges I	—	1
Liberal Arts Colleges II	18	3
Two-Year Colleges	43	4

[a]In addition, two public Research Universities I campuses have unions of teaching assistants only. On one campus the law faculty is organized, as is the medical faculty of one Research Universities I institution.

[b]There is a union of teaching assistants only on one public Research Universities II campus.

Source: "Fact-File: Faculty Bargaining Agents" (1979).

1975. Most of the institutions in states with enabling legislation are already organized; in states without such legislation, unionization has been very slow. (See following list of states with enabling legislation, based on data in Academic Collective Bargaining Information Service [1976].) The California legislature passed a law, which took effect on July 1, 1979, providing for faculty bargaining rights in four-year institutions. This may result in organizing activity in the state colleges and universities (although possibly not at the University of California), but unless other states enact such enabling legislation, widespread organizing activity does not seem likely.

Twenty-four states enabling faculty collective bargaining
in public postsecondary education:

Alaska (1972)
California (1975, 2-year institutions;
   1978, 4-year institutions)
Connecticut (1975)
Delaware (1970)
Florida (1974)
Hawaii (1973)
Iowa (1974)
Kansas (1970, 2-year institutions; and 1974, 1977)
Maine (1974, vocational and technical only; and 1975)
Massachusetts (1974)
Michigan (1973)
Minnesota (1974)
Montana (1975)
Nebraska (1972)
New Hampshire (1975)
New Jersey (1974)
New York (1967)
Oregon (1975)
Pennsylvania (1970)
Rhode Island (1973)
South Dakota (1973)
Vermont (1975)

Washington (1973, 2-year institutions only)
Wisconsin (1974, vocational and technical only)

By mid-1979, about one out of every six higher education institutions in the United States was organized, over 80 percent of them in the public sector. The percentage of unionized faculty among all faculty of the rank of instructor and above (full- and part-time) was 22 percent, and among full-time faculty was about 32 percent. About two-fifths of the unionized institutions were four-year colleges and universities, including about three-fifths of the covered faculty (see Tables H-5 and H-6).

The National Education Association, the agent on 294 campuses, leads the list of unions in terms of numbers of campuses organized, although most (228) of these are two-year campuses. The American Federation of Teachers is the agent on 222 campuses and leads in organizing four-year institutions (see Table H-7).

Faculty Hiring

The labor market for faculty members has virtually collapsed in many fields. At the peak of its activity, net additions to the professoriate were being made at the rate of 20,000 or more per year. The current level of net additions is about zero, and additions will remain at that level or become net reductions for most of the rest of this century. If student to faculty ratios should keep on rising (say, by 10 percent) on top of the rise in recent years of more than 10 percent, then net reductions of the professoriate may become quite substantial.

The impact of slowing enrollment growth on faculty hiring is becoming increasingly apparent, but it is not just the impact of enrollments that is likely to reduce the demand for new faculty members, but also the fact that *stable or declining enrollment follows a period of unprecedented growth.* The result is that there is a bulge of faculty members in the age range from about 33 to 47 years and a decided deficiency in the 55 and older bracket. Figure H-1 shows how the actual age distribution of full-time doctoral faculty members at Ph.D.-granting institutions differed from that which would prevail under steady-state

Table H-5. Newly unionized four-year institutions and their members,
1966 to September 30, 1979

	Total		*Public*		*Private*	
	Insti-tutions	*Persons*	*Insti-tutions*	*Persons*	*Insti-tutions*	*Persons*
1966	1	200	1	200	0	0
1967	1	90	0	0	1	90
1968	0	0	0	0	0	0
1969	24	18,369	23	18,299	1	70
1970	15	5,626	12	4,686	3	940
1971	45	19,994	41	18,694	4	1,300
1972	16	7,895	11	6,689	5	1,206
1973	20	4,794	7	2,895	13	1,899
1974	11	3,328	4	2,380	7	948
1975	29	6,670	15	4,602	14	2,068
1976	27	12,860	23	12,414	4[a]	446[a]
1977	9	1,197	6	810	3[a]	387[a]
1978	22	4,138	17	3,515	5	623
1979	3	398	0	0	3	398
Total	223	85,559	160	75,184	63	10,375

[a]Net of one decertification each year.

Note: An "institution" is essentially a campus with a president or chancellor or the equivalent as its chief executive officer. This is equivalent to the definition used in *Education Directory, Colleges and Universities, 1977-78,* U.S. National Center for Education Statistics (1978), except that system headquarters are not included.

Data on "persons" represented were collected by questionnaires, from newspaper reports, and election reports. Community colleges in comprehensive systems have been excluded. Six unionized law schools and one medical school in institutions in which no other faculty are organized were excluded.

Source: Garbarino (forthcoming).

conditions in 1978. A similar comparison for all faculty members at all institutions of higher education would not be very different, because enormously accelerated hiring occurred at all types of colleges and universities in the 1960s. Thus, the percentage of faculty members retiring or dying is very small compared with the retirement and mortality rates that would prevail

Table H-6. Unionized institutions of higher education, 1966 to
August 1, 1979, cumulative totals

	Total		*Four-year campuses*		*Two-year campuses*	
	Insti-tutions	*Faculty*	*Insti-tutions*	*Faculty*	*Insti-tutions*	*Faculty*
1966	23	5,200	1	200	22	5,000
1967	37	7,000	2	300	35	6,700
1968	97	11,300	2	300	95	11,000
1969	138	38,700	26	18,700	112	20,000
1970	178	48,200	41	24,300	137	23,900
1971	247	71,300	86	44,300	161	27,000
1972	285	81,900	102	52,200	183	29,700
1973	311	87,300	122	57,000	189	30,300
1974	327	92,400	133	60,300	194	32,100
1975	398	102,000	162	67,000	236	35,000
1976	450	117,800	189	79,800	261	38,000
1977	482	132,400	198	81,000	284	51,400
1978	515	140,100	220	85,200	295	54,900
1979	524	142,400	223	85,600	301	56,800

Sources: Four-year institutions and faculty: Garbarino (forthcoming). Two-year institutions and faculty: Garbarino and Lawler (1975, 1976, 1977, 1979).

Table H-7. Faculty bargaining agents on 648 campuses as of June 20, 1979

Agent	*Four-year campuses*			*Two-year campuses*			*Total*
	Public	Private	Total	Public	Private	Total	
American Association of University Professors (AAUP)	23	28	51	6	1	7	58
American Federation of Teachers (AFT)	72	21	93	123	6	129	222
National Education Association (NEA)	51	15	66	226	2	228	294
AAUP-AFT	14	—	14	—	—	—	14
AAUP-NEA	3	—	3	7	—	7	10

(continued on next page)

Table H-7 *(Continued)*

| Agent | Four-year campuses | | | Two-year campuses | | | Total |
	Public	Private	Total	Public	Private	Total	
Independent and other	5	12	17	32	1	33	50
Bargaining rejected	23	38[a]	61	13	3	16	77

[a]Includes one decertification of previously selected agent.

Source: "Fact-File: Faculty Bargaining Agents" (1979).

Figure H-1. **Actual and steady-state age distributions, full-time doctoral faculty at Ph.D.-granting institutions, 1978**

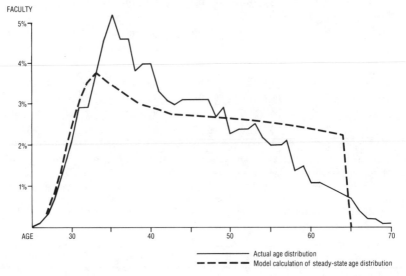

Source: National Research Council (1979, p. 18, based on data from the Survey of Doctorate Recipients).

under steady-state conditions. Table K-1 in Supplement K indicates combined death and retirement rates of faculty members in broad fields of science and engineering. In mathematics, for example, where the proportion of younger faculty members is particularly high, only 0.69 percent are expected to die or retire in 1980, but, as faculty members in mathematics grow older, the combined mortality and retirement rate is projected to rise to 2.84 percent by 2000.

Characteristics of Current Faculty Members

Before discussing projections of changes in the number of faculty members, we need to consider the characteristics of faculty members at present.

Nearly three-fourths of all faculty members teach at public institutions (Figure H-2). Moreover, in spite of the rapid growth of public two-year colleges in the last two decades, they accounted for only slightly more than one-fifth of all faculty members in 1978, although they accounted for nearly two-fifths of all students. This reflects their relatively high student-faculty ratios (see Supplement I).

About one-fourth of faculty members are women, but they are heavily concentrated at the lower ranks. Only 9 percent of full professors are women, and, in both public and private universities, the percentage is even smaller (about 6 percent). The percentage of women at the assistant professor level has increased substantially during the 1970s, but progress at the higher ranks has been slow, in part because older women on faculties, who were hired in the 1920s and 1930s, when the proportion of women was larger than it has been in recent decades, have been retiring and dying. We believe that a major effort should be made by colleges and universities to increase the proportion of women on their faculties, but, with limited overall hiring in the next two decades, progress in this respect will be difficult.

Only about 7 percent of faculty members in institutions of higher education were members of minority groups in 1975. Comprehensive universities and colleges, as well as liberal arts colleges, had slightly higher percentages than universities, but the difference was probably explained by the fact that most of the black colleges are in these two categories. Progress in increasing the percentage of minority group members on faculties is slow (except for Japanese- and Chinese-Americans), because historically there has been discrimination in higher education,

**Figure H-2. Selected characteristics of faculty members in
institutions of higher education**

DISTRIBUTION OF FULL-TIME FACULTY MEMBERS
BY TYPE AND CONTROL OF INSTITUTION, 1978

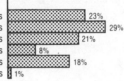

Public universities 23%
Public four-year colleges 29%
Public two-year colleges 21%
Private universities 8%
Private four-year colleges 18%
Private two-year colleges 1%

PERCENTAGE OF WOMEN AMONG FULL-TIME
FACULTY MEMBERS BY RANK, 1978

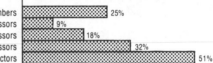

All full-time faculty members 25%
Full professors 9%
Associate professors 18%
Assistant professors 32%
Instructors 51%

PERCENTAGE OF MINORITY GROUP MEMBERS
AMONG FACULTY, BY TYPE OF INSTITUTION, 1975

All institutions 6.9%
Universities 5.8%
Comprehensive universities & colleges 7.5%
Liberal arts colleges 7.6%
Two-year colleges 7.1%

PERCENTAGE OF FACULTY MEMBERS WITH
DOCTOR'S DEGREE, 1975

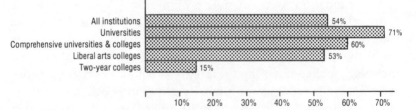

All institutions 54%
Universities 71%
Comprehensive universities & colleges 60%
Liberal arts colleges 53%
Two-year colleges 15%

10%   20%   30%   40%   50%   60%   70%

Sources: U.S. National Center for Education Statistics (1979, tables 3.13 and 3.14);
and Carnegie Council Surveys, 1975-1976.

but also because graduate education is prolonged and expensive for persons from low-income groups and often seems an unattractive alternative in today's job market when minority group college graduates can get jobs at good salaries. As we pointed out in our report, *Making Affirmative Action Work in Higher Education* (1975), the problem calls for efforts to increase the supply of minority group members with doctor's degrees as well as to open doors on the demand side in higher education.

In 1975, 54 percent of all faculty members had doctor's degrees, and, as would be expected, universities had the highest proportions of faculty members with doctorates, while two-year colleges continued to have a small (but clearly rising) percentage with doctorates. Whereas in the 1960s, when there were shortages of Ph.D.'s to meet the rising demand for faculty members, institutions frequently hired applicants who had not completed the work for a doctor's degree, this is clearly happening less frequently under the changed job market of the 1970s.

The Carnegie Commission's 1969 faculty survey indicated that only 40 percent of all faculty members had doctor's degrees, and the percentages were lower in some types of institutions, including two-year colleges, where only 5 percent of faculty members had doctor's degrees.

A major barrier to the hiring of young faculty members in the next two decades, of course, will be the rise in the percentage of faculty members with tenure. During the 1970s, the increase in the percentage with tenure has been pronounced—from about 50 percent of all faculty members in 1969 to 64 percent in 1978 (Figure H-3).[1] The rise has occurred at most types of institutions, but no increase occurred in liberal arts colleges between 1969 and 1975. This may well reflect a tendency on the part of liberal arts colleges—especially the less-selective colleges—to rely heavily on nontenured faculty in a period of

---

[1] Figure 15 (p. 81) and Figure H-3 indicate that 75 percent of the faculty members in four-year institutions have tenure in 1980. This is based on Fernandez' projection, developed before the 1978 data became available, and is probably somewhat too high.

Figure H-3. Percentage of faculty members with tenure, by type and
control of institution, actual, 1969, 1975, and 1978, and projected,
for four-year institutions, 1980 to 2000

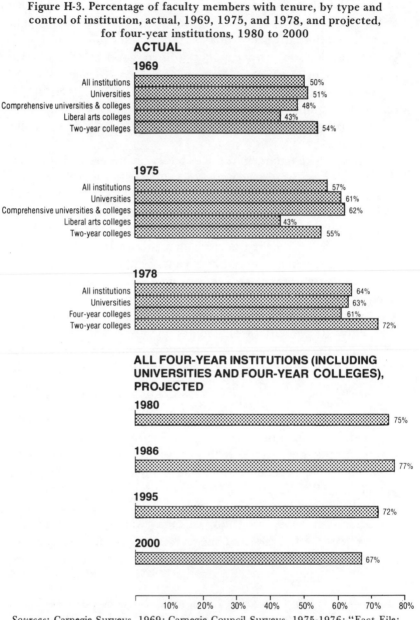

ACTUAL

1969

All institutions	50%
Universities	51%
Comprehensive universities & colleges	48%
Liberal arts colleges	43%
Two-year colleges	54%

1975

All institutions	57%
Universities	61%
Comprehensive universities & colleges	62%
Liberal arts colleges	43%
Two-year colleges	55%

1978

All institutions	64%
Universities	63%
Four-year colleges	61%
Two-year colleges	72%

**ALL FOUR-YEAR INSTITUTIONS (INCLUDING
UNIVERSITIES AND FOUR-YEAR COLLEGES),
PROJECTED**

1980   75%

1986   77%

1995   72%

2000   67%

10% 20% 30% 40% 50% 60% 70% 80%

Sources: Carnegie Surveys, 1969; Carnegie Council Surveys, 1975-1976; "Fact File:
Percentage of Faculty Members" (1979). Projections 1980 to 2000 prepared by L.
Fernandez for Carnegie Council based on Council staff enrollment projections.

slowing growth and financial stringency. A closer look at the 1978 data (not shown in Figure H-3) indicates that faculty members in private four-year colleges were less likely to have tenure (55 percent) than those in public four-year colleges (63 percent), and indeed the percentages with tenure tended to be smaller in all types of private institutions than in the public colleges and universities. The fact that faculty members in the public sector are more likely to be organized than those in the private sector is probably a factor in explaining this difference.

During the 1960s, the number of faculty members hired each year was unprecedentedly large, as colleges and universities attempted to serve the rapidly increasing student population. Some 30,000 to 35,000 FTE senior faculty members (instructor or above) were hired, on the average, each year (Figure H-4).[2] However, new hires include faculty members hired to replace those who die or retire or leave academic institutions, plus those hired to adapt to changing enrollment. Thus, net additions to faculty tend to be considerably smaller than total new hires. In

---

[2]The estimates of new hires presented in Figure H-4 must be regarded as rough approximations. NCES estimates of demand from 1963 to 1979 are based on the sum of estimated replacement demand plus demand related to increasing enrollment, and apply to all faculty members, including junior faculty, such as teaching assistants. We have adjusted the data to apply to senior faculty by assuming that there is a one-third turnover in junior faculty ranks each year—thus, we subtracted one-third of the annual number of junior faculty members from the NCES estimates of demand for FTE faculty. We also made some adjustments in the projections prepared for the Council by Luis Fernandez for the period from 1980 to 1999. Fernandez' projections related to four-year institutions and included, among other things, an assumption that there would be a net quit rate of nontenured faculty from four-year institutions rising from 5.8 percent in 1980 to 8.8 percent in 1986 and then gradually falling to 2.8 percent by 1999. We adjusted the projections to apply to all two-year and four-year institutions, by assuming that the proportion of FTE faculty in two-year institutions would remain constant and that new hires and net additions would fluctuate in the same manner as in four-year institutions. We also reduced Fernandez' assumed quit rate by half. Historically, at least in recent decades, there has been little or no net movement of faculty members out of academic institutions (Cartter, 1976, p. 119). Fernandez assumes that this pattern will be modified, because many young faculty members will fail to be granted tenure and will leave college teaching as a result, and because faculty salaries will be increasingly less attractive than salaries that can be received in government or industry. Although we believe that there may well be a net quit rate out of academic institutions, we consider Fernandez' net quit rate to be too high and have therefore reduced it.

Figure H-4. Estimated new hires of FTE senior faculty members
(instructor and higher ranks) in all institutions of higher education,
fall 1963 to fall 1999

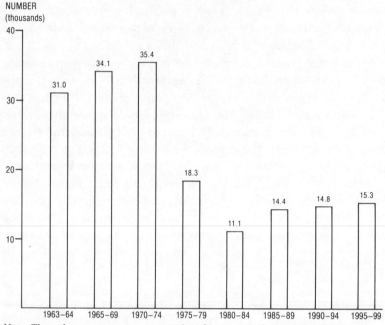

Note: These data assume a constant student-faculty ratio from 1980 to 1999.

Sources: Adapted from data in U.S. National Center for Education Statistics, *Projection of Education Statistics,* and from projections prepared by L. Fernandez based on our enrollment projections.

the 1960s, average net additions of FTE faculty were about 21,000, as we indicated in Figure 15 (p. 81). Net additions fell in the 1970s and are estimated to be close to zero in the first half of the 1980s, and to be negative for the period from 1985 on.

As we suggested earlier, the bleak outlook in the near-term demand for faculty is attributable not only to declining enrollment, but also to the bulge in the percentage of faculty members who are in the age range from about 33 to 47 years and the deficiency of those aged 55 and older. Thus, as we have seen, the replacement demand for faculty members who die or retire is currently very low. Fernandez' estimates of replacement demand for those who die or retire in all four-year institutions rise from 1.6 percent in 1980 to 3.5 percent in 2000. It is this rising replacement rate that largely explains the modest increase in estimated total new hires shown in Figure H-4 after 1984.

The Future for Faculty Development

The projections presented in Figure H-4 assume a constant student-faculty ratio in the 1980s and 1990s. However, we note in Supplement I that there has been a rising trend in the student-faculty ratio. This trend may well continue if institutions continue to face financial stringency, as many of them have in recent years. On the other hand, the student-faculty ratio might decline in a period of declining enrollment—probably chiefly because many institutions will not be able to reduce the size of their "tenured-in" faculties. For these reasons we have prepared two alternative projections, one of which assumes that the student-faculty ratio will gradually rise to 10 percent above its current level and the other of which assumes a decline to 10 percent below its current level. The results do not imply a dramatic change in new hires. Estimated new hires in 1995, for example, would be about 14,600 on the basis of a constant student-faculty ratio, 15,000 on the basis of a declining student-faculty ratio, and 14,100 on the basis of a rising student-faculty ratio.

Probably the most serious aspect of the outlook for faculty development in the next 20 years is the rise in the proportion of tenured faculty. We have seen that 64 percent of all faculty members had tenure in 1978, compared with 50 percent in 1969. Projections prepared by Fernandez for four-year institutions indicate a rise to 77 percent by 1986 and then a gradual and moderate decline to 67 percent by 2000 (Figure H-3). The dearth of openings for young scholars is one of the undesirable consequences of this trend, which we discuss fully in Supplement K. Another disadvantage is the difficulty that colleges and universities will face in adjusting their course offerings to changing demands of students by field. Clearly, there will have to be much more attention to policies designed to provide incentives for faculty members to shift their specialties (within fields) or to undertake retraining to prepare for teaching in neighboring fields. However, there are obvious limits to this type of adjustment. Professors of English literature could hardly be expected to retrain to give courses in physics, to cite an extreme example.

There will undoubtedly be efforts, also, to induce faculty members to retire early, so as to open up positions for young scholars. Even though colleges and universities will be under legal requirements not to provide for compulsory retirement before age 70 from 1982 on, they can, of course, attempt to induce voluntary early retirement by providing more attractive early retirement benefits. However, the prospects for success of such policies are much less favorable than they were only a few years ago, because of the exceedingly high rate of inflation now prevailing. Inflation rates of 12 to 13 percent a year can reduce the real incomes of retired persons very rapidly. Most retired faculty members receive the major portion of their retirement income from TIAA/CREF annuities, which are not indexed, or from institutional retirement plans, which are usually subject to little or no indexing, and a smaller proportion of their retirement income from social security benefits, which are indexed.

In fact, a rise in the average retirement age of faculty members may well occur, especially if a high rate of inflation continues. This would reduce the demand for new faculty members below even our projected levels for a few years, until the impact of the adjustment had run its course. Another highly probable development, along with increased unionization, may be greater efforts on the part of faculty members to obtain outside income through consulting or other types of remunerative activities, as Hansen (1979) has pointed out. This, of course, could be detrimental to the interests of students if it were widespread.

There is, however, one aspect of the outlook in the job market for Ph.D.'s that is not as bleak as predictions developed in the early 1970s implied. Although there is, and will continue to be, a surplus in the supply of young Ph.D.'s, the size of that surplus is not nearly as large as Cartter (1976) and others estimated. For one thing, graduate students have shifted out of Ph.D. programs to a greater extent than many projections indicated. The total number of Ph.D.'s awarded declined from a peak of nearly 34,800 in 1973 to 31,700 in 1977 (National Research Council, 1978, p. 3), and the prospects are for a continuing decline. Cartter had predicted a steady rise to about 42,000 in 1980.

An analysis by von Rothkirch (1978) projects steadily decreasing enrollment and completion in fields that have traditionally awarded the majority of doctorates: engineering-mathematics-physics, and arts-letters-social sciences. These fields are expected to represent less than one-third of all Ph.D.'s awarded within the next decade, whereas fields with promising employment opportunities in business, industry, and government can be expected to double their Ph.D. output, while fields with both academic and professional employment prospects are likely to produce a stable number of Ph.D.'s.[3]

References

Academic Collective Bargaining Information Service. *Analysis of Legislation in 24 States Enabling Faculty Collective Bargaining in Postsecondary Education.* Special Report #17 Update, May 1976.

Bowen, H. R. *Academic Compensation: Are Faculty and Staff in American Higher Education Adequately Paid?* New York: Teachers Insurance and Annuity Association/College Retirement Equities Fund, 1978.

Carnegie Council on Policy Studies in Higher Education. *Making Affirmative Action Work in Higher Education: An Analysis of Institutional and Federal Policies with Recommendations.* San Francisco: Jossey-Bass, 1975.

Cartter, A. M. *Ph.D.'s and the Academic Labor Market.* New York: McGraw-Hill, 1976.

"Coping with Adversity: The Economic Status of the Profession, 1971-72." *AAUP Bulletin,* June 1972, *58* (2), 178-243.

"An Era of Continuing Decline: Annual Report on the Economic Status of the Profession, 1978-79." *Academe,* Bulletin of the AAUP, Sept. 1979, *65* (5), 319-367.

"Fact File: Percentage of Faculty Members with Tenure, 1978-79." *Chronicle of Higher Education,* May 14, 1979, *18* (2).

"Fact File: Faculty Bargaining Agents on 648 Campuses." *Chronicle of Higher Education,* June 25, 1979, *18* (16).

---

[3]For more detailed analyses of the outlook for Ph.D.'s and faculty development, see selected monographs prepared for the Carnegie Council under the direction of Radner and Kuh, with the assistance of a grant from the Ford Foundation: Radner and Kuh (1977), Kuh (1977), Fernandez (1978), von Rothkirch (1978), and Radner and Kuh (1978).

Fernandez, L. *U.S. Faculty After the Boom: Demographic Projections to 2000.* Technical Report No. 4. Berkeley, Calif.: Carnegie Council on Policy Studies in Higher Education, 1978.

Garbarino, J. W. "Faculty Unionism: The First Ten Years." *Annals of the American Academy of Political and Social Science,* forthcoming.

Garbarino, J. W., in association with B. Aussieker. *Faculty Bargaining: Change and Conflict.* A Report Prepared for the Carnegie Commission on Higher Education and the Ford Foundation. New York: McGraw-Hill, 1975.

Garbarino, J. W., and Lawler, J. "Faculty Union Activity in Higher Education." An annual series of articles. *Industrial Relations,* Feb. 1975, *14* (1), 110-111; Feb. 1976, *15* (1), 119-120; Feb. 1977, *16* (1), 105-106; and Spring 1979, *18* (2), 244-246.

Hansen, W. L. "Academic Compensation: Myths and Realities." Paper presented at the Fourth Annual Academic Planning Conference, University of Southern California, Office of Institutional Studies, July 11-13, 1979.

Harris, S. E. *The Economics of Harvard.* New York: McGraw-Hill, 1970.

Kuh, C. V. *Market Conditions and Tenure for Ph.D.'s in U.S. Higher Education: Results from the 1975 Carnegie Faculty Survey and Comparison with Results from the 1973 ACE Survey.* Technical Report No. 3. Berkeley, Calif.: Carnegie Council on Policy Studies in Higher Education, 1977.

National Research Council, Commission on Human Resources. *Summary Report 1977: Doctorate Recipients from United States Universities.* Washington, D.C.: National Academy of Sciences, 1978.

National Research Council, Commission on Human Resources. *Research Excellence Through the Year 2000: The Importance of Maintaining a Flow of New Faculty into Academic Research.* Washington, D.C.: National Academy of Sciences, 1979.

"Nearly Keeping Up: The Economic Status of the Profession, 1975-76." *AAUP Bulletin,* Aug. 1976, *62* (2), 195-284.

Radner, R., and Kuh, C. V. *Market Conditions and Tenure in U.S. Higher Education: 1955-1973.* Technical Report No. 2. Berkeley, Calif.: Carnegie Council on Policy Studies in Higher Education, 1977.

Radner, R., and Kuh, C. V. *Preserving a Lost Generation: Policies to Assure a Steady Flow of Young Scholars Until the Year 2000.* A Report and Recommendations. Berkeley, Calif.: Carnegie Council on Policy Studies in Higher Education, 1978.

"Report on the Annual Survey of Faculty Compensation, 1977-78." *AAUP Bulletin,* Sept. 1978, *64* (3), 193-266.

Semas, P. W. "Faculty Unions Focusing on Job Security." *Chronicle of Higher Education,* Nov. 1, 1976, p. 3.

U.S. National Center for Education Statistics. *The Condition of Education, 1979 Edition.* Washington, D.C., 1979.

U.S. National Center for Education Statistics. *Projections of Education Statistics.* Washington, D.C., selected issues.

von Rothkirch, C. *Field Disaggregated Analysis and Projections of Graduate Enrollment and Higher Degree Production.* Technical Report No. 5. Berkeley, Calif.: Carnegie Council on Policy Studies in Higher Education, 1978.

Supplement I

Instructional Costs
and Productivity,
1930-1977

Higher education is a labor-intensive industry, as are other service sectors of the economy. In service sectors, it is much more difficult to achieve increases in productivity than in goods sectors, largely because there is much less opportunity to take advantage of technological changes.

It is not surprising, therefore, to find that real costs per student credit hour have not declined since 1930. In fact, they have shown a gentle rise (Table I-1). We shall return to a discussion of costs per student credit hour at a later point, basing our historical analysis on the pioneering statistical work of O'Neill (1971).

At this point, however, we need to refer to the data on educational expenditures per FTE student presented in Table 1 (p. 11). There we showed that real educational expenditures per student (in 1976-77 dollars) averaged about $2,500 in the 1960s and hovered at a figure slightly over $3,000 in the 1970s. In fact, if we consider the change from FY1960 to FY1970, we find that there was an increase from roughly $2,000 in 1960 to about $3,070 in 1970, representing an average annual rate of increase of about 4.4 percent. The decade of the 1960s was the only 10-year period from 1930 on in which there was an appre-

This supplement was prepared by Margaret S. Gordon, Associate Director, and Charlotte Alhadeff, Research Specialist.

Table I-1. Instructional costs per student credit hour,
all institutions of higher education, current and constant dollars,
1930 to 1977

Fiscal year	Current dollars	Constant dollars (1957-59 prices = $100)
1930	$ 14.6	$32.8
1932	14.1	35.0
1934	14.7	37.3
1936	13.8	34.2
1938	13.8	32.6
1940	13.9	32.8
1942	16.0	35.3
1944[a]	19.6	40.5
1946	17.3	31.5
1948	18.3	26.6
1950	21.6	29.8
1952	27.6	34.1
1954	32.0	37.5
1956	31.6	34.7
1958	35.7	36.3
1960	38.9	37.0
1962	41.2	36.6
1964	45.0	37.6
1966	47.0	35.9
1967	50.1	36.4
1968	55.1	37.8
1970	68.0	40.9
1972	76.3	40.8
1973	83.2	42.3
1974	89.3	42.3
1976	97.2	39.6
1977	107.6	41.0

[a]Credit-hour base includes estimated credits carried by military personnel enrolled in colleges and universities.

Source: Data from 1930 to 1967 are from O'Neill (1971, p. 97); data from 1968 to 1977 were developed by the Carnegie Council from enrollment and financial data of the U.S. National Center for Education Statistics (see notes to Figure I-1).

ciable rise in educational costs. In constant dollars, costs tended to be quite stable from 1930 to 1960 (although there was a drop in the immediate postwar years when heavy enrollment of veterans allowed institutions to take advantage of economies of scale, followed by a rise in the 1950s). Real costs have also tended to be fairly stable in the 1970s.

The rise in the 1960s was associated with a substantial increase in faculty salaries and fringe benefits, in library holdings, in scientific equipment, in counseling services, and in maintenance costs of vastly increased physical plant. There was also an increase in the contribution of research expenditures to graduate instruction. This higher level of expenditures built up in the 1960s was maintained in the 1970s, although real faculty salaries declined, because costs for energy, books, and many publicly mandated programs rose to offset the decline.

O'Neill's data on costs per student credit hour do not show as sharp a rise in the 1960s (Table I-1) as do our estimates of costs per FTE student. The difference is probably largely explained by the fact that we allocated 25 percent of expenditures for organized research to instructional costs, on the grounds that about that portion of research expenditures contributed to the education of graduate students. O'Neill did not include expenditures for organized research, which rose rapidly in the first half of the 1960s; in fact, she reduced expenditures on certain other categories somewhat to reflect contributions of overhead costs to research.[1] She also included an estimate of the contribution of capital costs to instructional costs.

---

[1]Specifically, O'Neill included current-funds expenditures for (1) instruction and departmental research, (2) libraries, (3) plant operation and maintenance, and (4) general administration. From the sum of these four categories, she deducted 5 percent of extension expenditures and 15 percent of organized research expenditures, on the ground that expenditures for libraries, plant operation and maintenance, and general administration include some expenses properly attributable to extension and public service and, also, to organized research (O'Neill, 1971, pp. 17-18). In our own estimates of costs per student credit hour since 1966-67, we have followed O'Neill's practice as closely as possible, making some adjustments for changes in reporting practices of the U.S. National Center for Education Statistics in order to ensure historical continuity. Our estimates of educational expenditures per FTE student, however, follow the definitions used in Carnegie Commission (1972), which attribute 25

In a general way, the gentle rise in costs per student credit hour over the decades, shown by O'Neill's data and the Carnegie Council's extension of her data to 1976-77, suggests a decline in productivity, although, as we suggest later, this is a generalization that is subject to qualifications. However, the fact that productivity in higher education has not increased helps to explain the fact that faculty salaries have declined in the face of accelerated inflation in recent years. It is difficult to grant large salary increases in a segment of the economy in which productivity is not rising, especially when there is strong consumer resistance to price (tuition) increases and strong legislative resistance to large increases in appropriations. It is particularly difficult, of course, as we suggested in Supplement H, when the demand for faculty is declining and faculty bargaining power is correspondingly weakened.

Another characteristic of the past few decades has been an upward trend in student-faculty ratios, although most of the increase occurred before 1970. Since 1972-73, there has been little change in the overall student-faculty ratio, but a pronounced contrast between its behavior in universities, where it has declined, and in four-year and two-year colleges, where it has risen.

Why have costs per student credit hour not fallen in a period when real faculty salaries have declined and the student-faculty ratio has been relatively stable overall? In view of the large proportion of expenditures of higher education represented by faculty salaries, one would expect them to fall when real faculty salaries are falling, in the absence of a decline in the student-faculty ratio. And, in fact, as we shall see, costs per credit hour in all institutions have fallen since 1973-74. Moreover, they have declined in those groups of institutions in which student-faculty ratios have risen.

---

percent of expenditures for organized research to instruction. Excluded from both definitions are current-funds expenditures for public service, student aid, auxiliary enterprises, hospitals, and independent operations. Excluded from our estimates of expenditures per FTE, but not from estimates of costs per student credit hour, is the contribution of capital costs to instruction.

There is, however, another factor that has been important in the 1970s and that helps to explain why it is dangerous to draw conclusions about the behavior of productivity from the behavior of aggregate costs per student credit hour. Institutions of higher education have been confronted with rising expenditures resulting from government regulations—occupational health and safety regulations, special provisions for the disabled, and affirmative action requirements. Although all of these regulations are related to important social goals, they have imposed new costs on colleges and universities. Moreover, expenditures on compensatory educational programs have risen, not only because of the opening of doors to more minority group students, who are sometimes poorly prepared, but also because of the general decline in student performance in basic language and numeracy proficiencies that has accompanied declining test scores. And, as we suggested earlier, costs for energy and books have risen sharply.

Another factor in rising costs has been the pronounced rise in social security payroll taxes, which has been especially important for private institutions, whose employees are compulsorily covered by social security, whereas not all public institutions are integrated with social security. To be sure, the institutions may be in a position to offset some of the increase in social security costs by holding down contributions to TIAA or to a separate retirement program, but it must be kept in mind that there has been a pronounced trend toward liberalization of fringe benefits, and in the face of this trend institutions are under considerable pressure to liberalize expected retirement income.

These considerations indicate that the behavior of aggregative measures, like student-faculty ratios, may conceal important changes that are occurring in the activities in which students and faculty are engaged. In fact, the estimated decline in institutional expenditures as a percentage of GNP, which we projected in Table 12 (p. 129), assumes that a decline in FTE enrollment will be accompanied by declining total instructional expenditures, but not on a one-to-one basis for each loss of an FTE student. We therefore suggest that, for each FTE student lost to the institution, there may be a decline in expenditure needs of about 60 to 80 percent of average expenditures per FTE. This estimate is based not only on the probability that marginal costs per FTE student will rise in a period of declining enrollment, but also that the trend toward rising costs associated with social goals and related government regulations is likely to continue.

Costs per Student Credit Hour

As we have already indicated, O'Neill found very little change in instructional costs per credit hour in constant dollars in higher education from 1929-30 to 1966-67—in fact, over the period as a whole, there was a slight increase, from $32.8 per credit hour in 1929-30 to $36.4 in 1966-67 (Table I-1 and Figure I-1). Indeed, the increase shows up only if we compare data for terminal years—it is not apparent in the behavior of costs in constant dollars over the period as a whole. Costs rose in current dollars, of course, along with increases in the Consumer Price Index (CPI), and, in fact, at a slightly higher rate than the CPI. The annual average rate of increase in costs in current dollars from 1929-30 to 1966-67 was 3.4 percent, compared with a 3.0 percent annual rate of increase in consumer prices.

This result has been generally interpreted to imply that there was no increase in productivity in higher education over this 37-year period. In fact, O'Neill herself was somewhat more cautious in appraising the significance of her results (O'Neill, 1971, p. 1):

> However, it is debatable whether changes in the credit-hours measure developed here can be taken to reflect changes in real output, since changes in the quality of credit hours could only be incorporated in a crude and possibly highly inadequate way.

Undoubtedly, for example, equipment used in laboratories in science departments and in medical schools became considerably more complex over this period. The percentage of students engaged in graduate study also increased, and this would be

Figure I-1. Instructional costs per student credit hour,[a] all institutions of higher education, in current and constant dollars, 1930 to 1977

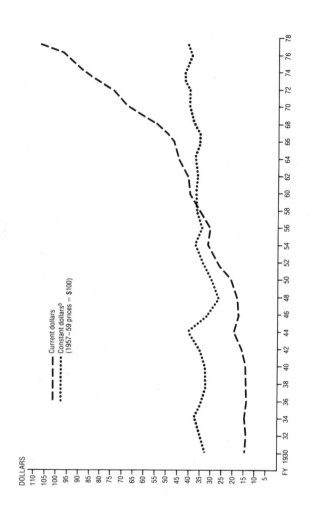

[a]Costs per credit hour are not weighted to reflect the higher cost of graduate education.

[b]In deflating educational costs for recent years, we have used the Higher Education Price Index (HEPI) developed by Halstead at the National Institute of Education (Halstead, selected issues).

Source: Data from 1930 to 1967 are from O'Neill (1971, p. 97); data from 1968 to 1977 were developed by the Carnegie Council from enrollment and financial data of the U.S. National Center for Education Statistics.

expected to result in increases in costs because of the larger inputs of faculty time required per student. O'Neill did, however, attempt to adjust for this change and found that it had virtually no effect on her overall results.

The behavior of costs in public and private institutions of higher education differed somewhat over the period (Figure I-2 and Table I-2). Costs per credit hour in private institutions were higher throughout and increased at a somewhat more pronounced rate—at an annual average rate in current dollars of 3.6 percent compared with 3.4 percent for the public institutions. This was partly, but not wholly, attributable to the relatively more pronounced increase in the percentage of graduate students in private universities.

Faculty salaries, as we noted in Supplement H, rose throughout most of this period at an annual average rate of 3.4 percent from 1929-30 to 1966-67, that is, at about the same rate as instructional costs per credit hour and at a somewhat more pronounced rate than the Consumer Price Index. Real incomes of faculty members, therefore, rose during this 37-year period. However, they rose at a considerably less pronounced rate than real incomes of average workers in the economy.

On the whole, the period studied by O'Neill was characterized, not only by phenomenal growth of higher education, but also by little evidence of pressure on institutions of higher education to hold down the increase in costs. The period since 1966-67, to which we now turn, has been quite different in significant ways.

Costs and Productivity in the 1970s

Probably the most significant contrast between the period since 1966-1967 and the period studied by O'Neill is the pronounced acceleration in the rate of inflation, which has created severe difficulties for many institutions of higher education and, perhaps, especially for those in the Northeast and Middle West that face heavy and rising heating costs in the winter. The average annual rate of increase in the Consumer Price Index of the U.S. Bureau of Labor Statistics was 6.0 percent from 1966-67 to 1976-77 and in the later part of this period was even higher,

Figure I-2. Instructional costs per student credit hour,[a] all public and all private institutions of higher education, in current and constant dollars, 1930 to 1977

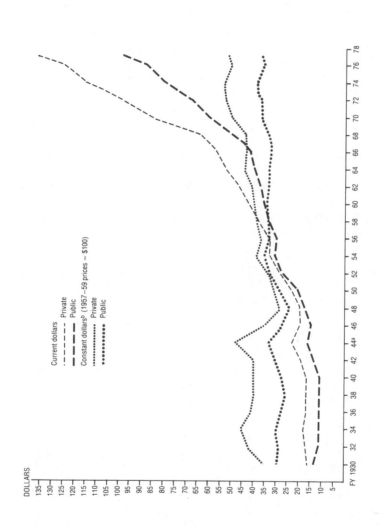

[a]Credit-hour base includes estimated credits carried by military personnel enrolled in colleges and universities.

[b]In deflating educational costs for recent years, we have used the Higher Education Price Index (HEPI) developed by Halstead at the National Institute of Education (Halstead, selected issues).

Source: Data from 1930 to 1967 are from O'Neill (1971, p. 97); data from 1968 to 1977 were developed by the Carnegie Council from enrollment and financial data of the U.S. National Center for Educational Statistics.

Table I-2. Instructional costs per student credit hour,
public and private colleges and universities, in current and constant
dollars, 1930 to 1977

	Current dollars		Constant dollars (1957-59 prices = $100)	
Fiscal year	Public	Private	Public	Private
1930	$13.3	$ 16.0	$29.6	$36.1
1932	11.7	17.0	28.7	42.3
1934	11.9	17.8	30.1	45.1
1936	11.3	16.7	27.7	41.6
1938	11.3	16.8	26.6	39.7
1940	11.5	16.8	27.2	39.8
1942	13.7	18.8	30.1	41.4
1944[a]	16.4	23.3	33.7	48.1
1946	15.2	19.6	27.6	35.7
1948	17.1	19.7	24.8	28.6
1950	20.4	23.1	28.1	31.8
1952	27.2	28.0	33.7	34.6
1954	31.2	33.0	36.6	38.7
1956	30.0	33.7	33.0	37.0
1958	33.8	38.6	34.3	39.2
1960	36.7	42.4	34.8	40.2
1962	37.7	46.9	33.5	41.7
1964	40.5	53.1	33.9	44.3
1966	42.0	57.0	32.2	43.6
1967	45.3	60.4	32.9	44.0
1968	50.6	65.5	34.7	44.9
1970	61.2	85.9	36.9	51.6
1972	68.4	99.5	36.6	53.0
1973	75.2	107.2	38.2	54.3
1974	80.8	115.3	38.4	54.6
1976	88.5	125.5	36.1	50.9
1977	98.5	136.1	37.6	51.8

[a]Credit-hour base includes estimated credits carried by military personnel enrolled in colleges and universities.

Source: Data from 1930 to 1967 are from O'Neill (1971, p. 97); data from 1968 to 1977 were developed by the Carnegie Council from enrollment and financial data of the U.S. National Center for Education Statistics.

compared with the 3.0 rate of increase for the period studied by O'Neill.

Table I-1 shows that costs per credit hour rose from $50.1 in 1966-67 to $107.6 in 1976-77, or at an annual average rate of 7.9 percent, substantially exceeding the rate of inflation. This meant, of course, that costs rose in constant dollars—from $36.4 to $41.0 over the period. However, the rise from 1966-67 to 1972-73 was even more pronounced, and a slight decline occurred after 1973-74. We will find evidence of intensified belt-tightening after 1973-74, which, it will be recalled, was the year of the first oil crisis.

Once again, there was a considerable difference in the behavior of costs in public and private institutions (Table I-2). The rise in terms of both current and constant dollars was considerably more pronounced in private institutions over the 10-year period as a whole. If we look more closely at the figures, however, we note that the rise for private institutions was especially sharp from 1967-68 to 1970-71 and that after that the increase slowed down and there was actually a reversal in constant dollars from 1973-74 to 1975-76. Similarly, in the public institutions a decline in costs in constant dollars occurred from 1973-74 to 1975-76.

The behavior of costs in private institutions over this period is particularly interesting in the light of the indications in studies by Cheit (1971) and others that substantial numbers of private colleges and universities were in financial difficulty at the beginning of the 1970s. We noted in Supplement A that a good many private institutions incurred deficits on current account at that time, wiped out the deficits in the following several years, and then faced deficits once more after 1973-74.

Table I-3 shows, however, that it is dangerous to generalize about private institutions, because the behavior of costs varied substantially among the three main types of private universities and colleges. Costs per credit hour increased steadily and at a comparatively pronounced rate in private universities. In private four-year colleges, on the other hand, costs in current dollars increased less than the rate of inflation after 1973-74 and de-

Table I-3. Instructional costs per student credit hour, by type and control of institution, 1968 to 1977

Fiscal year	In current dollars						In constant dollars (1967 = $100)[a]					
	Universities		Other four-year		Two-year colleges		Universities		Other four-year		Two-year colleges	
	Public	Private	Public	Private	Public	Private	Public	Private	Public	Private	Public	Private
1968	$71.9	$93.6	$57.0	$64.8	$40.1	$47.7	$67.8	$87.9	$53.8	$60.9	$37.7	$44.7
1970	85.2	121.0	70.6	86.0	52.0	57.7	70.4	99.9	58.4	71.0	43.0	47.4
1972	96.8	142.4	80.2	98.4	58.3	68.2	71.0	104.4	58.8	71.9	42.8	49.7
1973	105.9	152.1	88.9	106.1	64.8	75.5	73.7	105.6	61.9	73.7	45.1	52.5
1973 (new)	103.3	153.2	94.2	108.1	65.3	74.5	72.0	106.4	65.6	74.2	45.5	51.8
1974	110.9	167.1	103.9	114.4	68.1	78.4	72.1	108.4	67.6	74.2	44.7	50.9
1976	129.2	202.9	120.5	118.1	67.9	65.8	72.1	113.0	67.3	65.7	37.9	36.6
1977	142.0	221.6	132.3	127.6	77.4	76.7	74.4	115.6	69.3	66.6	40.5	40.0
Average annual rate of increase	7.9%	10.0%	9.8%	7.8%	7.6%	5.4%	1.0%	3.1%	2.9%	1.0%	0.8%	−1.0%

[a]Conversion to constant dollars on the basis of the Higher Education Price Index. Costs per credit hour are not weighted to reflect the higher cost of graduate education.

Note: The criteria for classification of institutions were changed in 1973. The first line for 1973 shows estimated costs using the same classification principles as in 1968-1972. The second line for 1973 (labelled "new") shows the estimated costs using the classification principles in use for 1974-1977.

Source: 1968 data computed from enrollment data of the U.S. National Center for Education Statistics and from data on instructional costs in O'Neill (1973, p. 11). Data for later years computed from enrollment and financial data of the U.S. National Center for Education Statistics.

clined in constant dollars. The private two-year colleges—on the whole, a rather weak group of institutions—were even more squeezed by inflation and experienced a sharp drop in constant dollars after 1973-74, as well as a net drop over the entire nine-year period.

Differences in the behavior of costs were somewhat less pronounced in the public sector, but the rise in both current and constant dollars was considerably more pronounced in public four-year colleges than in public universities or two-year colleges. Only in the public two-year colleges, moreover, was there evidence of a serious squeeze after 1973-74. However, in both public universities and public four-year colleges, increases in terms of constant costs were very slight after that year.[2]

Student-Faculty Ratios

Data on student-faculty ratios are available only from 1953-54 on, since that was the first year in which comprehensive data on faculty were collected. O'Neill (1971, p. 46) showed that there was a rising tendency in the student-faculty ratio throughout the period from 1953-54 to 1966-67 in all types of public institutions.[3] In private institutions, the ratio declined substantially in universities, probably reflecting the pronounced rise in the proportion of graduate students, but rose in four-year and two-year colleges. For all private institutions combined, the ratio remained virtually constant.

In Table I-4, we present data on student-faculty ratios from 1955-56 to 1976-77. They are not precisely comparable with O'Neill's data, which included both junior and senior faculty, whereas only senior faculty are included in computing the ratios in Table I-4. Nevertheless, the trends are consistent with those shown by O'Neill, except for the fact that the ratio in

[2]It should be noted that costs in constant dollars are based on 1967 prices rather than the 1957-1959 base used in previous tables and charts. Thus, they are considerably higher.

[3]O'Neill's measures were actually published in the form of faculty-student ratios, which declined over the period. We prefer to present the measures in terms of student-faculty ratios.

Table I-4. Ratios of full-time equivalent students to full-time
equivalent faculty,[a] by type and control of institution,
1955-56 to 1976-77

	Univer-sities[d]		Other four-year institutions[d]		Two-year colleges	
	Public	Private	Public	Private	Public	Private
Unweighted[b]						
1955-56	13.0	11.1	15.3	12.7	22.5	15.2
1967-68	15.7	11.3	17.9	14.3	20.3	17.2
1972-73	16.5	13.8	17.0	14.3	20.2	16.5
1972-73 (new)[d]	15.3	13.2	16.9	14.1	20.2	16.5
1976-77 (new)[d]	14.0	10.7	16.5	15.4	22.9	20.0
Weighted[c]						
1955-56	15.4	14.2	16.5	13.5		
1967-68	20.1	16.2	20.2	15.6		
1972-73	21.9	22.7	18.5	15.7		
1972-73 (new)[d]	20.3	21.5	18.3	15.4		
1976-77 (new)[d]	19.2	18.0	18.4	17.5		

[a]Senior faculty defined as all teachers above the level of teaching assistant.

[b]Graduates and undergraduates weighted equally.

[c]For 1955 and 1967, all graduate students weighted 3; undergraduates, 1. For 1972 and 1976, graduate students at universities weighted 3; other graduate students, 2; undergraduates, 1.

[d]Instruction and research staffs combined.

Sources: Data for 1955 and 1967 are from Carnegie Commission on Higher Education (1972, p. 65). Data for 1972 and 1976 have been developed by the Carnegie Council from HEGIS tapes of the U.S. National Center for Education Statistics.

private universities showed a rising tendency to 1972, after which there was a decline.

In interpreting the data for universities and other four-year institutions, the weighted data should be regarded as more significant than the unweighted data, since a change in the proportion of graduate students, who are usually enrolled in smaller classes and who require relatively more faculty time than undergraduates, can affect the need for faculty members. The weighted data show a decline in the student-faculty ratio in both public and private universities after 1972. This undoubtedly reflects the influence of the rise in the proportion of tenured faculty members, who will continue to hold their secure positions even when the rate of enrollment growth is declining, as well as the fact that university departments need adequate representation of the various specialities within each field more than do four-year and two-year colleges.

The behavior of student-faculty ratios in public and private four-year colleges has differed appreciably, with the public institutions showing a moderate decline after 1967-68 and the private institutions displaying a rising tendency. There were also differing trends between public and private two-year colleges, with the private institutions showing, on the whole, a fairly persistent rising tendency, while the public institutions experienced a decline in the ratio to 1972, followed by a rise.

If we view the entire period covered by Table I-4, however, focusing our attention on the weighted ratios in the case of universities and four-year colleges, we find that in all groups of institutions student-faculty ratios were higher in 1976 than in 1955, but the difference in the case of the public two-year colleges was very slight. Although we have not included combined data for all institutions in Table I-4, it is pertinent to note that the weighted ratios showed a rising tendency throughout the period in both public and private institutions.

Table I-5 compares the behavior of costs per credit hour with the behavior of student-faculty ratios for the six groups of institutions, for the period from 1972-73 to 1976-77, showing that the changes were generally consistent—where costs rose, the student-faculty ratio declined, and vice versa. The only exception was in the case of the public four-year colleges, where both costs per credit hour and the student-faculty ratio (on a weighted basis) rose.

When the student-faculty ratios were recalculated, however, for the more refined groups of institutions in the Carnegie Classification, we found that there were interesting differences between Research Universities I (1.1 in Table I-6) and other groups of universities. Between fall 1972 and fall 1976, the student-faculty ratio fell quite sharply in both public and private

Table I-5. Ratios of full-time equivalent students to full-time
equivalent faculty, and instructional costs per student credit hour
(in constant 1967 dollars), 1972-73 and 1976-77

	Univer-sities[c]		Other four-year institutions[c]		Two-year colleges[c]	
	Public	Private	Public	Private	Public	Private
Unweighted						
Instructional costs per credit hour						
1972-73	$72.0	$106.4	$65.6	$74.2	$45.5	$51.8
1976-77	$74.4	$115.6	$69.3	$66.6	$40.5	$40.0
Student (FTE)						
Faculty (FTE)[a]						
1972-73	15.4	13.1	16.5	14.1	20.2	17.2
1976-77	13.9	10.6	15.8	15.3	22.9	20.8
Weighted[b]						
Instructional costs per credit hour						
1972-73	$53.0	$ 65.3	$54.7	$61.5	$45.4	$51.8
1976-77	$53.6	$ 68.7	$55.5	$52.3	$40.6	$40.0
Student (FTE)						
Faculty (FTE)[b]						
1972-73	20.8	21.5	18.0	15.4	20.2	17.2
1976-77	19.3	17.9	18.3	17.5	22.9	20.8

[a]Research workers are included in faculty in both years.

[b]The weighting for student-faculty ratios is the same as in Table I-4. For the cost figures, all undergraduates were weighted 1, and all graduate students, 3.

[c]The "new" method of classification has been used here both for the cost data and for the student-faculty ratios.

Sources: Developed by the Carnegie Council from HEGIS tapes of the U.S. National Center for Education Statistics.

Research Universities I. It also fell in private Research Universities II (1.2) and, slightly, in private Doctorate-granting Universities I (1.3). It remained constant in public Doctorate-grant-

Table I-6. Ratios of full-time equivalent students to full-time equivalent faculty (weighted), by Carnegie classification and control of institution, fall 1972 and fall 1976

	Doctorate-granting Institutions				Compre-hensive Univer-sities and Colleges		Liberal Arts Colleges		Two-Year Colleges
	1.1	*1.2*	*1.3*	*1.4*	*2.1*	*2.2*	*3.1*	*3.2*	*4.1*
Public institutions[a]									
Fall 1972	20.4	20.5	22.1	20.6	19.2	17.3	—	17.7	20.1
Fall 1976	16.7	21.3	22.1	20.8	19.7	18.1	23.7	16.9	22.9
Private institutions[a]									
Fall 1972	18.3	21.8	21.1	23.6	19.2	16.7	12.7	14.0	17.2
Fall 1976	14.8	17.4	20.7	26.2	21.7	19.2	13.0	15.4	21.1
Public institutions[b]									
Fall 1972	22.8	22.7	22.6	21.8	19.4	17.4	—	17.8	20.1
Private institutions[b]									
Fall 1972	19.9	24.3	21.9	23.7	19.3	16.7	12.8	14.0	17.2

[a]Research workers included.

[b]Research workers excluded.

Sources: Developed by the Carnegie Council from HEGIS tapes of the U.S. National Center for Education Statistics.

ing Universities I and rose in varying amounts in the other groups of universities. The behavior of the student-faculty ratio in Research Universities I is of special interest, because we expect these groups of institutions to be least adversely affected by enrollment declines in the next two decades and, on the whole, to maintain the size of their faculties (see the discussion in Supplement K).

Another very interesting point brought out by our analysis is that universities and colleges increased the use of junior faculty to a rather marked extent in the period from fall 1972 to fall 1976 (Table I-7). This was presumably a way of economiz-

Table I-7. Ratios of full-time equivalent students to full-time equivalent
junior faculty, and ratios of full-time equivalent senior to full-time
equivalent junior faculty, fall 1972 and fall 1976

	Universities		Other four-year institutions		Two-year colleges	
	Public	Private	Public	Private	Public	Private
Students (FTE)						
Junior faculty (FTE)						
Fall 1972	54.0	68.8	275.0	399.2	1601.0	771.8
Fall 1976	38.4	39.5	157.9	265.9	797.3	1379.6
Senior faculty (FTE)						
Junior faculty (FTE)						
Fall 1972	3.51	5.24	16.66	28.42	79.45	44.84
Fall 1976	2.76	3.72	9.99	17.37	34.87	66.41

Source: Developed by the Carnegie Council from HEGIS tapes of the U.S. National Center for
Education Statistics.

ing on total faculty salary expenditures and is a trend that can
probably be expected to continue. Only in the private two-year
colleges was the tendency the reverse.

The Higher Education Price Index

Another revealing measure of the behavior of costs in higher
education is the Higher Education Price Index (HEPI), which
was developed by Halstead in the National Institute of Education in the late 1960s and which showed that, from 1967 to
1972-73, prices of services and commodities purchased by institutions of higher education rose at a more rapid rate than the
Consumer Price Index of the U.S. Bureau of Labor Statistics
(Table I-8). We have noted that faculty salaries rose faster than
the CPI during the 1960s, but there was also a tendency in the
late 1960s and early 1970s for such items as compensation of

Table I-8. Higher Education Price Index (HEPI) and
Consumer Price Index (CPI), 1968-1977 (1967 = $100)

Fiscal year	HEPI	CPI[a]	Annual rate of change in HEPI	CPI
1968	106.0	102.1	6.0%	2.1%
1969	113.2	107.0	6.8	4.8
1970	121.0	113.0	6.9	5.6
1971	128.6	118.8	6.3	5.1
1972	135.8	123.3	5.6	3.8
1973	143.0	129.2	5.3	4.8
1974	153.1	140.4	7.1	8.7
1975	166.2	154.4	8.6	10.0
1976	177.2	165.8	6.6	7.4
1977	188.6	176.0	6.4	6.2
Percentage change				
1977/1968	177.9%	172.4%		
1973/1968	134.9%	126.5%		
1977/1973	131.9%	136.2%		

[a]For the CPI, the calendar year series has been converted into a fiscal year series by averaging two adjacent calendar years.

Sources: Halstead, selected issues; and The President (1979).

nonfaculty employees and costs of library materials to rise even more rapidly than faculty salaries.

Since 1972-73, the comparative behavior of the HEPI has been significantly different. Costs in higher education have increased less rapidly than the CPI in three of the four years shown in Table I-8. This is undoubtedly primarily attributable to the failure of faculty salaries to rise as rapidly as the CPI. Institutions continue to face pronounced increases in compensation of nonfaculty employees and in such items as library costs.

In this connection, it should be pointed out that we used the CPI in computing constant dollars in Supplement H, when we were estimating the real change in faculty salaries, because the purchasing power of faculty salaries is best measured by the CPI. However, in computing instructional costs per credit hour as reported in this supplement, we used the HEPI as a deflator, since it is a more appropriate measure of changes in the costs of goods and services purchased by institutions of higher education.

Conclusions

It is clear that the period from the late 1960s to the present has been a period of greater financial strain for institutions of higher education than the preceding 37 years. By and large, the leading research universities show the least evidence of strain, while private four-year and two-year colleges appear to have been forced into the most stringent belt-tightening measures. Further analysis would doubtless reveal that, among private four-year colleges, the less-selective colleges have been the hardest hit.

On the other hand, it would be rash to conclude that higher education as a whole has suffered from this belt tightening. Clearly, some institutions have suffered much more than others, while some of the more selective institutions have been less severely affected. A rise in the overall student-faculty ratio in a large group of institutions does not necessarily imply a decline in the quality of instruction, given the ambiguous results of studies of the impact of class size on student performance. The situation of the faculty is less ambiguous. Faculty members as a whole are suffering a decline in real purchasing power, as we showed in Supplement H, after a long period in which they showed rather steady but also rather modest gains.

As we look toward the future, the prospect of continued severe inflation is the most unfavorable aspect of the outlook for the financial situation of higher education. This will continue to create difficulties for all institutions and for their faculty members, quite apart from changing enrollment prospects. However, the institutions with the least favorable enrollment prospects—less-selective private four-year and two-year colleges—will also have the most serious difficulties in meeting rising costs, because their revenues will be particularly precarious.

References

Carnegie Commission on Higher Education. *The More Effective Use of Resources: An Imperative for Higher Education.* New York: McGraw-Hill, 1972.

Carnegie Commission on Higher Education. *Higher Education: Who Pays? Who Benefits? Who Should Pay?* New York: McGraw-Hill, 1973.

Cheit, E. F. *The New Depression in Higher Education: A Study of Financial Conditions at 41 Colleges and Universities.* Sponsored by the Carnegie Commission on Higher Education. New York: McGraw-Hill, 1971.

Halstead, D. K. *Higher Education Prices and Price Indexes.* An annual series. Washington, D.C.: National Institute of Education, selected issues.

O'Neill, J. A. *Resource Use in Higher Education: Trends in Output and Inputs, 1930 to 1967.* Berkeley, Calif.: Carnegie Commission on Higher Education, 1971.

O'Neill, J. A. *Sources of Funds to Colleges and Universities.* Berkeley, Calif.: Carnegie Commission on Higher Education, 1973.

The President. *Economic Report of the President, January 1979.* Washington, D.C.: 1979.

Supplement J

A Comparative Review of Scholarly, Scientific, and Technological Progress in the United States

---

> No nation can maintain a position of leadership in the world of today unless it develops to the full its scientific and technological resources.
>
> —Harry S Truman,
> September 6, 1945

A Record of Achievement

President Truman's sentiments have guided this country's commitment to research and scholarship, and the payoff has been rich and far-reaching. Probably the least recognized benefit is the most direct—the creation of new knowledge—which helps us to better understand and appreciate our present and our past, which makes our world more comprehensible and our lives richer, which destroys our stereotypes and dispels our ignorance, and which equips us for fuller participation in a demo-

This supplement was prepared by Arthur Levine, Senior Fellow, and Rachel Volberg, Research Assistant.

cratic society. The United States has been a leader in the production of significant new knowledge. For example, a survey of this century's major social science advances, ranging from the contributions of E. L. Thorndike and C. Hull in learning theory to the work of C. Hitch and others in cost benefit analysis, indicates that one-fourth of the leading achievements of the 1900-1929 period, and four-fifths subsequently, originated in this country (Deutsch and others, 1971).

The indirect benefits of research and scholarship are numerous, too many to be listed here, but among the most outstanding are the following:

· Improvement in the quality of life

Research and scholarship have contributed to making the home more comfortable through television, electricity, and refrigeration; to bettering conditions in the workplace via improved technology and safety; to cleaning up our environment; and to bringing the average person luxuries that would in the past have been reserved for kings. Per capita income has risen annually since 1954 (U.S. Bureau of the Census, *Statistical Abstract of the United States,* 1979). And, as the largest investor in research and development (R&D) in the world, the United States produced 65 percent of 492 major technological innovations from 1953 to 1973 (Table J-1). (Several of the tables in this supplement indicate some decline in recent years. This will be discussed later.)

· Cures for disease and other social problems

Perhaps the most significant contribution has involved improvement in public health and sanitation. In this century polio and tuberculosis have been eliminated as major killers, vaccines for the measles and flu have been created, new miracle drugs have been produced, and a variety of methods have been offered for birth control. In 1976 health and community services comprised 15 percent of the federal government's research and development expenditures (U.S. National Science Board, *Science Indicators, 1978,* 146-147.)

· National economic productivity

Between 1960 and 1977, the real Gross Domestic Prod-

Table J-1. Major technological innovations by selected countries,
1953-55 to 1971-73, by years of market introduction

	United States	United Kingdom	West Germany	Japan	France	Five-nation total
Percentage of total						
1953-55	76%	13%	6%	—	5%	100%
1956-58	80	11	4	—	4	100
1959-61	69	19	2	2%	8	100
1962-64	66	18	5	11	0	100
1965-67	54	24	12	7	3	100
1968-70	56	20	7	14	4	100
1971-73	59	15	9	10	8	100
Number of innovations						
1953-55	63	11	5	—	4	83
1956-58	37	5	2	—	2	46
1959-61	36	10	1	1	4	52
1962-64	54	15	4	9	—	82
1965-67	37	16	8	5	2	68
1968-70	45	16	6	11	3	81
1971-73	47	12	7	8	6	80
Total	319	85	33	34	21	492

Note: Detail may not add to totals because of rounding.

Source: U.S. National Science Board, *Science Indicators, 1976,* 199.

uct per employed civilian was higher in the United States than in France, West Germany, Japan, the United Kingdom, or Canada (Table J-2). In 1976, 13 percent of federal research and development funding was targeted specifically for economic growth or development in such areas as agriculture, mining, construction, and transportation (U.S. National Science Board, *Science Indicators, 1978,* 146-147).

· National security

Between 1961 and 1976 national defense and space exploration were the primary national objectives of the United

Table J-2. Real Gross Domestic Product per employed civilian, for
selected countries compared with the United States, 1960 to 1977[a]
(Index, United States = 100)

	United States	France	West Germany	Japan	United Kingdom	Canada
1960	100	55.0	51.3	24.7	49.9	86.6
1965	100	61.3	55.2	32.2	48.2	85.6
1967	100	63.1	56.3	36.7	49.0	83.4
1970	100	71.4	67.0	48.7	52.6	88.6
1971	100	72.9	67.2	50.9	53.7	90.3
1972	100	74.5	67.9	54.0	53.5	90.2
1973	100	76.1	69.8	56.5	54.4	90.1
1974	100	80.5	73.9	58.1	56.1	92.1
1975	100	80.7	74.3	59.8	55.8	91.1
1976	100	83.1	77.1	60.8	55.6	92.2
1977	100	84.7	79.1	62.6	55.1	91.6

[a]Output based on international price weights to enable comparable cross-country comparisons.

Source: U.S. National Science Board, *Science Indicators, 1978,* 157.

States government research and development commitment
(U.S. National Science Board, *Science Indicators, 1978,* 146-
147).

· International economic advantage

Between 1966 and 1975, the United States had a positive patent balance of almost twice that of any other major
industrial nation (Table J-3). And between 1966 and 1976,
this country sold at least twice as much in R&D-intensive
manufactured goods as it imported every year (U.S. National
Science Board, *Science Indicators, 1976,* 203).

· National prestige and recognition

Between 1901 and 1978, the United States was honored
by having more Nobel Prize laureates in science than any
other nation in the world—a total of 132 in contrast to 212
for all other countries of the world combined. Between 1901
and 1929 the U.S. received 7 percent of the prizes; from

Table J-3. United States patent balance with selected countries, 1966 to 1976

	1966	1967	1968	1969	1970	1971	1972	1973	1974	1975	1976
Total:											
Balance	36,066	34,469	36,045	35,885	33,697	31,445	30,520	25,129	19,795	19,197	—
Granted to U.S.	45,633	44,385	45,168	47,825	45,918	47,311	47,359	41,391	38,096	37,482	—
Granted by U.S.	9,567	9,916	9,123	11,940	12,221	15,866	16,839	16,262	18,301	18,285	—
Canada:											
Balance	15,676	16,592	16,686	18,153	17,598	16,665	16,045	11,619	11,460	10,891	11,192
Granted to U.S.	16,614	17,583	17,583	19,147	18,663	17,992	17,289	12,964	12,785	12,220	12,411
Granted by U.S.	938	991	897	994	1,065	1,327	1,244	1,345	1,325	1,329	1,219
West Germany:											
Balance	−248	−360	362	−40	−1,552	−1,128	−1,153	−639	−2,243	−2,929	−2,200
Granted to U.S.	3,733	3,406	3,804	4,483	2,882	4,393	4,575	4,949	3,913	3,140	3,333
Granted by U.S.	3,981	3,766	3,442	4,523	4,434	5,521	5,728	5,588	6,156	6,069	5,533
Japan:											
Balance	3,561	2,008	3,439	2,505	2,149	1,667	794	546	−1,457	−1,421	−2,182
Granted to U.S.	4,683	3,432	4,903	4,657	4,774	5,700	5,948	5,485	4,432	4,918	4,029
Granted by U.S.	1,122	1,424	1,464	2,152	2,625	4,033	5,154	4,939	5,889	6,339	6,211
United Kingdom:											
Balance	11,440	10,877	10,107	9,503	9,776	9,226	9,837	8,866	7,831	8,436	8,373
Granted to U.S.	14,117	13,676	12,588	12,678	12,728	12,682	13,001	11,717	10,976	11,497	11,024
Granted by U.S.	2,677	2,799	2,481	3,175	2,952	3,456	3,164	2,851	3,145	3,061	2,651

Other E.E.C. countries[a]:

Balance	5,700	5,432	5,481	5,840	5,743	5,143	5,093	4,914	4,489	4,372	—
Granted to U.S.	6,483	6,253	6,225	6,777	6,670	6,346	6,287	6,071	5,783	5,455	—
Granted by U.S.	783	821	744	937	927	1,203	1,194	1,157	1,294	1,083	1,150
U.S.S.R.:											
Balance	−63	−80	−30	−76	−17	−128	−96	−177	−285	−152	—
Granted to U.S.[b]	3	35	65	83	201	198	259	205	207	252	—
Granted by U.S.	66	115	95	159	218	326	355	382	492	404	394

[a]Other European Economic Community (E.E.C.) countries included here are Belgium, Denmark, Ireland, Luxembourg, and The Netherlands. Data for France and Italy are not comparable for use in this indicator.

[b]Includes inventors' certificates.

Source: U.S. National Science Board, *Science Indicators, 1976*, 197; *Science Indicators, 1978*, 153, 155.

1930 to 1965 the U.S. was awarded 45 percent of the prizes; and in the period 1966 to 1978 the U.S. was given 57 percent of the prizes (*Information Please Almanac, 1979*).

The Conditions of Excellence

Neither America's historical achievements in scholarship and research nor those of any other nation are accidents. Integrally associated with quality in scholarship and research productivity are seven factors:

1. *High social priority.* This means that the value of new knowledge and the need for research to create it are recognized. Periods of national crisis such as World War II and the Soviet launching of Sputnik have been particularly supportive of knowledge production, especially in applied R&D.
2. *Financial support.* According to a sociologist of science, J. Ben-David (1971), its secure economic base is a key advantage of American research and scholarship over that of Europe's and pays large dividends in terms of innovation and creativity.
3. *Educated manpower.* Both a small number of great minds and a critical mass of trained researchers are required.
4. *Appropriate equipment and facilities.*
5. *Excited state or "takeoff point."* At certain points in history, particular branches or subfields of knowledge are "ripe"—on the verge of a major breakthrough. Familiar examples are psychology in the second half of the nineteenth century, atomic physics in the first decades of this century, and genetics in the 1950s. An excited state is not a precondition for an important contribution to knowledge, but it enhances the likelihood of such a breakthrough.
6. *Communication networks.* Knowledge production builds on previous knowledge production. Researchers must be able to locate easily, learn about, evaluate, and advance the research of others to support continuing excellence. Society must be able to use the fruits of knowledge production to improve itself and recoup its investment. Essential for this are established communication networks—a means of systematically

storing, disseminating, and sharing knowledge. Research libraries are of critical importance here.

7. *A supportive social environment.* When autonomy and academic freedom are high for knowledge producers, knowledge production tends to be qualitatively better. Characteristic of supportive environments are a high level of education, wealth, growth, and industrialization, and a low level of anti-intellectualism and imposition of ideological tests for research.

A Questionable Future

Recently the leadership of the United States in scholarship and research, once praised by Ben-David (1971, p. 165) for "setting the pace and forcing it on other countries," has deteriorated. In terms of the indicators of success, the following declines have been recorded:

- Between 1966 and 1976, the U.S. patent balance decreased with respect to the United Kingdom, Canada, West Germany, Japan, and the U.S.S.R. By 1975 it was negative for the last three (Table J-3).
- The proportion of the world's major technological innovations produced by the U.S. decreased from 80 percent in 1956-1958 to 59 percent in 1971-1973 (Table J-1).
- The real Gross Domestic Product per employed civilian decreased in the U.S. relative to France, West Germany, Japan, the United Kingdom, and Canada between 1960 and 1977 (Table J-2).
- The U.S. moved to last place in terms of gains in relative productivity (output/manhour) in the manufacturing industries in comparison to France, West Germany, Japan, the United Kingdom, and Canada between 1960 and 1977 (Table J-4).

Contributing to these declines have been recent changes in the degree to which the United States has satisfied the seven conditions necessary for research and scholarly excellence.

Table J-4. Relative productivity in manufacturing industries
by selected countries, 1960 to 1977
(Index, 1967 = 100)

	United States	France	West Germany	Japan	United Kingdom	Canada
1960	78.8	68.7	66.4	52.6	76.8	75.5
1961	80.7	71.9	70.0	59.3	77.4	79.6
1962	84.5	75.2	74.4	61.9	79.3	83.9
1963	90.4	79.7	78.4	67.1	83.6	87.1
1964	95.2	83.7	84.5	75.9	89.7	90.9
1965	98.2	88.5	90.4	79.1	92.4	94.4
1966	99.7	94.7	94.0	87.1	95.7	97.2
1967	100.0	100.0	100.0	100.0	100.0	100.0
1968	103.6	111.4	107.6	112.6	106.9	107.3
1969	104.9	115.4	113.8	130.0	108.4	113.3
1970	104.5	121.2	116.6	146.5	109.1	115.2
1971	110.3	127.5	122.5	151.7	114.3	122.9
1972	116.0	135.9	130.3	163.9	121.2	127.4
1973	119.4	142.2	138.6	184.3	128.1	132.2
1974	114.7	146.1	145.6	187.5	127.9	132.3
1975	114.9	139.8	150.4	181.7	123.9	134.0
1976	123.2	164.0	162.8	188.7	128.4	139.4
1977	126.1	172.6	169.6	199.2	126.3	146.1

Source: U.S. National Science Board, *Science Indicators, 1978,* 156.

1. High social priority. There is no evidence of how the public regards scholars and researchers, but public perceptions of the importance of science and technology are positive. The job of scientist was rated the most prestigious occupation by Americans in a 1977 Harris Poll; scientists finished ahead of doctors, ministers, and engineers ("Occupational Prestige," 1978, p. 36). In terms of the contributions of science, the vast majority of Americans (92 percent) believed in 1978 that science and technology were necessary to keep the country prosperous (Harris Survey, 1978). Nonetheless, the degree of public confidence in the scientific community changed significantly between 1966 and 1976, along with most other social institutions during the Watergate era. In 1966, 56 percent of Americans expressed a great deal of confidence in the scientific community. By 1973 the proportion dropped to 37 percent, but within three years it rose to 43 percent (U.S. National Science Board, *Science Indicators, 1976,* 171-172). Yet the public believes that science and technology could make a major contribution toward the solution of certain social problems—in the areas of health care (65 percent), reducing and controlling air pollution (56 percent), reducing crime (51 percent), finding new ways for preventing and treating drug addiction (48 percent), developing and improving methods of producing food (44 percent), and improving education (42 percent) (U.S. National Science Board, *Science Indicators, 1976,* 179). In summary, science remains a high priority for the public, although perhaps not as high as it once was. For government, knowledge production as a social priority has declined.

2. *Financial support.* Support for research is down.

* The proportion of the Gross National Product (GNP) spent on research and development (R&D) by all sources in the United States has decreased from 2.7 percent in 1964 to 2.25 percent in 1978. During this period, 1964 to 1977 specifically, the Soviet Union's investment has risen from 2.87 percent to 3.47 percent. Japan and West Germany have increased their relative support as well (Table J-5).
* Federal support for R&D has dropped in real dollars from $18.198 million in 1966 to $15.824 million in 1979, a decline of 13 percent (Table J-6).
* Support for different types of research has been erratic. The number of real dollars provided for basic research rose in 1968, 1972, 1976, 1977, and 1978, and dropped in 1969, 1970, 1971, 1973, 1974, and 1975. The drops involved declines of as much as $225 million in a single year. One result is that expensive research equipment is underutilized, research teams must be hastily assembled and then broken up before they have a chance to finish their work, and needed

Table J-5. National expenditures for performance of R&D as a percentage
of Gross National Product (GNP) by country, 1961 to 1978

	France	West Germany	Japan	United Kingdom	United States	U.S.S.R.
1961	1.38%	n.a.	1.39%	2.39%	2.74%	n.a.
1962	1.46	1.25%	1.47	n.a.	2.73	2.64%
1963	1.55	1.41	1.44	n.a.	2.87	2.80
1964	1.81	1.57	1.48	2.30	2.97	2.87
1965	2.01	1.73	1.54	n.a.	2.91	2.85
1966	2.03	1.81	1.48	2.32	2.90	2.88
1967	2.13	1.97	1.53	2.33	2.91	2.91
1968	2.08	1.97	1.61	2.29	2.83	n.a.
1969	1.94	2.05	1.65	2.23	2.74	3.03
1970	1.91	2.18	1.79	n.a.	2.64	3.23
1971	1.90	2.38	1.84	n.a.	2.50	3.29
1972	1.86	2.33	1.85	2.06	2.43	3.58
1973	1.77	2.32	1.89	n.a.	2.34	3.66
1974	1.81	2.26	1.95	n.a.	2.32	3.64
1975	1.82	2.39	1.94	2.05	2.30	3.69
1976	1.78	2.28	1.94	n.a.	2.27	3.55
1977	1.79	2.26	n.a.	n.a.	2.27	3.47
1978	n.a.	2.28	n.a.	n.a.	2.25	n.a.

n.a. = not available.

Source: National Science Board, *Science Indicators, 1978,* 14.

research is interrupted or sometimes not completed. (See
Table J-6.)

· Since 1968 real federal support for basic research has
  dropped slightly, while support for applied research has increased (Table J-6). Basic research or "advancement of
  knowledge" is now a significantly smaller proportion of the
  U.S. research budget than that of Japan, West Germany,
  France, United Kingdom, and Canada (U.S. National Science
  Board, *Science Indicators, 1976,* 146-147).
· Federal support for universities, the prime performers of
  basic research (69 percent), has been erratic, increasing gener-

Table J-6. Federal support for research, total and type, from 1953 to 1979
(constant 1972 dollars, in $ millions)

	Total	Basic	Applied	Development	Percentage basic	Percentage applied	Percentage development
1953	4.675	.426	1.268	2.981	9.1%	27,1%	63.7%
1954	5.247	.474	1.337	3.436	9.0	25.4	65.5
1955	5.743	.496	1.342	3.907	8.6	23.3	68.0
1956	7.714	.574	1.570	5.569	7.4	20.3	72.1
1957	9.397	.657	1.945	6.795	6.9	20.6	72.3
1958	10.262	.724	2.178	7.360	7.0	21.2	71.7
1959	11.917	.929	2.358	8.630	7.8	19.8	72.4
1960	12.725	1.041	2.458	9.226	8.2	19.3	72.5
1961	13.351	1.261	2.531	9.558	9.4	18.9	71.6
1962	14.048	1.603	2.930	9.515	11.4	20.8	67.7
1963	15.651	1.831	2.968	10.850	11.7	18.9	69.3
1964	17.241	2.196	3.296	11.748	12.7	19.1	68.1
1965	17.508	2.434	3.396	11.678	13.9	19.4	66.7
1966	18.198	2.578	3.364	12.256	14.2	18.5	67.3
1967	18.217	2.764	3.438	12.015	15.2	18.9	65.9
1968	18.077	2.802	3.441	11.835	15.5	19.0	65.5
1969	17.176	2.796	3.242	11.138	16.3	18.9	64.8
1970	16.055	2.685	3.365	10.005	16.7	21.0	62.3
1971	15.509	2.535	3.243	9.731	16.4	20.9	62.7
1972	15.755	2.553	3.172	10.030	16.2	20.1	63.6
1973	15.415	2.495	3.284	9.636	16.2	21.3	62.5
1974	14.440	2.436	3.153	8.851	16.9	21.8	61.3
1975	14.276	2.428	3.167	8.681	17.0	22.2	60.8
1976	14.674	2.508	3.433	8.733	17.1	23.4	59.5
1977[a]	15.288	2.652	3.482	9.153	17.3	22.9	59.9
1978[b]	15.678	2.758	3.479	9.440	17.6	22.2	60.2
1979[b]	15.824	n.a.	n.a.	n.a.	—	—	—

n.a. = not available.

[a]Preliminary data.

[b]Estimated by Carnegie Council.

Sources: U.S. National Science Foundation (1977, tables B-5, B-6, B-7, B-8; and 1979).

ally, but moving up and down from year to year throughout the 1970s (Table J-7). In addition, support is smaller: in 1966 the federal government provided 73.6 percent of college and university expenditures for research, but by 1978 support had been reduced to 67.1 percent.[1]

· In general, faculty (77 percent) believe it is harder to get research support now than it was a few years ago (Carnegie Council Surveys, 1975-76). There is a serious danger that this will discourage them from proposing new and creative approaches to research and that they will concentrate instead on the safe, tried, and true, which may be good for getting support, but is bad for research.

· Support for particular fields is inadequate. Between 1973 and 1976 real federal monies targeted for social science research declined by 27 percent (U.S. National Science Board, *Science Indicators, 1978,* 233-234). Even more serious is the plight of the humanities, which in 1976 received only $18.6 million for scholarships from the federal government (National Endowment for the Humanities, 1978).

3. Educated manpower. The pool of educated manpower for research has shrunk. The number of scientists and engineers in the U.S. engaged in R&D per 10,000 labor force fell from 66.9 in 1968 to 56.3 in 1974 but then began to rise again. During the period from 1968 to 1977, the number in the U.S.S.R. rose from at least 53.5 to 81.9, and the number in Japan increased from 31.1 to 49.9 (Table J-8). The decline is most serious among young university researchers who are needed to train the scholars of tomorrow. This problem is discussed more fully in Supplement K.

4. Facilities and equipment. The Ford Foundation's report from 15 university presidents (1978, p. 41) states:

> The most serious reduction has occurred in funds for new equipment and facilities and for upgrading exist-

---

[1]Data obtained from U.S. National Science Foundation by telephone.

Table J-7. Federal support for research, total and by recipient
(Current dollars in $ millions)

	Total Amount	Federal government		Industry		Universities and colleges		Federally funded R&D centers		Nonprofit institutions	
		Amount	Percentage	Amount	Percentage	Amount	Percentage	Amount	Percentage	Amount	Percentage
1953	$ 2.753	$1.010	36.7%	$ 1.430	51.9%	$ 138	5.0%	$ 121	4.4%	$ 54	1.9%
1954	3.132	1.020	32.6	1.750	55.9	160	5.1	141	4.5	61	1.9
1955	3.502	905	25.8	2.180	62.2	169	4.8	180	5.1	68	1.9
1956	4.852	1.040	21.4	3.328	68.6	213	4.4	194	4.0	77	1.6
1957	6.110	1.220	20.0	4.335	70.9	229	3.7	240	3.9	86	1.4
1958	6.779	1.374	20.3	4.759	70.2	254	3.7	293	4.3	99	1.5
1959	8.046	1.640	20.4	5.635	70.0	306	3.8	338	4.2	127	1.6
1960	8.738	1.726	19.8	6.081	69.6	405	4.6	360	4.1	166	1.9
1961	9.250	1.874	20.3	6.240	67.5	500	5.4	410	4.4	226	2.4
1962	9.911	2.098	21.2	6.435	64.9	613	6.2	470	4.7	295	3.0
1963	11.204	2.279	20.3	7.270	64.9	760	6.8	530	4.7	365	3.3
1964	12.536	2.838	22.6	7.720	61.6	916	7.3	629	5.0	433	3.5
1965	13.012	3.093	23.8	7.740	59.5	1.073	8.2	629	4.8	477	3.7
1966	13.969	3.220	23.1	8.332	59.6	1.262	9.0	630	4.5	525	3.8
1967	14.395	3.396	23.6	8.365	58.1	1.409	9.8	673	4.7	552	3.8
1968	14.926	3.493	23.4	8.560	57.3	1.573	10.5	719	4.8	582	3.9

(continued on next page)

Table J-7 (continued)

	Total Amount	Federal government		Industry		Universities and colleges		Federally funded R&D centers		Nonprofit institutions	
		Amount	Percentage	Amount	Percentage	Amount	Percentage	Amount	Percentage	Amount	Percentage
1969	$14.895	$3.503	23.5%	$ 8.451	56.7%	$1.600	10.7%	$ 725	4.9%	$ 616	4.1%
1970	14.668	3.855	26.3	7.779	53.0	1.648	11.2	737	5.0	649	4.4
1971	14.892	4.156	27.9	7.666	51.5	1.724	11.6	716	4.8	630	4.2
1972	15.755	4.482	28.4	8.017	50.9	1.839	11.7	764	4.8	653	4.1
1973	16.309	4.619	28.3	8.145	49.9	2.038	12.5	817	5.0	690	4.2
1974	16.754	4.815	28.7	8.220	49.1	2.032	12.1	865	5.2	822	4.9
1975	18.152	5.397	29.7	8.605	47.4	2.288	12.6	987	5.4	875	4.8
1976	19.628	5.710	29.1	9.345	47.6	2.501	12.7	1.147	5.8	925	4.7
1977[a]	21.649	6.142	28.4	10.419	48.1	2.717	12.5	1.384	6.4	987	4.6
1978[b]	23.815	6.565	27.6	11.750	49.3	3.075	12.9	1.375	5.8	1.050	4.4
1979[b]	25.715	6.940	27.0	13.000	50.5	3.315	12.9	1.425	5.5	1.035	4.0

[a]Preliminary data.

[b]Estimated by Carnegie Council.

Source: National Science Foundation, National Patterns of R&D Resources, 1953-1977, table B-1; updated by telephone.

Table J-8. Scientists and engineers engaged in research and development,
by country, 1965 to 1978

	France	West Germany	Japan	United Kingdom	United States	U.S.S.R. (low est.)	U.S.S.R. (high est.)
Scientists and engineers[a] engaged in R&D per 10,000 labor force population							
1965	21.0	22.6	24.6	21.4	64.1	44.8	48.2
1966	23.0	22.3	26.4	n.a.	66.1	47.1	51.4
1967	25.3	23.9	27.8	n.a.	66.1	50.7	55.3
1968	26.4	25.9	31.1	17.2	66.9	53.5	58.8
1969	27.2	28.8	30.8	n.a.	66.1	56.5	62.1
1970	27.3	30.8	33.4	n.a.	63.6	58.4	64.2
1971	27.8	33.5	37.5	n.a.	60.6	63.0	69.1
1972	28.1	35.7	38.1	27.8	58.3	66.5	73.2
1973	28.4	37.4	42.5	n.a.	56.8	73.5	81.5
1974	28.8	38.2	44.9	n.a.	56.3	74.5	82.9
1975	29.3	39.4	47.9	30.6	56.4	78.2	87.5
1976	29.9	40.0	48.4	n.a.	56.7	80.7	90.9
1977	n.a.	40.5	49.9	n.a.	57.4	81.9	92.7
1978	n.a.	n.a.	n.a.	n.a.	58.0	n.a.	n.a.
Scientists and engineers engaged in R&D (in thousands)							
1965	42.8	61.0	117.6	54.6	494.5	521.8	561.4
1966	47.9	60.0	128.9	n.a.	521.1	556.5	607.6
1967	52.4	63.0	138.7	n.a.	534.4	607.8	662.6
1968	54.7	68.0	157.6	43.6	550.4	650.8	715.2
1969	57.2	76.3	157.1	n.a.	556.6	698.8	767.5
1970	58.5	82.5	172.0	n.a.	546.5	733.3	806.9
1971	60.1	90.2	194.3	n.a.	526.4	804.2	881.8
1972	61.2	96.0	198.1	71.1	518.5	862.5	950.1
1973	62.7	101.0	226.6	n.a.	517.5	966.7	1,072.1
1974	64.1	102.5	238.2	n.a.	525.4	995.8	1,108.0
1975	65.3	103.9	255.2	78.8	534.8	1,061.2	1,187.6
1976	67.0	104.5	260.2	n.a.	549.9	1,113.7	1,254.5
1977	n.a.	105.5	272.0	n.a.	571.1	1,147.8	1,299.1
1978	n.a.	n.a.	n.a.	n.a.	595.0	n.a.	n.a.

(continued on next page)

Table J-8 *(continued)*

	France	West Germany	Japan	United Kingdom	United States	U.S.S.R.
Total labor force (in thousands)						
1965	20,381	27,034	47,870	25,498	77,178	116,494
1966	20,522	26,962	48,910	25,632	78,893	118,138
1967	20,676	26,409	49,830	25,490	80,793	119,893
1968	20,744	26,291	50,610	25,378	82,272	121,716
1969	20,996	26,535	50,980	25,370	84,239	123,584
1970	21,465	26,817	51,530	25,300	85,903	125,612
1971	21,638	26,910	51,860	25,123	86,929	127,672
1972	21,817	26,901	52,000	25,194	88,901	129,722
1973	22,083	26,985	53,260	25,545	91,040	131,610
1974	22,282	26,797	53,100	25,602	93,240	133,600
1975	22,310	26,397	53,230	25,795	94,793	135,767
1976	22,440	26,148	53,780	26,093	96,917	137,987
1977	22,468	26,051	54,520	26,327	99,534	140,140
1978	n.a.	n.a.	n.a.	n.a.	102,537	n.a.

n.a. = Not available.

Note: Estimates are shown for most countries for latest years and for the United States for 1966 and 1967. A range has been provided for the U.S.S.R. because of the difficulties inherent in comparing Soviet scientific personnel data to those of other countries.

[a]Includes all scientists and engineers engaged in R&D on a full-time equivalent basis (except for Japan, whose data include persons primarily employed in R&D, and the United Kingdom, whose data include only the government and industry sectors).

Source: U.S. National Science Board, *Science Indicators, 1978,* 143.

ing plant. In 1971 it was estimated that $275 million was needed to remedy then-existing deficiencies in research equipment. Federal funds available to universities for new research facilities plummeted in constant dollars from $168 million in 1966 to $34 million in 1974. In the mid-sixties, the National Science Foundation and the National Institutes of Health allocated approximately 11 percent of their project grants for permanent laboratory equipment. Today they are able to provide only about 5 percent for these purposes. These declines in resources have coincided with rapid increases in the sophistication and cost of experimental apparatus.

Measured in constant 1972 dollars, federal expenditures for R&D plant for all performers has dropped from $1.450 billion in 1965 to $1.030 billion in 1978 (U.S. National Science Foundation, *Federal Funds,* 1976, 1977, and 1978).

5. Takeoff point. There are always ripe fields for research. Among today's are international economics, leisure, demography, biological nitrogen fixation, neurochemistry, and tropical biology. There is also public interest in research on environment and solar energy. And certain fields like psychology and education are dependent upon new discoveries in the life sciences for significant future advances.

6. Communication networks. The volume of knowledge being produced is increasing quickly. For example, the number of scholarly and technical journals grew from 1,598 to 2,013 between 1961 and 1974 (King Research Inc., 1978); the number of books published annually increased from 18,060 to 42,780 between 1961 and 1977 (U.S. Bureau of the Census, *Statistical Abstract of the United States,* 1975, and 1972 through 1978); the number of general periodicals increased from 9,275 to 9,732 between 1961 and 1977 (U.S. Bureau of the Census, op. cit., 1975; *Ayer Directory of Publications*); and the percentage of households with televisions increased from 88 percent to 98 percent between 1961 and 1977 (U.S. Bureau of the Census, op. cit., 1975; *Broadcasting Yearbook, 1977*).

The primary concern here is the sustenance of research libraries. Rising costs and increasing knowledge production are at the root of the problem. "During the two decades from 1950 to 1970, expenditures for books doubled every six or seven years with costs for salaries and wages increasing at a rate only slightly lower. The number of books added annually to collections doubled every ten or eleven years" (The Ford Foundation, 1977, p. 92). Between 1967 and 1977, the costs of books rose more than 240 percent and scholarly journals by more than 300 percent, yet library budgets for acquisitions increased only 220 percent. From 1968 to 1977, student enrollments grew by 60 percent, but professional library staff increased only 26 percent and nonprofessional staff by 37 percent (*Bowker Annual of Library and Book Trade Information,* 1969; 1978). Research libraries have not been able to keep up the pace. Many, many have fallen critically far behind.

7. A supportive social environment. A serious problem is the rising tide of government regulation. Between 1967 and 1977, federal government regulations for education increased tenfold from 92 pages to nearly 1,000 ("Califano Cautions Against Education Dependence," 1978, p. 1). The result has been a decline in the health and vitality of the American research and scholarship enterprise. Part of the difficulty has been added expense. President Bok of Harvard University (1976) estimated the cost of complying with five mandated, but noneducationally oriented, government programs to be $4.6 to $8.3 million per year for his institution.

The American Council on Education made a study of 12 federally mandated programs applying to colleges and universities as business entities rather than as educational institutions (Van Alstyne and Coldren, 1976). At the six colleges and universities examined, they found that: (1) the cost of compliance ran 1 to 4 percent of total institutional operating budgets, a relatively large sum compared to income from endowment and gifts and the deficits suffered by colleges; (2) as new mandated programs were legislated between 1965 and 1975, their costs increased much faster than instructional costs or total institutional revenues; (3) the costs of mandated programs have risen from a negligible amount to as much as one-eighth to one-fourth of general administrative costs; and (4) mandated programs have contributed substantially to financial instability at the schools studied and have compounded difficulties in fiscal management and budget balancing. Certain programs have proved to be considerably more expensive and debilitating than others. For instance, Section 504 of the 1973 Rehabilitation

Act, which forbids discrimination against the handicapped by federal aid recipients, is estimated by HEW's National Center for Educational Statistics (NCES) to involve costs to colleges and universities of $561 million, a staggering sum which will not be shared equally by institutions ("HEW estimates Section 504 compliance costs at $561 million," 1979). This is an unfortunate situation because much of the new regulation is intended for socially laudable purposes, but colleges are in the unique position of being unable to pass the added costs on to the consumer.

Another difficulty is time: "At Harvard, for example, compliance with federal regulations consumed over 60,000 hours of faculty time in 1974-75 alone" (Bok, 1976). This time could have been applied to research.

A third difficulty is the increasing bureaucratization of colleges and universities, which is incompatible with research and scholarly productivity. The pattern is one of increasing numbers of administrators, growing levels of administration, and expanding volumes of newly promulgated rules and regulations. For instance, Stanford University was recently compelled to add 33 staff positions in a single year to deal with business and finances, including 28 positions in accounting and law ("New Rules on How to Spend Research Aid," 1979, p. 1).

And Now for the Good News

The past need not determine the future. Although there has been marked decay in U.S. resources for scholarship and research, there is no reason for the American future to be characterized by continued decline or even maintenance of the status quo. The following discussion shows five areas where remedial action is both possible and necessary.

Improving support for research. Of upmost importance here is a reversal in the trend of investing declining percentages of the Gross National Product (GNP) in research and scholarship. It would be desirable to target minimal federal support at the average 1960s level of approximately 1.8 percent of GNP. (See Table J-9.)

Table J-9. Expenditures for research by the federal government
as a percentage of Gross National Product, 1955-1959 to 1975-1977

	Average level	High (year)	Low (year)
1955-1959	1.32%	1.66% (1959)	.88% (1955)
1960-1964	1.83	1.98 (1964)	1.73 (1960)
1965-1969	1.78	1.90 (1965)	1.60 (1969)
1970-1974	1.34	1.50 (1970)	1.19 (1974)
1975-1977	1.17	1.20 (1975)	1.15 (1977)

Sources: U.S. Bureau of the Census, *Statistical Abstract,* 1978; U.S. National Science Foundation, *National Patterns of R&D Resources, 1953-1977* (1977).

Another concern is this nation's commitment to basic research. This type of research should be at the heart of a leading industrial nation's R&D endeavor, but, as noted earlier, United States support is lagging far behind that of other nations. Additionally, the level of support declined between 1969 and 1975. It is in the interest of the United States to follow the lead of other industrial countries and invest at least 20 percent of its R&D budget in basic research. President Carter has begun moving in this direction.

In pursuing basic research, universities have proved to be excellent locations, primarily because they offer many advantages that other performers lack:

- Universities are the only performers that train the researchers and scholars of tomorrow. Without a vital basic research environment, scientists and humanists could simply not be educated.
- The spirit of academic communities at their best allows ample intercommunication and cross-fertilization among disciplines.
- Universities are committed to freedom of research, meaning that faculty can engage in whatever research they choose. This is quite impossible in a profit-making or mission-oriented organization.
- Universities are a mix of the young and the old, living and

working together. This allows for new and creative scholarly approaches tempered by the experience of age—a unique combination.

- Universities are not only producers of research and scholarship, but also the most active disseminators of new knowledge through teaching and publications (U.S. National Science Foundation, Advisory Council, 1978).
- Universities have the most extensive experience in basic research.
- Universities have exceptional capacity to perform research because they have within them numerous centers of incomparable excellence. Ben-David and Zloczower (1962) described the hallmarks of a successful academic system as adaptiveness and innovativeness. In their opinion universities perform best when they are nonhierarchic, nonauthoritarian, decentralized, and flexible. And in these respects the authors found the American system to be superior to that of Great Britain, West Germany, the Soviet Union, and France.

For these reasons, which are elaborated upon by Wolfle (1972), it would seem desirable that universities remain the principal locale for American basic research.

Other concerns for research in the United States are the inconsistency in federal funding and the neglect of certain research areas.

Wiesner (1978) has criticized the rapid, "yoyo-like" fluctuations in government support for research for their detrimental and sometimes destructive impact on the research enterprise. Two mechanisms might be useful in curbing this tendency. The first would be to tie changes in scholarship and research support to a three-year moving average annual rate of growth in GNP. The second, recommended by 15 university presidents (The Ford Foundation, 1977, p. 53), would involve utilizing "a range of funding methods including step funding [project support for several years, but at declining levels], roll forward funding [full funding guaranteed for several years, with possible annual additions], and longevity funding . . . in federal grant procedures, to encourage long-term planning and to promote the greatest possible degree of stability, flexibility, and effectiveness in federally aided research projects."

The funding of several research areas is below the sustenance level. At present, the manpower level for the academic disciplines is largely enrollment-driven and their funding partially so. This does not serve the national interest well and is inconsistent with the demands of quality research. The condition of the humanities is particularly distressing; that of the social sciences is only marginally better. It is necessary that federal government support for each be quickly and substantially increased if the humanities and social sciences are to thrive in this country.

Improving research facilities and equipment. Plummeting federal support for facilities and equipment has been debilitating to colleges and universities. They are in immediate need of funding for renovation, maintenance, and new facilities and equipment. A report from 15 university presidents (The Ford Foundation, 1977) estimated the backlog at $275 million in 1977. To combat the problem the presidents urged two actions (pp. 56, 57):

> We propose that Congress provide additional funding of $100 million a year for the next three years to be allocated to academic departments or research centers for the purchase of equipment. In addition we recommend a federal policy of increasing the percentage of project awards devoted to equipment from the present 5 percent level to the 10-15 percent range of a few years ago. The increased grants devoted to equipment should come from new funds, rather than from the reallocation of money previously used for other aspects of a research project, such as the support of personnel. Investigators seeking grants for equipment should be required to submit their case for rigorous review by disinterested peers. (p. 56)

> We recommend that the government allocate $150 million a year to the renovation of university research

facilities (including renovation designed to reduce operation costs and energy consumption). To assist the government in the administration of this program, such an organization as the Association of American Universities or the National Academy of Sciences should be encouraged to establish a task force to make an overall assessment of the need for the modernization and improvement of research space in the universities.

With the same purposes in mind, the White House has proposed an annual $50 million authorization under Title VII of the Higher Education Act to provide research universities with the facilities and equipment they need. The spirit of this legislation is certainly appropriate, but the funding is inadequate. The university presidents' proposals are more realistic in this regard.

Saving the research libraries. Research libraries have five priority needs: (a) increasing funds to keep up with the cost of library materials, (b) increasing skilled library manpower, (c) improving facilities, (d) preserving existing and future library materials, and (e) improving patron access to bibliographic resources and patron acceptance of changes in the world of libraries.

Toward this end, the eminent National Enquiry on Scholarly Communication, following a two-year study, has urged two major initiatives worthy of support—the creation of a linked national bibliographic center and the establishment of a national periodicals center (1979). The National Enquiry recommended that "research libraries, scholarly associations, and organizations currently engaged in producing bibliographic services join with the Library of Congress in creating a linked national bibliographic center," whose purpose it would be "to permit scholars to identify information pertinent to their work and indicate how and where that information can be most readily obtained" (p. 16). Efforts in this direction are currently being led by the Council on Library Resources with assistance from the Library of Congress and the National Endowment for the Humanities.

Over $5 million in grants have been pledged to support the first five years of work.

The National Enquiry not only recommended the establishment of a national periodicals center (NPC), but specifically endorsed the plans for its development, operation, management, and financing prepared by the Council on Library Resources (National Enquiry, 1979). The proposed functions of the NPC are the following (pp. 18, 19):

1. To provide a reliable method of access to a comprehensive collection of periodical literature.
2. To reduce the overall costs of acquiring periodical material by interlibrary loan.
3. To reduce the time required to obtain requested material.
4. To assure that, for any document delivered through the NPC, all required copyright fees and obligations will have been paid.
5. To act, under appropriate conditions, as a distribution agent for publishers.
6. To provide libraries with additional options as they establish their own collection development and maintenance policies.
7. To promote the development of local and regional resource sharing.
8. To contribute to the preservation of periodical material.
9. To provide a base for the development of new and imaginative publication strategies.
10. To provide a working example of a national access service that might be extended to other categories of materials.

The Carnegie Council supports the National Enquiry's call for federal legislation establishing and authorizing such a center.

The Council also commends the federal government for taking the first steps needed to insure the research library's survival. In 1975, the Council (1975) urged the establishment of a new federal program to assist major research libraries. Legislation for such a program—seeking to maintain and strengthen institutional, independent, and public research libraries and help them make their collections available to other libraries and borrowers—is incorporated in the Education Amendments of 1976.

In addition to supporting research libraries directly, this legislation also created programs of indirect aid seeking to strengthen general library resources and library training and research. The Carnegie Council concurs with this country's lawmakers who stated in framing this legislation—"the nation's major research libraries are often an essential element in undergraduate education and are essential to advanced and professional education and research," but that of late "unprecedented demands [have been made] upon research libraries requiring programs and services that strain their capabilities . . . and are beyond the financial competence of individual or collective library budgets." The Council believes that Title II, Part C, of the 1976 Education Amendments, focusing on strengthening research libraries, should be fully funded at its $20 million au-. thorization for fiscal year 1979, rather than the $6 million approved by Congress for fiscal year 1980. It would also be desirable to expand this legislation to allow for funding of comprehensive cooperative library services under the auspices of existing organizations, such as the Council on Library Resources, the National Commission on Libraries and Information Science, and the Association of Research Libraries in order to encourage regional and national consortial arrangements and collaborative efforts among libraries.

Higher education can also make a major contribution to saving the research library. Colleges and universities, their libraries, and their library schools can do a better job in initiating consortial relationships around common library needs and in educating a new breed of librarians, capable of seeing beyond the single institution and the short-term solution. There is a critical need for individuals capable of managing large libraries.

Preserving the autonomy and academic freedom of the research enterprise. In the post-Watergate/Proposition 13 era, there is a growing tension between demands for public accountability and research's need for academic freedom and autonomy. Both are necessary. To protect the balance between them, the federal government might consider the following steps. It might require of all proposed regulations or legislation with regulatory intent a "Regulatory Impact Statement" of the type described in Section 7 of this report. It might additionally consult with colleges and universities in developing, drafting, implementing, and evaluating regulations. Formal advisory committees could be created within regulatory agencies and departments where now absent.

Institutions of higher education and higher education associations also have an active part to play in protecting public accountability and insuring academic freedom and institutional autonomy. Colleges and universities must not cry "Wolf" and claim that every new regulation that is formulated violates their academic freedom or autonomy.

Extending linkages. A serious problem in research and scholarship can be isolation. Researchers and scholars are too often closed off from one another in colleges and universities by disciplinary or departmental walls. This is partially an organizational phenomenon and partially a matter of predilection. Scholarship, research, and their many beneficiaries suffer from the isolation, however, because many critical, researchable questions do not fit comfortably or even adequately into a single discipline or department. The consequence too often is both duplication and neglect. Some questions are examined independently in a variety of locations, while others equally, or more, important fail to be asked or answered. Colleges and universities need to encourage interdisciplinary scholarship and teaching, and the federal government should provide increased support for such work.

Cooperation between institutions of higher education and industry should also be strengthened. Each complements the other—universities emphasizing basic research and industry specializing in applied research and development—yet in recent years ties between the two have been attenuated. For example, industrial support of university scholarship declined from 8.6

percent of total higher education R&D funding in 1958 to 3.3 percent in 1978, a decrease of more than 60 percent (U.S. National Science Foundation, 1978, tables B-1, 2, 3, 4). Baer (1977) discusses a number of valuable ways to reinvigorate the relationship. With the goal of encouraging collaborative research, he recommends direct corporate funding of university research projects, cost sharing for joint research programs, university/industry research consortia, and joining industry and university laboratories. To improve knowledge transfer, he suggests wider use of staff exchanges and consulting, technology licensing and technological brokers, joint university/industry libraries, extension services, industrial associates programs, industrial parks, innovation centers, and small business institutes. There is every reason to hope that current improvements in the labor market for college graduates will provide both institutions and industry with an incentive for renewed collaboration.

Who Should Do What?

Federal government

- Target federal support for research at the average 1960s level of approximately 1.8 percent of the U.S. Gross National Product (GNP).
- Reduce "yoyo-like" fluctuations in government support for research by tying support to a three-year moving average of the GNP and utilizing a variety of stable, yet flexible, funding methods including step funding, roll forward funding, and longevity funding.
- Maintain university research support at 12 to 13 percent of total federal research and development funding.
- Retain the university as the principal locale for America's basic research.
- Introduce a policy to support research libraries and other related research services, such as computer resources, by including within research contracts a standard 5 percent allowance for this purpose.
- Increase support quickly for historically neglected research areas, such as the humanities and social sciences.

- Provide immediate funding for desperately needed renovation, maintenance, and new facilities and equipment by allocating $100 million a year for three years for the purchase of equipment, providing $150 million a year for renovation of university research facilities, and increasing the percentage of project awards devoted to equipment from the 5 percent level to the 10-15 percent range of a few years ago as part of the recommended federal R&D spending level of 1.8 percent of GNP.
- Pass legislation creating a national periodicals center (NPC).
- Fund Title II, Part C, of Education Amendments of 1976 at its $20 million authorization level for fiscal year 1979 and expand this legislation to allow for the funding of comprehensive library services under the auspices of existing organizations such as the Council on Library Resources, the National Commission on Libraries and Information Sciences, and the Association of Research Libraries in order to encourage regional and national consortial arrangements and collaborative efforts between libraries.
- Require of all proposed regulations or legislation a "Regulatory Impact Statement."
- Create formal advisory committees within regulatory agencies and departments where now absent.
- Support interdisciplinary scholarship.

Colleges and universities

- Maintain and enhance those characteristics that make the university a prime locale for basic research.
- Do a better job in initiating consortial relationships around common library needs and in educating a new breed of librarians capable of managing large libraries and seeing beyond the single institution and the short-term solution.
- Avoid complaints about violations of academic freedom or autonomy with every new regulation that is formulated.
- Encourage interdisciplinary scholarship and teaching.
- Strengthen research ties with industry by encouraging collaborative research and improving knowledge transfer.

Business and industry

· Strengthen research ties with higher education by supporting university R&D, encouraging collaborative research, and improving knowledge transfer.

Annotated Bibliography

Ben-David, J. *Centers of Learning: Britain, France, Germany, United States*. New York: McGraw-Hill, 1977. Sponsored by the Carnegie Commission on Higher Education. This book examines the evolution of higher education and advanced learning in four countries—Britain, France, West Germany, and the United States. Among the topics considered are education for the professions, general higher education, research and training for research, social criteria, and furthering social justice and equality.

Ford Foundation, The. *Research Universities and the National Interest: A Report from Fifteen University Presidents*. New York: 1977. This book written by the presidents of several of America's most eminent research universities examines a full range of critical issues facing research enterprises and universities in particular, and offers a number of valuable and innovative solutions.

National Enquiry on Scholarly Communication. *Scholarly Communication*. Baltimore, Md.: Johns Hopkins University Press, 1979. After a two-year study, an eminent panel issued this important report on the state of American scholarly communications. Useful recommendations are offered on research libraries, scholarly journals, scholarly books, and presses.

Smith, B. L., and Karlesky, J. J. *The State of Academic Science: The Universities in the Nation's Research Effort*. New Rochelle, N.Y.: *Change* Magazine Press, 1977. This book, based on a wide variety of data and visits to 36 research institutions, is must reading. It covers trends in research support and performance, the changing relationship between universities and other performers, current developments in academic science and engineering, and emerging issues in academic research.

U.S. National Science Board. *Science Indicators*. Washington, D.C. These biennial reports contain commentary and all the basic data on science in the U.S. with a comparative perspective. The subjects discussed include international indicators of science and technology, resources for research and development, basic research, indicators of innovation in R&D, science and engineering personnel, and public attitudes toward science and technology.

Wiesner, J. "Text of Wiesner's Warning: Remarks by Jerome B. Wiesner at Annual Meeting of the National Council of University Research Administrators." *Chronicle of Higher Education*, Nov. 13, 1978, *17* (11), 1. In this speech, a scientific statesman outlines articulately the interrelated problems of the university, science, and the federal government.

Wolfle, D. *The Home of Science: The Role of the University*. Sponsored by the Carnegie Commission on Higher Education. New York: McGraw-Hill, 1972. This book is exactly what its title suggests—a chronicle of the university and its evolution as the principal locus of America's basic scientific research.

References

Association of Research Libraries. *Academic Library Statistics.* Washington, D.C.: annual.

Baer, W. S. "The Changing Relationships: Universities and Other R&D Performers." In B. L. Smith and J. J. Karlesky (Eds.), *The State of Academic Science: Background Papers.* New Rochelle, N.Y.: *Change* Magazine Press, 1977.

Bell, D. *The Coming of Post-Industrial Society: A Venture in Social Forecasting.* Ch. 3: "The Dimensions of Knowledge and Technology." New York: Basic Books, 1973.

Ben-David, J. *The Scientist's Role in Society: A Comparative Study.* Englewood, N.J.: Prentice Hall, 1971.

Ben-David, J. *Centers of Learning.* 1977. *See* Annotated Bibliography.

Ben-David, J., and Zloczower, A. "Universities and Academic Systems in Modern Societies." *European Journal of Sociology,* 1962, *3* (1), 45-84.

Bok, D. "The President's Report: 1974-1975." *Harvard Gazette,* March 1976.

"Califano Cautions Against Education Dependence on the United States." *Higher Education and National Affairs,* Aug. 25, 1978.

Carnegie Council on Policy Studies in Higher Education. *The Federal Role in Postsecondary Education: Unfinished Business, 1975-1980.* San Francisco: Jossey-Bass, 1975.

Deutsch, K., and others. "Conditions Favoring Major Advances in the Social Sciences." *Science,* Feb. 5, 1971, *171* (1970), 456-457.

Ford Foundation, The. *Research Universities and the National Interest.* 1977. *See* Annotated Bibliography.

Harris Survey, Nov. 1978.

"HEW Estimates Section 504 Compliance Costs at $561 Million." *Higher Education Daily,* May 8, 1979, p. 1.

King Research, Inc. "The Journal System of Scientific and Technical Communication in the United States." Draft. Rockville, Md.: Nov. 1978.

Machlup, F. *The Production and Distribution of Knowledge in the United States.* Princeton, N.J.: Princeton University Press, 1972.

National Enquiry on Scholarly Communication. *Scholarly Communication.* 1979. *See* Annotated Bibliography.

"New Rules on How to Spend Research Aid." *San Francisco Chronicle,* March 5, 1979, p. 1.

Nobel Foundation. *Nobel: The Man and His Prizes.* Third edition. New York: American Elsevier, 1972.

"Occupational Prestige." Survey by Louis Harris and Associates, Oct. 8-16, 1977. Reported in *Public Opinion,* March/April 1978, p. 36.

Oleson, A., and Brown, S. C. *The Pursuit of Knowledge in the Early American Republic.* Baltimore: Johns Hopkins University Press, 1976.

Press, F. "Who Decides What Research We Do?" Panel 4 Abstract, Sixty-first Annual Meeting of the American Council on Education, Oct. 12, 1978.

Price, D. J. de S. *Little Science, Big Science.* New York: Columbia University Press, 1961a.

Price, D. J. de S. *Science Since Babylon.* New Haven: Yale University Press, 1961b.

Smith, B. L., and Karlesky, J. J. *The State of Academic Science.* 1977. *See* Annotated Bibliography.

Terleckyj, N. (Ed.). *The State of Science and Research: Some New Indicators.* Boulder Colo.: Westview Press, 1977.

U.S. Bureau of the Census. *Historical Statistics of the United States, Colonial Times to 1970.* Bicentennial Edition. Washington, D.C.: 1975.

U.S. Bureau of the Census. *Social Indicators, 1976.* An annual series. Washington, D.C.: 1977, and selected issues.

U.S. Bureau of the Census. *Statistical Abstract of the United States.* Washington, D.C.: annual.

U.S. National Board on Graduate Education. *Outlook and Opportunities for Graduate Education.* Washington, D.C.: 1975.

U.S. National Center for Education Statistics. *Digest of Education Statistics.* An annual series. Washington, D.C.: selected issues.

U.S. National Endowment for the Humanities. *Annual Reports.* Washington, D.C.: selected issues.

U.S. National Science Board. *Science Indicators. See* Annotated Bibliography.

U.S. National Science Foundation. *National Patterns of R&D Resources, Funds, and Manpower in the United States, 1953-1978/79.* Washington, D.C.: annual.

U.S. National Science Foundation, Advisory Council. *Continued Viability of Universities as Centers for Basic Research.* Report of Task Group No. 1. Washington, D.C.: Oct. 20, 1978.

U.S. National Science Foundation. *Federal Funds for Research, Development, and Other Scientific Activities.* Washington, D.C.: annual.

Van Alstyne, C., and Coldren, S. L. *The Costs of Implementing Federally Mandated Social Programs at Colleges and Universities.* Washington, D.C.: American Council on Education, 1976.

Wiesner, J. "Text of Wiesner's Warning." 1978. *See* Annotated Bibliography.

Wolfle, D. *The Home of Science.* 1972. *See* Annotated Bibliography.

Smoothing Out the Flow of Young Scientists into Universities

The next two decades are likely to be a critical period for scientific progress. There are indications that important breakthroughs may be near at hand in such fields as genetic research and the search for the causes of cancer. The energy crisis creates a critical need for both basic and applied research relating to possible uses of new forms of energy. Slowing economic growth and intensified international competition underscore the need for technological innovations.

In the recent past, the United States has maintained a position of leadership in science largely because of a combination of favorable conditions: (1) the greatly increased flow of federal funds into research and development (R&D) from the early 1950s to the mid-1960s; (2) the concentration of basic research in universities and, more generally, the position of leadership of research universities in scientific progress; and (3) the opening up of large numbers of faculty positions in research universities for promising young scientists, stimulating some of the most able young people to train for advanced scientific research. Whether this country will maintain its position of leadership is now somewhat doubtful, as much of the data in Supplement J suggests.

This supplement was prepared by Margaret S. Gordon, Associate Director.

Not only has federal support of research lagged since the mid-1960s (though recovering somewhat in the past few years), but the number of positions becoming available for young scholars has been declining precipitously in a number of fields in the 1970s, and this situation is likely to become more serious in the 1980s. As this occurs, the leadership of research universities in basic research may be threatened.

The Impending Shortage of Faculty Positions

The dearth of faculty positions for young scholars is in part attributable to the slowing rate of growth of enrollment. As the rate of growth of enrollment declines, so, also, does the rate of growth of additions to faculties. But it is not only the declining rate of growth of enrollment—and the prospect of an actual decline in enrollment from the early 1980s on—that has created the shortage of new positions for faculty members. It is also the fact that *this period of slowing growth was preceded by the unprecedented growth of the late 1950s and the decade of the 1960s.* The result is an age distribution among existing faculty members that deviates markedly from the age distribution that would be characteristic of a "steady-state" (no growth) faculty, as Figure H-1 shows.

Thus, the impending shortage of positions for young faculty members is not exclusively dependent on predictions of an actual decline in enrollment—it would prevail even under conditions of stable enrollment or of any rate of growth much below the abnormally high rates of the 1960s. Moreover, the shortage of positions for young scholars may begin to become less serious before enrollment passes its trough. This is because retirement and mortality rates of faculty members will begin to rise in the late 1980s, as Table K-1 shows.

The situation varies substantially by fields. This is indicated not only by the data in Table K-1, but also by data from several sources showing changes in the age distribution of faculty members in the 1970s.

For example, a special survey conducted by the American Council on Education for the National Science Foundation showed that the percentage of young doctoral faculty among

Table K-1. Projected combined death and retirement rates as a
percentage of total faculty, by broad fields of science and engineering,
1976 to 2000

	Mathematics	Physical sciences	Engineering	Life sciences	Social sciences
1976	1.06%	1.11%	1.07%	1.27%	1.20%
1977	.94	1.41	.79	1.28	1.21
1978	.93	1.22	.61	1.35	1.26
1979	.71	1.13	.61	1.21	1.23
1980	.69	1.05	.72	1.22	1.34
1981	.67	1.03	.80	1.21	1.31
1982	.76	1.16	.80	1.22	1.24
1983	.81	1.30	.96	1.40	1.48
1984	1.12	1.38	.98	1.44	1.64
1985	1.04	1.49	1.29	1.44	1.73
1986	.98	1.49	1.40	1.74	1.97
1987	1.02	1.88	1.48	1.68	2.21
1988	1.57	2.15	1.55	2.08	2.19
1989	1.45	1.97	1.67	1.97	2.30
1990	1.43	2.14	1.90	1.98	2.45
1991	1.58	1.96	1.78	2.18	2.71
1992	1.53	2.24	2.28	2.05	2.73
1993	1.96	2.50	2.13	2.23	2.80
1994	2.06	2.46	2.05	2.52	2.98
1995	1.98	2.53	2.33	2.45	2.90
1996	2.07	2.64	2.22	2.47	3.00
1997	2.32	2.58	2.34	2.70	3.24
1998	2.44	2.98	2.63	2.70	3.08
1999	2.57	2.95	2.54	2.60	3.16
2000	2.84	3.03	2.50	2.55	3.12

Source: National Research Council (1979); data based on special tabulations prepared by Charlotte Kuh.

total full-time faculty in Ph.D.-granting institutions (persons
within 7 years of having received the Ph.D. were defined as
young doctoral faculty) fell from 30.4 percent in the spring of
1974 to 23.7 percent in the academic year 1977-78 (Table K-2).

Table K-2. Full-time doctoral faculty and young doctoral faculty: departments providing data for 1974, 1975, and 1977-78 (unweighted)

Field	Number of departments	Spring 1974 Doctoral faculty		December 1975 Doctoral faculty		1977-78 Doctoral faculty		Change in percentage points from 1974 to 1977-78
		Total number	Percentage young	Total number	Percentage young	Total number	Percentage young	
Biochemistry	24	363	23.1%	363	20.9%	383	15.9%	-7.2%
Biology	42	987	28.1	1,033	29.8	988	24.1	-4.0
Botany	17	303	25.7	306	24.5	346	17.6	-8.1
Chemical engineering	24	333	18.9	312	18.6	322	18.3	-0.6
Chemistry	90	2,189	21.8	2,194	19.6	2,255	18.2	-3.6
Economics	50	1,129	36.8	1,131	35.4	1,180	33.1	-3.7
Electrical engineering	51	1,129	29.1	1,161	27.4	1,251	19.8	-9.3
Geology	39	628	23.6	614	22.6	645	22.2	-1.4
Mathematics	71	2,401	37.0	2,472	31.4	2,569	27.8	-9.2
Microbiology	13	171	24.0	179	26.8	173	19.1	-4.9
Physics	81	2,070	19.8	2,031	16.8	2,067	13.2	-6.6
Physiology	9	137	33.6	157	28.7	154	26.0	-7.6
Psychology	66	1,628	42.5	1,673	39.4	1,719	31.5	-11.0
Sociology	50	955	46.4	972	40.7	1,002	34.8	11.6
Zoology	22	508	29.9	515	28.7	510	26.7	-3.2
All fields	649	14,931	30.4	15,113	27.9	15,564	23.7	-6.7

Source: Spring 1974 data from U.S. National Science Foundation (1975); Dec. 1975 data from Atelsek and Gomberg (1976); 1977-78 data from Atelsek and Gomberg (1979).

The rate of decline varied from field to field and was steepest in sociology, psychology, electrical engineering, and mathematics, in that order. However, the fields with the smallest proportions of young doctoral faculty in 1977-78 were physics, biochemistry, botany, chemistry, and chemical engineering—all fields in which the percentage of young doctoral faculty was already quite low in 1974.

Table K-3 provides several indicators of shortages of positions for new faculty in all Ph.D.-granting institutions and in major research universities. It shows that the situation in major research universities does not differ greatly from that in all Ph.D.-granting institutions.[1]

A particularly sensitive measure is the annual rate of change in young doctoral faculty as a percentage of total doctoral faculty, showing that the rate of decline is particularly pronounced in mathematics, physics, chemistry, and engineering (Table K-3). Although the percentage of young doctoral faculty in mathematics was high in 1977, the Commission on Human Resources (National Research Council, 1979) considered that percentage to be somewhat deceptive, reflecting a substantial proportion of instructors who were not on a tenure track. In these same fields (except for chemistry), the percentage of elderly faculty is particularly low, indicating that few positions will be opening up because of retirement or deaths.

Data based on the Carnegie Commission 1969 faculty survey and the Carnegie Council 1975 faculty survey show that the average age of faculty members in natural and social sciences in research universities rose significantly between 1969 and 1975. There were also substantial increases in the percentages of faculty members with tenure (Table K-4). By 1975, these percentages were high and were likely to become much higher.

According to Grodzins (1979 and n.d.), who has been studying the situation in physics throughout most of the last

---

[1]Note that in a number of fields the percentage of young doctoral faculty is higher than that shown in Table K-2, apparently because the data for all Ph.D.-granting institutions differ from the data for those institutions that reported data for each of the years shown in Table K-2.

Table K-3. Indicators of severity of shortages of positions for new faculty, by field, 1977

	All fields	Mathematics	Physics	Chemistry	Earth sciences	Engineering	Agriculture	Biological sciences	Psychology	Social sciences	Steady-state value
All Ph.D.-granting institutions											
Young doctoral faculty as percentage of total doctoral faculty, 1977	33.7%	36.5%	20.7%	23.2%	31.6%	26.7%	29.2%	34.1%	36.0%	44.5%	33.0%
Full-time faculty aged 61 and over as percentage of total full-time faculty, 1977	5.5	4.5	3.3	8.0	7.4	4.0	7.5	5.9	4.7	6.2	9.2
Annual rate of change in young doctoral faculty as percentage of total doctoral faculty, 1973-1977	-4.6	-7.2	-9.4	-6.0	-2.7	-10.4	-2.0	-2.1	-4.6	-2.1	0
Annual rate of change of total doctoral faculty, 1975-1977	3.4	0.8	1.7	2.2	0	2.8	0	4.0	0	10.0	0
Major research universities											
Young doctoral faculty as percentage of total doctoral faculty, 1977	32.3	35.4	23.5	23.0	35.7	26.2	28.1	32.1	35.0	41.5	33.0

(continued on next page)

Table K-3 (*continued*)

	All fields	Mathematics	Physics	Chemistry	Earth sciences	Engineering	Agriculture	Biological sciences	Psychology	Social sciences	Steady-state value
Full-time faculty aged 61 and over as percentage of total full-time faculty, 1977	6.3%	4.5%	3.2%	6.8%	6.5%	4.8%	8.2%	6.8%	5.7%	7.6%	9.2%
Annual rate of change in young doctoral faculty as percentage of total doctoral faculty, 1973-1977	-3.9	-7.0	-7.1	-7.0	0	-8.3	-0.8	-2.8	-3.1	-1.9	0
Annual rate of change of total doctoral faculty, 1975-1977	3.1	0	6.6[a]	0	2.0	2.2	0	3.2	0	10.1	0

[a]This high growth rate from 1975 to 1977 follows a significant drop in faculty size in physics at major research universities in the preceding two years. The annual growth rate in physics faculties in these institutions over the four years 1973 to 1977 was 2.4 percent.

Source: National Research Council (1979, p. 105; data based on the Survey of Doctorate Recipients of the NRC).

Table K-4. Percentages of faculty members with tenure, natural and social sciences, Research Universities I and II, by field, 1969 and 1975

Field and year	Research Universities		Field and year	Research Universities	
	I	*II*		*I*	*II*
Total[a]			Geology		
1969	63.2%	59.8%	1969	68.0%	56.3%
1975	67.0	71.0	1975	78.8	65.1
Bacteriology			Physics		
1969	64.2	66.7	1969	64.0	56.8
1975	73.0	69.1	1975	65.8	70.4
Biochemistry			Psychology		
1969	64.0	61.9	1969	55.8	46.2
1975	65.1	78.0	1975	58.5	70.5
Biology			Anthropology		
1969	67.5	64.6	1969	61.2	53.7
1975	75.6	72.6	1975	50.0	77.8
Botany			Economics		
1969	71.7	77.8	1969	60.9	64.6
1975	87.5	87.5	1975	68.8	73.5
Anatomy			Political science		
1969	58.1	64.4	1969	55.9	56.7
1975	54.7	70.5	1975	76.7	60.8
Zoology			Sociology		
1969	77.2	63.7	1969	62.5	49.4
1975	72.7	75.0	1975	49.1	71.1
Chemistry					
1969	70.2	64.7			
1975	73.6	82.8			

[a]Total includes faculty members in miscellaneous fields, not shown separately, but excludes those not reporting tenure status or age; also excluded are instructors, lecturers, etc.

Sources: Carnegie Commission Surveys, 1969; Carnegie Council Surveys, 1975.

decade and has more complete data than are available for virtually any other field, the decline in the demand for Ph.D.'s in physics, which has been apparent since 1968, has led to a variety of adjustments in supply. For one thing, the number of Ph.D. recipients in physics and astronomy fell from a peak of 1,737 in 1971 to 1,066 in 1978. (Because many of those in the

pipeline continue until they receive their degrees, the number of
Ph.D. recipients did not begin to decline until several years after
the drop in demand was apparent.) Second, there has been a rise
in the percentage of Ph.D. recipients who are foreign citizens
and who leave the United States after receiving their degrees.
Another type of adjustment is mobility into other fields. In
spring 1975, for example, only about 70 percent of those who
had received their Ph.D.'s in 1974 (and had not left the country) were employed in physics. Among those getting jobs in
other fields, the largest numbers were in engineering, mathematics, and earth sciences (in that order). Thus, the number
who actually enter the physics/astronomy labor force is smaller
than the number of recipients of doctor's degrees.

Grodzins (1979 and n.d.) concludes that the overall demand in traditional physics and astronomy employment will
about match the supply of new entrants into the labor force by
the mid-1980s, but that throughout the 1980s the demand in
academic institutions will be far below the supply of those seeking faculty positions. The number of tenure openings per year
in doctorate-granting physics/astronomy departments will probably be no greater than 100 in 1986, and thus only about 15
percent of the projected 750 new entrants into the Ph.D. labor
force will attain permanent positions in doctorate-granting departments. In recent years this percentage has been as low as 8
percent. Physicists are obtaining jobs in industrial laboratories,
but outside of academic institutions the demand for theoretical
physicists is less than one-half the demand for experimental
physicists.

Numerous projections of the demand for faculty members
have been developed in recent years, including that prepared by
Radner and Kuh (1978) for the Carnegie Council (with support
from a Ford Foundation grant). Most of the projections, however, relate to the demand for faculty in all four-year colleges
and universities, whereas the central issue with which we are
concerned here is maintaining the flow of young scholars into
faculty positions in research universities, where most academic
research activity—and especially basic research activity—occurs.

We believe, as do a number of other analysts, that major

research universities will not be faced with serious problems of declining enrollment in the 1980s and 1990s. This is because they tend to have high ratios of applicants to admissions and will be in a position to maintain their enrollments even if these ratios decline substantially. Even so, they are clearly experiencing a declining demand for young faculty and will undoubtedly continue to do so for some years to come, because the age distributions of their faculty members show the same bulge in the central age range that is characteristic of faculties in general. On this question, the Commission on Human Resources concluded in its recent report (National Research Council, 1979, p. 38):

> Even if enrollments and numbers of faculty stay constant and R&D support keeps up with inflation—and more optimism than that would be unwarranted even at the most prestigious institutions—the current age distribution of the faculty implies a significant reduction in new hires over the next ten years in some fields. The extent of the enrollment problem at the major research producers remains somewhat speculative; the faculty age distribution problem is clear and present.

The problem in the United States is by no means unique. Most other Western industrial countries face a similar problem of a dearth of opportunities for young scholars. In a special report prepared for the Commission on Human Resources, National Research Council, Kidd (1979) reviewed the situation in the Federal Republic of Germany, France, the Netherlands, Great Britain, Denmark, Norway, Sweden, and Canada. All of these countries face a decline in the 18-year-old population at some time in the 1980s or 1990s, but the timing and prospective severity of the decline differ somewhat. What is common to all of them is that they experienced a sharp increase in the number of faculty members and, in many cases, of research personnel in research institutions in the 1960s, and that the increase has slowed markedly in recent years. Faculty members and scientists employed in research institutions tend to be compara-

tively young. And yet the combined impact of slowing enrollment growth in universities and reduced real government research expenditures has greatly reduced the number of new
positions opening up. Thus, opportunities for young researchers
both in universities and in government-supported research institutions are very poor.

The Role of Young Scholars

It is sometimes argued that it is important to maintain a flow of
young scholars into faculty positions because creativity peaks at
a relatively early age in some fields, such as mathematics and
physics, and relatively fewer important research findings are
attributable to the work of older scholars. In fact, earlier evidence of peak creativity at relatively young ages has been
shown, on the basis of more recent studies, to be based on
flawed methodology in a number of cases, and more recent
studies indicate that age is a relatively unimportant variable in
explaining differences in research output among scientists in
various disciplines. Much more important than age are such factors as training, type of institution in which employed, and
access to research support. Moreover, a number of studies have
provided evidence of bimodal curves in age differences in research output, with the first peak occurring in the late thirties
and a second peak occurring in the late forties, after a slump in
the intervening years (National Research Council, 1979, Appendix C).

In fact, the case for maintaining a flow of young scholars
does not depend on evidence that creativity peaks early, but
rather on several other considerations:

1. Evidence both in the United States and in other countries indicates that young scholars are more likely to become
   involved in innovative types of research than older scholars
   and, frequently, also more likely to influence their more
   mature colleagues into innovative research patterns.
2. Failure to prevent the development of an extreme shortage of
   young scholars on university faculties will mean the emergence by the 1990s of a severe generation gap problem, in

which faculties will be dominated by older men who, all too often, will not be familiar with the most recent developments in their fields. Knowledge of recent developments, for example, in methodology, is frequently disseminated by young scholars who have benefited by receiving their doctoral training from some of the most eminent and innovative faculty members in their fields.

The Role of Research Universities

In the absence of opportunities for young scholars in research universities, some of the ablest young people, especially those who aspire to a career in basic research, are likely to be discouraged from entering advanced training. Others who complete the work for a Ph.D. may be attracted by positions in government or industrial laboratories. Under these circumstances, the relative position of research universities as centers for basic research could be weakened.

We are not referring here to the decline in graduate enrollment in some academic fields or to the shift of graduate enrollment to professional fields where job prospects are much better; these are healthy reactions to a changing job market. The question is whether the most able students will be motivated to prepare for careers in teaching and research. According to Grodzins (1979), the opinion is widely held in the field of physics that the brightest minds are not being attracted to the field as they were in its period of spectacular growth.

It has long been recognized that the great strength of the United States in scientific research is attributable in part to the central role of the leading research universities, especially in basic research. As Wolfle (1972, p. 83) put it:

> The university gave scientists freedom to explore ideas to their limits in order to find their flaws or their new implications. It provided mutual stimulation of teachers and inquiring students, with the resulting need to clarify ideas, explain reasons and objectives, and improve methods. It offered a kind of benign anarchy in which merit could be quickly

recognized. And always, after about 1880, there were scientists in a number of universities, and scientists in other institutions as well, competing with and challenging each other, sometimes verifying another's new findings and sometimes demonstrating error. These are conditions that are conducive to broad and rapid progress and to intellectual creativity.

An excellent summary of the major strengths of universities as centers for basic research was included in the Report of Task Group No. 1 of the National Science Foundation Advisory Council (1978, pp. 8-10):

1. *Continuity and tradition.* Fiscally, psychologically, and morally, good universities have great momentum. Paradoxically, individual departments can have great fragility, but, generally speaking, departments that are superior tend to remain so for long periods, and not-so-good departments find it very difficult to improve themselves. . . .

2. *Freedom of research.* At a good university, the senior research-oriented scientist turns his or her attention to those research problems that seem most important. Subject to the need for equipment and staff funding, the search for truth can go on largely untouched by the passions of politics, convention or prejudice, or even by transient disciplinary fads. . . .

3. *Interactions among different disciplines.* At the best universities, discussions among scholars in different fields often yield unexpected and abundant harvests.

4. *Students.* The presence of extremely bright, active, questioning, ambitious graduate students gives universities part of their special character. The entering student just may see something that the senior professor neglected. . . .

5. *Dual responsibilities of universities.* Traditionally,

universities are responsible not only for contributing new knowledge of all kinds but also for maintaining the knowledge of the past and imparting it to students. As a consequence, scientists in universities are surrounded with colleagues who have an appreciation of the value of new knowledge.

Whereas universities and colleges account for only about 10 percent of national R&D expenditures, they are responsible for 52 percent of expenditures for basic research (National Research Council, 1979, p. 71). Interestingly, this was not always so. In 1953, when the big rise in federal R&D expenditures was just getting under way, universities and colleges accounted for only 26 percent of basic research expenditures. Thus, one of the results of the rise in federal R&D expenditures, whether planned or not, was to bring about a pronounced increase in basic research activity in universities.

We emphasize these points about the role of research universities, because we see the need to smooth out the flow of young scholars and the need for adequate support of university research as inseparable problems. Some of the vitality and capacity for innovation of leading university research departments and centers may be lost if there is a "lost generation" of young scholars.

Proposals by Others

During the past several years, since the Carnegie Council first became concerned with this problem, a number of groups have developed proposals for maintaining the flow of young scholars. We will review these proposals briefly here, along with several proposals or policies in other countries summarized in the Kidd (1979) report.

1. The Radner-Kuh proposal (Radner and Kuh, 1978). This proposal focuses on junior faculty and new Ph.D.'s in the approximately 100 leading doctorate-granting institutions in the country. It is concerned particularly with faculty in the sciences and ensures that a minimal level of academic (teaching or junior scholar) jobs will be available to each cohort of new Ph.D.'s. It is also designed so that those who participate in the Junior Scholar Program (JSP) can eventually be absorbed into jobs as teaching faculty. Junior scholar positions would be short-term and limited to numbers that could later be fed back into regular academic positions when academic hiring picks up. The number of such positions would rise from 300 in 1984 to 3,769 in 1986, but then, with an anticipated rise in academic hiring, they would be fed back into regular academic positions. The program would be re-implemented in 1990 with 1,650 junior scholars and would rise to 15,000 in 1995, when no new Ph.D.'s would be hired into teaching positions. Then academic hiring would pick up, and all junior scholars would be absorbed into regular faculty positions by 2000.

This proposal is closely linked to the Radner-Kuh projections of enrollment and of demand for new faculty. The revival of faculty hiring after 1986 would be in response to a temporary increase in the number of 18-year-olds from 1985 to 1990. In our own projections of demand for faculty (see Supplement B), we have assumed that colleges and universities will not increase their hiring of faculty appreciably in response to this temporary increase in enrollment, since they will be anticipating a second, steeper decline from 1990 on (Figure 11, p. 47).

2. Report of Task Group No. 1 (U.S. National Science Foundation, 1978). This report was concerned, not only with the problem of young scholars, but with the broader issue of adequate support of university research. We include here only the proposals that were especially designed to maintain the flow of young scholars.

- *Postdoctoral fellowships.* The National Science Foundation (NSF) should establish a national postdoctoral fellowship program with three-year awards to candidates who at the time of their applications have not had their Ph.D. degree for more than one year.
- *Research career development awards.* The NSF should insti-

tute "Research Career Development Awards" to universities on behalf of specified young scientists who have already demonstrated their research potential but are not yet established as independent investigators.

- *National research professorships.* The NSF should establish "National Research Professorships" based on university nominations of internationally distinguished scientists whose contributions to basic research would be enhanced through full-time scientific activity. The full salary of the professor would be paid by NSF for the remainder of his or her active career. Nominations would be made by universities on behalf of individuals and departments and would require that the salary savings through the award would be devoted to the employment of young faculty members in the same department.

3. Klitgaard, Kennedy School of Government, Harvard University (1979). In a carefully prepared report, Klitgaard urges caution in adopting governmental measures that might be premature. He emphasizes the uncertainty about existing enrollment projections, in view of the fact that participation rates vary, adults may increasingly enter or re-enter higher education, and foreign students are growing in importance. Enrollments, he argues, should not go below the levels of the early 1970s, and new hires may resemble those in the late 1950s. (These predictions are quite similar to ours.)

He suggests that, in two years or so, "more facts and a better climate may lead to a more successful call to action" (p. iii). Among various possible types of governmental intervention, he indicates that "the idea of temporary governmental subsidies for additional tenured openings fares well compared to the others, although the mechanics of implementing it are problematic and its cost is likely to be quite high (perhaps more than $100 million per year)" (p. iii).

4. Commission on Human Resources of the National Research Council (1979). Although prepared under the auspices of the commission, the report was actually the work of the Committee on Continuity in Academic Research Performance, under the chairmanship of Robert M. Bock. It is notable for the thoroughness with which it has brought together all of the existing data relating to the problem of young scholars.

Although the report includes several other recommendations, the *Research Excellence Awards program,* to be administered by NSF, is the central recommendation and the one that is given by far the greatest emphasis. The program would provide a five-year stipend in support of salary to award recipients selected from existing faculties, with the released university funds to support the employment of new faculty members.

Nominations would be made by departments and would be required to include a staff development plan prepared by the department and endorsed by the university. Award recipients would be expected to serve as regular members of their departments and especially to carry out innovative research. A department receiving an award would undertake to hire a new faculty member in a nontenured tenure-track position, in addition to those who would have been hired in the absence of the award. (Requirements for monitoring this obligation are spelled out in some detail.) The award would include an annual fixed sum equivalent to the salary and fringe benefits of a new faculty member at a research university (currently about $22,000 to $24,000) plus the cost of a two-months' summer research appointment plus an 8 percent allowance for indirect costs to the department.

The proposal contemplates some awards to recent Ph.D.'s and some to more experienced scientists and also states: "In determining the balance of awards between younger and older scientists, the special importance of encouraging the contributions of younger scholars should be recognized" and "NSF should make clear that nominations of women and minorities are to be vigorously encouraged" (ibid., p. 101).

The report specifically recommended that the program be started immediately only in mathematics and physics, with 30 awards in each field, but contemplated that it would later be extended to other fields. Costs of the program were estimated to rise from $2.1 million in the first year to a peak of $39 million in 1991-92 (when shortages of positions due to low retirement rates would begin to ease in most fields) and to decline from then to 2000. Total costs over the 19 years of the program's existence would be $381 million (in 1979 dollars), not including NSF's administrative costs. However, the costs might have to be larger if enrollment declined significantly at research universities. The report also recommended that the program be partly financed from new funds appropriated to NSF for this purpose and partly from funds advanced by the individual research directorates.

5. *France.* According to the Kidd (1979) report, France is the only country that has actually established a program designed to maintain the flow of young scholars, although plans have been proposed in West Germany and Norway and are under discussion elsewhere.

The French program is designed to sustain the entry of young people into research in universities and government research establishments. Two-year stipends are granted to 1,500 students (no older than 24) per year, to permit them to work full time on completion of an advanced thesis. At the same time, the budget provides for the creation of new positions at a constant 3 percent increment per year. This resulted in the creation of 937 positions in 1976. Measures have also been adopted to permit earlier entry into the system and to promote mid-career shifts out of the system (through the provision of severance pay).

6. *West Germany.* According to Kidd (1979), a proposal, the so-called Heisenberg Program, has been put forward by the presidents of the major research organizations (the Deutsche Forschungsgemeinschaft, the West Deutsche Rektorenkonferenz, and the Wissenschaftsrat). The program consists of two parts: (1) the appointment of 200 promising young scholars (aged 25 to 30) per year for each of 10 years, to be given annual stipends plus allowances for travel and books, and to be permitted to study in any field; and (2) the appointment of 300 Heisenberg professors per year for a period of 10 years, to be given tenure.

7. *Norway.* The Norwegian proposals were made by Hans Skoie of the Norwegian Research Council for Science and the

Humanities and include a variety of measures aimed at sustaining the vitality of research staffs and increasing the number of academic openings for young persons (Kidd, 1979). Particularly pertinent are proposals to reallocate vacant posts, achieve economies in nonessential items in university budgets to permit creating more faculty positions, and arrange for employment of a few of the most eminent researchers by research councils on long-term contracts.

The Council's Recommendation

Our proposed Fund for the Encouragement of Young Scientists (pp. 125-126) resembles the proposal of the Committee on Continuity in Academic Research Performance but is somewhat more flexible. Under our proposal, the amounts spent each year would rise to a peak in 1991-92 and then decline to the year 2000, but would be somewhat higher each year than the amounts proposed by the committee. We suggest some awards directly to recent Ph.D.'s, along with 10-year awards to establish scholars during the first decade of the program (the duration of awards to be gradually reduced after that, as the shortages of positions become less serious). Expenditures under our proposal would not exceed $100 million in the peak years. We also suggest augmentation of funds for the National Endowment for the Humanities and the National Endowment for the Arts for similar programs.

On the whole, we believe that primary emphasis should be placed on awards to established scholars, following the precedent of the program of the National Institutes of Health. They are easier to identify, and the university would be obligated to commit some of its own funds. Moreover, we believe that foundations (including major corporate foundations) and large corporations should consider developing private award programs for the purpose of encouraging young scholars, in view of the national interest in encouraging the development of research talent. There are indications that the problem of choosing among fields and institutions may be politically troublesome for the federal government.

References

Atelsek, F. J., and Gomberg, I. L. *Young Doctorate Faculty in Selected Science and Engineering Departments, 1975 to 1980.* Higher Education Panel Report No. 30. Washington, D.C.: American Council on Education, 1976.

Atelsek, F. J., and Gomberg, I. L. *Young Doctoral Faculty in Science and Engineering: Trends in Composition and Research Activity.* Higher Education Panel Report No. 43. Washington, D.C.: American Council on Education, 1979.

Fiske, M. D. *The Transition in Physics Doctoral Employment, 1960-1990.* Report of the Physics Manpower Panel, American Physical Society. New York: 1979.

Grodzins, L. *Supply and Demand for Ph.D. Physicists, III, Doctoral-Granting Physics Departments, 1979 to 1990.* Cambridge, Mass.: Massachusetts Institute of Technology, 1979. Duplicated.

Grodzins, L. *Supply and Demand for Ph.D. Physicists, 1977 to 1986.* Cambridge, Mass.: Massachusetts Institute of Technology, n.d. Duplicated.

Kidd, C. V. *The Prospects for New Academic Positions in Western Europe and Canada, 1980-2000.* Prepared for the Committee on the Continuity of Academic Research Performance. Washington, D.C.: Graduate Program in Science, Technology, and Public Policy, George Washington University, 1979.

Klitgaard, R. E. *The Decline of the Best? An Analysis of the Relationships Between Declining Enrollments, Ph.D. Production, and Research.* Cambridge, Mass.: John Fitzgerald Kennedy School of Government, Harvard University, 1979.

National Research Council, Commission on Human Resources. *Research Excellence Through the Year 2000: The Importance of Maintaining a Flow of New Faculty into Academic Research.* A Report with Recommendations of the Committee on Continuity in Academic Research Performance. Washington, D.C.: National Academy of Science, 1979.

Radner, R., and Kuh, C. V. *Preserving a Lost Generation: Policies to Assure a Steady Flow of Young Scholars Until the Year 2000.* A Report for the Carnegie Council on Policy Studies in Higher Education. Berkeley, Calif.: 1978.

U.S. National Science Foundation. *Young and Senior Science and Engineering Faculty, 1974: Support, Research Participation, and Tenure.* Report No. 75-302. Washington, D.C.: 1975.

U.S. National Science Foundation, Advisory Council. *Continued Viability of Universities as Centers for Basic Research.* Howard K. Schachman, chairman. Report of Task Group No. 1. Washington, D.C.: 1978. Duplicated.

Wolfle, D. *The Home of Science: The Role of the University.* Sponsored by the Carnegie Commission on Higher Education. New York: McGraw-Hill, 1972.

Supplement L

State Support
of Higher Education

State Expenditures

In Supplement A, we have shown that the relative role of state and local governments in the financing of higher education has been increasing. This is true whether we are considering sources of institutional income or sources of total monetary outlays for higher education; on the basis of both types of measures, the increase in the relative role of the state and local governments has occurred in the period since World War II. The primary reason for this change, of course, is the increase in the proportion of enrollment in public institutions. If we consider sources of institutional funds for public and private institutions separately (as in Tables A-2 and A-3), we find that the percentage of support for public institutions from both state and local governments has been remarkably stable, while the percentage of support for private institutions derived from these sources has been very small and has not changed very much, although there has been some tendency for institutional support to be replaced by expenditures on state scholarship programs.

Once we consider the situation in individual states, however, we find that there is enormous variation from state to state in financial support for higher education, regardless of what measure of relative state support is used. We turn first to

This supplement was prepared by Margaret S. Gordon, Associate Director, and Charlotte Alhadeff, Research Specialist.

state and local expenditures per capita (Table L-1), since we recommend that these expenditures should remain stable in constant dollars in the next several decades. On the basis of this measure, state and local expenditures ranged from $31.68 per capita in New Hampshire to $141.17 in Alaska in 1976-77—a difference of more than $100. If one considers the characteristics of states ranking high and those ranking low on the basis of this measure, one notes that the states with relatively high expenditures per capita in 1976-77 were chiefly in the West (and to some extent in the Middle West), while those that ranked low were chiefly in the Northeast. But, as we have noted in earlier reports (especially in *The States and Private Higher Education,* 1977), the historic predominance of private higher education in the Northeast and of public higher education in the West and in many of the middle western states is an important factor in explaining these differences. By and large, the states with low ranks have relatively large private sectors (though not as large, relatively, as they once were), while those with high ranks have very large proportions of their total enrollments in public institutions.

This relationship is brought out clearly in Table L-2, which shows that expenditures per capita tend to decline quite steadily with increases in the proportion of enrollment in private institutions among the states. New York, with a relatively large private sector and comparatively large expenditures per capita on higher education, has tended to be something of an exception to this pattern, in part because it has one of the most liberal programs of support of private higher education, including a substantial state scholarship program and a program of institutional support.

Rankings of states, however, tend to change over the years, and some of the states with very large percentage changes in real per capita expenditures from 1967-68 to 1976-77 had comparatively small expenditures in the former year. In Table L-3, we have ranked the states in order of their percentage increases in real expenditures per capita between the two fiscal years. Among the states ranking high on this basis are a number of Southern states that had comparatively low expenditures per

Table L-1. Changes in state and local government expenditures on higher education per capita, by state, 1967-68 and 1976-77, in current dollars and constant (1977) dollars (states arranged in order of per capita expenditures in 1976-77)

		Current dollars			Constant (1977) dollars		
		1967-68	1976-77[a]	Percentage change	1967-68	1976-77[a]	Percentage change
Alaska	(1)	$27.33	$141.17	417%	$47.14	$141.17	199%
California	(2)	37.33	114.35	206	64.39	114.35	78
Wyoming	(3)	41.60	106.64	156	71.76	106.64	49
Wisconsin	(4)	30.17	103.34	243	52.04	103.34	99
Arizona	(5)	32.41	98.76	205	55.91	98.76	77
Hawaii	(6)	35.44	91.96	159	61.13	91.96	50
Washington	(7)	36.50	88.62	143	62.96	88.62	41
Oregon	(8)	34.48	87.14	153	59.48	87.14	47
Kansas	(9)	28.22	85.86	204	48.68	85.86	76
Nebraska	(10)	22.91	84.60	269	39.52	84.60	114
Utah	(11)	27.70	83.52	202	47.78	83.52	75
North Dakota	(12)	31.08	83.41	168	53.61	83.41	56
Idaho	(13)	25.45	83.31	227	43.90	83.31	90
Iowa	(14)	30.94	82.67	167	53.37	82.67	55
Texas	(15)	20.08	78.19	289	34.64	78.19	126
Colorado	(16)	30.55	77.09	152	52.70	77.09	46
New York	(17)	24.14	75.28	212	41.64	75.28	81
North Carolina	(18)	17.32	71.71	314	29.88	71.71	140
UNITED STATES AVERAGE		22.86	69.19	203	39.43	69.19	75

Illinois	(19)	27.71	69.04	149	47.80	69.04	44
Michigan	(20)	27.02	68.91	155	46.61	68.91	48
South Carolina	(21)	16.85	68.88	309	29.07	68.88	137
New Mexico	(22)	25.06	68.09	172	43.23	68.09	58
Delaware	(23)	18.77	67.69	261	32.38	67.69	109
Minnesota	(24)	20.42	67.55	231	35.22	67.55	92
Nevada	(25)	27.41	64.26	134	47.28	64.26	36
Montana	(26)	28.50	63.70	124	49.16	63.70	30
Kentucky	(27)	22.26	63.42	185	38.40	63.42	65
Alabama	(28)	15.71	62.44	297	27.10	62.44	130
Maryland	(29)	21.01	62.08	195	36.24	62.08	71
Rhode Island	(30)	21.89	62.07	184	37.76	62.07	64
Mississippi	(31)	18.10	61.78	241	31.22	61.78	98
Indiana	(32)	25.65	55.86	118	44.25	55.86	26
Florida	(33)	20.84	55.78	168	35.95	55.78	55
Virginia	(34)	14.18	55.56	292	24.46	55.56	127
Oklahoma	(35)	18.71	55.09	194	32.27	55.09	71
Missouri	(36)	22.00	53.33	142	37.95	53.33	41
West Virginia	(37)	24.52	51.64	111	42.30	51.64	22
South Dakota	(38)	32.31	51.31	59	55.73	51.31	−8
Arkansas	(39)	17.02	51.30	201	29.36	51.30	75
Louisiana	(40)	25.32	50.22	98	43.68	50.22	15
New Jersey	(41)	11.80	50.02	324	20.35	50.02	146
Georgia	(42)	18.29	49.62	171	31.55	49.62	57
Tennessee	(43)	17.47	48.68	179	30.14	48.68	62

(continued on next page)

Table L-1 *(continued)*

		Current dollars			Constant (1977) dollars		
		1967-68	*1976-77*[a]	*Percentage change*	*1967-68*	*1976-77*[a]	*Percentage change*
Pennsylvania	(44)	$15.28	$ 48.54	218%	$26.36	$ 48.54	84%
Ohio	(45)	13.31	47.92	260	22.96	47.92	109
Connecticut	(46)	16.80	43.46	159	28.98	43.46	50
Massachusetts	(47)	13.49	42.39	214	23.27	42.39	82
Vermont	(48)	20.68	41.29	100	35.67	41.29	16
Maine	(49)	14.06	36.99	163	24.25	36.99	53
New Hampshire	(50)	14.70	31.68	116	25.36	31.68	25

[a]Data for 1976-77 include state and local government allocations to institutions of higher education plus state student aid expenditures; data for 1967-68 do not include student aid expenditures, because comprehensive data on state student aid expenditures were not gathered until 1969-70.

Sources: U.S. National Center for Education Statistics (1970; 1979); National Association of State Scholarship and Grant Programs (1976); and *Statistical Abstract of the United States, 1972* (p. 14), and *1978* (p. 14).

Table L-2. State and local government expenditures per capita,
by percentage of FTE enrollment in private institutions, 1976-77

Expenditures per capita	Percentage of FTE enrollment in private institutions				
	0-9%	*10-19%*	*20-29%*	*30-39%*	*40% and over*
$100 and over	2	2			
$80 to $99	4	4	2	2	
$70 to $79	1	1	1		
$60 to $69	2	6	2		1
$50 to $59		6	3	1	
$40 to $49			3	1	3
Less than $40			1		1
AVERAGE	$88.33	$67.40	$59.54	$65.75	$45.19

Source: Computed from data in Table L-1 and U.S. National Center for Education Statistics, unpublished enrollment tables for fall 1976.

capita in 1967-68. The pronounced increases in these states reflect two changes that have been occurring: (1) a tendency (which we have noted in earlier analyses of enrollment) for the most pronounced increases in enrollment to occur in states that had very low enrollment rates in higher education historically and (2) the relatively rapid rate of economic growth in the Southern states in the 1970s.

Also worthy of comment is the pronounced increase in real per capita expenditures in New Jersey, a state which historically ranked near the bottom in expenditures on higher education, but which has made substantial progress in developing its public system of higher education in the last several decades. Massachusetts is a somewhat similar case, but its percentage increase in real per capita expenditures was not as large as that of New Jersey. Even so, both of these states continue to rank low in relative expenditures per capita, although New Jersey has moved up somewhat in recent years.

Some of the states that rank low in Table L-3 nevertheless ranked moderately well in terms of actual expenditures per capita in 1976-77. These include Washington, Illinois, Nevada, and Montana. On the other hand, New Hampshire, West Vir-

Table L-3. Percentage changes in state and local government expenditures
on higher education per capita, in constant dollars, 1967-68 to 1976-77
(states arranged in order of percentage change in per capita expenditures)

		Percentage change			*Percentage change*
Alaska	(1)	199%	Rhode Island	(26)	64%
New Jersey	(2)	146	Tennessee	(27)	62
North Carolina	(3)	140	New Mexico	(28)	58
South Carolina	(4)	137	Georgia	(29)	57
Alabama	(5)	130	North Dakota	(30)	56
Virginia	(6)	127	Iowa	(31)	55
Texas	(7)	126	Florida	(32)	55
Nebraska	(8)	114	Maine	(33)	53
Delaware	(9)	109	Hawaii	(34)	50
Ohio	(10)	109	Connecticut	(35)	50
Wisconsin	(11)	99	Wyoming	(36)	49
Mississippi	(12)	98	Michigan	(37)	48
Minnesota	(13)	92	Oregon	(38)	47
Idaho	(14)	90	Colorado	(39)	46
Pennsylvania	(15)	84	Illinois	(40)	44
Massachusetts	(16)	82	Washington	(41)	41
New York	(17)	81	Missouri	(42)	41
California	(18)	78	Nevada	(43)	36
Arizona	(19)	77	Montana	(44)	30
Kansas	(20)	76	Indiana	(45)	26
Utah	(21)	75	New Hampshire	(46)	25
Arkansas	(22)	75	West Virginia	(47)	22
Maryland	(23)	71	Vermont	(48)	16
Oklahoma	(24)	71	Louisiana	(49)	15
Kentucky	(25)	65	South Dakota	(50)	−8

Note: Where states appear to have equal percentage increases, ranking is based on unrounded percentages.

Source: Table L-1.

ginia, Louisiana, and Vermont not only have increased their expenditures very little, but also continue to rank very low in
terms of expenditures in 1976-77. South Dakota, with declining
real expenditures per capita, is a somewhat special case. It has

actually lost enrollment in its public institutions of higher education in the 1970s, especially in its state colleges, which have been oriented toward teacher training.

Although one might expect high-income states to support higher education more generously than low-income states, it has long been known that there is no consistent relationship between per capita income and state support of higher education. Figure L-1 shows that this continues to be the case. Arizona, which spent the most on higher education in 1976-77 in relation to its per capita income, ranked 32nd in personal income per capita. Mississippi, which has long had the lowest per capita income of any of the states, ranked 11th in the percentage spent on higher education. Near the bottom of the chart, with the lowest expenditures in relation to per capita income, were two of the wealthiest states in the nation, New Jersey, ranking second in per capita income, and Connecticut, ranking third. In fact, Figure L-1 displays, in general, the same pattern as that in Table L-1, with the highest expenditures in relation to per capita income in the states with large public sectors, and the lowest expenditures in states with sizable percentages of their enrollment in private institutions. And this relationship, in general, continues to prevail despite the rapid increase in expenditures on state scholarship programs in recent years. Two of the states with relatively large state scholarship expenditures, Pennsylvania and New Jersey, rank quite low in expenditures as a percentage of per capita income.

Expenditures per FTE Enrollment

Another highly significant measure of state effort, of course, is expenditure per full-time equivalent (FTE) enrollment. In Table L-4, we present data on state and local expenditures per FTE enrollment in both public and private institutions for 1971-72 and 1976-77, as well as on percentage changes between the two years. In both years, expenditures per FTE were far higher in Alaska than in any other state, reflecting the high level of prices and salaries in Alaska, as well as the fact that a number of its public institutions are quite small and cannot benefit from economies of scale.

In Figure L-2, states are ranked by state and local expendi-

Figure L-1. State and local expenditures per capita as percentage
of personal income per capita, 1976-77, compared with state rank[a]
in terms of personal income per capita (in parentheses)

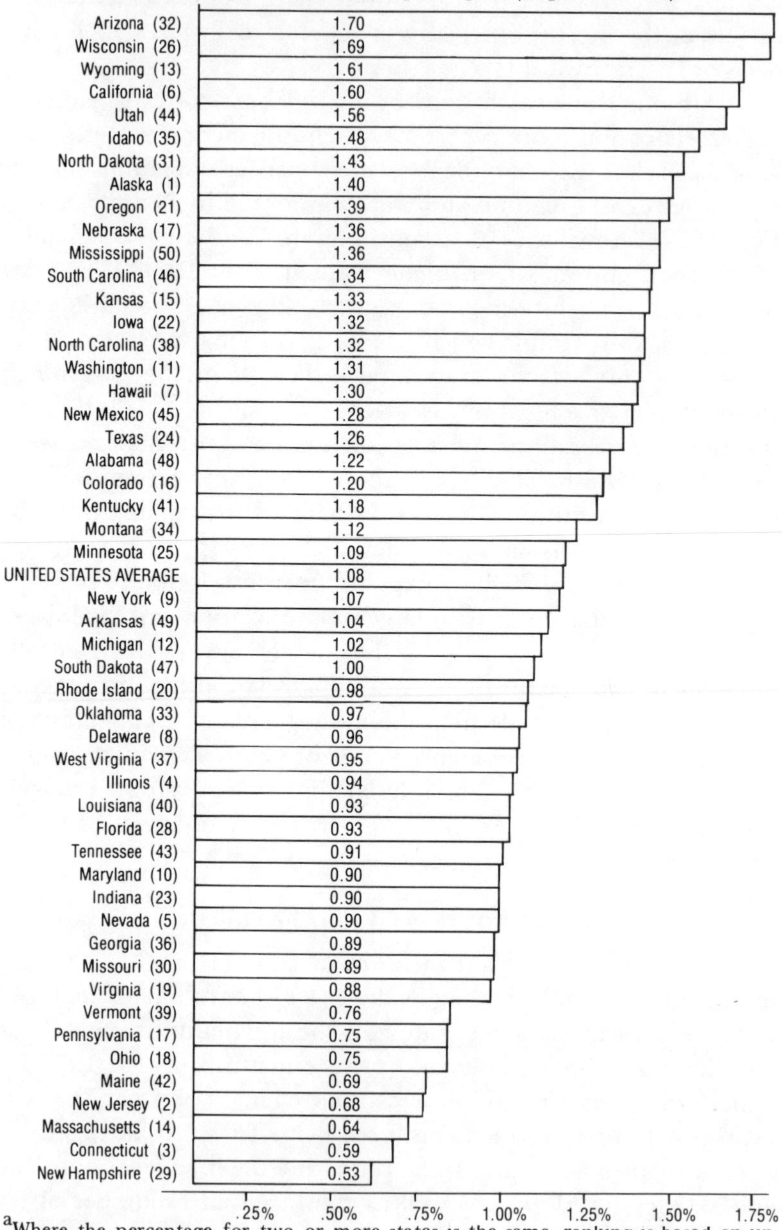

State (rank)	Value
Arizona (32)	1.70
Wisconsin (26)	1.69
Wyoming (13)	1.61
California (6)	1.60
Utah (44)	1.56
Idaho (35)	1.48
North Dakota (31)	1.43
Alaska (1)	1.40
Oregon (21)	1.39
Nebraska (17)	1.36
Mississippi (50)	1.36
South Carolina (46)	1.34
Kansas (15)	1.33
Iowa (22)	1.32
North Carolina (38)	1.32
Washington (11)	1.31
Hawaii (7)	1.30
New Mexico (45)	1.28
Texas (24)	1.26
Alabama (48)	1.22
Colorado (16)	1.20
Kentucky (41)	1.18
Montana (34)	1.12
Minnesota (25)	1.09
UNITED STATES AVERAGE	1.08
New York (9)	1.07
Arkansas (49)	1.04
Michigan (12)	1.02
South Dakota (47)	1.00
Rhode Island (20)	0.98
Oklahoma (33)	0.97
Delaware (8)	0.96
West Virginia (37)	0.95
Illinois (4)	0.94
Louisiana (40)	0.93
Florida (28)	0.93
Tennessee (43)	0.91
Maryland (10)	0.90
Indiana (23)	0.90
Nevada (5)	0.90
Georgia (36)	0.89
Missouri (30)	0.89
Virginia (19)	0.88
Vermont (39)	0.76
Pennsylvania (17)	0.75
Ohio (18)	0.75
Maine (42)	0.69
New Jersey (2)	0.68
Massachusetts (14)	0.64
Connecticut (3)	0.59
New Hampshire (29)	0.53

.25% .50% .75% 1.00% 1.25% 1.50% 1.75%

[a]Where the percentage for two or more states is the same, ranking is based on unrounded data.

Sources: Table L-1; and "State Personal Income Revisions, 1971-76" (1977, p. 17).

Table L-4. State and local government expenditures[a] per FTE student in higher education, in 1976-77 dollars

	Support per FTE student in 1971-72			Support per FTE student in 1976-77			Total support per FTE student in 1976-77		Percentage change in total support per FTE student 1971-72 to 1976-77
	Public institutions	Private institutions	Total	Public institutions	Private institutions	Total	Rank	Relative to U.S. (=100%)	
Alabama	$1,609	$ 90	$1,363	$2,003	$113	$1,739	30	−3	+28
Alaska	4,472	251	4,033	6,646	0	6,354	1	+256	+58
Arkansas	1,834	0	1,537	2,288	20	1,931	14	+8	+26
Arizona	1,850	170	1,810	1,918	0	1,848	21	+3	+2
California	2,126	177	1,861	2,476	309	2,205	6	+23	+18
Colorado	1,577	0	1,382	1,833	0	1,652	33	−8	+20
Connecticut	2,277	1	1,390	1,974	134	1,253	45	−30	−10
Delaware	1,686	0	1,416	1,827	46	1,559	36	−13	+10
Florida	1,988	116	1,616	2,207	143	1,797	25	+1	+11
Georgia	2,014	7	1,617	2,145	19	1,714	31	−4	+6
Hawaii	2,190	0	1,982	2,290	0	2,142	8	+20	+8
Idaho	1,861	0	1,419	2,802	0	2,167	7	+21	+53
Illinois	2,621	422	1,962	2,367	464	1,838	22	+3	−6
Indiana	2,169	1	1,624	2,203	231	1,684	32	−5	+4
Iowa	2,474	167	1,668	3,103	338	2,244	5	+26	+35
Kansas	1,748	6	1,514	2,356	285	2,084	11	+17	+38
Kentucky	2,491	0	1,994	2,558	43	2,101	10	+18	+5
Louisiana	1,707	14	1,457	1,720	173	1,501	38	−16	+3
Maine	2,039	0	1,390	1,667	65	1,207	47	−32	−13
Maryland	2,093	218	1,727	2,027	267	1,764	28	−1	+2

(continued on next page)

Table L-4 (*continued*)

| | Support per FTE student in 1971-72 | | | Support per FTE student in 1976-77 | | | Total support per FTE student in 1976-77 | | Percentage change in total support per FTE student 1971-72 to 1976-77 |
	Public institutions	Private institutions	Total	Public institutions	Private institutions	Total	Rank	Relative to U.S. (=100%)	
Massachusetts	$2,444	$ 58	$ 819	$1,892	$ 62	$ 860	48	−52	+5
Michigan	2,073	220	1,804	2,071	388	1,824	24	+2	+1
Minnesota	1,979	17	1,591	2,292	231	1,790	26	0	+13
Mississippi	1,797	0	1,593	1,945	0	1,741	29	−3	+9
Missouri	1,948	13	1,420	2,105	62	1,476	39	−17	+4
Montana	1,700	0	1,553	2,019	0	1,827	23	+2	+18
Nebraska	1,770	19	1,382	2,624	11	2,119	9	+19	+53
Nevada	2,186	0	2,170	2,256	0	2,379	4	+33	+10
New Hampshire	1,320	0	707	1,323	0	763	50	−57	+8
New Jersey	2,480	271	1,778	2,270	384	1,782	27	0	0
New Mexico	1,593	24	1,483	2,006	74	1,863	18	+4	+26
New York	3,015	576	2,014	2,798	567	1,850	19	+4	−8
North Carolina	2,296	10	1,636	2,396	66	1,846	20	+3	+13
North Dakota	1,362	0	1,302	2,125	11	1,981	13	+11	+52
Ohio	1,561	177	1,204	2,869	199	1,473	40	−18	+22
Oklahoma	1,225	1	1,031	1,550	28	1,317	44	−26	+28
Oregon	1,609	78	1,406	2,167	122	1,896	16	+6	+35
Pennsylvania	2,240	506	1,479	2,211	578	1,523	37	−15	+3
Rhode Island	2,102	1	1,112	2,482	92	1,227	46	−31	+10
South Carolina	2,229	6	1,534	2,415	323	1,925	15	+8	+25
South Dakota	1,490	0	1,055	1,900	5	1,337	43	−25	+27

Tennessee	1,805	23	1,310	1,887	36	1,395	42	−22	+7
Texas	1,902	98	1,581	2,271	366	2,004	12	+12	+27
Utah	1,705	0	1,025	2,300	0	1,428	41	−20	+39
Vermont	1,869	68	1,005	1,313	100	783	49	−56	−22
Virginia	1,744	0	1,396	1,859	58	1,579	34	−12	+13
Washington	1,904	14	1,677	2,123	28	1,871	17	+5	+12
West Virginia	1,858	9	1,516	1,828	104	1,565	35	−12	+3
Wisconsin	2,423	248	2,089	2,882	380	2,519	3	+41	+21
Wyoming	1,986	0	1,964	2,968	0	2,968	2	+66	+51
United States	2,089	223	1,617	2,253	276	1,786	0	0	+10

[a]Defined as appropriations from state and local governments to the institutions of higher education in their state plus state student assistance.

Source: Data on state and local expenditures per FTE in 1971-72 and 1976-77 were kindly provided to us by Charles Byce of the Washington, D.C., office of the College Entrance Examination Board.

Figure L-2. State and local government expenditures[a] per FTE student in public and private institutions of higher education, 1976-77

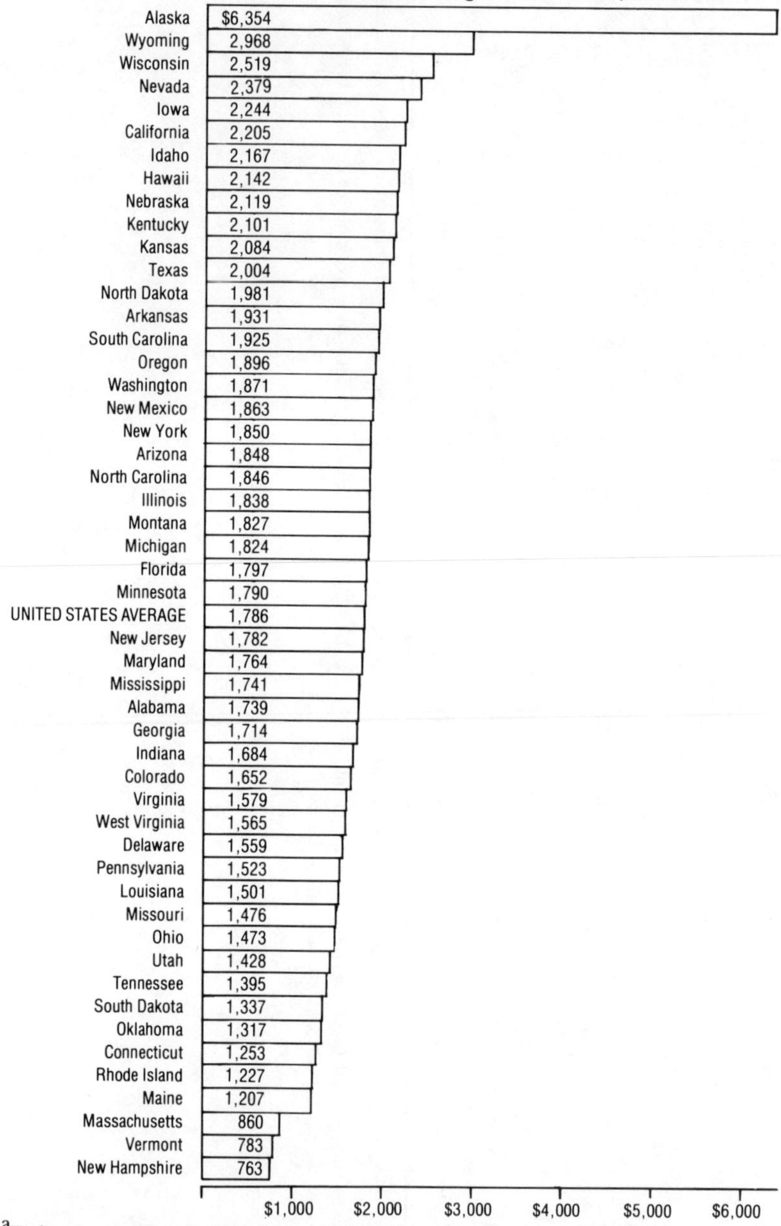

State	Expenditure
Alaska	$6,354
Wyoming	2,968
Wisconsin	2,519
Nevada	2,379
Iowa	2,244
California	2,205
Idaho	2,167
Hawaii	2,142
Nebraska	2,119
Kentucky	2,101
Kansas	2,084
Texas	2,004
North Dakota	1,981
Arkansas	1,931
South Carolina	1,925
Oregon	1,896
Washington	1,871
New Mexico	1,863
New York	1,850
Arizona	1,848
North Carolina	1,846
Illinois	1,838
Montana	1,827
Michigan	1,824
Florida	1,797
Minnesota	1,790
UNITED STATES AVERAGE	1,786
New Jersey	1,782
Maryland	1,764
Mississippi	1,741
Alabama	1,739
Georgia	1,714
Indiana	1,684
Colorado	1,652
Virginia	1,579
West Virginia	1,565
Delaware	1,559
Pennsylvania	1,523
Louisiana	1,501
Missouri	1,476
Ohio	1,473
Utah	1,428
Tennessee	1,395
South Dakota	1,337
Oklahoma	1,317
Connecticut	1,253
Rhode Island	1,227
Maine	1,207
Massachusetts	860
Vermont	783
New Hampshire	763

$1,000 $2,000 $3,000 $4,000 $5,000 $6,000

[a]Defined as appropriations from state and local governments to the institutions of higher education in their state plus state student assistance.

Source: Data were kindly provided by Charles Byce of the Washington, D.C., office of the College Entrance Examination Board.

tures per FTE in 1976-77. The results indicate, as in the case of expenditures per capita, that the states with large proportions of enrollment in public institutions tend to rank at the top, while those with large private sectors tend to rank at the bottom—once again, New York is an exception to this pattern. A striking aspect of this array is that all 6 New England states are at the bottom of the list.

If, however, we rank the states by expenditures per FTE in public higher education, we find some significant changes in the ranking. The 10 highest states on this basis, in order, are:

Alaska	Idaho
Iowa	New York
Wyoming	Nebraska
Wisconsin	Kentucky
Ohio	Rhode Island

Of these states, 7 also ranked in the top 10 in expenditures per FTE in public and private institutions combined, but 3 have moved up quite decisively from their ranking in Figure L-1— Ohio, New York, and Rhode Island.

On the other hand, the 10 lowest states in terms of expenditures per FTE in public institutions are, in reverse order of their expenditures:

Vermont	Delaware
New Hampshire	West Virginia
Oklahoma	Colorado
Maine	Virginia
Louisiana	Tennessee

One of the reasons for Vermont's ranking at the bottom is the fact that its public institutions of higher education have long had the highest tuition charges of those in any state. Oklahoma's low ranking, on the other hand, reflects its capacity— noted in earlier reports (for example, Carnegie Council, 1976)—to operate its public system at very low cost. Of interest, also, is the fact that 3 of the New England states remain in the bottom 10 on this basis, but Rhode Island's position rises dramatically, while Connecticut and Massachusetts move up to a position slightly below the national average.

In terms of support per FTE student in private institutions, the 10 highest ranking states, in order, are:

Pennsylvania	Wisconsin
New York	Texas
Illinois	Iowa
Michigan	Kansas
New Jersey	Maryland

States at the bottom of the array on this basis had zero expenditures per FTE student in private institutions in 1976-77, but it should be noted that Wyoming has no private institutions. Since 1976-77, all the states that had no scholarship programs at that time have adopted them, and in nearly all states some of the scholarship funds now flow to students in private institutions. There is, however, enormous variation in amounts per FTE student expended for this purpose.

The data in Table L-4 are consistent with our finding in Supplement I that real expenditures per student have been rising somewhat, although here, of course, we are dealing only with the portion of educational expenditures stemming from state and local government appropriations. Total support per FTE rose 10 percent in the nation as a whole in constant dollars between 1971-72 and 1976-77, but there were very wide differences among the states in the extent of the change. States ranking in the top 10 on the basis of their percentage increases are:

Alaska	Utah
Idaho	Kansas
Nebraska	Oregon
North Dakota	Iowa
Wyoming	Oklahoma

Once again, the states heading the list on this basis tend to be states with large percentages of their enrollment in public insti-

tutions. This is not surprising, since in all states, even those with substantial support for private higher education like New York and Pennsylvania, expenditures flowing to private institutions are a small proportion of total expenditures.

At the bottom of the list, in reverse order of their percentage changes, are:

Vermont	New Jersey
Maine	Michigan
Connecticut	Arizona
New York	Pennsylvania
Illinois	Louisiana

This list includes a good many states with sizable private sectors. Even so, the 6 leaders on this list all experienced substantial declines in support per FTE in public institutions.

It should be noted that the impact of Proposition 13 was not felt in California higher education until 1978-79 and thus is not reflected in Table L-4.

The Fiscal Outlook of the States

The fiscal position of the states tends to fluctuate over the course of the business cycle. Fiscal stringency and deficits were serious problems in the states in the 1974-75 recession, but surpluses built up rapidly as the economy recovered, and in early 1978 the total budgetary surplus of the states was about $8.4 billion (Peirce, 1979; and Levin, 1978). Then, as economic growth slowed down, the situation rapidly deteriorated, and by the spring of 1979 the states had a cumulative deficit of about $6.1 billion. In part, this pronounced shift was explained by the enactment of Proposition 13 in California, which led to the appropriation of much of that state's large surplus to relieve the impact of the loss in property tax revenues on local governments and school districts.

On the whole, despite these fluctuations, the long-run outlook for the fiscal position of the states in the next few decades appears to be favorable. There are several reasons for this: (1) expenditures on education and welfare, which are important in state budgets, are population-related and will benefit from a declining rate of population growth (we have shown in Table 12 [p. 129] how expenditures on higher education are likely to decline as a percentage of GNP as real GNP increases and enrollment declines); (2) some of the states that had regressive tax structures have recently adopted income taxes that bring in relatively more revenue with rising incomes, and other states may well move in that direction in the future; and (3) although Congress is adopting a more skeptical attitude toward general revenue sharing with state and local governments, recent trends toward larger federal grants-in-aid to meet urban problems (including housing grants, funds for CETA programs, and larger federal contributions to welfare expenditures) are likely to continue.

On the other hand, the repercussions of the current antitax revolt might turn out to be serious. California voters have recently adopted Proposition 4—a second tax-slashing measure following Proposition 13—by a huge margin, and similar measures are being approved in other states. While Proposition 13 limited property taxes to 1 percent of the value of property, Proposition 4 limited both state and local expenditures (with certain exceptions) to increases that would be proportional to the growth of population in the state and increases in the cost of living. Still a third initiative, which would reduce state income taxes by one-half, will be on the ballot in June 1980.

Even so, there is evidence that the wrath of the voters is not directed toward expenditures on education. Supporters of tax-cutting measures emphasize the need to cut out the "waste" in government, while polls conducted after enactment of Proposition 13 indicated that voters had particularly adverse attitudes toward welfare expenditures.

So far as higher education is concerned, slowing enrollment growth, with actual declines in many of the states, should ease the burden of adequate support from state governments. The real danger in the situation, as we point out in Section 7, may be a tendency on the part of state budget analysts to accept exaggerated projections of declines in enrollments in higher education and to recommend commensurate slashing of appropriations. Institutions of higher education can guard against this contingency by insisting on more carefully developed projections of enrollment in their states and cooperating in the development of such projections. Interstate cooperation on a regional basis is particularly needed in this connection.

Some Carnegie Priorities

We conclude this supplement by calling attention again to certain important programs that have been emphasized in earlier reports by the Carnegie Council and by its predecessor, the Carnegie Commission.

First among these is the development of *open-door community colleges* in communities where they do not exist. The case for these colleges—along with a strong recommendation that their programs be comprehensive—was stated fully in Carnegie Commission (1970b), and our most recent review of needs for new community colleges was included in the Supplement to Carnegie Foundation for the Advancement of Teaching (1976).

Second, we are immensely pleased with the progress that has been made during the 1970s in the development of Area Health Education Centers (AHECs), which were recommended in the Carnegie Commission's (1970a) report, *Higher Education and the Nation's Health.* The 11 AHECs (in as many states) that were awarded the first federal contracts for the development of AHECs have recently been evaluated for the Carnegie Council by Odegaard (1980a and 1980b), who found that the best of these programs—in North Carolina, South Carolina, Illinois, and California—were making important contributions to attracting health manpower to underserved communities. The other seven programs were also making a variety of contributions but suffered in differing ways from administrative and other deficiencies that in most cases could be corrected. Our most recent review of AHECs was included in Carnegie Council (1976) and indicated that there were examples of decentralized medical and other health professional training programs in 33 states.

A particularly significant finding of Odegaard's report is that federal funds to support the development of AHECs have admirably fulfilled the function of "seed money" in several states. As the programs have developed in these states, the state government has increasingly perceived the value of the programs and has increased the amount of state support, so that, in several states, support from the state government now very substantially exceeds federal support. In North Carolina, particularly, state support has been important from the beginning.

The third priority to be emphasized here is the need for expansion of state scholarship programs where, as in most of the states, appropriations for these programs are far smaller than would be required to meet the needs of low-income students. Our most recent review of these programs was in Carnegie Council (1977). The adequacy of state scholarship programs will play an important role in encouraging the survival of many private colleges and universities in the next 20 years.

Finally, we reemphasize the recommendation in Section 7 (p. 120) that the states generally should be prepared to maintain real per capita contributions to higher education at current levels. As we noted there, such a policy will create some leeway, as public enrollments decline, to provide more aid for private colleges and to offset the higher cost per student for overhead as enrollments decrease. States with declining populations (and therefore total expenditures if they maintain per capita real expenditures) are also likely to have relatively large enrollment declines.

We also believe that states with particularly low per capita expenditures in fiscal 1977—those at the bottom of Table L-3—should increase their expenditures per capita. Several of these states (particularly Indiana, New Hampshire, Vermont, Louisiana, and South Dakota) also rank low on some of the other measures discussed here.

References

Carnegie Commission on Higher Education. *Higher Education and the Nation's Health: Policies for Medical and Dental Education.* New York: McGraw-Hill, 1970a.

Carnegie Commission on Higher Education. *The Open-Door Colleges: Policies for Community Colleges.* New York: McGraw-Hill, 1970b.

Carnegie Council on Policy Studies in Higher Education. *The States and Private Higher Education: Problems and Policies in a New Era.* San Francisco: Jossey-Bass, 1977.

Carnegie Council on Policy Studies in Higher Education. *Progress and Problems in Medical and Dental Education: Federal Support Versus Federal Control.* San Francisco: Jossey-Bass, 1976.

Carnegie Foundation for the Advancement of Teaching. *The States and Higher Education: A Proud Past and a Vital Future. Supplement.* Berkeley, Calif.: Carnegie Council on Higher Education, 1976.

Levin, D. J. "State and Local Government Fiscal Position in 1978." *Survey of Current Business,* Dec. 1978, *58* (12), 19-22.

National Association of State Scholarship and Grant Programs. *Eighth Annual Survey: 1976-77 Academic Year.* Deerfield: Illinois State Scholarship Commission, 1976.

Odegaard, C. E. *Area Health Education Centers: The Pioneering Years, 1972-1978.* Berkeley, Calif.: Carnegie Council on Policy Studies in Higher Education, 1980a.[a]

Odegaard, C. E. *Eleven Area Health Education Centers: The View from the Grass Roots.* Berkeley, Calif: Carnegie Council on Policy Studies in Higher Education, 1980b. Duplicated.[a]

Peirce, N. R. "Hard Times Threaten the Euphoria of Tax Cutters." *Sacramento Bee,* Sept. 24, 1979.

"State Personal Income Revisions, 1971-76." *Survey of Current Business,* Aug. 1977, *57* (8), 15-31.

U.S. Bureau of the Census. *Statistical Abstract of the United States, 1972.*

U.S. Bureau of the Census. *Statistical Abstract of the United States, 1978.*

U.S. National Center for Education Statistics. *Financial Statistics of Institutions of Higher Education, 1967-68.* Washington, D.C.: 1970.

U.S. National Center for Education Statistics. *Financial Statistics of Institutions of Higher Education, Fiscal Year 1977: State Data.* Washington, D.C.: 1979.

[a]Persons interested in obtaining copies of the two Odegaard reports should write to Charles Odegaard, President Emeritus, University of Washington, Seattle, WA 98195.

Appendix A

Carnegie Council Surveys

The Carnegie Council on Policy Studies in Higher Education has made an extensive and continuous effort to keep in touch with developments on the nation's campuses. As a part of that effort, it has sponsored or conducted a series of special studies. The latest of these are the Carnegie Council's Surveys of Institutional Adaptations to the 1970s conducted in 1978. These surveys are described in some detail in this Appendix. Before presenting that description, however, it may be useful to review the contributions made by several prior surveys conducted under the sponsorship or direction of the Carnegie Commission on Higher Education or the Carnegie Council on Policy Studies in Higher Education. In chronological order, with their full titles, and the text reference used to identify them in this and other reports,[1] these surveys are as follows:

In 1968–69, under Carnegie Commission sponsorship, Harold Hodgkinson conducted studies of changes in higher education during the previous decade. Much of his data was gathered from governmental sources. This was supplemented, however, by a survey of 1,230 presidents of institutions of higher education. This questionnaire focused on specific changes that had taken place. Hodgkinson supplemented his survey findings with data gathered in case studies of five institutions. The results were reported in *Institutions in Transition* (Hodgkinson, 1971).

---

[1]See References for titles of publications in which survey findings are reported.

Date	Survey Title	Text Reference
1969	Survey of Institutions in Transition	Hodgkinson, 1971
1969	Carnegie Commission Surveys of Undergraduates, Graduate Students, and Faculty Members*	Carnegie Surveys, 1969
1974	Survey of Changes in Enrollments and Financing	Glenny, Shea, Ruyle, and Freschi, 1976
1974	Survey of Changing Practices in Undergraduate Education	Blackburn and others, 1976
1975	Carnegie Council Catalog Study	Catalog Study, 1976 (not published)
1975	Carnegie Council Surveys of Graduate Students and Faculty*	Carnegie Surveys, 1975
1976	Carnegie Council Survey of Undergraduates*	Carnegie Survey, 1976
1978	Carnegie Council Surveys of Institutional Adaptations to the 1970s	Carnegie Council Surveys, 1978
1979	Carnegie Council Site Visits	Site Visits, 1979 (not published)

*Collectively referred to as Carnegie Surveys, 1969-70, 1975-76.

In 1969, a survey of undergraduates, graduate students, and faculty members was conducted under the sponsorship of the Carnegie Commission on Higher Education and the American Council on Education with support from the U.S. Office of Education. Usable questionnaires were received from approximately 60,000 faculty members, 30,000 graduate students, and 70,000 undergraduates. Some of the findings were reported in *Teachers and*

Students, edited by the director of the project, Martin Trow (1975). Data from the survey are now accessible through the Survey Research Center at the University of California, Berkeley.

In summer 1974, a "Survey of Presidents' Response to Changes in Enrollments and Financing" was conducted for the Council by Lyman Glenny and members of the staff of the Center for Research and Development in Higher Education at the Universtiy of California, Berkeley. Usable responses were received from 1,227 institutions and yielded information on changes that took place on American campuses between 1968 and 1974. The basic report of this study (Glenny and others, 1976), was published as a technical report of the Council. Many of the findings were also reported in *More than Survival* (The Carnegie Foundation for the Advancement of Teaching, 1975) and other publications of the Council.

Under the Council's sponsorship, Robert Blackburn and his associates at the University of Michigan conducted detailed studies of the catalogs of 271 representative colleges and universities to determine trends and changes in their curricula between 1967 and 1974. The findings of this study were released in a technical report (Blackburn and others) published by the Council in 1976. The Council's staff conducted further catalog studies to update the findings of Blackburn and his colleagues and to identify trends in educational practices. There has been no formal written report of the findings from the staff studies, although the information that was obtained was reported extensively in *Missions of the College Curriculum* (The Carnegie Foundation for the Advancement of Teaching, 1977) and *Handbook on Undergraduate Curriculum* (Levine, 1978).

In order to examine once again the experiences and attitudes of undergraduates, graduate students, and faculty members in American colleges and universities, national surveys were conducted in 1975 and 1976 under the direction of Martin Trow at the Survey Research Center of the University of California, Berkeley. Tabulations of data from this survey drew on responses from about 25,000 individuals in each survey group. The information that was yielded included demographical descriptions of the participants in higher education, perceptions of their roles in governance, political and religious orientations, views on certain social questions of current interest, work and study practices, and many other significant matters. These surveys were particularly useful because, to a considerable extent, they updated the surveys of undergraduates, graduate students, and faculty members conducted under Professor Trow's direction in 1969. The information provided by the Carnegie Council's National Surveys of 1975 and 1976 has been utilized in several of the Council's reports. A technical report (Roizen, Fulton, and Trow, 1978) on these surveys is available from the Center for Studies in Higher Education, University of California, Berkeley. A few reproductions of the marginals for each of the surveys are available from The Carnegie Foundation for the Advancement of Teaching. Inquiries concerning access to the survey data should be addressed to the Center for Studies in Higher Education at the University of California, Berkeley.

In this final report of the Carnegie Council and in two of the technical reports that are associated with it (Levine, forthcoming; Stadtman, forthcoming), reference frequently is made to the Carnegie Council Surveys of 1978. These are formally known as the Council's Surveys of Institutional Adaptations to the 1970s. To some extent they update information obtained in the surveys conducted by Lyman Glenny in 1974, but they are considerably more comprehensive and involved responses not only from college and university presidents but also from deans of student affairs and chief academic, financial, or planning officers of each institution. The surveys were conducted under the direction of Verne A. Stadtman, associate director, and Arthur E. Levine and John Shea, senior fellows of the Carnegie Council. Technical coordination was provided by Sura Johnson. Staff assistance was also provided by Steven Archibald, C.E. Christian, Sandra Elman, Sandra Loris, Lillian North, Rachel Volberg, Claudia White, Keith Wilson, and Mitch Zeftel. We deeply appreciate the cooperation of the Educational Testing Service (E.T.S.), and particularly Richard Millard, Michael Walsh, and Judith Hirabayashi, all members of the E.T.S. staff, for counsel and assistance throughout the project and in providing data processing services. We are particularly appreciative of the presidents, other administrators, and students whose participation was crucial to the survey's success. We realize that, in many cases, their cooperation involved a considerable investment of time. Their contribution to our understanding of what is happening to higher education on the eve of the 1980s has been immense.

The surveys were pretested by members of the Council's staff at 11 California institutions—American River College, California State University-Hayward, Dominican College, Grossmont College, International University, Los Medanos College, Merritt College, Mills College, University of California at Davis, University of the Pacific, and University of San Diego. The Council expresses its thanks to these institutions for their contribution to the effectiveness of the final survey instruments.

In all, administrators of 870 American colleges and universities were invited to answer the questionnaires. The questionnaire directed to college and university presidents (Questionnaire A) was concerned with general trends, changes in control, internal governance, collective bargaining, and relationships with the outside community and with state and federal governments. The questionnaire also asked for the presidents' generalized perceptions of the most important positive and negative changes at their institutions during the past decade, and their views of the major issues that higher education will face between now and the end of this century. To provide a different perspective on the matters reported by student affairs officers, presidents also were queried about student attitudes and asked to describe college students in the late 1970s.

The questionnaire directed to vice presidents of financial affairs or planning officers (Questionnaire B) explored the impact of changes in enrollment on faculty and student recruiting; personnel and tenure policies; admissions, guidance, and retention policies; selectivity; curriculum; scheduling and location; student/faculty ratios; use of available funds and student aid funds.

The questionnaire directed to student affairs officers (Questionnaire C) sought information about how undergraduates had changed and how institutions had responded to these changes; how students were involved in governing themselves and their institutions; what they were interested in (as revealed by their participation in various clubs and activities); how and what they protested. To provide perspective on the information supplied by planning officers, questions on retention policy and curriculum flexibility also were asked. The questionnaires were printed and first mailed at the end of March 1978.

From *A Classification of Institutions of Higher Education: Revised Edition* (1976), a classification of 3,072 campuses of higher education listed by the U.S. Office of Education, the staff rejected (1) all specialized and nontraditional institutions, (2) all religious schools training clergy only for religious functions, and (3) all schools not located in the 50 states or the District of Columbia. The remaining 2,481 campuses, divided by the *Carnegie Classification of Institutions of Higher Education* (1976) into 17 control (public and private) and classification categories, constituted the study universe. Seeking information from at least 30 campuses in each Carnegie classification and control category and assuming a 50 percent response rate, the staff chose at least 60 campuses from each Carnegie classification and control category for the sample. In each category with fewer than 60 campuses in the universe, every campus in the universe was chosen. This was the case for Research Universities I and II, Doctorate-granting Universities I and II, and public Liberal Arts Colleges II. Left with 2, 313 campuses in other categories from which to draw our sample, the staff decided to use 120 campuses in the largest category (public Two-Year Colleges and Institutes) because of an anticipated low response rate among these institutions. The size of the sample in all remaining categories with between 60 and 909 campuses in the universe was determined by extrapolation, using a table of random numbers to select the first campus and then every third, fifth, or whatever. The resulting "original sample" contained 799 institutions. Five pretest institutions were eliminated, and the sample was adjusted in other minor ways until it stood at 794 campuses.

Questionnaires were mailed in March 1978 to liaison officers at institutions whose presidents had agreed to participate in the survey. In April, it was determined that an insufficient number of postcard responses was being received in three categories: private Comprehensive Universities and Colleges I, public Comprehensive Universities and Colleges II, and private Comprehensive Universities and Colleges II. By adding 20, 28, and 28 campuses respectively to these control categories in the "original sample," the sample was increased to 870 campuses.[2]

---

[2]Questionnaires also were sent to and received from 130 additional women's and black institutions, but their responses were not included in basic tabulations (unless otherwise specified).

The achieved response rate,[3] that is, the proportion of institutions eligible and able to participate in our study and choosing to do so (before the cutoff date), was 68.7 percent for complete and partial respondents; 66.9 percent for Questionnaire A; 67.6 percent for Questionnaire B; and 68.1 percent for Questionnaire C.

Response rates for each questionnaire varied only slightly because 95 percent of the institutions returning at least one questionnaire returned full sets of three questionnaires. However, response rate by Carnegie type and control shows greater variation (Table A-1), from 47.1 percent for private Two-Year Colleges (sample number= 71) to 94.7 percent for private Doctorate Universities I (sample number = 19). Still, the variation is not great; except for private two-year colleges, Carnegie control and classification types returned questionnaires at a rate of close to 60 percent or higher, and the average rate of return (exclusive of private Two-Year Colleges) was 74.9 percent. With a response rate of 47.1 percent, private Two-Year Colleges stand apart as markedly more reluctant to participate in the survey, probably because the lengthy and detailed questionnaires were unsuited to their type of institution: some of these schools are very small with limited staff resources; others offer a specialized curriculum (for example, funeral services or dental hygiene) or mission (preparing clergy for their duties).

The different sample ratios and different response rates within the 17 control and Carnegie types made a differential weighting of institutions necessary. A series of weights was developed for each Carnegie type and control category. The "weight unadjusted for nonresponse" is the reciprocal of the sampling ratio; the "weight adjusted for nonresponse" is the reciprocal of the ratio of respondents to the "revised universe" within the appropriate sampling stratum.

Looking for possible sampling or response bias, the universe of 2,481 institutions, our sample of 870 institutions, and the 591 respondents to our survey were compared. These three-way comparisons concerned control, regional distribution by control, enrollment size by control, relative changes in enrollment (between 1969

---

[3]Achieved response rates were calculated as the number of responding institutions divided by the number of sampled institutions minus those 10 schools that might well have been eliminated from the sample because of aggregate responses (schools listed separately by the U.S. Office of Education that consider themselves one unit and returned a single set of questionnaires) or closings and mergers.

Table A-1. Response rates for Carnegie Surveys, 1978

	Public & Private	Public	Private
Research Universities I			
Universe	51	29	22
Sample	50	28	22
Respondents	40	23	17
Research Universities II			
Universe	47	33	14
Sample	47	33	14
Respondents	37	27	10
Doctorate-granting Universities I			
Universe	56	38	18
Sample	56	38	18
Respondents	44	29	15
Doctorate-granting Universities II			
Universe	30	19	11
Sample	29	19	10
Respondents	25	18	7
Comprehensive Universities and Colleges I			
Universe	375	247	128
Sample	154	70	84
Respondents	116	48	68
Comprehensive Universities and Colleges II			
Universe	207	101	106
Sample	179	88	91
Respondents	112	51	61
Liberal Arts Colleges I			
Universe	123	—	123
Sample	66	—	66
Respondents	47	—	47
Liberal Arts Colleges II			
Universe	459	11	448
Sample	98	11	87
Respondents	61	9	52
Two-Year Colleges			
Universe	1134	904	228
Sample	191	120	71
Respondents	109	76	33
Total			
Universe	2481	1383	1098
Sample	870	407	463
Respondents	591	281	310

The N's for the universe are the number of institutions actually listed for each designated Carnegie classification and control type in *A Carnegie Classification of Institutions: Revised Edition* (1976) minus the number of schools not located in the 50 states or in Washington, D.C.

and 1977) by control. In addition, the responding institutions and the full sample were compared along the dimensions of selectivity and age. The resulting tabulations satisfied us that our sample and respondents adequately represent American higher education.[4]

Soon after the first tabulations of the written responses were available, members of the Council's staff visited 28 institutions across the country to obtain a first-hand impression of the ways in which campuses were adapting to current trends and circumstances. These visits also provided an opportunity to clarify ambiguous responses to items in the questionnaires, and to obtain more detailed information about certain programs and practices that came to our attention through the surveys. On each campus, the staff members visited with the president, the official who had responded to the questionnaire for vice presidents or planning officers, and a group of from five to ten students. Many of the findings from these site visits have been presented in this and related reports of the Council.

Copies of the questionnaires used in the Carnegie Council's 1978 survey may be obtained from The Carnegie Foundation for the Advancement of Teaching, which also retains the master tapes on the survey.

[4]Greater detail about these comparative tabulations will be available in a technical report being prepared for the custody of The Carnegie Foundation for the Advancement of Teaching.

Appendix B

Glossary and Abbreviations

FTE enrollment: "Full-time equivalent" enrollment. FTE enrollment is defined as the number of full-time students plus some fraction (usually 1/3) of the number of part-time students.

Headcount enrollment: In this form of enumeration, each student, whether attending school full-time or part-time, counts as one enrollment. See *FTE enrollment* for contrast.

FTE faculty: "Full-time equivalent" faculty. FTE faculty is defined as the number of full-time faculty members plus a fraction (usually 1/3) of the number of part-time faculty members.

Educational and general expenditures: Usually includes all the activities performed at institutions of higher education directly connected with instruction and research. Indirectly connected activities, such as providing residence halls, feeding students, and other services, and construction are excluded from educational and general expenditures.

Monetary outlays for higher education: The net expenditure for educational and general functions of the institutions of higher education and the outlays of students and their families for tuition and living expenses, including student aid.

Disposable income: Personal income minus that portion paid in income taxes.

Real per capita contributions: State expenditures for contributions to higher education divided by the total population of the states and adjusted for changes in consumer prices.

Instructional costs: The sum of current operating expenditures and capital costs. Current operating expenditures include funds expended for instruction and departmental research, libraries, plant operation and maintenance, and an allowance for overhead. Capital costs consist of depreciation of the buildings and equipment plus an allowance for the income that could have been earned on the capital investment. Student aid, organized research, auxiliary enterprises, and sales and services are not included in instructional costs.

Forgone earnings: The wages or salaries that would have been paid to students if they were not enrolled in school and were employed full-time.

Total economic costs: The sum of the current costs expended by the institutions for instruction, the living costs of the students, and the foregone earnings of students.

BEOG: Basic Educational Opportunity Grants. These are federally funded grants available for needy undergraduate students.

SEOG: Supplemental Educational Opportunity Grants. These are federally funded grants made directly to institutions of higher education who then award funds to students of exceptional financial need.

SSIG: State Student Incentive Grants. The SSIG program provides for federal matching grants to the states for "need-based" state scholarships and grant programs.

FIPSE: Fund for the Improvement of Post-Secondary Education. There is a federal FIPSE designed to promote innovation, and several states have adopted similar programs.

References

Academy for Educational Development. (J.D. Millett, Director.) *319 Ways Colleges and Universities Are Meeting the Financial Pinch.* New York: 1971. (Reprinted in Mayhew, 1979.)

Academy for Educational Development. (J.D. Millett, Director.) *A Strategic Approach to the Maintenance of Institutional Financial Stability and Flexibility in the Face of Enrollment Instability or Decline.* Washington, D.C.: June 1979.

Ashby, Sir E. "Ivory Towers in Tomorrow's World." *Journal of Higher Education,* Nov. 1967, *38.*

Astin, A.W., King, M.R., and Richardson, G.T. *The American Freshman: National Norms for Fall 1978.* Washington, D.C.: American Council on Education, Cooperative Institutional Research Program, 1978.

Bailey, S.K. *Academic Quality Control: The Case of College Programs on Military Bases.* Washington, D.C.: American Association for Higher Education, 1979a.

Bailey, S.K. "Marketing Perspectives: Student and National Interests." Address at Wingspread Conference Center, Racine, Wisc., Nov. 8, 1979b.

Balderston, F.E. *Managing Today's University.* San Francisco: Jossey-Bass, 1974.

Baldridge, J.V., and Tierney, M.L. *New Approaches to Management: Creating Practical Systems of Management Information and Management by Objectives.* San Francisco: Jossey-Bass, 1979.

Behn, R.D. *The End of the Growth Era in Higher Education.* Raleigh, N.C.: Center for Educational Policy, Duke University, June 1979.

Ben-David, J. *The Scientist's Role in Society: A Comparative Study.* Englewood Cliffs, N.J.: Prentice-Hall, 1971.

Ben-David, J., and Zloczower, A. "Universities and Academic Systems in Modern Societies." *European Journal of Sociology,* 1962, *3*(1), 45-84.

Blackburn, R., and others. *Changing Practices in Undergraduate Education.* Berkeley, Calif.: Carnegie Council on Policy Studies in Higher Education, 1976.

Boulding, K.E. "The Management of Decline." *AGB Reports,* Sept./Oct. 1975, *17*(8), 4-9.

Boulding, K.E. *Ecodynamics.* Beverly Hills, Calif.: Sage Publications, 1978.

Boulding, K.E. "Science and Uncertain Futures." *Technology Review,* June-July 1979, *81*(7), 8-9.

Bowen, H.R. *Investment in Learning: The Individual and Social Value of American Higher Education.* San Francisco: Jossey-Bass, 1977.

Bowen, H.R. "Academic Compensation." *Academe: Bulletin of the AAUP,* Sept. 1979.

Bowen, H.R., and Douglas, G.K. *Efficiency in Liberal Education: A Study of Comparative Instructional Costs for Different Ways of Organizing Teaching-Learning in a Liberal Arts College.* Prepared for the Carnegie Commission on Higher Education. New York: McGraw-Hill, 1971.

Burn, B.B. *Expanding the International Dimension of Higher Education.* Prepared for the Carnegie Council on Policy Studies in Higher Education. San Francisco: Jossey-Bass, 1980.

Bush, V. *Science the Endless Frontier.* Washington, D.C.: U.S. Office of Scientific Research and Development, July 1945.

Carnegie Commission on Higher Education. *The Open Door Colleges: Policies for Community Colleges.* A Special Report and Recommendations. New York: McGraw-Hill, 1970a.

Carnegie Commission on Higher Education. *Higher Education and the Nation's Health: Policies for Medical and Dental Education.* New York: McGraw-Hill, 1970b.

Carnegie Commission on Higher Education. *New Students and New Places: Policies for the Future Growth and Development of American Higher Education.* A report and recommendations. New York: McGraw-Hill, 1971.

Carnegie Commission on Higher Education. *The Fourth Revolution: Instructional Technology in Higher Education.* New York: McGraw-Hill, 1972a.

Carnegie Commission on Higher Education. *The More Effective Use of Resources: An Imperative for Higher Education.* New York: McGraw-Hill, 1972b.

Carnegie Commission on Higher Education. *Priorities for Action: Final Report of the Carnegie Commission on Higher Education.* New York: McGraw-Hill, 1973a.

Carnegie Commission on Higher Education. *Higher Education: Who Pays? Who Benefits? Who Should Pay?* New York: McGraw-Hill, 1973b.

Carnegie Commission on Higher Education. *The Purposes and the Performance of Higher Education in the United States: Approaching the Year 2000.* New York: McGraw-Hill, 1973c.

Carnegie Commission on Higher Education. *A Digest of Reports of the Carnegie Commission on Higher Education.* New York: McGraw-Hill, 1974.

Carnegie Commission on Higher Education. *Sponsored Research of the Carnegie Commission on Higher Education.* New York: McGraw-Hill, 1975.

Carnegie Council on Policy Studies in Higher Education. *More Than Survival: Prospects for Higher Education in a Period of Uncertainty.* A Commentary with recommendations of the Carnegie Foundation for the Advancement of Teaching. San Francisco: Jossey-Bass, 1975a.

Carnegie Council on Policy Studies in Higher Education. *The Federal Role in Postsecondary Education: Unfinished Business, 1975-1980.* San Francisco: Jossey-Bass, 1975b.

Carnegie Council on Policy Studies in Higher Education. *A Classification of Institutions of Higher Education: Revised Edition.* Berkeley, Calif.: 1976.

Carnegie Council on Policy Studies in Higher Education. *The States and Private Higher Education: Problems and Policies in a New Era.* San Francisco: Jossey-Bass, 1977.

Carnegie Council on Policy Studies in Higher Education. *Fair Practices in Higher Education: Rights and Responsibilities of Students and Their Colleges in a Period of Intensified Competition for Enrollments.* San Francisco: Jossey-Bass, 1979a.

Carnegie Council on Policy Studies in Higher Education. *Next Steps for the 1980s in Student Financial Aid: A Fourth Alternative.* San Francisco: Jossey-Bass, 1979b.

Carnegie Council on Policy Studies in Higher Education. *Giving Youth a Better Chance: Options for Education, Work, and Service.* San Francisco: Jossey-Bass, 1979c.

Carnegie Council on Policy Studies in Higher Education. *The Carnegie Council on Policy Studies in Higher Education: A Summary of Reports and Recommendations.* San Francisco: Jossey-Bass, forthcoming.

Carnegie Foundation for the Advancement of Teaching. (A. Pifer, President.) *Seventieth Annual Report for the Year Ended June 30, 1975.* New York: 1975.

Carnegie Foundation for the Advancement of Teaching. *Missions of the College Curriculum: A Contemporary Review with Suggestions.* San Francisco: Jossey-Bass, 1977.

Cheit, E.F. *The New Depression in Higher Education: A Study of Financial Conditions at 41 Colleges and Universities.* A Report for the Carnegie Commission on Higher Education and the Ford Foundation. New York: McGraw-Hill, 1971.

College Entrance Examination Board. *Using the Student Search Service Effectively, 1979-80.* New York: 1979.

"Colleges Make Big Use of Television, Study Shows." *Higher Education Daily,* Nov. 8, 1979, 7(216), 3-4, 5-8.

Connecticut Board of Higher Education. *Anticipating the 1980s: Report and Recommendations to the General Assembly on Higher Education in Connecticut.* Hartford, Conn.: 1979.

Council for Interinstitutional Leadership. *Costing Collegiate Cooperation: A Report on the Costs and Benefits of Interinstitutional Programs.* Washington, D.C.: Oct. 1979.

Creager, J.A., and others. *National Norms for Entering College Freshmen, Fall 1969.* Washington, D.C.: American Council on Education, 1969.

Cross, K.P. *Beyond the Open Door: New Students to Higher Education.* San Francisco: Jossey-Bass, 1971.

Doermann, H. *Toward Equal Access.* New York: College Entrance Examination Board, 1978.

Dubin, R., and Taveggia, T.C. *The Teaching-Learning Paradox: A Comparative Analysis of College Teaching Methods.* Eugene, Ore.: Center for the Advanced Study of Educational Administration, 1968.

Easterlin, R.A. *Population, Labor Force, and Long Swings in Economic Growth.* New York: National Bureau of Economic Research, 1968.

Easterlin, R.A. "Implications of Recent Twists in Age Structure." *Demography*, Nov. 1978, *15*(4), 397-432.

Embling, J. *A Fresh Look at Higher Education: European Implications of the Carnegie Commission Reports.* Amsterdam, The Netherlands: Elsevier, 1974.

Ford Foundation. *Research Universities and the National Interest: A Report from Fifteen University Presidents.* New York: 1978.

Froomkin, J. *Needed: A New Federal Policy for Higher Education.* Washington, D.C.: Institute for Educational Leadership, George Washington University, 1978.

Garbarino, J. "Faculty Unionism: The First Ten Years." *Annals of the American Academy of Political and Social Science,* forthcoming.

Glenny, L.A. "Demography and Related Issues for Higher Education in the 1980s." Paper presented at the Center for the Study of Democratic Institutions, Santa Barbara, Calif., Nov. 17, 1978. (Revised July 1979)

Glenny, L.A., Shea, J.R., Ruyle, J.H., and Freschi, K.H. *Presidents Confront Reality: From Edifice Complex to University Without Walls.* San Francisco: Jossey-Bass, 1976.

Golladay, M. *The Condition of Education, 1977.* Vol. 3, part 1. Washington, D.C.: U.S. National Center for Education Statistics, 1977.

Gordon, M. S. (Ed.) *Higher Education and the Labor Market.* Prepared for the Carnegie Commission on Higher Education, New York: McGraw-Hill, 1974.

Grant, G., and Riesman, D. *The Perpetual Dream: Reform and Experiment in the American College.* Chicago: University of Chicago Press, 1978.

Halstead, D. K. *Tax Wealth in Fifty States.* Washington, D.C.: National Institute for Education, 1978.

Harris, S. *The Economics of Harvard.* New York: McGraw-Hill, 1970.

Hartnett, R. T., and Centra, J. A. "The Effects of Academic Departments on Student Learning." *Journal of Higher Education,* Sept.-Oct. 1977, *48*(5), 491-507.

Henry, D. D. *Challenges Past, Challenges Present: An Analysis of American Higher Education Since 1930.* Prepared for the Carnegie Council on Policy Studies in Higher Education. San Francisco: Jossey-Bass, 1975.

Hesburgh, T.M. *The Hesburgh Papers: Higher Values in Higher Education.* Kansas City: Andrews and McMeel, 1979.

Higher Education Daily, Sept. 10, 1979, 7(174), 1.

Hodgkinson, H. *Institutions in Transition: A Profile of Change in Higher Education (Incorporating the 1970 Statistical Report).* Prepared for the Carnegie Commission on Higher Education. New York: McGraw-Hill, 1971.

Jaffe, A. J., with Adams, W. "Trends in College Enrollment." *College Board Review,* Winter 1964-1965, *55*, 27-32.

Jencks, C., and Riesman, D. *The Academic Revolution.* New York, N.Y.: Doubleday, 1968.

Kerr, C. "The Moods of Academia." In Hughes, J.F. (Ed.), *Education and the State.* Washington, D.C.: American Council on Education, 1975.

Kramer, M. *The Venture Capital of Higher Education: The Public and Private Sources of Discretionary Funds.* Carnegie Council on Policy Studies in Higher Education, forthcoming.

Lee, E. C., and Bowen, F. M. *The Multicampus University: A Study of Academic Governance.* Prepared for the Carnegie Commission on Higher Education. New York: McGraw-Hill, 1971.

Lee, E. C., and Bowen, F. M. *Managing Multicampus Systems: Effective Administration in an Unsteady State.* Prepared for the Carnegie Council on Policy Studies in Higher Education. San Francisco: Jossey-Bass, 1975.

Levine, A. *Handbook on Undergraduate Curriculum.* Prepared for the Carnegie Council on Policy Studies in Higher Education. San Francisco: Jossey-Bass, 1978.

Levine, A. *When Dreams and Heroes Died: A Portrait of Today's College Student.* Prepared for the Carnegie Council on Policy Studies in Higher Education. San Francisco: Jossey-Bass, forthcoming.

McConnell, T. R. *A General Pattern for American Public Higher Education.* New York: McGraw-Hill, 1962.

Mayhew, L. B. *The Smaller Liberal Arts College.* New York: Center for Applied Research in Education, 1962.

Mayhew, L. B. *The Carnegie Commission on Higher Education: A Critical Analysis of the Reports and Recommendations.* Prepared for the Carnegie Council on Policy Studies in Higher Education. San Francisco: Jossey-Bass, 1973.

Mayhew, L. B. *Surviving the Eighties: Strategies and Procedures for Solving Fiscal and Enrollment Problems.* San Francisco: Jossey-Bass, 1979.

Millett, J. D. *Mergers in Higher Education: An Analysis of Ten Case Studies* Washington, D.C.: Academy for Educational Development, 1976.

Mingle, J. R. *Black Enrollment in Higher Education: Trends in the Nation and the South.* Atlanta, Ga.: Southern Regional Education Board, 1978.

Mood, A. M., and others. *Papers on Efficiency in the Management of Higher Education.* Berkeley, Calif.: Carnegie Council on Policy Studies in Higher Education, 1974.

Mortimer, K. P. *The Selection of College and University Trustees: A Policy Paper.* Washington, D.C.: Association of Governing Boards of Universities and Colleges, forthcoming.

Nason, J. W. *The Future of Trusteeship: The Role and Responsibilities of College and University Boards.* Washington, D.C.: Association of Governing Boards of Universities and Colleges, 1974.

Nason, J. W. *Presidential Search: A Guide to the Process of Selecting and Appointing College and University Presidents.* Washington, D.C.: Association of Governing Boards of Universities and Colleges, 1979.

Nason, J. W. *Presidential Assessment: Improvement of Institutional Performance.* Washington, D.C.: Association of Governing Boards of Universities and Colleges, forthcoming.

Odegaard, C. E. *Area Health Education Centers: The Pioneering Years, 1972-1978.* Berkeley, Calif.: Carnegie Council for Policy Studies in Higher Education, 1979.

Orwell, G. *1984.* New York: Harcourt Brace Jovanovich, 1949.

Perkins, J. A. *The University in a Restless Decade.* New York: International Council for Educational Development, 1972.

Pifer, A. *See* Carnegie Foundation for the Advancement of Teaching (1975).

Pyke, D. L. "The Future of Higher Education: Will Private Institutions Disappear in the United States?" *The Futurist,* Dec. 1977, *11*(6).

Radner, R., and Miller, L. S., with the collaboration of Adkins, D. L., and Balderston, F. E. *Demand and Supply in U.S. Higher Education.* Prepared for the Carnegie Commission on Higher Education. New York: McGraw-Hill, 1975.

Riesman, D. *On Higher Education.* Prepared for the Carnegie Council on Policy Studies in Higher Education. San Francisco: Jossey-Bass, forthcoming.

Roizen, J., Fulton, O., and Trow, M. *Technical Report: 1975 Carnegie Council National Surveys of Higher Education.* Berkeley, Calif.: Center for Studies in Higher Education, University of California, Berkeley, 1978.

Ruyle, J. H., and Glenny, L. A. *State Budgeting for Higher Education Trends in State Revenue Appropriations From 1968 to 1977.* Berkeley, Calif.: Center for Studies in Higher Education, University of California, Berkeley, 1978.

Smith, J. P., and Welch, F. "*The Overeducated American?* A Review Article." *The Rand Paper Series.* Santa Monica, Calif.: The Rand Corporation, Nov. 1978.

Spaeth, J. L., and Greeley, A. M. *Recent Alumni and Higher Education: A Survey of College Graduates.* Prepared for the Carnegie Commission on Higher Education. New York: McGraw-Hill, 1970.

Spence, D. S. *A Profile of Higher Education in the South in 1985.* Atlanta, Ga.: Southern Regional Education Board, 1977.

Stadtman, V. A. *Academic Adaptations: Higher Education Prepares for the 1980s and 1990s.* Prepared for the Carnegie Council on Policy Studies in Higher Education. San Francisco: Jossey-Bass, forthcoming.

The President. *Economic Report of The President, 1979.* Washington, D.C.: 1979.

The President's Commission on Foreign Languages and International Studies. (J. A. Perkins, Chairman) *Strength Through Wisdom: A Report to The President from the President's Commission on Foreign Languages and International Studies.* Washington, D.C.: Government Printing Office, Nov. 1979.

Thomson, S., and DeLeonibus, N. *Guidelines for Improving SAT Scores.* Reston, Va.: National Association of Secondary School Principals, 1978.

Trow, M. "The Public and Private Lives of Higher Education." *Daedalus,* Winter 1975, *11,* 113-127.

Trow, M. (Ed.). *Teachers and Students: Aspects of American Higher Education.* New York: McGraw-Hill, 1975.

U.S. Bureau of the Census. *U.S. Census of the Population: 1960. Subject Reports: School Enrollment.* Final Report PC(2)-5A. Washington, D.C.: 1964.

U.S. Bureau of the Census. *Current Population Reports.* Series P-20, no. 222. Washington, D.C.: 1971.

U.S. Bureau of the Census. *Historical Statistics of the United States, Colonial Times to 1970.* Bicentennial Edition, Part I. Washington, D.C.: 1975.

U.S. Bureau of the Census. *Statistical Abstracts, 1978.* Washington, D.C.: 1978.

U.S. Bureau of the Census. *Current Population Reports: Illustrative Projections of State Populations by Age, Race, and Sex: 1975 to 2000.* Series P-25, no. 796. Washington, D.C.: March 1979a.

U.S. Bureau of the Census. *Current Population Reports.* Series P-20, no. 333, Washington, D.C.: 1979b.

U.S. Congress, Congressional Budget Office. "Estimated Per Capita Federal Expenditures for Youth Aged 14-22." Preliminary study for Senator Harrison Williams, June 28, 1979.

U.S. Department of Commerce. *Survey of Current Business.* August 1979.

U.S. Department of Health, Education, and Welfare, Office of Education. "Statistics of Higher Education 1955-56: Faculty, Students, and Degrees." *Biennial Survey of Education in the United States, 1954-56.* Chap. 4, sect. 1. Washington, D.C.: 1958.

U.S. Department of Health, Education, and Welfare, Office of Inspector-General. *Annual Report.* Washington, D.C.: March 31, 1978.

U.S. Department of Health, Education, and Welfare. *Monthly Vital Statistics Report,* August 13, 1979, 27 (13).

U.S. General Accounting Office, Comptroller General. *Report to the Congress of the United States.* Washington, D.C.: Sept. 19, 1978.

U.S. National Center for Education Statistics. *Fall Enrollment in Higher Education, 1969—Supplementary Information, Summary Data.* Washington, D.C.: 1970.

U.S. National Center for Education Statistics. *Fall Enrollment in Higher Education, 1970—Supplementary Information, Summary Data.* Washington, D.C.: 1971.

U.S. National Center for Education Statistics. *Projections of Educational Statistics to 1980-81.* Washington, D.C.: 1972.

U.S. National Center for Education Statistics. *Financial Statistics of Institutions of Higher Education, Current Funds Revenues and Expenditures, 1969-70.* Washington, D.C.: 1973.

U.S. National Center for Education Statistics. *Fall Enrollment in Higher Education, 1976: Final Report.* Washington, D.C. 1978a.

U.S. National Center for Education Statistics. *Digest of Education Statistics, 1977-78.* Washington, D.C.: 1978b.

U.S. National Center for Education Statistics. *Fall Enrollment in Higher Education, 1977.* Washington, D.C.: 1978c.

U.S. National Center for Education Statistics. *Projections of Education Statistics to 1986-87.* Washington, D.C.: 1978d.

U.S. National Center for Education Statistics. *Digest of Education Statistics, 1979.* Washington, D.C.: 1979a.

U.S. National Center for Education Statistics. *Financial Statistics of Institutions of Higher Education, Current Funds Revenues and Expenditures, Fiscal Year 1977: State Data.* Washington, D.C.: 1979b.

U.S. National Center for Education Statistics. *Fall Enrollment in Higher Education, 1978: Final Report.* Washington, D.C.: 1979c.

U.S. National Center for Education Statistics. *Fall Enrollment in Colleges and Universities, 1979: Preliminary Estimates.* Washington, D.C.: Oct. 31, 1979d.

Wolfle, D. *The Home of Science.* New York: McGraw-Hill, 1972.

Wren, S. C. *The College Student and Higher Education Policy: What Stake and What Purpose?* New York: The Carnegie Foundation for the Advancement of Teaching, 1975.

Index